First Edition

biography
for
beginners

World Explorers

Laurie Lanzen Harris,
Editor

Favorable Impressions

P.O. Box 69018 • Pleasant Ridge, MI 48960

Laurie Lanzen Harris, *Editor*

Dan Robert Harris and Claire Rewold, *Contributing Editors*

Design, Layout and Maps by
Mary Ann Stavros-Lanning, MASWEL Group

Library of Congress Cataloging-in-Publication Data

Biography for beginners : world explorers / Laurie Lanzen Harris, editor.
p. cm.
Summary: Profiles 100 world explorers, from 500 B.C. when Carthaginian explorer Hanno colonized West Africa, to such present-day adventurers as astronaut Neil Armstrong and ocean explorer Sylvia Earle.
Includes bibliographical references.
ISBN 1-931360-20-0 (alk. paper)
1. Explorers — Biography — Encyclopedias, Juvenile. 2. Discoveries in geography — Biography — Encyclopedias, Juvenile. [1. Explorers — Encyclopedias. 2. Discoveries in geography — Encyclopedias.]
I. Title: World explorers. II. Harris, Laurie Lanzen.
G175.B555 2003
910'.92'2 — dc21

2003001942

The information in this publication was compiled from the sources cited and from other sources considered reliable. While every possible effort has been made to ensure reliability, the publisher will not assume liability for damages caused by inaccuracies in the data, and makes no warranty, express or implied, on the accuracy of the information contained herein.

(∞)

This book is printed on acid-free paper meeting the ANSI Z39.48 Standard. The infinity symbol that appears above indicate that the paper in this book meets that standard.

Printed in the United States

Contents

Preface vii

Introduction vii

Dedication xxi

World Explorers

Alexander the Great (356 B.C. - 323 B.C.) 1
King of Macedonia and Military Leader Who Conquered and Explored Lands in
the Middle East, Asia, and Africa

Roald Amundsen (1872 - 1928) 6
Norwegian Explorer of the Arctic and Antarctica Who Discovered the South Pole

Neil Armstrong (1930 -) 14
American Astronaut and First Person to Walk on the Moon

William Baffin (1584? - 1622) 23
English Navigator Who Explored the Canadian Arctic

Vasco Núñez de Balboa (1475 - 1519) 26
Spanish Conquistador and Explorer, First European to See the Pacific Ocean

Robert Ballard (1942-) 30
American Oceanographer and Explorer Who Discovered the *Titanic*

Joseph Banks (1743 - 1820) 39
English Naturalist and Explorer Who Traveled with James Cook

Willem Barents (1550? - 1597) 43
Dutch Explorer Who Looked for the Northeast Passage

Gertrude Bell (1868 - 1926) 46
English Archeologist, Explorer, and Writer Who Explored the Middle East

Benjamin of Tudela (1100s) 49
Spanish Rabbi Who Traveled to the Jewish Communities in Europe, Africa,
and the Middle East

Vitus Bering (1681-1741) **51**
Danish Explorer, Navigator, and Mapmaker Who Led Two Expeditions to
Alaska for Russia

Isabella Bird Bishop (1831-1904) **55**
English Traveler, Writer, and Explorer

Daniel Boone (1734-1820) **60**
American Explorer and Frontiersman Who Built the Wilderness Road in the
Cumberland Gap

Etienne Brulé (1591?-1632?) **66**
French Explorer Who Lived Among the Indian Tribes of North America

Richard Francis Burton (1821-1890) **70**
English Explorer of India, Africa, and the Middle East; First European to
Discover Lake Tanganyika

Richard E. Byrd (1888-1957) **75**
American Naval Officer and Explorer of Antarctica, First to Fly Over the
North and South Poles

Alvar Núñez Cabeza de Vaca (1490?-1560?) **81**
Spanish Explorer of Texas and Northern Mexico

John Cabot (1450?-1499?) **86**
Italian Navigator, Explorer, and Mapmaker Who Explored the New World for
England

Sebastian Cabot (1476?-1557) **92**
Italian Explorer and Mapmaker Who Searched for the Northwest Passage in
Canada

Pedro Alvares Cabral (1467?-1519?) **97**
Portuguese Explorer Who Discovered Brazil

Kit Carson (1809-1868) **100**
American Frontiersman, Explorer, and Soldier Who Explored the American West

Jacques Cartier (1491-1557) **106**
French Navigator Who Explored Canada and Discovered the Saint Lawrence River

Samuel de Champlain (1567?-1635) **113**
French Explorer of Canada and the Upper Northeastern United States, Founder
of Quebec and "The Father of New France"

William Clark (1770-1838) **121**
American Explorer, Military Officer, and Co-Leader of the Lewis and Clark
Expedition

Christopher Columbus (1451?-1506) 133
Italian Explorer Who Was the First European to Discover the New World,
Opened North and South America to European Exploration and Colonization

James Cook (1728-1779) 151
English Explorer, Navigator, and Naval Officer Who Explored the Pacific Ocean
and Its Islands, as well as Alaska and Canada

Francisco Vázquez de Coronado (1510-1554) 161
Spanish Conquistador Who Explored the Southwest United States

Hernando Cortes (1485-1547) 165
Spanish Conquistador and Explorer Who Conquered Mexico

Jacques Cousteau (1910-1997) 172
French Ocean Explorer, Film Producer, and Inventor

Vasco da Gama (1460?-1524) 177
Portuguese Explorer and the First European to Sail around Africa to India

Charles Darwin (1809-1882) 183
English Scientist and Explorer Who Developed the Theory of Evolution

Alexandra David-Neel (1868-1969) 190
French Explorer of Asia and First European Woman to Enter Lhasa, Tibet

Hernando de Soto (1496?-1542) 194
Spanish Conquistador Who Explored the Southeastern United States and the
First European to Discover the Mississippi River

Bartholomew Dias (1450?-1500) 200
Portuguese Navigator Who Led the First European Expedition to the
Cape of Good Hope

Sir Francis Drake (1540?-1596) 204
English Navigator and Explorer and the Second Person to Circumnavigate
the World

Sylvia Earle (1935-) 212
American Marine Botanist, Oceanographer, and Explorer of the Oceans

Erik the Red (950A.D.?-1000A.D.?) 220
Norwegian Viking and Explorer Who Founded the First European Settlement
on Greenland

Leif Erikson (b. 980?-d.1020?) 225
Norwegian Viking Explorer and the First European to Reach North America

Faxian (374?-462?) 233
Chinese Buddhist Monk Who Traveled to India and Asia

v

Matthew Flinders (1774-1814) **235**
English Explorer and Navigator, the First European to Circumnavigate Australia

John Franklin (1786-1847) **239**
English Officer and Explorer Who Searched for the Northwest Passage

Simon Fraser (1776-1862) **244**
Canadian Explorer Who Searched for the Northwest Passage

John Charles Frémont (1813-1890) **248**
American Soldier, Explorer, and Politician Who Explored and Mapped the
American West

Martin Frobisher (1540?-1594) **253**
English Explorer Who Explored the Canadian Arctic and Searched for the
Northwest Passage

Yuri Gagarin (1934-1968) **259**
Russian Cosmonaut and the First Person to Travel in Space

John Glenn (1921-) **264**
American Astronaut and Politician, First American to Orbit the Earth

Hanno (c.500 B.C.) **272**
Carthaginian Who Explored the West Coast of Africa

Sven Anders Hedin (1865-1952) **275**
Swedish Explorer and Geographer of Central Asia

Louis Hennepin (1626-1701) **278**
French Missionary and Explorer of the Great Lakes Region with La Salle

Prince Henry the Navigator (1394-1460) **282**
Portuguese Prince Who Founded a School to Train Explorers, and Started the
European Age of Exploration

Matthew Henson (1866-1955) **286**
African-American Explorer Who Traveled to the North Pole in 1909 with
Robert E. Peary

Herodotus (484 B.C.? to 420 B.C.?) **291**
Greek Historian, Geographer, and Traveler, Called "The Father of History"

Hsuan Tsang (600-664) **294**
Chinese Monk Who Traveled to Asia and India

Henry Hudson (1565?-1611) **297**
English Navigator and Explorer of the Arctic Ocean and North American Coast

Alexander von Humboldt (1769-1859) **304**
German Scientist and Explorer of South America, Mexico, and the United States

Ibn Battuta (1304 - 1368?) 310
Islamic Moroccan Traveler Who Visited All of the Muslim Nations of His Time

Mae Jemison (1956 -) 315
American Scientist and Doctor Who Was the First African-American Woman to
Travel in Space

Louis Jolliet (1645 - 1700) 320
French Explorer and Cartographer Who Explored the Mississippi River with
Jacques Marquette

Mary Henrietta Kingsley (1862 - 1900) 325
English Explorer of West and Central Africa

Rene-Robert Cavelier, Sieur de La Salle (1643 - 1687) 329
French Explorer of the Mississippi River Who Claimed the Region for France

Leo Africanus (1485? - 1554?) 336
Arab Traveler Who Explored Africa South of the Sahara Desert

Meriwether Lewis (1774 - 1809) 339
American Explorer and Co-Leader of the Lewis and Clark Expedition

David Livingstone (1813 - 1873) 353
Scottish Missionary and Explorer of Africa

Alexander Mackenzie (1764 - 1820) 361
Scottish Explorer Who Was the First European to Reach the Pacific Ocean
Overland

Ferdinand Magellan (1480 - 1521) 366
Portuguese Navigator and Explorer Who Led the First Expedition to
Circumnavigate the World

Jacques Marquette (1637 - 1675) 375
French Missionary and Explorer of the Mississippi River with Louis Jolliet

Fridtjof Nansen (1861 - 1930) 380
Norwegian Arctic Explorer, Scientist, and Statesman

Adolf Erik Nordenskiöld (1832 - 1901) 386
Finnish-Born Swedish Explorer and Scientist Who Was the First to Navigate
the Northeast Passage

Francisco de Orellana (1511? - 1546) 390
Spanish Explorer Who Was the First European to Navigate the Amazon River

Mungo Park (1771 - 1806) 394
Scottish Explorer of the Niger River in Africa

William Edward Parry (1790 - 1855) 397
English Navigator and Explorer of the Canadian Arctic

Robert E. Peary (1856 - 1920) **403**
American Arctic Explorer Who Claimed to Be the First Person to Reach the
North Pole

Ida Pfeiffer (1797 - 1858) **409**
Austrian Traveler and Writer Who Traveled Around the World and Wrote
about her Journeys

The Phoenicians **414**

Zebulon Pike (1779 - 1813) **416**
American Explorer and Soldier Who Explored the American West

Francisco Pizarro (1475? - 1541) **421**
Spanish Conquistador Who Explored Peru and Ecuador and Conquered
the Incas

Marco Polo (c.1254 - 1324) **428**
Venetian Merchant and Traveler Who Explored Asia

Juan Ponce de León (1460? - 1521) **437**
Spanish Explorer and the First European to Reach Florida, Searching for the
"Fountain of Youth"

John Wesley Powell (1834 - 1902) **442**
American Scientist and Explorer of the Grand Canyon and the Colorado
and Green Rivers

Ptolemy (100 A.D.? to 165 A.D.?) **450**
Greek Astronomer, Geographer, and Mathematician Whose Maps Were
Used for 1,000 Years

Pytheas (345 B.C.? to 300 B.C.?) **453**
Greek Navigator and Explorer of Europe and the British Isles

Sir Walter Raleigh (1554? - 1618) **457**
English Explorer, Statesman, and Soldier

Sally Ride (1951-) **463**
American Astronaut and Scientist Who Was the First American Woman
to Travel in Space

James Clark Ross (1800 - 1862) **469**
English Navigator and Explorer of the Arctic and Antarctic

Sacagawea (c. 1778 - 1812) **477**
Shoshone Indian Guide and Translator for the Lewis and Clark Expedition

Robert Falcon Scott (1868 - 1912) **486**
English Naval Officer and Explorer of Antarctica Who Led an Expedition to
the South Pole

Ernest Shackleton (1874 - 1922)...493
Irish-Born English Explorer of Antarctica

May French Sheldon (1847 - 1936) 502
American Explorer of East Africa

Alan Shepard (1923 - 1998) 505
American Astronaut Who Was the First American to Travel in Space

John Hanning Speke (1827 - 1864) 513
English Explorer Who Discovered the Source of the Nile River

Henry M. Stanley (1841 - 1904) 517
English-American Explorer and Journalist Who Explored Africa and
Rescued David Livingstone

Abel Janszoon Tasman (1603 - 1659) 524
Dutch Explorer and Navigator Who Was the First European to Discover
Tasmania, New Zealand, the Fiji Islands, and Tonga

Valentina Tereshkova (1937-) 528
Russian Cosmonaut and the First Woman to Travel in Space

David Thompson (1770 - 1857) 532
English Explorer and Geographer Who Explored and Mapped the
Canadian West

George Vancouver (1757 - 1798) 537
English Explorer and Navigator Who Surveyed the Pacific Coast of
North America

Giovanni da Verrazzano (1485? - 1528?)..................540
Italian Navigator Who Explored for France, the First European to Sight
New York Harbor

Amerigo Vespucci (1451 - 1512).............................543
Italian Explorer of South America

The Vikings...549

Alfred Russel Wallace (1823 - 1913) 552
English Naturalist and Explorer Who Developed the Theory of Evolution

Francis Xavier (1506 - 1552)....................................556
Spanish Missionary Who Traveled to India, Indonesia, Japan, and China

Xenophon (430 B.C.? to 350 B.C.?).........................559
Greek Historian and Military Leader Who Explored the Middle East

Zheng He (1371-1433?) **562**
   Chinese Diplomat and Admiral Who Led Sea Voyages to Southeast Asia,
   the Middle East, and Africa

Photo and Illustration Credits **567**

Glossary **569**

Appendixes:
   Explorers by Nationality **577**
   Explorers by Area of Exploration. **579**
      (Includes Maps of Area of Exploration)
   Timeline of World Exploration **587**

Subject Index **595**
   (Names and Key Words)

Preface

Welcome to *Biography for Beginners: World Explorers*. Since we began *Biography for Beginners* in 1995, I've received requests from librarians for reference books written for early readers on such high-interest topics as U.S. Presidents, world explorers, famous women in history, and African-American leaders. The positive response to our first effort in this area, *Biography for Beginners: Presidents of the United States*, has encouraged us to go on to the fascinating world of exploration.

The Plan of the Work

Like *Biography for Beginners* and *Biography for Beginners: Presidents of the United States, World Explorers* is written for early readers, ages 7 to 10. The volume is especially created for young students in a format they can read, understand, and use for assignments. The 102 entries are arranged alphabetically. Each entry begins with a heading listing the explorer's name, birth and death dates, nationality, and a brief description of the individual's importance to the history of exploration. Boldfaced headings lead readers to information on birth, youth, growing up, education, marriage and family, and the nature of the individual's discovery. However, in the case of some explorers, information is not available in every category. Every effort has been made to use only solid historical data in composing the biographical profiles. Whenever there is not definitive historical data, or if the information available is largely derived from legend or lore, that is clearly stated in the text.

Some entries end with a list of World Wide Web sites. These sites have been reviewed for accuracy and suitability for use by young students. A bibliography of works used in the compilation of the entries follows the Preface.

The entries also include portraits of the explorers, when available, as well as paintings, photos, and other illustrations to enhance the reader's understanding of the individuals. Maps that outline the routes of some of the explorers also illustrate the text. For context, the maps contain both historical and current place names. For example, a map of Champlain's expedition of 1608 contains place names used in his time ("Stadacona") and in the present ("Quebec"). For further reference, the Appendix contains maps of the continents, which include major countries and physical features.

Audience

This book is intended for young readers in grades two through five who are studying world explorers for the first time. Most children will use this book to study one explorer at a time, usually as part of a class assignment. For this reason, standard information about exploration, including the development of navigational tools, and such concepts as the search for the Northwest Passage or the importance of the Silk Road to the exploration of Asia, are repeated in several entries.

We have tried to give variant forms and spellings of names from non-English alphabets, such as Chinese and Arabic. Pronunciations are also given for many names and places unfamiliar to young readers. In many cases, the names by which a place was known in ancient times is not the name by which it is known today. For that reason, we have often described a place using both the ancient and current names, in the text and in the maps.

Some of these topics are also described and defined in the "Glossary" section of the volume. The Glossary also includes entries on the instruments of navigation and transportation used from ancient times to the present, including definitions for tools like the astrolabe and the chronometer. It also includes descriptions of the types of vessels used by explorers of different eras, such as Viking longships, Chinese junks, and European caravels. Glossary topics are bold-faced in the entries, as are the names of other explorers who appear in the volume.

The term "Indian" is used in the text to describe the many diverse Native American tribes encountered by the European explorers of North and South America. This term is similarly used in the encyclopedias and other reference sources consulted for this volume; dictionaries do not denote the term as pejorative. Therefore, "Indian" is used interchangeably with "Native American" and "native peoples" throughout the text.

Appendix

The Appendix contains an alphabetical lists of explorers by nationality, a list of explorers by area of exploration, and a timeline of world exploration. It also includes a set of maps of the continents, with major countries and physical features.

Index

An Index covering names and key words concludes the volume. The Index has been created with the young reader in mind, and therefore contains a limited number of terms that have been simplified for ease of research.

Our Advisors

Biography for Beginners: World Explorers was reviewed by an Advisory Board that included school librarians, public librarians, and elementary students. I would particularly like to thank the students of McDougle Elementary School in Chapel Hill, NC, and their media coordinator, Nancy Margolin. The thoughtful comments and suggestions of all the Board members have been invaluable in developing this publication. Any errors, however, are mine alone. I would like to list the members of the Advisory Board and to thank them again for their efforts.

Linda Carpino   Detroit Public Library, Detroit, MI
Nancy Margolin   McDougle Elementary School, Chapel Hill, NC
Laurie Scott   Farmington Hills Community Library, Farmington Hills, MI

Your Comments Are Welcome

Our goal is to provide accurate, accessible biographical information for early readers. Please write or call me with your comments.

Acknowledgments

I would like to thank the staffs of the Mariner's Museum in Newport News, Virginia, the National Archives of Canada, the Royal Geographical Society of England, and the Library of Congress for their help in obtaining illustrations. Thank you to Mary Ann Stavros-Lanning of the Maswel Group for outstanding design and layout. Thanks to Cherie Abbey for editorial assistance, Shaina Liberson and Catherine and Joseph Harris for research support.

Bibliography

This is a listing of works used in the compilation of the biographical profiles. Most of the works cited here are written at the middle school or high school reading level and are generally beyond the reading level of early elementary students. However, many librarians consider these reliable, objective points of departure for further research.

Adams, Simon. *Exploration and Discovery.* Exploring History Series, Lorenz Books, 2000.
Columbia Encyclopedia, 2000 edition.
Compton's Encyclopedia, 2002 edition.
Encyclopedia Britannica, 2001 edition.
Explorers: From Ancient Times to the Space Age. Macmillan Reference, 1999.
Mason, Antony. *The Children's Atlas of Exploration.* Millbrook Press, 1993.
Matthews, Rupert. *Explorer.* Eyewitness Books Series, Dorling Kindersley, 2000.

Laurie Harris, *Editor and Publisher*

Introduction

It is hard for us to imagine how the early explorers viewed their world. In our modern age, where information flows over the Internet at thousands of bytes per second, where all the land masses have been explored, and where astronomers are mapping the realms of space, it is difficult to imagine what it would have meant to become an explorer. Where did they find the courage to set out across the ocean, when many believed that the world was flat, and that a ship would simply fall off the edge and disappear forever? Maybe that is why explorers continue to fascinate us. As we try to understand who they were, what motivated them, how they viewed the world, and how that world view changed with each discovery, we learn about ourselves, too. For it is part of what it is to be human to want to explore, discover, and extend the boundaries of our world.

What Is an "Explorer"?

When we call someone an "explorer," what do we mean? Do we mean a European explorer, like **Christopher Columbus**, who traveled to what he thought was India, "discovering" America instead? And what do we mean by "discovery"? When Columbus "discovered" America, there were Native American tribes who had been living in North and South America for thousands of years. So what did Columbus discover? And whom did he "discover" it for?

Why does someone become an explorer? What motivated the men and women profiled in this book on their journeys of discovery? There are as many different reasons as there are explorers. Some explored for the sheer joy of discovery. Some wanted money and fame. Others sought to claim new lands for king or queen, or to spread their religious faith. And some were merchants who wanted to establish trade routes among diverse peoples and countries.

This book will try to answer these kinds of questions, to examine the who, what, when, where, and why of the people we call explorers. For the purposes of this book, we will define an "explorer" as someone from past 2500 years, from about 500 B.C. to the present, who left his or her native land and traveled to an area that was unknown to them. They left their impressions of their discoveries in historical writings, in ship's logs, maps, illustrations, and photographs. So we have included as our earliest explorer the Carthaginian **Hanno**, who explored the coast of Africa in around 500 B.C. And we continue to explorers of the present day, including ocean explorers **Sylvia Earle** and **Robert Ballard**, who are still actively involved in their quests to chart and understand the undersea world, and astronauts like **Neil Armstrong** and **Sally Ride**, whose realm is the huge expanse of space.

We have purposely been very broad in our definition of explorers to include the earliest explorers of the ancient world, the more well-known explorers of the so-called Age of Exploration, and the explorers of the most recent century, whose discoveries took them to the last places on Earth left unexplored, the polar regions, as well as today's explorers of the oceans and space. We have also included scientists, like **Charles Darwin**, whose discoveries led to major changes in the way we think about our world. Also included are astronomers and mapmakers, like **Ptolemy,** whose maps were used for more than 1400 years. We have also included summary entries on groups like the **Phoenicians** and the **Vikings**, whose collective contributions are important to the history of discovery.

An Introduction to the Ages of Exploration

Explorers from Ancient Times to 1400

Who were the earliest explorers? Most likely they were people from thousands of years ago, who traveled from their homes in search of food. Over thousands of years, as people learned to farm and raise animals, cities and civilizations began to develop. These people became interested in trading the goods they produced. Some of these early traders came from cities around the Mediterranean Sea—from Egypt, North Africa, Greece, and the Middle East—and traveled by boat. Around 1100 B.C., the **Phoenicians** began to explore the Mediterranean area. The Phoenecians were a people who lived along the coast of modern-day Lebanon, Syria, and Israel. They were great sailors and made settlements in ports as far as the coasts of West Africa. Many historians consider the Phoenecians the first explorers.

It was from the Phoenician port of Carthage that one of the earliest explorers, **Hanno**, made his voyage to the west coast of Africa, around 500 B.C. On his return, he wrote of his discoveries. His report was read by people for hundreds of years. In around 400 B.C., the Greek historian **Herodotus** traveled through most of the known world of his time and wrote of what he saw, sharing his understanding of the cultures he encountered. The Greek soldier **Xenophon** fought battles in the Middle East and was forced to travel home by an unknown route. He, too, wrote down and shared his experience of the new cultures he encountered with his fellow Greeks.

Perhaps the most famous explorer of this early period was **Alexander the Great**. He conquered peoples from the edge of the Mediterranean in the west to India in the east. Another Greek explorer of the early era, **Pytheas,** lived in a Greek colony in what is now southern France. Setting sail from there, he explored the Atlantic coasts of France and Spain and reached Britain and Ireland. He may have even reached Iceland.

In the early centuries A.D., the Chinese explorer **Faxian** traveled to India and Asia to learn about Buddhism. He later wrote about his journey, describing the lands and peoples he had visited, sharing information about a land unknown to most of the world. Other Asian explorers of the first 1000 years A.D. include two Chinese explorers, **Hsuan Tsang**, who traveled in India, and **Zheng He**, whose wide-ranging explorations led him to Asia, India, the Middle East, and Africa. The most important Arabic explorer of the era, **Ibn Battuta**, traveled in the Middle East, Africa, and the Mediterranean.

The Viking explorers of the era included two of the best-known men of early European exploration, **Erik the Red** and **Leif Erikson**. From Venice, **Marco Polo** left on a journey to Asia, where he lived and explored for many years. Like Herodotus and Faxian, Polo wrote about his time in Asia, and provided his and later eras with a record of life in a land totally unknown to them.

The Age of Exploration and Discovery: 1400 to 1900

The era of exploration most familiar to young readers began in the late 1400s. In a span of about 400 years, men and women explored all but the polar regions and the ocean depths. The Age of Exploration and Discovery is dominated by the European explorers who sailed for Portugal, Spain, France, and England.

It began with the Portuguese explorers trained by **Prince Henry the Navigator,** including **Bartholomew Dias** and **Vasco da Gama**, who rounded the Cape of Good Hope in Africa. Da Gama's travels around the Cape and on to India established Portugal as the ruler of that water route to the riches of the East. Portugal also sent explorers to claim parts of the **New World**. **Pedro Alvarez Cabral** claimed what is now Brazil for Portugal.

In the late 1400s Spain began its quest for a sea route to the East. **Christopher Columbus** sailed west from Europe, and, thinking he'd reached Asia, landed in what became known as the "**New World**." He and later Spanish explorers claimed much of what is now the Caribbean, Central America, and portions of North and South America for Spain. Mexico was explored by **Francisco Coronado, Hernando Cortes**, and **Alvar Núñez Cabeza de Vaca**; **Columbus** and **Ponce de León** explored the Caribbean, and **Ponce de León** went on to what is now the southeastern U.S., as did **Cabeza de Vaca** and **Hernando de Soto**. **Giovanni da Verrazano** explored the east coast of the U.S. In Central America, **Vasco Núñez de Balboa, Columbus,** and **Francisco Pizarro** explored Panama. **Pizarro** also traveled to what is now South America, conquering the Incas in Peru. **Amerigo Vespucci** explored the coast of South America; his first name would provide mapmakers with the term for the continents of the **New World**: the "Americas." Although he first sailed for his native Portugal, in 1519 **Ferdinand Magellan** began the first successful circumnavigation of the globe for Spain.

The French sent several expeditions to the **New World**, where they explored the St. Lawrence River region of what would become Canada, and the Atlantic coast and Great Lakes region of what would later be the U.S. These Frenchmen included **Etienne Brulé, Jacques Cartier, Samuel de Champlain, Louis Hennepin, Louis Jolliet, Rene-Robert Cavelier Sieur de La Salle,** and **Jacques Marquette; Jolliet, Marquette, and La Salle** also explored the Mississippi River.

The English also sent explorers to what would become Canada and the northeastern U.S., including **John and Sebastian Cabot, Simon Fraser, Martin Frobisher, Henry Hudson, Alexander Mackenzie, David Thompson,** and **George Vancouver.** The Englishman **Francis Drake** became the second man to circumnavigate the globe in 1580, stopping at several points on the Pacific coast of South and North America on his journey.

The fabled **Northwest Passage** became a potent lure for explorers from several nations for hundreds of years. From the late 15th century to the 20th, explorers searched for the elusive route through the Canadian Arctic. **Sebastian Cabot, Jacques Cartier, Martin Frobisher, Henry Hudson, William Baffin, John Franklin, Simon Fraser, Alexander Mackenzie, William E. Parry,** and **James Clark Ross** are some of the explorers who sought the passage, which was finally discovered in the early 20th century by **Roald Amundsen.** The **Northeast Passage** drew a number of explorers, too, including **Willem Barents, Vitus Bering, Henry Hudson,** and **Nils Nordenskiöld.**

Australia attracted explorers of many eras, including **Abel Tasman, Matthew Flinders, James Cook,** and **Joseph Banks**. Some of these explorers also explored the waters and islands of the Pacific.

In the 19th century, Americans began to explore their own country, especially after the Louisiana Purchase doubled the size of the nation. This era begins with perhaps the two most famous U.S. explorers, **Meriwether Lewis** and **William Clark**, who, aided by the Indian guide **Sacagawea**, tried to find a water route to the Pacific. Other American explorers of the West include **Kit Carson, John Charles Frémont, Zebulon Pike,** and **John Wesley Powell.**

Africa became a source of fascination for European explorers in the 19th century. **Richard Francis Burton, John Hanning Speke, David Livingstone,** and **Henry M. Stanley** all became renowned for their African explorations, especially in their quest for the source of the Nile. Later in the century, several woman made their names as the first European woman to journey into Africa, including **Mary Henrietta Kingsley** and **May French Sheldon**.

Nineteenth-century scientists were also drawn to exploration. **Charles Darwin, Alfred Russel Wallace,** and **Alexander von Humboldt** all explored South America, making discoveries that changed the world of science.

Slavery

The history of exploration is also bound to the shameful legacy of slavery. **Alexander the Great** routinely enslaved the populations he conquered. **Henry the Navigator** financed the first slaving missions of the Portuguese explorers. Spanish conquistadors enslaved populations they conquered in Mexico, the Caribbean, and South America. **Francis Drake** captained the first English boat to bring slaves to the **New World**. Even in the 19th century, explorer and fervent abolitionist **David Livingstone** fought Portuguese slave traders to free captive Africans. The depth of the connection between slavery and exploration is perhaps shocking, yet it is part of the history of discovery. Even young readers need to learn, and to understand, this aspect of the past.

Explorers of the Modern Age: 1900 to the Present

The first decades of the 20th century brought the great age of polar exploration. **Robert Falcon Scott, Robert E. Peary, Roald Amundsen, Fridtjof Nansen, Ernest Shackleton, Richard E. Byrd, Matthew Henson,** and others sought and found the North and South Poles, and explored the forbidding regions of the polar ice caps.

Technological advances led to the exploration of the ocean floors, including the SCUBA equipment invented by **Jacques Cousteau.** Cousteau, along with **Sylvia Earle** and **Robert Ballard,** was responsible for opening up the oceans to discovery.

Technology also brought about the exploration of space for the first time. In 1957, the Soviet Union launched *Sputnik*, the first space probe. The race was on to put the first human into space. The Soviets won that part of the race, launching **Yuri Gagarin** into space in 1961. The American astronauts **Alan Shepard** and **John Glenn** followed several months later. The Soviets scored a first in the space race again in 1963, when they sent the first woman into space, cosmonaut **Valentina Tereshkova.** It would take the Americans 20 years to match that, when, in 1983, **Sally Ride** made history by becoming the first American woman in space. **Mae Jemison** made history in 1992, when she became the first African-American woman to travel in space. And one of the most phenomenal events of exploration, the landing of humans on the Moon, occurred in 1969, when **Neil Armstrong** became the first person to make that "one small step for man, one giant leap for mankind."

The history of exploration is by no means complete. The next millennium will most likely find humans reaching out into the depths of space, searching to discover, understand, and learn more about our place on Earth and in the universe. What they find will astound and enrich those future generations, adding to the history of discovery and continuing the very human need to explore.

Dedication

The rich history of exploration is full of human drama. It contains success and failure, vanity and purity of purpose, adventure and challenge. If there is a characteristic that unites explorers of all eras, it is their courage to face great risk.

The history of exploration is also marked by those who gave their lives in their quest; from Magellan to Captain Cook, from Franklin to Scott, the names of those lost in pursuit of the unknown speak to us across the ages.

It is in this spirit that we both mourn and celebrate the seven astronauts of the space shuttle *Columbia*, who lost their lives on February 1, 2003, as they returned to Earth. We grieve for them, yet we also honor their achievements and the bravery of their quest. This volume is dedicated to them: to David M. Brown, Rick D. Husband, Laurel Black Salton Clark, Kalpana Chawla, Michael P. Anderson, William C. McCool, and Ilan Ramon.

World Explorers

Alexander the Great

356 B.C. - 323 B.C.
King of Macedonia and Military Leader
Conquered and Explored Lands in the Middle East,
Africa, and Asia

ALEXANDER THE GREAT WAS BORN in Pella in what is now Greece. At the time, Pella was in a country called Macedonia. His father was King Phillip II of Macedonia. His mother was named Olympias. She was a princess from Epirus. Philip divorced Olympias when Alexander was young and married another woman. Alexander and his mother left Philip's court.

1

ALEXANDER THE GREAT GREW UP first in Pella, then in Epirus, where his mother's family lived. He was always very close to his mother. She told him that he was descended from the famous Greek warrior Achilles. Achilles was the hero of the ancient Greek poem *The Iliad*. Alexander kept a copy of *The Iliad* with him on his journeys of conquest and discovery.

Alexander also claimed that he was descended from Hercules, one of the Greek gods. With such a remarkable background, he grew up thinking he was destined for greatness.

As he grew up, Alexander returned to live with his father. He showed signs of great intelligence and ability. Many stories and legends grew up around him. In one, he bet his father he could tame the wild horse, Bucephalus (bew-CEF-ah-lus.) He tamed the horse and rode it for his father. Philip supposedly said, "Get yourself another kingdom, my boy, for Macedonia is not big enough to hold you!"

ALEXANDER THE GREAT WENT TO SCHOOL as the student of one of the wisest men of the ages. His tutor was the famous philosopher Aristotle. Aristotle was the most learned man in Greece. He taught Alexander medicine, science, and philosophy. Alexander thought of Aristotle as a father. Aristotle had a great influence on his young pupil.

KING OF MACEDONIA: Philip had conquered and united much of what is modern Greece while Alexander was growing up. Then, in 336 B.C., Philip was murdered. Alexander quickly took the throne. He fought several battles against those who rebelled against his rule. Then he pursued his father's plan to conquer the greatest power of the time, the Persians.

LEADING ARMIES OF CONQUEST: In 334 B.C., Alexander led an army of 44,000 soldiers against the Persians. Over the next several years he fought battles and conquered their armies in modern-day Turkey, Lebanon, Egypt, Iraq, and Iran.

Alexander moved swiftly and his army was often overpowering. Many of the cities they conquered had been held by the Persians for years. The conquest of these lands wasn't always easy. It took them months to take over the ancient city of Tyre, in what is now Lebanon. Alexander could be cruel and ruthless. After conquering Tyre, he had all the women and children sold into slavery. He sometimes had a terrible temper, and he could turn against his own men. On several occasions, he had his own close advisers put to death, when he thought they were disloyal.

But Alexander was also one of the greatest military commanders of all time. Through brilliant strategy, and the growing strength and

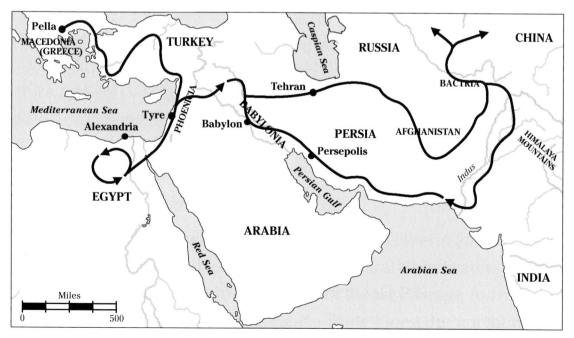

Alexander the Great's expeditions, 334 B.C. to 323 B.C.

numbers of his soldiers, he created the largest empire of the ancient world.

In Egypt, Alexander was welcomed as a liberator. The Egyptians had always resented the Persians. They made Alexander a pharaoh. He founded the city of Alexandria in Egypt. It became one of the great cities of the ancient world.

By 329 B.C., Alexander ruled all the lands that once belonged to Persia. Next, he and his army moved to the east. They ventured into the lands of modern-day Afghanistan. They crossed the forbidding mountains called the Hindu Kush. They reached the Indus River, traveling as far as India.

EXPLORING: Alexander had led his men as far as anyone from his part of the world had ever ventured. He wanted to find an ocean that people believed circled the world. Wherever he traveled, Alexander brought geographers and mathematicians. They developed maps that were used for centuries.

Alexander was ready to press on, but his men refused. They had loyally followed him for years, but they wanted to go home. Alexander finally agreed. He divided the army into three parts. One group built ships and took a sea route home. They traveled down the Indus, through the Arabian Sea and the Persian Gulf, and back to the Middle East. Another group took a land route home.

Alexander led the third group south along the Indus River. They headed west toward home, along the shore. But when the area became mountainous, they headed inland. Over the next months, they marched over desert. There wasn't enough food or water, and almost half the army died.

Finally, the weary army reached home. Their journey had lasted almost ten years and covered some 25,000 miles.

THE DEATH OF ALEXANDER: Over the next few years, Alexander tried to keep his huge empire together. But his realm was vast, and he was not well. He became ill after a banquet in 323 B.C. He died several days later, at the age of 32.

HIS DISCOVERY: Without Alexander at the helm, the empire fell apart. Yet his influence continued. He brought Greek language, culture, and thought to all the areas he conquered. The people of the areas he conquered continued to travel and trade for centuries. His mapmakers and geographers added a great amount of geographical information to what was known at the time about the world.

MARRIAGE AND FAMILY: In his mid-20s, Alexander married a Persian princess named Roxanne. They had two sons. One of them, Alexander IV, became king after his father's death. He was killed by enemies around 310 B.C. By 300 B.C., Alexander the Great's vast empire had split into many small states.

WORLD WIDE WEB SITE:

http://www.mpt.org/programsinterests/mpt/alexander

Roald Amundsen
1872 - 1928
Norwegian Explorer of the Arctic and Antarctica
Discovered the South Pole

ROALD AMUNDSEN WAS BORN on July 16, 1872, near Oslo, Norway. His name is pronounced "ROO-ahl AHM-uhn-suhn." His father was a sea captain who owned a fleet of ships. Roald was the youngest of four boys.

ROALD AMUNDSEN GREW UP around his father's shipyard. He learned all he could about ships and sailing. He was fascinated by tales of explorers and exploration. He was especially interested in the Arctic and Antarctica and the search for the **Northwest Passage**.

By the end of the 19th century, most of the surface of the planet had been explored. What remained were the North and South Polar regions. When Amundsen was growing up, **Fridtjof Nansen** had become a national hero for his polar discoveries. Amundsen had also read about the centuries-old search for the **Northwest Passage.** From the early 1500s, many explorers had tried to find a sea route linking the Atlantic and Pacific Oceans through the islands of the Canadian Arctic. Amundsen read about explorers of the Passage like **Sir John Franklin**. He was determined that he, too, would make an attempt someday.

ROALD AMUNDSEN WENT TO SCHOOL at the local schools. His father died when he was 14. His mother hoped he would become a doctor. She insisted he go to medical school. But when he was 21, his mother died, and he left medical school. He began his career as one of the great polar explorers.

FIRST VOYAGE TO THE ARCTIC: Amundsen's goal was to command his own Arctic expedition. He exercised to make his body strong. He learned all he could about navigating ships and leading men. His first taste of Arctic exploration was aboard a seal-hunting ship in 1894. He learned how to survive in the cold, vast reaches of the Arctic.

FIRST VOYAGE TO ANTARCTICA: In 1897, Amundsen served as first mate aboard the Belgian ship *Belgica*. The expedition's goal was to explore the Antarctic coast. But soon after crossing the

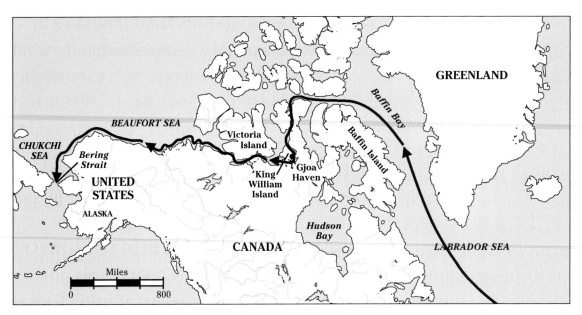

Amundsen's Northwest Passage expedition, 1903-1906.

Antarctic Circle the ship became frozen in the ice. Many of the crew became ill and developed scurvy. The *Belgica* didn't become free of the ice until 1899. By then, the captain was too ill to lead the return voyage. It was Amundsen who led the vessel out of the ice and toward home. He hadn't planned it, but he became part of the first crew to spend the winter in Antarctica. It was one of many "firsts" in his career.

SAILING THE NORTHWEST PASSAGE: Amundsen was eager to lead his own expedition. He decided to attempt to sail the entire Northwest Passage. He studied the paths of previous expeditions. He readied a new boat, the *Gjoa*, and hired a crew of six. On June 16, 1903, they left Norway, with provisions to last five years.

They sailed across the Atlantic, then along the west coast of Greenland. They headed around Baffin Island and then turned south. They found a cove that Amundsen named Gjoa Haven. They spent two years there. They got to know the local Inuit people.

From them, they learned to build igloos, what kinds of clothes to wear, and how to use sled dogs.

Amundsen and his crew also made important scientific measurements. They located the magnetic **North Pole**, which had been found by **James Clark Ross** in 1831. They made the important discovery that the magnetic Pole shifts location.

When the ice cleared in 1905 Amundsen continued on his course through the Northwest Passage. They spent another winter in the ice, then in 1906, took their ship through the Bering Strait. They were the first ship ever to travel the entire Northwest Passage.

Amundsen's ship the Gjoa, *1906.*

Amundsen.

Amundsen returned to Norway a hero. He was ready to explore again. He gave a series of lectures to raise money for his next journey. This time he wanted to reach the North Pole. He planned to use the *Fram*, Nansen's boat that had taken him across the Arctic. But while Amundsen was preparing for his journey in 1909, he received surprising news. On April 1909, **Robert E. Peary** had reached the North Pole. Amundsen had to change his plans.

THE RACE TO THE SOUTH POLE: By 1909, there were several expeditions trying to reach the **South Pole. Ernest Shackleton** had recently returned from a trip to Antarctica where he had almost reached the Pole. And **Robert Falcon Scott** was already heading to Antarctica to set up a camp and reach the Pole.

In June 1910, Amundsen left Norway. Only his brother knew his destination. He sailed to Antarctica aboard the *Fram*. He set up his base camp at the Bay of Whales. It was only several hundred miles from Scott's base camp at McMurdo Sound.

By that point, Amundsen had declared his goal to the world: to beat Scott to the South Pole. Over several months, Amundsen

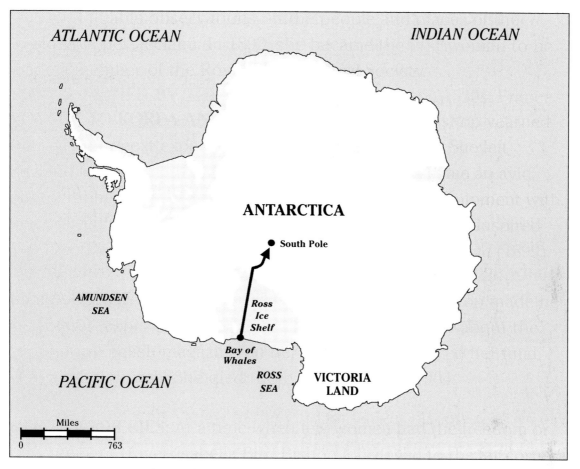

Amundsen's route to the South Pole, 1911.

planned his route. He set up supply camps he would use as stopping points on his journey.

Finally, on October 19, 1911, Amundsen set out for the Pole with a crew of four men. They traveled on four dog sleds. The weather was good, and they traveled quickly. They reached the South Pole on December 14, 1911, the first people to achieve that goal. Scott's crew wouldn't reach it for another 35 days.

Amundsen returned to his base camp on January 25, 1912. They had made their record-breaking journey in 99 days, covering more than 1,800 miles. The Amundsen crew rejoiced in their triumph.

The Norge.

They didn't yet know the horrible fate of Scott's crew, who all perished on their return journey.

THE *MAUD*: Amundsen returned to Norway a world-famous explorer. Yet he still yearned for more. He raised money for another expedition to the Arctic. In 1918, he built a new ship, the *Maud*, hoping to drift across the North Pole. But that was not to be. Instead, he traveled the **Northeast Passage**. Over two years, he navigated the passage through the Arctic along the coast of Russia and Siberia.

FLYING OVER THE NORTH POLE: In 1925, Amundsen and fellow explorer Lincoln Ellsworth attempted to be the first people to fly over the North Pole. But their attempt ended in failure when their plane had trouble and had to land short of their destination. In 1926

Richard E. Byrd became the first to fly over the North Pole. (Byrd's claim has been debated for several years.)

AIRSHIPS: Shortly after Byrd's 1926 flight, Amundsen, Ellsworth, and Umberto Nobile flew over the North Pole in a blimp, the *Norge*. Their path took them from Spitsbergen, Norway, over the Pole, to Alaska. They dropped the flags of their countries over the North Pole. When they landed in Alaska, Nobile tried to take all the credit for the expedition's success. That angered Amundsen, and he and Nobile quarreled.

SEARCHING FOR NOBILE: In 1928, Nobile crashed while flying a blimp across the Arctic. Despite their earlier argument, Amundsen immediately went to Nobile's rescue. The great Norwegian explorer was last seen on June 18, 1928, when his plane left on its rescue mission. His plane was never found.

In an interview he gave in the last year of his life, Amundsen tried to explain his love of the polar regions. "If only you knew how splendid it is up there," he said. "That's where I want to die."

HIS DISCOVERY: Amundsen is considered one of the greatest polar explorers. He was the first to navigate the Northwest Passage and the first to reach the South Pole. He may have also been the first to fly over the North Pole. Recent research indicates that Byrd never reached the North Pole. If that is true, then Amundsen's string of "firsts" includes that achievement, too.

WORLD WIDE WEB SITES:

http://www.mnc.net/norway/roald.html
http://www.south-pole.com/p0000101.htm

Neil Armstrong
1930-
American Astronaut
First Person to Walk on the Moon

NEIL ARMSTRONG WAS BORN on August 5, 1930, in Wapakoneta, Ohio, on his grandparents' farm. His parents were Stephen and Viola Armstrong. His father worked for the finance department of the state of Ohio. That meant that Neil moved often when he was young.

NEIL ARMSTRONG GREW UP in several communities in Ohio. His love of flying began at the age of two. His dad took him to the

National Air Races in Cleveland, Ohio. Neil loved the planes. He took his first plane ride at six, and he became determined to become a pilot.

Armstrong began taking flying lessons at 15. He worked at the local airport to pay for his lessons. He actually got his pilot's license before his car driver's license.

NEIL ARMSTRONG WENT TO SCHOOL at the local public schools. After graduating from Blume High School in Wapakoneta in 1947, he went to Purdue University on a Navy scholarship. Armstrong studied aeronautical engineering.

FLYING FOR THE NAVY: Armstrong left Purdue in 1949. He trained as a Navy fighter pilot, then flew missions in the Korean War. The U.S. was part of a United Nations (U.N.) military force fighting on the side of South Korea in their civil war. Armstrong flew 78 combat missions before returning to the U.S. He finished his bachelor of science degree in 1955, and began to work for **NASA** (National Aeronautics and Space Administration).

NASA: Armstrong worked for NASA for 17 years. He worked first as a NASA engineer in Ohio, then moved to California where he became a test pilot.

BECOMING A TEST PILOT: Like most of the early astronauts, Armstrong was a test pilot. He tried out some of the newest, fastest, and most advanced aircraft in the world. He tested over 200 different models, including the X-15, which could travel at 4,000 miles per hour. Armstrong was a scientist and engineer as well as a pilot. He helped develop, test, and make adjustments to these powerful

Apollo 11 *takeoff, July 16, 1969.*

aircraft. He also completed a master's degree in aerospace engineering at the University of Southern California.

16

THE COLD WAR: When Armstrong worked for NASA, the Soviet Union and the U.S. were locked in what was called the "Cold War." After World War II, the Soviet Union and the U.S. became the two strongest nations in the world. They represented two very different political systems. The U.S. was a democracy; the Soviet Union was a Communist state. The two "superpowers" also had powerful nuclear weapons. The relationship between the two nations was very important. For more than 40 years, the hostilities between them affected world politics.

SPUTNIK **AND THE SPACE RACE:** On October 4, 1957, the Soviets launched the very first satellite, *Sputnik 1*. It was the beginning of the Space Age and the Space Race.

Because of its military importance, the Space Race between the U.S. and the Soviet Union was always about much more than exploration. The Space Race was also about domination. Each country was afraid that the other would develop the weapons and technology to dominate them. The U.S. was astonished at the success of *Sputnik*. U.S. military leaders had no idea that the Soviets had the technology to launch a satellite. And the same technology that could launch a satellite could launch a missile. But *Sputnik* wasn't the only tremendous "first" for the Soviet space program.

YURI GAGARIN: On April 12, 1961, Soviet cosmonaut Yuri Gagarin became the first person to travel in space. Aboard the space capsule *Vostok 1*, he orbited the Earth once. He reached an altitude of 188 miles, traveling at 18,000 miles an hour. His flight lasted 108 minutes.

Once again, the Americans had been beaten by the Soviets.

ALAN SHEPARD: The U.S. entry into the space race came just three weeks later. **Alan Shepard** blasted into space on the morning of May 5, 1961. His flight carried him 116 miles into space and lasted 15 minutes. After traveling 302 miles, his capsule fell into the Atlantic Ocean.

After the success of Shepard's flight, President John F. Kennedy announced: "I believe this nation should commit itself to the goal, before the decade is out, of landing a man on the Moon and returning him safely to Earth." Now, the race to the Moon was on. Neil Armstrong would play the lead role in that race.

BECOMING AN ASTRONAUT: In 1962, Armstrong joined the astronaut program as part of the Apollo program. The goal of Apollo was to put a man on the Moon. Armstrong moved to Houston, Texas. He spent the next four years preparing for his trip to the Moon.

THE FLIGHT OF *GEMINI VIII*: Armstrong's first flight as an astronaut came on March 16, 1966. He shot into space as the captain of *Gemini VIII*. With him aboard *Gemini VIII* was astronaut David Scott. The goal of the mission was to dock their capsule, in space, with another orbiting spacecraft. Things went according to plan for the first part of the mission. But after the two spacecraft were connected, they began to gyrate. Shepard had to undock the two craft. He and Scott made an emergency landing, unhurt.

***APOLLO 11*:** Armstrong's next mission is the one for which he is famous. He was selected as commander of *Apollo 11*—the first mission to land a man on the Moon. Previous Apollo missions had orbited the Moon, but hadn't landed. Instead, they tested equipment and orbiting techniques, and made other preparations for *Apollo 11*.

Armstrong's fellow astronauts were Michael Collins and Edwin (Buzz) Aldrin. Collins was the pilot in charge of flying the Command

Armstrong and Buzz Aldrin place the U.S. flag on the Moon, July 1969.

Module. Aldrin piloted the Lunar Module. That was the space craft that would launch from the Command Module and take him and Armstrong to the Moon's surface.

Apollo 11 left Earth on July 16, 1969. People the world over watched the voyage on television. When they landed on the Moon, Armstrong piloted the Lunar Module to the surface.

FIRST PERSON TO WALK ON THE MOON: On July 20, 1969, Neil Armstrong became a part of history. He climbed down the ladder

Armstrong's footprint on the Moon's surface, July 1969.

from the Lunar Module and set foot on the Moon. As he stepped onto the surface, he spoke these words:

"That's one small step for man, one giant leap for mankind."

Aldrin joined Armstrong on the Moon, and they spent nearly 3 hours on the surface. They gathered rock and soil samples. They also placed a plaque on the Moon. It said: "Here men from the planet Earth first set foot upon the Moon. July 1969 A.D. We came in peace for all mankind."

The crew of *Apollo 11* returned to Earth on July 24, 1969, as heroes. Armstrong received many awards, from the U.S. government and NASA. He continued to work for NASA for two years. He didn't go into space again.

LEAVING NASA: Armstrong left NASA in 1971. From 1971 to 1979, he taught engineering at the University of Cincinnati. After leaving teaching, he served on the boards of several businesses.

The Earth, as seen from the Moon, July 1969.

Armstrong also served on a commission that planned the future of the NASA space program. And after the crash of the **space shuttle** *Challenger* in 1986, President Ronald Reagan named Armstrong to the commission that investigated the disaster.

NEIL ARMSTRONG'S HOME AND FAMILY: Armstrong married Janet Shearon in 1956. They have two sons, Eric and Mark. The Armstrongs live quietly on their farm in Lebanon, Ohio.

HIS DISCOVERY: Armstrong was the first person to walk on the Moon. It was an astonishing feat of exploration, and is considered one of the greatest in human history.

WORLD WIDE WEB SITES:

http://starchild.gsfc.nasa.gov/docs/StarChild/shadow/whos_who_
    level2/armstrong.ht ml
http://www.grc.nasa.gov/WWW/PAO/html/neilabio.html
http://www.jsc.nasa.gov/BIOS/htmlbios/armstrong-na.html

William Baffin

1584? - 1622
English Navigator and Explorer
Explored the Canadian Arctic
Baffin Bay and Baffin Island Are Named for Him

WILLIAM BAFFIN WAS BORN in England around 1584. Nothing is known about his early life.

FIRST VOYAGE: Baffin probably took his first voyage in 1612. He was the pilot of a ship captained by James Hall. They were searching for the **Northwest Passage**.

NORTHWEST PASSAGE: From the early 1500s, many people believed that a passage from Europe to Asia existed through what is now Canada. They were looking for a sea route linking the Atlantic and Pacific Oceans through the islands of the Canadian Arctic. Many of these explorers were English. At that time, Spain and Portugal controlled the sea routes closer to the equator. England wanted to find a route to control and use for trade with Asia.

Baffin's 1612 voyage met with disaster when Captain Hall was killed by Indians. Baffin returned home to England and wrote about his voyage.

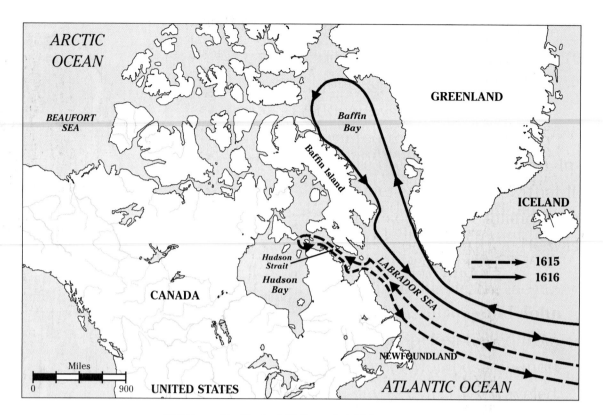

William Baffin's 1615 and 1616 voyages.

VOYAGE OF 1615: In 1615 Baffin went to sea again, this time with Robert Bylot, who had sailed with **Henry Hudson**. They sailed in Hudson's old ship, the *Discovery*. Looking for the Northwest Passage, they explored the Hudson Strait. At the northern portion of the strait, Baffin measured the tides. He wrote later that he could tell by the tides that "there could be no passage in this place."

On this voyage, Baffin attempted to measure the **longitude** of his location by observing where the moon was in the night sky. At that time, there was not an instrument that could measure longitude. Baffin's is the first recorded attempt to determine it. Modern mapmakers are amazed at his ability to determine longitude and his notes on the tides. (You can read about **latitude** and **longitude** in the Glossary.)

A later Arctic explorer, **William Parry**, named Baffin Bay and Baffin Island after the early English navigator. He, too, was impressed with the precision of Baffin's measurements.

VOYAGE OF 1616: In 1616, Baffin sailed into the bay that bears his name. He was once again the pilot aboard the *Discovery*, with Bylot as captain. But they didn't find a Northwest Passage to the east. Instead, the way was blocked with ice.

VOYAGES TO THE EAST: Baffin's next voyage was not to the west, but to the east. In 1617, he sailed to the Red Sea in the Middle East as part of a trading mission. There, he made maps of the Red Sea and the Persian Gulf. From there, he went on to India, then back to England.

Baffin made another journey to the Persian Gulf in 1620 as pilot on the *London*. But Portuguese and Dutch ships were waiting for them, ready to attack. They fought, and the captain of Baffin's ship was killed.

In 1621, Baffin was again in the Middle East taking measurements on an island off the coast of what is now Iran. He was killed during a sea battle between the English and the Portuguese.

HIS DISCOVERY: Baffin is remembered as a brilliant navigator. Without modern tools, he attempted to measure longitude. His mapping of the Canadian Arctic was later found to be very accurate. The naming of Baffin Island and Baffin Bay in his honor is a lasting tribute to his discoveries.

WORLD WIDE WEB SITES:

http://www.baughen.demon.co.uk/HallFame.htm
http://collections.ic.gc.ca/arctic/explore/baffin.htm

VASCO NUÑEZ DE BALBOA.

Descubridor del Mar del Sur. Nació en
Xeréz de Estremadura en el año de 1475.
y fué muerto en Acla en 1517.

Vasco Núñez de Balboa

1475 - 1519
Spanish Conquistador and Explorer
First European to See the Pacific Ocean
from the New World

VASCO NÚÑEZ DE BALBOA WAS BORN in 1475 in the city of Jerez
de los Caballeros in Spain. Very little is known about his early life. He

was from a poor family and left Spain in his mid-20s for adventure in the **New World**.

VOYAGE TO THE NEW WORLD: Around 1501, Balboa sailed for the New World aboard a ship captained by Rodrigo de Bastidas (bah-STEE-dahs). Like many explorers of that time, Bastidas had heard of the success of **Christopher Columbus**. He sailed in search of treasure.

Bastidas took the crew to present-day Colombia. There, they explored the coast. Balboa then landed on Hispaniola (now Haiti and the Dominican Republic). He became a farmer, but by 1510 his farm failed and he was deeply in debt.

According to legend, Balboa stowed away aboard a ship to avoid paying his debts. The ship was captained by Martin Fernandez de Enciso. It was bound for the Spanish colony of San Sebastian, in what is now Colombia. When he was discovered, Balboa convinced Enciso that he was a good sailor and soldier.

On their way to San Sebastian, they met the ship of **Francisco Pizarro.** He told them that San Sebastian was destroyed. They traveled together to the site of the colony and discovered that it was in ruins.

On his earlier voyage with Bastidas, Balboa had seen a site close to San Sebastian, in what is now Panama. He suggested they start a new settlement there. So the crew moved to the area, called Darien. There, Balboa founded the town of Santa Maria de la Antigua. They took the land and belongings of the native people living there, including food and gems.

Balboa became one of the leaders of the colony. He also began to hunt for gold. He used whatever means he had to, including enslaving and torturing the natives, to get what he wanted. He had Enciso sent back to Spain, and continued to build his power.

Balboa learned from some of the local natives that there was a huge body of water nearby, and possibly gold. He decided to go look for it. He sent messengers to Spain to request men and money. But King Ferdinand of Spain had heard bad reports about Balboa. He didn't send the men.

Balboa decided to go on his own. He left Santa Maria with nearly 200 Spaniards and 1,000 natives. They sailed to an area near the isthmus of Panama. They landed at a place called Acla. There, they found the place where the land is narrowest between the Atlantic and Pacific Oceans.

They set out through the tropical rain forest. The weather was hot and humid, and the Spaniards traveled in heavy armor. They fought natives along the way, but also found gold and slaves. It took them 26 days, but they finally made it through the dense, steaming jungle and over mountains.

SEEING THE PACIFIC OCEAN: On September 27, 1513, Balboa became the first European to see the Pacific Ocean from the **New World**. He and his men took several more days to reach the shore of the ocean. He called it the "South Sea." They planted a cross and Balboa claimed the land and sea for Spain.

The expedition returned to Santa Maria in January 1514. Balboa was a hero for a while, but trouble was brewing. King Ferdinand had sent a man named Pedro Avias de Avila, called Pedrarias (pay-DRAR-ee-ahs), to Santa Maria. He was to be the new ruler, instead of Balboa. Pedrarias was jealous of Balboa and plotted against him.

Balboa still had grand ideas. He wanted to go back to the Pacific. He built ships and had natives carry them, piece by piece, through the jungle and over the mountains. They reached the Pacific, and Balboa led an expedition to the nearby islands.

Pedrarias was still full of hatred for Balboa. He lured him back to Santa Maria. He sent Pizarro to find Balboa and tell him to return. The unsuspecting Balboa returned to Santa Maria. Pedrarias arrested him and had him tried for rebellion and treason. The charges were false, but the court was under Pedrarias's control. Balboa was convicted and sentenced to death. He was executed in January 1519.

HIS DISCOVERY: Balboa was a fearless and often ruthless explorer. He is remembered for his trip through some of the most dense jungle in the world, and for being the first European to see the Pacific. In modern Panama, there is still no road in the area where Balboa forged a path through the rain forest.

WORLD WIDE WEB SITES:

http://campus.northpark.edu/history/webchron/Americas/
  Balboa.html
http://www.win.tue.nl/~engels/discovery/balboa.html

Robert Ballard

1942-
American Oceanographer and Explorer
Who Discovered the *Titanic*

ROBERT BALLARD WAS BORN on June 30, 1942, in Wichita, Kansas. His full name is Robert Duane Ballard. His parents were Chester and Harriet Ballard. Chester was an engineer who built jets. Harriet was a homemaker. Ballard has a brother named Richard and a sister named Nancy.

ROBERT BALLARD GREW UP in San Diego, California. His family had moved there when he was little. Some of his earliest memories are of exploring the beaches and ocean outside San Diego.

"As long as I can remember, I've been fascinated by the sea," he says. "As a boy, I was always collecting shells and driftwood that the ocean washed up on the beaches. I also loved to watch the creatures that lived underwater in tidal pools. As a teenager, instead of becoming a surfer like most of my friends, I took up scuba diving and began to explore the world just beneath the ocean surface."

He also loved to visit the Scripps Institution of Oceanography in San Diego. He spent hours watching the many exotic fish in the aquarium.

Ballard also loved to read. His favorite book was *20,000 Leagues under the Sea*. That's a science fiction classic by Jules Verne written over 100 years ago. It tells the story of Captain Nemo and his crew of ocean explorers.

ROBERT BALLARD WENT TO SCHOOL at the local public schools in San Diego. When he was 11, the family moved to Downey, California, outside Los Angeles. Ballard was a good student, and an athlete, too. At Downey High, he played football, basketball, and tennis.

Ballard always found time to continue exploring the ocean nearby. The summer he was 17, he got a job at the Scripps Institution. He sailed on a research ship. Once, they got caught in a fierce storm. The boat was damaged, and they nearly sunk. But Ballard loved the sea. He knew that when he grew up, he wanted to explore the ocean.

In 1960, Ballard graduated from high school. He went to the University of California at Santa Barbara for college. There, he studied science. He also trained to be a military officer in the ROTC (Reserve Officers Training Corps). After graduating from college in 1965, he went on to the University of Hawaii. He studied marine geology. He also had a part-time job training dolphins for Sea Life Park. "I spent hours teaching dolphins to dive through hoops," he recalls.

In 1967, Ballard was called up to serve in the Navy. He moved to Massachusetts, where he worked for the Office of Naval Research. He also worked at the famous Woods Hole Oceanographic Institute. There, he did research on submarines.

After his Navy service, Ballard got a job with Woods Hole. They paid for him to finish his Ph.D. in oceanography. He spent four years on his degree, completing it in 1974. Next, he began a career that has made him one of the most famous explorers of modern times.

BEGINNING THE LIFE OF AN EXPLORER: In the early 1970s, Ballard became part of the team working on the submarine *Alvin*. The *Alvin* was small—it held just three people. Ballard and his team spent two years studying a section of the Atlantic Ocean floor.

Ballard designed a small, remote-control submarine for the project. Called the *Argus*, it could take pictures thousands of feet below the ocean surface. In 1976, Ballard went to the Cayman Trough in the Caribbean. That's an ocean canyon in the Atlantic that is 24,000 feet deep. Ballard used the *Alvin* to make a map of the area. He also collected rocks. They are the deepest rock samples ever found.

Ballard with students from the JASON Project on the big island of Hawaii.

In 1977 Ballard took part in an expedition to the Galapagos Islands. That is a group of islands in the Pacific Ocean off the coast of Ecuador. Scientists wanted to know what caused warm water temperatures in the area.

The group discovered that there are heat vents on the ocean floor. These release hot water from under the ocean. The warm currents are full of minerals that feed a large and unusual group of marine animals. These strange creatures include giant clams and eight-foot long tube worms. Later explorations found "black smokers," heat vents that released lava from undersea volcanoes.

Ballard's discoveries amazed the world. And they spurred him on to further ocean quests.

THE *ARGO-JASON* SUBMARINES: Part of that search included building submarines that could go deeper and farther into the ocean depths. Ballard developed two remote-control subs, the *Argo* and the *Jason*. The *Argo* had three video cameras and could operate in almost total darkness. The *Jason* launched with the *Argo,* then detached itself to explore the ocean with its mechanical arms.

FINDING THE *TITANIC:* In 1985, using the *Argo* and the *Jason*, Ballard made one of the greatest discoveries of modern times. He located the famous sunken ship, the *Titanic*.

The luxury steamship *Titanic* was on its first voyage when it struck an iceberg and sank in 1912. More than 1,500 people died. The boat had never been found. Everything about the *Titanic* fascinated Ballard. "My idea was to pursue her remains in the spirit of exploration," he said. In 1984, using the *Argo* and *Jason,* he put together a team to find the lost ship.

"I knew it wasn't going to be easy," he said. After the *Titanic* sank, "the area had the biggest earthquake ever recorded underwater. It triggered an avalanche of moving mud about the size of New England." The *Titanic* could be beneath all that mud.

But on September 1, 1985, Ballard and his team found the *Titanic*. The *Argo* sent back pictures of the boiler of the ship. Over several days, the cameras sent back photos of the ship outside and inside. Inside the sunken ship, china, furniture, and personal items were clearly visible.

Ballard's discovery made him famous. He appeared on television shows and in newspapers and magazines. He wrote a best-seller about his experiences, too. He said that he was pleased to "make science exciting" for the public.

Ballard with students from the JASON Project at NASA's Johnson Space Center in Houston, Texas.

For Ballard, finding the *Titanic* was "the beginning of a new era in exploration. The *Titanic* is the first pyramid to be found in the deep sea. There are thousands of others, waiting to tell their tales."

OTHER FAMOUS SHIPWRECKS: Since the *Titanic*, Ballard has discovered the sites of many of the most famous shipwrecks in history. In 1989, he found the *Bismarck*. That is a German warship from World War II. In 1993, he explored the *Lusitania*. That ship had been sunk by the Germans in World War I. And in 1998, he discovered the *U.S.S. Yorktown*. That is a U.S. warship that went down in the battle of Midway, one of the most important battles of World War II.

Ballard next to the Amazon River in Peru for the JASON Project.

In 2000, Ballard explored the wreckage of Pearl Harbor. In December 1941, the Japanese destroyed most of the U.S. naval fleet in Pearl Harbor, Hawaii. After the attack, the U.S. declared war on Japan and World War II began.

In July 2002, Ballard announced another amazing discovery. He found the remains of *PT 109*. That was a torpedo boat captained by John F. Kennedy in World War II. Kennedy saved most of his men when the boat was sunk by the Japanese. In 1960 he became President. Ballard will not move the *PT 109*. Instead, it will remain a memorial to the two crew members who died in the attack.

THE JASON PROJECT: Ballard started the JASON project in 1989. After discovering the *Titanic*, he'd received thousands of letters from kids. He wanted to encourage them to share exploring with him. Each year, the JASON project chooses an underwater site where kids in grades four to nine work with scientists. Kids all over the world are connected to the site through the Internet. They can ask the scientists questions and keep up with research.

The JASON project has connected kids with scientists to explore shipwrecks in Lake Ontario, coral reefs in the Caribbean, Florida marine life, and other places. "We have seen less than one-tenth of one percent of the planet beneath the oceans," says Ballard. "We know more about the mountain ranges on Mars than we do about the mountain ranges beneath our own oceans. But technology has opened the door."

INSTITUTE FOR EXPLORATION: In 1997 Ballard started to build the Institute for Exploration in Mystic, Connecticut. It's a place where he can share the results of his exploration. There's a model of the *Jason* you can climb into to get the feeling of what it's like to explore in a little submarine.

Also in 1997 Ballard made a major discovery in the Mediterranean Sea. He found eight ancient ships. Some were from the Roman empire of 2,000 years ago. Some were **Phoenician** ships, from an ancient culture that flourished in the Mediterranean 2,500 years ago. Many were still upright, and he was even able to explore the cargo they were carrying when they sank.

In 1999 Ballard traveled to the Black Sea. He was in search of evidence of a flood that may have occurred 7,500 years ago. That flood may have been the basis for the story of Noah's Ark that appears in the Bible.

ROBERT BALLARD'S HOME AND FAMILY: Ballard has been married twice. With his first wife, Marjorie Hargas, he had two sons, Todd and Douglas. They divorced in 1990. In 1991, Ballard married Barbara Earle. They have two children, William and Emily. Barbara works with Ballard, and they have produced film documentaries on their work. When they're not out on the oceans, the Ballard family lives in Connecticut.

HIS DISCOVERY: Ballard is one of the most important ocean explorers of modern times. His discoveries have added to our understanding of science and of history, and he plans to explore for years to come.

"I am an explorer who's a geologist," he says. "I'm an explorer who loves the ocean. And I'm an explorer who loves technology. To be an explorer I had to be a scientist. I love science. I love the pursuit of anything, and the pursuit of the truth is noble."

WORLD WIDE WEB SITE:

http://www.jasonproject.org

Joseph Banks

1743 - 1820
English Naturalist and Explorer
Traveled with James Cook
Collected Plants in North and South America, on Pacific Islands, Australia, and Iceland

JOSEPH BANKS WAS BORN on February 13, 1743, in London, England. His parents were wealthy landowners in Lincolnshire, where he grew up.

JOSEPH BANKS WENT TO SCHOOL at home until he was nine. He was then sent to Harrow, an exclusive private boys' school. According to the records at Harrow, he enjoyed playing games more than studying. When he was 13, he was sent to Eton, a famous private high school for boys.

For college, Banks went to Christ Church, part of Oxford University. He loved botany, which is the study of plants. He studied at Oxford for several years. When his father died in 1761, Banks inherited his money and land. He became a very wealthy young man.

BECOMING A NATURALIST AND AN EXPLORER: Banks decided to devote the rest of his life to science. He wanted to become a "naturalist" — a scientist who studies plants and animals.

He also wanted to study plants and animals in their natural environment. When he was 23, he traveled to Newfoundland and Labrador in Canada. There, he collected plants. He discovered that he loved to explore.

EXPLORING WITH CAPTAIN COOK: When Banks returned to England, he joined the Royal Society. That is an organization that promotes studying science and the arts. In 1768, they were putting together an expedition to Tahiti led by **James Cook**. (For a map of this expedition, see the Cook entry.)

Cook was taking a group of scientists who wanted to observe a solar eclipse. The best place to view the eclipse was on the Pacific island of Tahiti. Banks wanted to go on the expedition, too. It was a chance unlike any other to study plants in unknown lands. In some ways, it was like a modern-day scientist getting a chance to travel to another planet.

Banks spent the equivalent of $1 million of his own money on the expedition. He used the money to bring along other scientists, helpers, and an artist to draw pictures of the plants.

The expedition left England in 1768, with Banks serving as Senior Scientific Officer. They first stopped and explored in South America. They visited Tierra del Fuego, at the tip of South America. Banks took samples of plants never seen before in Europe.

From South America the ship headed to Tahiti. While the scientists observed the eclipse, Banks gathered plants and explored the island. He made detailed observations of the plants, and the people, too.

AUSTRALIA: From Tahiti, the Cook expedition headed to what is now Australia. Banks called the point at which they landed "Botany Bay" because it was full of plant treasures. He saw a kangaroo for the first time. By the end of the expedition, Banks had identified an incredible 1,300 new species of plants. He had also been part of Cook's circumnavigation of the globe. He returned to England in 1771 and was greeted as a hero. He was eager to explore again.

ICELAND: In 1772, Banks went on another voyage of discovery. This time he visited Iceland and the Hebrides and Orkney Islands off the coast of Scotland. It would be his final voyage as an explorer.

When Banks returned to England, King George III asked him to direct the Royal Gardens. He also was elected President of the Royal Society. In that position, he helped organize scientific expeditions all over the world. Some of the explorers he helped were **George Vancouver, Mungo Park,** and **Matthew Flinders**.

41

Banks also remained deeply involved with Australia. He helped organize settlers to move to the new country. He was involved with choosing the colony's leaders.

JOSEPH BANKS'S HOME AND FAMILY: Banks married a woman named Dorothea Hugessen in 1779. They had no children. Banks died in England on June 19, 1820, at the age of 77.

HIS DISCOVERY: Banks is remembered as one of the first and most important scientific explorers. He was so important to the development of Australia that the country was almost named for him. His vast collection of plants formed a major part of the Natural History Museum in London.

WORLD WIDE WEB SITES:

http://www.anbg.gov.au/biography/banks.biography.html
http://www.asap.unimelb.edu.au/bsparcs/biogs/P000037b.htm
http://www.slnsw.gov.au/banks/intro/biognote.htm

Willem Barents

1550? - 1597
Dutch Explorer Who Looked for the Northeast Passage

WILLEM BARENTS WAS BORN around 1550 on Terschelling Island, in the Netherlands. Little is known about his life until he became an explorer.

THE NORTHEAST PASSAGE: Barents spent his career looking for the **Northeast Passage**. In the 1500s, Portugal and Spain controlled the sea routes from Europe to the riches of the East. Other countries, especially England and the Netherlands, wanted to find a sea route to Asia by a northern route, following the Russian coast of the Arctic Ocean. They wanted to use the passage as a trade route to Asia. Early explorers like **Sebastian Cabot** of England and Barents traveled north from Europe and explored the Arctic looking for the passage.

FIRST JOURNEY: Barents's first expedition to the Arctic took place in 1594. He left Amsterdam, sailed north through the North Sea and reached as far as Novaya Zemlya. Novaya Zemlya is an island and now part of Russia. It lies north of the mainland between the Kara Sea and what was then called the Murmean Sea. In 1594, Barents sailed as far as the northern tip of the island. The weather became too harsh, and he sailed for home.

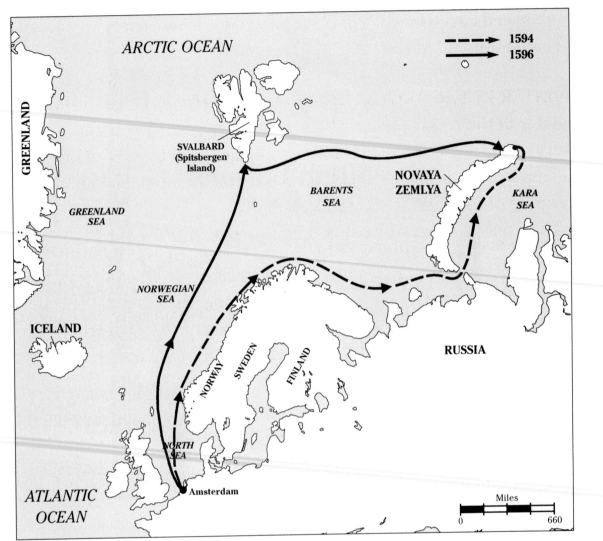

Barents's 1594 and 1596 expeditions.

SECOND JOURNEY: Barents led a second expedition in 1595. This trip included seven ships, loaded with goods to trade in China. But the ships had to turn back when they reached the northwest Russian coast and found the way blocked by ice.

THIRD JOURNEY: Barents led a final expedition in 1596. This time, he and his two ships discovered Spitsbergen Island (now part of Svalbard). They thought they had reached Greenland. Barents's ship sailed east to the tip of Novaya Zemlya, where the ship became trapped in the ice.

WINTER IN THE ARCTIC: Barents and his crew of 17 spent the winter in the Arctic. With grit and determination, 15 of them survived. They built a cabin with a fireplace, and they lived on animals they caught. Throughout the winter, Barents kept careful records of the weather and geography.

When spring came, Barents's boat remained trapped in the ice. The crew took the small boats from the larger ship. They set out for home, but Barents didn't survive. He died one week into the voyage. The rest of the crew sailed and rowed their way to the northern Russian coast, some 1,600 miles. They were greeted in Europe as heroes.

BARENTS'S JOURNAL: Barents's winter cabin and his journal were found in 1875. The modern world learned even more about the bravery and ability of this early Dutch explorer.

HIS DISCOVERY: On his three journeys in the Arctic, Barents gathered valuable information on geography and weather. He is one of the most important early explorers of the Arctic. The Murmean Sea, which he had explored on all three of his expeditions, was renamed the Barents Sea in his honor in 1853.

WORLD WIDE WEB SITES:

http://library.thinkquest.org/C001692/english/index.php3?
  subject=explorers/
http://www.ub.uit.no/northernlights/eng/wbarentsz.htm

Gertrude Bell

1868-1926
English Archeologist, Explorer, and Writer
Archeological Explorer of the Middle East

GERTRUDE BELL WAS BORN on July 14, 1868, in Durham, England. She grew up in a wealthy family with one brother.

GERTRUDE BELL WENT TO SCHOOL at home, then at a school in London. She went to Oxford University for college. She completed her degree in just two years. She graduated with a "first," the highest honors, at age 20.

STARTING A LIFE OF TRAVEL: Bell traveled to Persia (now Iran) in 1888. She stayed with her uncle, who was the English ambassador. She found she loved the Middle East, and travel.

TRAVELING AROUND THE WORLD: Bell traveled around the world twice, from 1897 to 1898, and from 1902 to 1903. She also became an excellent mountain climber.

THE MIDDLE EAST: Bell especially loved the land and the people of the Middle East. She traveled throughout the region, exploring on archeology expeditions. She went on "digs" in Turkey, Syria, and other parts of the Middle East.

Bell learned Arabic, Persian, and other languages spoken in the area. She got to know the various tribes well. They called her "daughter of the desert." She traveled, accompanied by a few male guides, where European women had never been. She knew the land so well that the Royal Geographical Society gave her the Gold Medal for exploration.

Bell wrote about her discoveries. In books like *The Thousand and One Churches*, she wrote about exploring ancient ruins. These were often illustrated with her own photographs.

GOVERNMENT SERVICE: In 1914, World War I broke out. Because she knew the land and the people of the Middle East so well, Bell worked for the British government during the war. After the war, she served on a commission headed by Winston Churchill on the future of the Middle East. She was the only woman on a commission of 40.

IRAQ: Bell helped to establish the boundaries for what became modern-day Iraq. She also helped to establish Prince Faisal as its first ruler. She was a close political advisor to the prince. Bell was often called the "Uncrowned Queen of Iraq." She even helped to write the laws for the new country.

Bell spent the rest of her life in Iraq. She became head of the Iraq Museum in Baghdad. She was also responsible for collecting and storing the ancient art of the country. She was one of the first archeologists to insist that artifacts found in a country should stay in the country, as part of a nation's treasures.

At her death in 1926, Bell left money to continue the study of archeology in her adopted country.

HER DISCOVERY: Bell is remembered as a powerful force in the forming of modern-day Iraq. Her explorations helped to build and protect the country's collection of artifacts.

WORLD WIDE WEB SITE:

http://www.gerty.ncl.ac.uk/HOME/Intro.htm

Benjamin of Tudela
1100s
Spanish Rabbi Who Wrote of His Travels to the Jewish Communities of Europe, North Africa, and the Middle East

EARLY LIFE: Little is known about the early life of Benjamin of Tudela. He was a Jewish rabbi from Tudela, a city in northern Spain.

Benjamin lived in the second half of the 1100s. During that time, many Jews faced discrimination because of their religious beliefs. Most of the countries of Europe were Christian nations. Jews were often threatened and could not live in safety. Some were even forced from their homes.

THE TRAVELS OF BENJAMIN OF TUDELA: Benjamin traveled throughout Europe, North Africa, and the Middle East visiting Jewish communities. He wanted to find safe places for Jewish people if they were forced to leave Europe.

Benjamin began his journey around 1160. He left Spain and traveled north to France. He visited several Jewish communities there. Next, he went to Italy and Greece. From there he traveled to Turkey, noting the way of life of Jews, Christians, and Muslims alike.

From Europe he traveled to the Middle East. There he visited modern-day Lebanon, Syria, and Israel. He traveled to Iraq, Iran, and Egypt. Everywhere he went, he noted the treatment of Jews, the size of their communities, and their religious practices. He saw many of the great cities of the ancient world, including Baghdad, Alexandria, and Damascus. He noted that in some cities Jews were treated with great respect, while in others they were segregated and physically threatened.

THE TRAVELS OF BENJAMIN OF TUDELA: Benjamin returned to Spain in 1173. He set down his observations in a book that has been read for centuries. Benjamin's remarkable record was called *The Travels of Benjamin of Tudela*. Benjamin wrote his book in Hebrew. It was read and enjoyed from that time by Jewish readers. In the 1500s it was translated into Latin, and many Europeans read it. It has since been translated into many other languages.

HIS DISCOVERY: Benjamin's *Travels* are still valued by modern readers. Even though historians think he may have exaggerated some things — he sometimes wrote down legends as if they were real — his record is important. People of his own time learned about other people and lands they knew little about. People of modern times can glimpse into a world now 1,000 years in the past.

WORLD WIDE WEB SITES:

http://www.pbs.org/wgbh/nova/israel/losttribes.html
http://www.us-israel.org/jsource/biography/BenjaminTudelo.html
http://www.uscolo.edu/history/seminar/benjamin.htm

Vitus Bering

1681-1741
Danish Explorer, Navigator, and Mapmaker
Led Two Expeditions to Alaska for Russia

VITUS BERING WAS BORN on August 12, 1681, in Horsens, Denmark. His full name was Vitus Jonassen Bering. Very little is known about his early life.

GOING TO SEA: When he was a young adult, Bering began to make his living as a sailor. He visited India and other countries in Asia. In 1703, he joined the Russian Navy. He fought in sea battles for Russia and rose to the rank of captain.

FIRST EXPEDITION: In 1724, Czar Peter the Great of Russia asked Bering to lead an expedition across Siberia all the way to Alaska. Peter wanted to know more about the eastern part of his vast empire. He wanted maps drawn that described the land. He wanted to know what kinds of people lived there.

But most of all he wanted to know whether Siberia and Alaska were connected by land, or if they were separated by water. The Russians were interested in finding a **Northeast Passage** to trade goods with Asia. They wanted to use a route along the northern coast of Siberia through the Arctic Ocean.

Bering and a crew of 100 left St. Petersburg, Russia, in 1725. They spent the next two years traveling across the enormous expanse of Siberia. After traveling more than 5,000 miles, they arrived at the city of Okhotsk, on the eastern coast of Russia. They spent the next year building ships and getting ready for the next part of their journey.

DISCOVERING THE BERING STRAIT: In the summer of 1728, they sailed across the Sea of Okhotsk and reached the Kamchatka Peninsula. Next, they sailed north up the coast of the peninsula. In August 1728, Bering came to the water strait that separated the two land masses. The fog was so thick, he could not see the land across the water from Russia. But he was convinced that it was another continent, separated from Russia by water. He was right. It was Alaska.

Bering sailed north through the strait and into the Arctic Ocean. Then, he turned back, sailed through the strait again, and headed back to Kamchatka. The waterway he had sailed between Russia and North America was later named for him, the Bering Strait.

SECOND EXPEDITION: Bering returned to St. Petersburg in 1730. In 1733, he was chosen to lead another expedition. This was called the Great Nordic Expedition. Bering began this second exploration in 1733, with more than 3,000 men. Over the course of the next several years, they mapped most of the Arctic coast of Siberia.

Bering reached Kamchatka in 1740. He and his crew spent the winter there. In the summer of 1741, they set out for Alaska in two ships, the *St. Peter* and the *St. Paul.* The ships became separated during a storm. The *St. Peter*, captained by Bering, set out for Alaska. They reached land off the Gulf of Alaska.

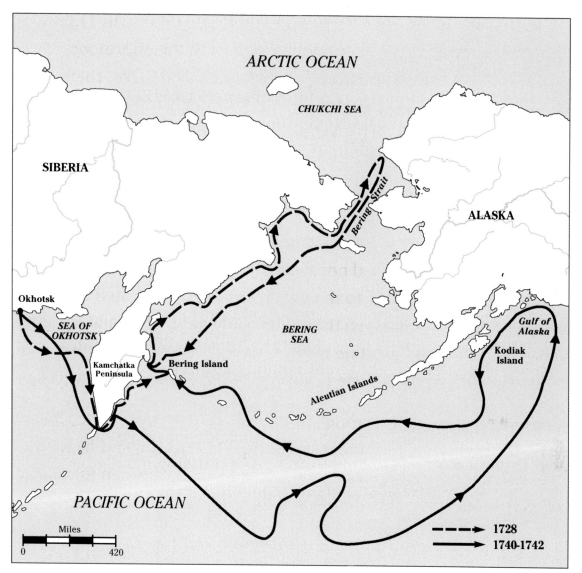

Bering's voyages, 1728 and 1740-1742.

Their stay was short, because they were running out of food. The trip back to Kamchatka was difficult, but Bering finally sighted land in November 1741. They thought they had made it to Kamchatka, but they had landed on a deserted island, later named Bering Island. The men built crude huts for shelter, but over the winter they faced starvation and freezing weather. Bering was among 32 men who died that winter.

In the spring, the remaining crew rebuilt their ship and sailed for Kamchatka, arriving in August 1742.

HIS DISCOVERY: Bering is remembered as a brave and able explorer. He is noted for exploring the strait that bears his name, for his mapmaking, and for opening up Alaska as a source of trade for Russia.

No one really knows what Bering looked like. In 1991, an expedition of Danish and Russian scientists went to Bering Island to search for the remains of his second voyage. They found the cannons from the *St. Peter*, several huts, and graves. The skeletons from the graves were analyzed, and one was determined to be Bering's. From that, artists made a drawing of him. After their examinations were over, his remains were returned and buried on Bering Island.

WORLD WIDE WEB SITES:

http://www.horsenmuseum.dk/bering/ber_en.htm
http://www.um.dk/english/danmark/danmarksbog/kap6/6-23.asp

Isabella Bird Bishop
1831-1904
English Traveler, Writer, and Explorer
First Female Member of the Royal Geographical Society

ISABELLA BIRD BISHOP WAS BORN on October 15, 1831, in North Yorkshire, England. "Bishop" became her last name when she married. Her name when she was born was Isabella Lucy Bird. Her parents were Edward and Dora Bird. Her father was a minister. She had one sibling, a younger sister named Henrietta. The two were very close.

ISABELLA BIRD BISHOP GREW UP in a comfortable home. Her parents were very religious. Isabella was educated at home. Her mother taught her literature, French, history, and drawing. Her father taught her poetry, chemistry, and biology. Isabella loved to ride horses. She and her father would ride near their home, while he told her about farming, raising livestock, and other practical things about life in the country.

Isabella was an active, curious child. But by the time she reached her 20's, she was often sick. Her doctor recommended travel.

VOYAGE TO NORTH AMERICA: Isabella's father agreed with the doctor. He decided Isabella should travel to North America. In 1854, Isabella Bird traveled alone, by ship, to Canada and the U.S. She toured the countries by stagecoach and by train.

When Bishop returned home, her father was ill. After his death, she reviewed the letters she had written home about her travels. She decided to turn them into a book. *The Englishwoman in America,* published in 1856, was a success.

Bishop, her sister, and her mother moved to Edinburgh, Scotland. Her mother died in 1866. Bishop once again became ill. Once again, her doctor encouraged her to travel.

VOYAGE TO AUSTRALIA, HAWAII, AND THE U.S.: Bishop traveled to Australia in 1872. After several months there and in New Zealand, she sailed for Hawaii.

Bishop loved Hawaii. She climbed volcanoes and rode horseback over the mountains. From Hawaii, she sailed for San Francisco. She traveled east, to Colorado, and spent time climbing the Rockies. She met a man named "Mountain Jim" Nugent. Together, they explored the Rockies and climbed Long's Peak, 14,000 feet high. Bishop was only the second woman ever to climb the mountain.

Bishop, far right, on her travels.

On her return to England, Bishop wrote two books about her adventures, *The Hawaiian Archipelago* (1875) and *A Lady's Life in the Rocky Mountains* (1879). The two books were eagerly read by many people in Europe and the U.S.

VOYAGE TO JAPAN: In 1878, Bishop visited Japan. She traveled throughout the country and stayed at Christian missions. She also explored distant peasant villages, rarely seen by outsiders. From Japan, she traveled in China and Malaysia. These journeys inspired her next two books, *Unbeaten Tracks in Japan* (1880) and *The Golden Chersone* (1883). After Bishop returned to Scotland, she didn't travel for 10 more years. These years were taken up with more traditional, domestic concerns.

ISABELLA BIRD BISHOP'S HOME AND FAMILY: In 1880, Bishop's beloved sister Henrietta died. Bishop grieved deeply. Many of her books had been based on her letters to Henrietta.

Still in mourning, Bishop accepted a marriage proposal from Dr. John Bishop. He had known Isabella for years, and had asked her to marry him several times. He once said "I have only one formidable rival in Isabella's heart, and that is the highland of Central Asia." They married on March 8, 1881. But their married life would be brief. John Bishop became ill and was an invalid for several years. He died on March 8, 1886. Bishop spent several years mourning for her husband and sister.

VOYAGE TO INDIA AND THE MIDDLE EAST: In 1889, Bishop was ready to travel again. She went first to India. There, she looked for places to build mission hospitals in memory of her husband and sister. She also visited Tibet, the remote country in the Himalaya Mountains.

By this time, Bishop's writings had made her a famous woman. She was asked to travel to Persia (now Iran). Bishop had to cover herself in traditional Muslim women's clothing to be part of the mission. She did, but she was happier when she left the group to travel alone again. Then, on a trip to Isfahan, she took off her scarf and veil and rode her horse full-speed. She was stopped and detained by Islamic officials. After her was release, she decided to travel north.

Bishop journeyed to the Black Sea, then on to Turkey and Kurdistan. These travels led her to write *Journeys in Persia and Kurdistan*. They also inspired the British government to ask her to speak to the House of Commons. In June 1891, she reported on the conditions of Christians in Persia.

Her valuable observations on the people and places of the world won her acclaim. In 1892, she became the first woman to be made a member of the Royal Geographical Society.

VOYAGE TO KOREA AND CHINA: Even in her 60s, Bishop yearned to travel. Her next expedition was to Korea and China. She left England in 1894 and traveled for three years. She became an avid photographer. She took her cameras and developing equipment with her, to keep a visual record of her travels. These journeys inspired *Korea and her Neighbors* (1898) and *The Yangtze and Beyond* (1899).

LAST VOYAGE — TO MOROCCO: At the age of 70, Bishop made her last voyage. This time, she visited Morocco. She wrote about the trip for an English magazine on her return. Bishop lived her final years in Edinburgh. She died there on October 7, 1904.

HER DISCOVERIES: At a time when few women had the freedom or the money to travel, Isabella Bird Bishop journeyed to the far corners of the world. Many women of her time, in England or the U.S., were uneducated. They were further restricted by cultures that defined women only by their relationships to fathers or husbands.

Bishop believed "in a women's right to do what she can do well." Unfettered by others expectations, she paved the way for later women to explore. Her books brought the remote worlds of Asia and the Middle East to life for Westerners.

WORLD WIDE WEB SITE:

http://www.ganesha-publishing.com/bird_intro.htm

Daniel Boone

Daniel Boone

1734 - 1820
American Explorer and Frontiersman
Built the Wilderness Road in the Cumberland Gap

DANIEL BOONE WAS BORN on November 2, 1734, in Bucks County, Pennsylvania, near Reading. His parents were Squire and Sarah Boone. Squire was a farmer, weaver, and blacksmith. Daniel was the sixth of 11 children.

DANIEL BOONE GREW UP in Pennsylvania helping out on the farm. He loved life in the backwoods and became an excellent hunter. He didn't go to school, but he did learn to read and write.

When he was 15, Boone's family moved to North Carolina. They settled on the Yadkin River. Boone made his living as a hunter and farmer. In 1755, he fought with English forces in the French and Indian War. He fought in a famous battle at Pittsburgh.

Around this time, Boone met a young woman named Rebecca Bryan. They married in 1756. Their family grew to include 10 children. They moved often, as Boone's explorations took them ever further into the west.

BEGINNING TO EXPLORE: In 1765, Boone left North Carolina to explore Florida. But Rebecca had no interest in moving there. Instead, they moved to western North Carolina, near Wilkesboro.

FIRST EXPEDITION TO KENTUCKY: In 1769, Boone traveled west with five friends. Over the next two years, he and his friends braved a series of adventures. He and a companion were captured by the Shawnee Indians. He escaped, but his companion was killed.

Boone lived alone in the wilderness for months. In June 1769, he saw the Kentucky territory for the first time. (It would not become the state of Kentucky for many years.) In his autobiography, he remembered that first glimpse. "I had gained the summit of a commanding ridge, and, looking round with astonishing delight, beheld the ample plains, the beauteous tracts below."

Boone explored the Kentucky territory as far west as the Ohio Falls. He returned home to North Carolina in 1771.

Boone's cabin, High Bridge, Kentucky.

FIRST ATTEMPT TO CREATE A SETTLEMENT IN KENTUCKY:
In 1773, Boone led a group of settlers, including his family, to the Kentucky territory. Indians attacked the group, and Boone's oldest son, James, was killed. The settlers returned to North Carolina.

THE WILDERNESS ROAD: In 1775, Boone led a group of men into Kentucky to the Cumberland Gap. That is a famous natural pass through the Appalachian Mountains. They had been hired by the Transylvania Company to build a trail through the Gap. That trail became known as the "Wilderness Road." It stretched from eastern Virginia into Kentucky and became the major route taken by settlers and adventurers to the west. Boone helped to establish the first settlements in the area, including one named for him, Boonesborough.

In 1776, the Revolutionary War began. Boone served as a captain in the Virginia militia. He also moved his family to Kentucky. But once again, the family had to fight off Indian attacks. Boone's daughter Jemima and two others were captured by Shawnees in July 1776. Boone soon rescued them.

In 1778, Boone was captured by Indians again. This time, he was taken by the Shawnee. After several months, he escaped. He reached Boonesborough in time to warn them of a planned Shawnee attack. Boone then traveled back to North Carolina, where his family had moved after his capture.

In 1779, Boone was back in Kentucky. He led a group of settlers and started a new town, Boone's Station.

ELECTED TO THE VIRGINIA LEGISLATURE: The tireless explorer and woodsman made time for politics, too. At that time, Kentucky was not a state, but a part of Virginia. In 1781 he was elected to the Virginia Assembly. Over the next ten years, he served three terms in the Virginia legislature.

A FAMOUS EXPLORER: In 1784, on his 50th birthday, Daniel Boone's autobiography was published. It really wasn't an autobiography, because he didn't write it. Instead, it was written by a friend named John Filson. It was called *The Adventures of Colonel Daniel Boone, Formerly a Hunter.* It was a wildly popular book. People all over the country read it, and Boone became a famous man.

In the 1780s, Boone moved his family to Limestone, on the Ohio River. He became a surveyor and bought land. They moved again,

DANIEL BOONE PROTECTS HIS FAMILY.

to Charleston, West Virginia, in 1792, and to Brushy Fork, Kentucky, in 1795. In 1799, Boone decided to follow his son Daniel to Missouri. Missouri was then under Spanish control. The Spanish governor granted Boone land, and he made his living hunting and trapping.

But Boone had trouble holding on to his land. He was never a good businessman, and because of problems with documents and deeds, he lost land he thought he owned in Kentucky. Then he lost his land in Missouri. Boone appeared before the U.S. Congress in 1809. He asked them to grant him land, in exchange for his service to the country. Finally, in 1814, the Congress granted Boone a tract of land in Missouri.

The celebrated explorer and frontiersman died near St. Louis, Missouri, on September 26, 1820. He was 85 years old.

DANIEL BOONE'S HOME AND FAMILY: Boone married Rebecca Bryan in 1756. They had 10 children: James, Israel, Susannah, Jemima, Levina, Rebecca, Daniel, Jesse, William, and Nathan.

HIS DISCOVERY: Boone is remembered as an explorer of Kentucky who helped to settle the area. He helped to build the Wilderness Road, which was taken by thousands of settlers to the west.

WORLD WIDE WEB SITES:

http://earlyamerica.com/lives/boone
http://www.louisville.edu/library/ekstrom/govpubs/states/
  kentucky/kyhistory/boone. html
http://memory.loc.gov/ammem/today/jun07.html
http://www.americanwest.com/pages/boone.htm

Etienne Brulé

1591? - 1632?
French Explorer Who Lived Among the Indian Tribes of North America
First European to Sight Four of the Great Lakes

ETIENNE BRULÉ WAS BORN around 1591 near Paris, France. His name is pronounced "ay-tee-EHN brew-LAY." Very little is known about his life. He never wrote about his travels. Most of what we know is from the accounts of other early explorers of **New France** (the lands in North America claimed by the French, including much of the St. Lawrence River Valley).

COMING TO NEW FRANCE: Brulé probably came to the **New World** with **Samuel de Champlain** in 1608. Champlain had founded the colony of **New France**. Brulé spent two years in Quebec with Champlain.

EXPLORING NEW FRANCE: In 1610, Champlain sent Brulé into the area west of the Lachine Rapids, just beyond Quebec. Brulé wanted to live among the Algonquin Indian tribe. He wanted to learn their language and way of life.

In 1611, Brulé met Champlain again. He had lived among the Algonquin for one year. Champlain described him as "dressed in the manner of the savages." He had also learned the language well enough to become an interpreter for the Indians and the French.

AMONG THE HURON: Around 1615, Brulé next traveled to the Georgian Bay area. That is a large bay connected to Lake Huron. Brulé was probably the first European to see Lake Huron.

Brulé wanted to travel south, to meet the tribe called the Andastes. Champlain agreed. Brulé traveled to what is now Buffalo, New York. There, he was probably the first European to see Lakes Erie and Ontario. Then he traveled down the Susquehanna River, through what is now Pennsylvania. He was probably the first European to see Pennsylvania.

CAPTURED: Brulé headed back to New France. But on the way he was captured by the Iroquois. The Iroquois had been at war with

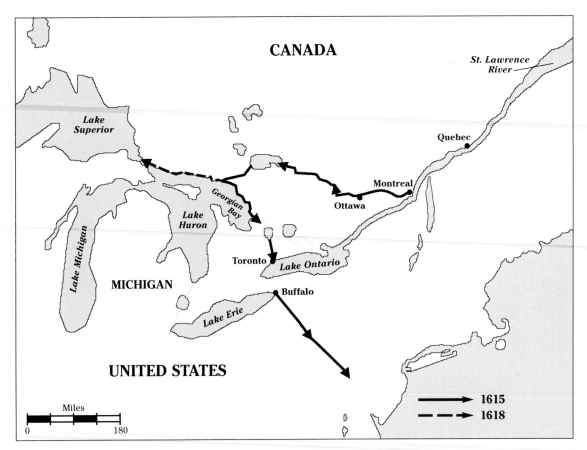

Brulé's voyages of 1615 and 1618.

the French and other Indian tribes for years. Now they kept Brulé as a prisoner. He was tortured, but he was finally let go.

BACK TO NEW FRANCE: Brulé returned to Quebec in 1618. He was eager to explore again. Champlain sent him west, where he explored Lake Huron, reaching Lake Superior. He was probably the first European to see Superior, the largest of the Great Lakes.

BETRAYING HIS COUNTRYMEN: In 1629, Quebec fell to the English in a battle. Brulé betrayed Champlain and joined the English. He went back to live among the Huron. He was killed by Huron Indians sometime around 1632. No one ever learned why. Champlain learned of the death of his countryman when he returned to Quebec in 1633.

HIS DISCOVERY: Brulé is remembered for his exploration of New France, the Great Lakes, and the Susquehanna Valley. His decision to live among the Native American tribes and learn their language and way of life also sets him apart from other early explorers. Yet why he betrayed his countrymen, and how he died at the hands of the Huron, make Brulé a mysterious figure in the history of exploration.

WORLD WIDE WEB SITE:

http://www.civilization.ca/vmnf/explor/brule_e2.html

Richard Francis Burton

1821 - 1890
English Explorer and Scholar
Discovered Lake Tanganyika and Explored India,
Africa, and the Middle East

RICHARD FRANCIS BURTON WAS BORN on March 19, 1821, in Devonshire, England. His parents were Joseph and Martha Burton. Joseph Burton was a retired Army officer. Richard had a brother and a sister.

RICHARD FRANCIS BURTON GREW UP in France and Italy. Even though he was English, he spent very little time in England. Instead, he traveled with his family through Europe.

RICHARD FRANCIS BURTON WENT TO SCHOOL at home for most of his young life. Learning languages came very naturally to him. By the time he went to college in 1840, he knew French, Italian, Latin, and Greek. During his life as an explorer, he learned 25 languages.

Burton went to Trinity College at Oxford University in England. After two years, he was expelled for bad behavior. He decided to join the Army.

INDIA: The Army sent Burton to India in 1842. He lived in many places, including Bombay and Karachi. He continued to learn more languages and worked as an Army spy.

After eight years in India, Burton returned to England. He'd become very ill with cholera. It took him several years to recover. He lived for three years in France with his mother and sister. While recuperating, he wrote books on his travels.

MECCA AND MEDINA: For his next voyage, Burton disguised himself as an Arab Muslim. In 1853, he joined a group of Muslims traveling to the Islamic holy cities of Mecca and Medina. (They are both in modern-day Saudi Arabia.) Burton visited the holy shrines, which he sketched in secret. He made careful observations of the Muslim way of life. Back in England, his book *Pilgrimage to El-Medinah and Mecca* was a great success.

In 1854, Burton went to Africa. This time he wanted to visit the city of Harar, Ethiopia. It was also a Muslim city, and non-Muslims were forbidden to enter. But Burton was able to get in. He became the first European to visit Harar and live to tell about it. He described this adventure in *First Footsteps in East Africa.*

Burton next turned his attention to one of great quests of 19th century exploration—the search for the source of the Nile.

THE NILE: The Nile River is 4,160 miles long—the longest river in the world. People have been fascinated with the great river for centuries. Many people had tried to find its "source"—the point where the river begins. But by the 19th century no one had found it.

What Burton and others were actually looking for was the source of the White Nile. The Nile's two main tributaries are the

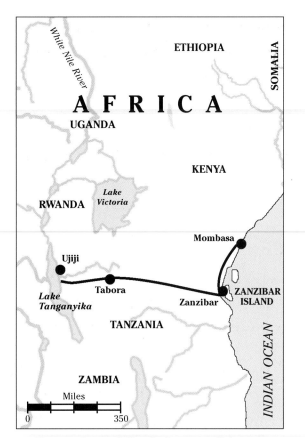

Burton's and Speke's expedition to Lake Tanganyika, 1856 to 1858. (For a full-scale map of Africa, see the Appendix)

Blue Nile and The White Nile. The White Nile forms the longest segment of the Nile River system. What Burton wanted to know was exactly where the White Nile began. In his time, explorers knew that it started somewhere inland from the east coast of Africa. He was determined to find it.

In 1856, Burton and **John Hanning Speke** started from the city of Mombasa, in modern-day Kenya. They traveled south to Zanzibar, then headed inland into what is now Tanzania. They were looking for a large lake that local legend said was the source of the Nile. They explored East Africa and became the first Europeans to reach Lake Tanganyika.

But disaster struck before they could find the Nile's source. Burton developed malaria, and Speke became blind from a tropical disease. Luckily, Speke's blindness was temporary. He left Burton in Tabora to recover and traveled on alone.

Speke headed north from the city of Tabora. On July 30, 1858, he reached the great lake. He had found the source of the Nile. He called it "Lake Victoria" in honor of England's Queen. Speke returned to Burton to tell him of his success. But Burton didn't believe him.

Speke returned to England and was greeted by some as a hero. Others doubted he had found the Nile's source, especially Burton. The Royal Geographical Society sponsored Speke on another expedition to prove his discovery.

In 1860, Speke returned to Africa, accompanied by explorer James Grant. Together they reached Lake Victoria and mapped parts of it. They returned to England, where Burton still doubted their discovery. Burton challenged Speke to a public debate on the issue. But the day before the debate, Speke shot and killed himself in a hunting accident. Later explorations proved Speke had indeed discovered the Nile's source.

THE LIFE OF A DIPLOMAT: In 1862, Burton began working as a diplomat for England. His first post was on the island of Fernando Po, off the coast of West Africa. He made frequent trips to Africa, where he continued to explore. He wrote about the people and cultures he observed in several books.

In 1864, Burton was sent to Brazil. He lived in the city of Santos from 1864 to 1868. He continued to explore, and to write about the culture. His next job was in Damascus, Syria. He lived and worked there until 1871.

From Syria, Burton moved to Trieste, Italy. He lived there until his death in 1890. He continued to write books and also began to translate. Among his translations is an English edition of *The Arabian Nights*.

RICHARD FRANCIS BURTON'S HOME AND FAMILY: Burton married Isabel Arundell in 1861. They had no children.

HIS DISCOVERY: Burton is remembered for his explorations of the Middle East and Africa. His most important discovery was Lake Tanganyika.

WORLD WIDE WEB SITE:

http://www.win.tue.nl/~engels/discovery/alpha/b.html

Richard E. Byrd

1888 - 1957
American Naval Officer and Explorer of Antarctica
First to Fly Over the North and South Poles

RICHARD E. BYRD WAS BORN on October 25, 1888, in Winchester, Virginia. His full name was Richard Evelyn Byrd. His parents were Richard and Eleanor Byrd. His father was a lawyer and his mother was a homemaker. He had a brother named Harry.

RICHARD E. BYRD GREW UP in a very wealthy family. He dreamed of being an explorer when he was just a boy. He traveled more that most children ever do. When he was just 12, his parents let him travel around the world alone.

RICHARD E. BYRD WENT TO SCHOOL at Shenandoah Valley Military Academy, then to Virginia Military Institute. He spent two years at the University of Virginia before going on to the United States Naval Academy. He was a good student and an outstanding athlete.

THE NAVY: After graduating from the Naval Academy in 1912, Byrd began his career in the Navy. He was assigned to several different ships in his first years. In 1916, he injured his foot so badly that he had to retire from active duty. He remained in the Navy for many more years.

STARTING TO FLY: Despite his injury, Byrd wanted to serve, and to learn to fly. He joined the Navy flying school in Pensacola, Florida. Soon, he was learning to fly some of the earliest Navy planes.

When the U.S. entered World War I in 1918, Byrd commanded a Naval air station in Canada. He experimented with new techniques in flying. He learned to navigate and land a plane at night, on the ocean.

Byrd helped establish a special section of the Navy devoted to aeronautics — the study of flying. He helped develop a special kind of flying boat — the NC series. One of these made the Navy's first trip across the Atlantic Ocean in 1919.

EXPEDITION TO GREENLAND: Byrd's first trip to the Arctic came in 1925. He traveled to Greenland with D.B. MacMillan. While there,

Byrd became the first pilot to fly over Ellesmere Island and parts of Greenland.

FLYING OVER THE NORTH POLE: In 1926, Byrd was back in the Arctic. He led an expedition funded by Edsel Ford, John D. Rockefeller, and other private sources. The goal was to fly over the **North Pole**. They flew a plane named the *Josephine Ford*. It was equipped with skis.

On May 9, 1926, with pilot Floyd Bennett, Byrd took off from Spitsbergen, Norway. They returned 15 ½ hours later, claiming to have flown over the North Pole. Since that time, some historians have challenged Byrd's claim. But at the time, they were hailed as heroes. Byrd and Bennett became famous and received many awards, including the Medal of Honor.

Byrd's next major flying feat took place in June 1927. He commanded the first flight of a tri-motor plane across the Atlantic Ocean. He and his crew of two men crashed off the coast of France, after 42 hours in the air. They swam to shore, and were soon ready to fly again. Next, the tireless pilot and explorer turned his attention to Antarctica.

FIRST EXPEDITION TO ANTARCTICA: Byrd set out for the first of his five expeditions to Antarctica in September 1928. On this first trip he established a base camp he called 'Little America," at the edge of the Ross Ice Shelf. He began a series of flights over the continent. One section he named for his wife, Marie Byrd.

FLYING OVER THE SOUTH POLE: On November 28, 1929, Byrd and a crew of three attempted the first flight over the **South Pole**. They took off from Little America and rose over the Queen Maud

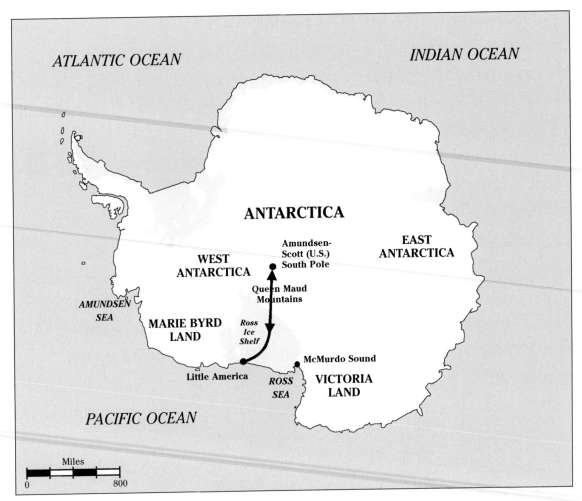

The route of Byrd's flight to the South Pole, November 28, 1929.

Mountains. As they climbed over the mountains, they had to throw many things overboard to lighten the plane. Finally, they cleared the mountains and reached the Pole. They returned to Little America, making the round trip in 19 hours.

Byrd brought to Antarctica the most advanced airplanes, cameras, vehicles, and data-gathering equipment available. Over the two years of the expedition, he and his crew made important scientific discoveries, recording data on weather, geology, and climate.

SECOND EXPEDITION — 1933-1935: In 1933, Byrd returned to Antarctica. Once again he based his explorations in Little America. He explored and mapped regions of Marie Byrd Land and other areas. From March to August 1934, Byrd lived alone in a small hut at a place called Bolling Advance Base. He continued to make weather and other scientific observations, but he became extremely ill. Byrd hadn't realized that his hut didn't allow in enough fresh air. He was rescued in August 1934, nearly dead from breathing carbon monoxide fumes.

THIRD EXPEDITION — 1939-1941: Byrd was back in Antarctica in 1939. He'd been named Commander of the U.S. Antarctic Service by President Franklin D. Roosevelt. He established new bases and explored and mapped new areas. In addition to ships and planes, Byrd had a new vehicle, "The Snow Cruiser." It was a huge snow-going vehicle, with sleeping quarters for four, a science lab, a radio room, a map room, and a galley. Unfortunately, it broke down soon after they arrived.

FOURTH EXPEDITION — "OPERATION HIGHJUMP": In 1946, Byrd returned to Antarctica as head of "Operation Highjump." It was the largest Antarctic expedition ever attempted. It included 4,700 men, 13 ships, and 25 airplanes. Over two years, the expedition mapped 537,000 miles of Antarctica. They surveyed sections of the coastline and interior that had never been seen before.

FINAL EXPEDITION — OPERATION DEEP FREEZE: Byrd's final trip to Antarctica took place in 1955. He helped lead "Operation Deep Freeze," which explored and conducted scientific research. It was part of an international effort to prepare for the International

Geophysical Year of 1957. Byrd made his final flight over the South Pole on January 8, 1956. Byrd was awarded the Medal of Freedom one month before his death on February 21, 1957.

RICHARD E. BYRD'S HOME AND FAMILY: Byrd married Marie Ames in 1915. He named a large section of Antarctica for her.

HIS DISCOVERY: Byrd is remembered for his commitment to the exploration of Antarctica. His first achievements included his flights over the North and South Poles, and he was an outstanding aviator. But perhaps most importantly, he brought public attention—and funding—to the exploration of Antarctica. He also introduced 20th-century technology to exploration. Through the use of airplanes, modern ships, and scientific tools, Byrd helped expand our knowledge of the last continent to be explored.

WORLD WIDE WEB SITES:

http://www-bprc.mps/ohio-state.edu/AboutByrd/bio.html
http://www.south-pole.com/p0000107.htm

Alvar Núñez Cabeza de Vaca
1490? - 1560?
Spanish Explorer
Explored Texas and Northern Mexico

ALVAR NÚÑEZ CABEZA DE VACA WAS BORN in Jerez (huh-RAYS), Spain, in about 1490. Very little is known about his early life. His father was Francisco de Vera and his mother was Teresa Cabeza de Vaca. Both parents were from noble families.

HOW DID HE GET HIS NAME? The family name, "Cabeza de Vaca," means "head of the cow" in Spanish. According to family legend, an ancestor had marked an unguarded path with a cow's skull during a battle between the Spanish and the Moors. The Spanish used the path and surprised the Moors. The Spanish won the battle. As a reward for his service, the ancestor was given a new name, "Cabeza de Vaca." It is pronounced "cah-BAY-zah day VAH-cah."

SOLDIER: When he was a young man, Cabeza de Vaca joined the Spanish army. He fought in battles in Spain and Italy. Then, in 1527, he joined an expedition to the Spanish settlement of Santo Domingo (now in the Dominican Republic).

FIRST EXPEDITION: Cabeza de Vaca traveled as the treasurer with a Spanish expedition headed by Panfilo de Narvaez (nar-vie-YEZ).

They left Spain with five ships and 600 men. After they landed in Santo Domingo, many of the crew quit.

Narvaez sent Cabeza de Vaca to Trinidad for supplies. When he arrived, the island was hit by a hurricane. The storm killed many sailors and destroyed their ship. Narvaez rescued as many men as he could and planned another journey.

In 1528, the remaining crew set out for what is now Tampa Bay, Florida. They needed food. The local natives told them to travel north, toward a city called Apalachen. There, they would find abundant food, and gold, too.

Narvaez divided his men into two groups. One, under his command (and including Cabeza de Vaca), traveled on foot in search of Apalachen. The other group followed by boat. It was a bad decision. The group that traveled on foot clashed with unfriendly Indians. They had little food, and many men became ill and died. When they reached Apalachen, they found only corn.

Meanwhile, the group on the ship had searched the coast and couldn't find the land crew. They abandoned their mission. With his men dying of starvation, Narvaez decided to sail from the Florida coast for **New Spain** (now Mexico). The men built boats with the meager supplies they had, but they weren't seaworthy. In September 1528, about 250 men set out along the Florida coast. They sailed west from Florida along what is now the coast of Mississippi and Louisiana. They faced storms and starvation, and most were lost at sea.

TEXAS: After almost two months at sea, Cabeza de Vaca and about 80 men reached the coast of what is now Texas, near the city of

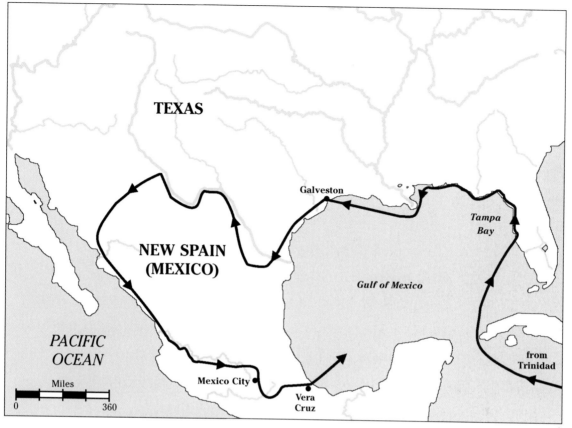

The expedition of Cabeza de Vaca, 1528-1536.

Galveston. He named it "Isle of Misfortune." It would be his home for the next five years.

The Spaniards were found by local natives, the Karankawas, who brought them food. Much of what we know about Cabeza de Vaca's explorations comes from a book he wrote. It details his life among the many Indian tribes he met over the next ten years.

KARANKAWAS: In his book, Cabeza de Vaca told about the Karankawas's way of life. He wrote about what they ate, how they lived, how they treated one another, and their religion. He noted that the natives considered the Spaniards to be "medicine men." They thought that the Spaniards could heal the sick and bless their food.

During the next several years, many Spaniards died of disease. Others headed south, toward the settlements in New Spain. But Cabeza de Vaca was too ill to travel. When he was better, the Karankawas wouldn't let him leave. He was held captive and forced to work for the natives for a year.

EXPLORING TEXAS AND NORTHERN MEXICO: In 1535, Cabeza de Vaca escaped. Three other Spaniards got away with him. These men were named Dorantes, Castillo, and Esteban. Esteban was an African slave. The four headed inland, traveling south through Texas then west through what is now northern Mexico. They may have also reached what is now New Mexico and Arizona. They traveled west to the Pacific coast of Mexico. Then they traveled south and east, to the settlement in Mexico City. In 1536, when Cabeza de Vaca and his men finally reached Mexico City, they were greeted as heroes.

In his book Cabeza de Vaca described the land and the people they encountered on their long journey. They traveled through deserts and over mountains. They met friendly and hostile natives. Among the tribes they met were the Caddoes, Atakapans, Jumanos, Conchos, Pimas, and Opatas. His descriptions of these people and their way of life were the first to reach Europe. Cabeza de Vaca also described the Zuni and their legends of the Seven Cities of Cibola. These were supposedly cities full of gold and silver. The legend inspired later explorers, especially **Hernando de Soto** and **Francisco Coronado.**

RETURNING TO SPAIN: In 1537, Cabeza de Vaca returned to Spain. He spent three years there, then returned to the **New World**.

PARAGUAY: In 1540, Cabeza de Vaca was sent to what is now Paraguay. To reach the area, he had to travel for months through the Brazilian forest. He served as governor of the Spanish settlement there. But he was challenged by a rebel governor, who arrested Cabeza de Vaca and sent him back to Spain for trial.

RETURNING TO SPAIN: Back in Spain, the former hero wrote the book for which he became famous. It took years for his case to be settled. Finally, in 1548, he was convicted and banished to Africa. But the King of Spain pardoned him. Cabeza de Vaca died around 1556 in Spain.

HIS DISCOVERY: Cabeza de Vaca is remembered for his vivid record of life among the native peoples of the **New World**. He also inspired other explorers to journey to the west. As an explorer, he was also a man of bravery and strength. He survived hunger and illness to travel, and to tell his tale.

WORLD WIDE WEB SITES:

http://www.english.swt.edu/CSS/vacaindex.html
http://www.pbs.org/weta/thewest/resources/archives/one/cabeza.htm
http://www.tsha.utexas.edu/handbook/online/articles/view/CC/
  fca6.html

DISCOVERY OF NORTH AMERICA, BY JOHN AND SEBASTIAN CABOT.

John Cabot

1450? - 1499?
Italian Navigator, Explorer, and Mapmaker
Explored the New World for England
First European to Reach North America after Leif Erikson

JOHN CABOT WAS BORN around 1450, probably in the city of Genoa in Italy. His name is written as "Giovanni Caboto" in Italian, the language of his birthplace. We know him as "John Cabot," the English form of his name, because he made his discoveries exploring for the King of England.

Many of the facts of Cabot's life are unknown. We don't know exactly when or where he was born. We don't know about his parents, or his education. We do know that he moved to Venice sometime around 1460. He became a citizen of Venice and worked there as a sailor.

Sometime in the 1470s, Cabot traveled to the Middle East. He visited Mecca, then a thriving center for trade. He saw the wealth of items traded in Mecca — gold, jewels, and especially spices. Spices came from the East — from Asia. Cabot began to dream about sailing to Asia and becoming part of the spice trade. But like **Christopher Columbus**, Cabot wanted to sail *west*. He thought that by heading west from Europe, he could reach the riches of Asia.

Cabot believed the world was round. He reasoned that the distance between Europe and Asia was widest at the equator. The same journey would be shorter at the northern portion of the globe. Cabot visited the Kings and Queens of Portugal and Spain to ask for funding. They weren't interested.

MOVING TO ENGLAND: Cabot moved to England sometime in the 1490s. He and his family settled in the port city of Bristol. Cabot presented his plan to King Henry VII. By now, the successful voyages of Columbus were known throughout Europe. King Henry wanted the riches and power that came with trade for England.

Henry agreed to permit Cabot and his sons to go on their voyage. He wrote a letter allowing them to sail to all parts of the "eastern, western, and northern sea." They were to "find, discover, and investigate whatsoever islands, countries, regions or provinces" they wished. But they were not to claim lands already under Spanish control.

Cabot meets with King Henry VII.

Money for the trip came from the merchants of Bristol. These trading men also wanted to find a successful route to the East.

Cabot made his first attempt to cross the Atlantic in 1496. The voyage ended in failure. A man named John Day wrote a letter to Christopher Columbus telling him of Cabot's problems. He said Cabot had bad weather and problems with his crew. Cabot had much better luck on his next voyage. It would make him a famous explorer.

VOYAGE OF 1497: In May 1497, Cabot set off from England in one ship, the *Matthew*. His crew was made up of 18 men. Cabot had three sons, including one, **Sebastian**, who also became an explorer. It's possible that they, too, went on the voyage.

Cabot left Bristol and landed in Ireland, then set off across the Atlantic. Cabot was a great navigator. He set his course to sail on the same **latitude** across the ocean. He checked his course with a **compass** and **quadrant**.

LANDFALL IN NORTH AMERICA: Cabot sighted land on June 24, 1497. The journey had taken 33 days. Even though his path across the Atlantic was shorter than Columbus's, Cabot's trip took longer. That is because he traveled in the north, where the weather is harsher and the winds are less favorable.

WHERE DID THEY LAND? No one knows for sure where Cabot and his crew landed. Most historians think it was in Canada, on what is now Newfoundland. Others think he might have reached Cape Breton or Labrador. They were the first Europeans to land in the area since **Leif Erikson**.

Cabot and his men went ashore and discovered what looked like a settlement. But they saw no people. Cabot claimed the land for England, raising a cross and the flags of England and Venice. The crew did not spend a long time on the island. Instead, Cabot probably led them along the coast of Newfoundland.

Although Cabot didn't find any spices, he discovered other kinds of riches. The waters were full of fish. The crew let down buckets, and when they pulled them up they were brimming with fish.

Cabot returned to England. The voyage back took just 15 days. He made a map outlining his discoveries and took it to King Henry.

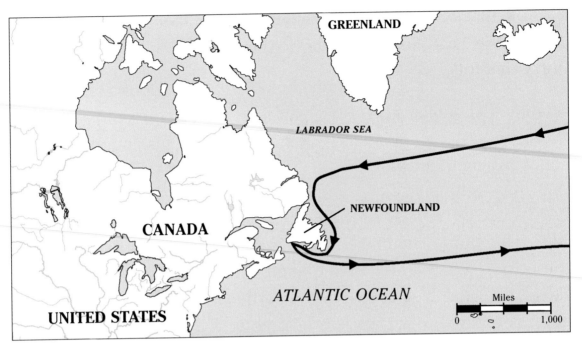

Possible route of John Cabot's 1497 Expedition.

Henry was delighted with Cabot's success. He was willing to fund another voyage to this "newe founde lande," which is where the name "Newfoundland" comes from.

VOYAGE OF 1498: Still convinced he'd reached the East, Cabot was anxious to find the riches of Asia. He left England in May 1498. This time, he headed a crew of six ships and 200 men. They headed west for what they thought was Japan.

THE DISAPPEARANCE OF CABOT: John Cabot was never seen again. He and his crew were probably lost at sea, but no one knows for sure what happened.

SEBASTIAN CABOT: Sebastian Cabot carried on his father's trade as an explorer and mapmaker. But Sebastian was a curious man. He took credit for his father's discoveries. No one knows why, but he claimed that it was he and not his father who had led the voyage of 1497 to the **New World**. (Read more about **Sebastian Cabot** in the entry that follows.)

JOHN CABOT'S HOME AND FAMILY: Cabot's wife's name was Mattea, and they had three sons, Sebastian, Ludovico, and Sancio.

HIS DISCOVERY: Cabot is remembered as a skilled navigator and mapmaker. He opened up North America to English exploration and discovery.

WORLD WIDE WEB SITES:

http://www.mariner.org/age/cabot.html
http://www.heritage.nf.ca/exploration/cabot.html
http://www.matthew.co.uk/history/jcabot.html

Sebastian Cabot

1476? - 1557
Italian Explorer and Mapmaker
Searched for the Northwest Passage in Canada

SEBASTIAN CABOT WAS BORN in Venice, Italy, around 1476. His father was the famous explorer **John Cabot** and his mother was Mattea Cabot. Sebastian had two brothers, Ludovico and Sancio.

MOVING TO ENGLAND: When Sebastian was a young boy, his father moved the family to England. John Cabot had tried to interest the kings of Spain and Portugal in his exploration plan. Like **Christopher Columbus,** Cabot wanted to sail *west* to the riches of the East. But the kings of Spain and Portugal weren't interested.

John Cabot moved to Bristol, England. The merchants of Bristol were involved in trade for spices and riches from the East. They were interested in funding Cabot's plan to sail west across the Atlantic to reach Asia. The king of England, Henry VII, was also interested in Cabot's voyage. He wrote a letter granting Cabot and his sons the rights to the lands they discovered.

THE VOYAGE OF 1497: John Cabot's first voyage took place in 1497. Sebastian may have been on board with his father. That mission took them not to Asia, but to North America—the **New World.** They landed on what was probably Newfoundland in June 1497.

The next year, 1498, John Cabot went on another voyage to the New World. This time, Sebastian did not go with him. And this time, the great explorer was lost at sea. He was never heard from again.

THE CURIOUS CASE OF SEBASTIAN CABOT: A curious thing happened after John Cabot's death. Sebastian Cabot became a mapmaker and explorer like his father. He also began to take credit for his father's discoveries. It took hundreds of years of research for historians to discover that it was John, not Sebastian, who had led the expedition to Newfoundland.

THE SEARCH FOR THE NORTHWEST PASSAGE: In 1508, Sebastian Cabot led his first expedition. He was sent by the King of England to find the **Northwest Passage.** At that time, many people believed that a passage to Asia existed north of where the Cabots had previously explored. They thought that a sea route existed that linked the Atlantic and Pacific Oceans through the islands north of Canada. For 400 years, explorers sought—and died—looking for the Northwest Passage.

Cabot left England in 1508. He kept no written record of his voyage, so no one is exactly sure of his route or how far he explored. One source, written years after the voyage, says he reached Newfoundland. He sailed north from there, reaching perhaps as far as Hudson Bay. He thought Hudson Bay was the Northwest Passage, and returned home.

A FAMOUS MAPMAKER: After he returned to England, Cabot became the chief mapmaker for the new king, Henry VIII. He would go on to become one of the finest mapmakers, or cartographers, of all time.

IN THE SERVICE OF SPAIN: Henry VIII was not very interested in sea explorations. So in about 1512 Cabot moved to Spain. He held the job as Pilot Major. That meant that he recorded the results of Spanish expeditions to the **New World**.

VOYAGE TO SOUTH AMERICA: Cabot again headed an expedition in 1526. He wanted to find a trade route to Asia that was shorter than that found by **Ferdinand Magellan** in 1521.

Cabot set out in April 1526 with four ships and 200 men. Taking a southwest route from the Canary Islands off the African coast, they sailed across the Atlantic. They landed in June 1526 in what is now Recife, in Brazil.

Cabot found a sailor who'd been stranded from an earlier voyage. He told Cabot of a city that was full of silver. (Some

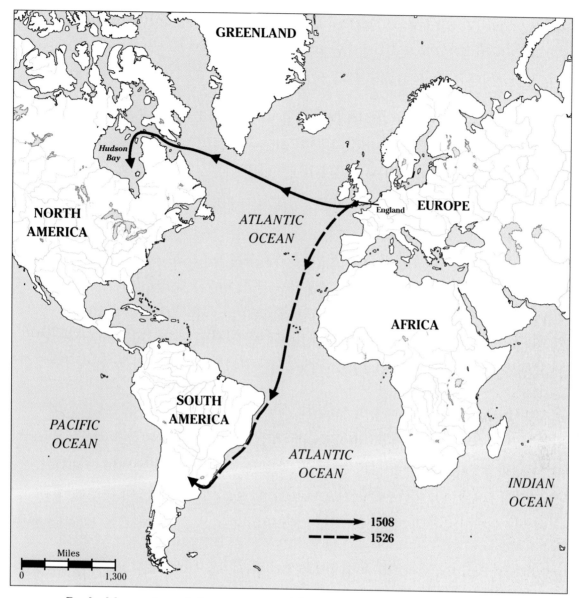

Probable routes of the voyages of Sebastian Cabot, 1508 and 1526.

historians believe this was one of the first references to the Inca civilization. The Incas, based in Peru, had large amounts of silver and gold.) Cabot decided to abandon the mission to find a route to Asia. He wanted to find silver instead.

Cabot sailed toward what is now Argentina. He entered a river he called "Rio de Plata," or "river of silver." He began his quest for

95

riches, sailing up the Uruguay and Parana Rivers. But he found no silver. Soon, the expedition began to run out of food. The local natives were hostile, and they destroyed the fort Cabot had built.

Cabot returned to Spain in 1530, empty-handed. The king was angry with him for abandoning his original mission. Cabot was sent into exile to Africa for two years.

After his exile, he returned to Spain. He created a map of the world that is still considered important. In 1547 he returned to England, at the request of the king. There, he founded the Muscovy Company. It was supposed to find trade routes, specifically the **Northeast Passage**. Like the Northwest Passage, the Northeast Passage was a hoped-for sea route to Asia through the waters off the Russian coast of the Arctic Ocean.

In the 1550s, Cabot put together expeditions whose purpose was to discover the Northeast Passage. The passage wasn't found by Cabot's expeditions, but the voyages did bring about trade between Russia and England.

HIS DISCOVERY: Sebastian Cabot never achieved the greatness of his father as an explorer. But he is praised for his mapmaking. Why he tried to claim his father's accomplishments as his own is a question people still wonder about. He remains something of a mystery in the history of exploration.

WORLD WIDE WEB SITES:

http://www.mariner.org/age/cabot.html
http://www.heritage.nf.ca/exploration/sebcabot.html

Pedro Alvares Cabral
1467? - 1519?
Portuguese Explorer Who Was the First
European to Discover Brazil

PEDRO ALVARES CABRAL WAS BORN around 1467 in Belmonte, Portugal. His parents were Fernao Cabral and Isabel de Gouveia. Very little is known about his early life.

THE RISE OF PORTUGAL AS A SEA POWER: When Cabral was growing up, Portugal was becoming one of the world's great sea powers. In the early 1400s, **Prince Henry the Navigator** of Portugal began the search for a sea route around Africa. He wanted to find a route by water instead of by land to reach Asia. Portugal would use the sea route to trade goods with Asian countries.

At around the age of 17, Cabral was sent to the court of King John II. King John, Henry's nephew, continued his uncle's dream of a Portugese sea empire. In 1487, **Bartholomew Dias** sailed as far as the Cape of Good Hope, at the southern tip of Africa. And in 1497, the new king, Manuel, sent **Vasco Da Gama** all the way to India.

Da Gama's voyage was so successful that Manuel wanted to send another expedition right away. He chose Cabral to sail to India.

VOYAGE TO INDIA — AND DISCOVERY OF BRAZIL: In March 1500, Cabral set out from Portugal with 13 ships and 1,000 men. One of

Cabral's voyage to Brazil, 1500.

the ships was captained by Dias. Da Gama had told Cabral to follow his path of sailing far west of the African coast. They were blown off course, and, by accident, to the coast of what we now call Brazil.

In April 1500, Cabral landed on an island off the coast of modern-day Rio de Janeiro. He called it "the land of the true cross." Later, it became known as Brazil for the brazilwood that grew there and was used to make red dye.

Cabral planted a cross on the island and met with natives. He claimed the land for Portugal. After about 10 days, the ships left Brazil, sailing east for the southern coast of Africa. But on the way they faced terrible storms. Four ships were lost, including the one captained by Dias.

Cabral and the remaining ships sailed for India. They reached the trading city of Calicut in September. The Muslim merchants controlled most of the trade in the city. They didn't like the Portuguese trying to take over their business. When Cabral built a fort, a Muslim army attacked it and killed Portuguese soldiers.

Cabral responded by seizing Muslim ships and killing their crews. He also bombarded Calicut. Then, he took his remaining crew to ports south of Calicut. There, in Cochin, Cabral loaded his ships with spices and gems. They sailed for home in January 1501.

On the way back, Cabral stopped in the Cape Verde Islands. There, he met **Amerigo Vespucci**. Cabral described the land he had recently discovered, while on his journey from Portugal to India. Vespucci thought they'd seen the same land—what we now call Brazil. And he thought that land was *not* Asia. Later, Vespucci claimed it was a new continent—the **New World**.

Cabral returned to Portugal in July 1501. The King greeted him as a hero. He had brought back much wealth and shown the possibilities of trade with India. But Cabral's first voyage was his last. No one knows why, but the next mission to India was headed by Da Gama.

PEDRO ALVARES CABRAL'S HOME AND FAMILY: Cabral retired to his home in the city of Santarem. He married and had six children. He died there in about 1519.

HIS DISCOVERY: Cabral is praised in both Portugal and Brazil as the discoverer of Brazil. Even though Vespucci and other explorers may have reached it before him, he is still considered its founder. This may be because he was the first to go ashore in what is now the center of the country, near Rio de Janeiro.

WORLD WIDE WEB SITE:

http://www.win.tue.nl/~engels/discovery/alpha/c.html

Kit Carson

1809 - 1868
American Frontiersman, Explorer, and Soldier
Explored the American West

KIT CARSON WAS BORN on December 24, 1809, in Madison County, Kentucky. His parents were Lindsey and Rebecca Carson. His first name was Christopher, but his father called him "Kit." He was known by that name all his life. Kit was the youngest of 11 children. His father's first wife had died, so Kit had five older half-siblings: William, Sarah, Andrew, Moses, and Sophie. His other siblings were Elizabeth, Nancy, Robert, Matilda, and Hamilton.

KIT CARSON GREW UP first in Kentucky, then in Missouri. His father moved the family to Boone's Lick, Missouri, in 1811. There, Kit learned hunting and other ways of the frontier from his father and brothers. That included protecting the family from unfriendly Indians.

KIT CARSON WENT TO SCHOOL only briefly. He was more interested in frontier life than in school. In his autobiography he said, "I was a young boy in the school house when the cry came, 'Injuns!' I jumped to my rifle and threw down my spelling book, and thar it lies." He didn't learn to read and write until he served in the Civil War.

When Kit was nine, his father died. His mother remarried, but Kit didn't get along with his stepfather. He was sent to Franklin, Missouri, to work for a saddlemaker when he was 14.

RUNNING AWAY: Kit loved to listen to the fur trappers who traveled through Franklin. He heard marvelous tales of life in the West. When he was 17, he decided to run away with a group of trappers heading west. He went first to Santa Fe, then to Taos, New Mexico. Taos would be his main home for the next 40 years.

THE LIFE OF A FUR TRADER: Carson spent more than 10 years trapping and fur trading. He traveled as far west as California, and as far north as Idaho. He crossed mountains and deserts, enduring heat, cold, even hunger. The life was sometimes harsh but always exciting, and he loved it. He made a good deal of money, and he enjoyed spending it. He remembered "spending money freely—never thinking that our lives were risked gaining it."

LIVING AMONG THE PEOPLE OF THE WEST: In his travels, Carson got to know many different Indian tribes. He learned their languages and their ways. Carson had his share of skirmishes with Indians. Indian tribes felt threatened by white people taking their land and their way of life. They responded by fighting to preserve what was theirs. But in his dealings with Indians, as a trapper and later as an Indian agent, Carson was deeply respected by the Indian tribes, who trusted him as an honest man.

Even though he couldn't read or write, he could speak many languages. He knew Navajo, Apache, Cheyenne, Crow, Blackfoot, and other Indian languages. Living among the Mexicans in Taos, he learned Spanish. Because he trapped and traded with many French-Canadians, he learned French, too.

EXPLORING WITH FRÉMONT: In 1842, Carson was traveling on a Missouri Riverboat when he met **John Charles Frémont**. Frémont was about to begin his first expedition to the West. He hired Carson on the spot to be his guide. (See the map in the Frémont entry.)

That year, Carson led the group into the Oregon Territory. Frémont mapped what later became the Oregon Trail, which was followed by many later settlers. In 1843, Frémont and Carson headed west again. Frémont completed mapping the Oregon Trail all the way to the mouth of the Columbia River. Carson's friend, the famed mountain man Tom Fitzpatrick, accompanied them. On the return trip, the group headed south, then east, crossing the Sierra Nevada Mountains in winter.

THE YOUTH'S COMPANION HISTORIC MILESTONES

KIT CARSON · · HUNTER AND TRAPPER · · IMPLACABLE FOE OF HOSTILE INDIANS BUT FRIEND AND PROTECTOR OF THOSE THAT WERE PEACEFUL · · TRAIL MAKER · PATHFINDER · GUIDE · · INCOMPARABLE SCOUT AND LOYAL AND EFFICIENT SOLDIER · · THE LAST OF THE OLD FRONTIERS-MEN AND ONE OF THE GREATEST

A POPULAR EXPLORER: Back east, Frémont published books about his travels. They were colorful and exciting tales, and the American public loved them. Frémont included vivid accounts of Carson, praising his courage as he blazed trails over the mountains or fought off Indians. Along with Frémont, Carson became a national hero.

A FAMOUS FRONTIERSMAN: Thanks to Frémont and others, Carson became a famous man. He was the subject of "dime novels," sensational little books that exaggerated the facts of his life. Carson found all the attention embarrassing, and he never got used to it.

Carson aided Frémont again in his expedition to California in 1845. At that time, California was under Mexican control. Frémont went to California with the goal of turning the area into U.S. territory. He encouraged Americans in California to rebel against the Mexican authorities. He and Carson led a group of Americans who declared their independence from Mexico. They claimed allegiance to their own nation, which they called the Bear Flag Republic.

In 1846, Mexico declared war on the U.S. Carson carried important military information to Washington. He also fought in battles against the Mexicans. After the Mexicans surrendered, he went back to New Mexico and became a rancher. He also worked as an Indian agent.

THE CIVIL WAR: When Civil War was declared in 1861, Carson was made a colonel. He was in charge of the New Mexican Volunteers. But he spent most of the war handling Indian problems. The U.S. wanted the tribes to move to reservations. The Indians wanted to stay on their own land, and they fought the soldiers who tried to force them.

Against his orders, officers under Carson's command attacked and killed many Indians. They also destroyed their homes and crops.

Carson has been accused of these crimes, but most historians believe he never gave the orders that led to so many deaths. Still, he was the officer in charge, and some of the blame must fall to him.

After the Civil War, Carson moved his family to Colorado. He commanded Fort Garland for a few years, then left the Army and moved to Boggsville, Colorado. He died there in 1868.

KIT CARSON'S HOME AND FAMILY: Carson married three times. His first wife, Waanibe, was an Arapaho Indian. They married in 1835 and had one daughter, Adaline. Waanibe died in 1838. His next wife was a Cheyenne woman who lived with him briefly, then left him.

Carson's third wife was Josefa Jaramillo. She was from a wealthy Taos family. She and Carson were married in 1843 and had eight children. Seven of those children lived to adulthood. Their names are William, Teresina, Christobal, Charles, Rebecca, Estifanita, and Josefita.

Josefa Carson died after the birth of Josefita, and Kit died one month after her, on April 23, 1868. He was 59 years old, and was memorialized as a great American hero.

HIS DISCOVERY: Carson's reputation as a brave and able frontiersman made him a legend in his own time. Frémont's books about his expeditions with Carson made him hugely popular with the American public. Those stories were full of the possibilities of life in the West, and they drew thousands of people to settle in the western U.S.

WORLD WIDE WEB SITES:

http://www.ku.edu/heritage/families/kitcarsn.html
http://www.pbs.org/weta/thewest/people/a_c/carson.htm

Jacques Cartier

1491 - 1557
French Navigator Who Explored Canada
Discovered the Saint Lawrence River and
Founded a French Colony

JACQUES CARTIER WAS BORN in the sea port of Saint-Malo, France, in 1491. Very little is known about his early life. Some historians think he might have traveled with **Giovanni da Verrazzano** on his voyage to the **New World** (North America) in

1524. No one is sure how he got his training, but he was a skilled navigator by the time he was chosen to explore for France.

COMMISSIONED BY THE KING OF FRANCE: By the 1530s, France wanted to take part in the exploration of the **New World**. In 1534, King Francis I selected Cartier to lead an expedition to North America.

The king had several goals in mind. He wanted Cartier to discover the **Northwest Passage**. In the early 1500s, many people believed that a passage from Europe to Asia existed through what is now Canada. They sought a sea route linking the Atlantic and Pacific Oceans through the islands of the Canadian Arctic. That would be a shorter route to the riches of China, and not require sailing around the South American continent.

King Francis also knew of the gold and silver discovered by Spanish and Portuguese explorers. He wanted Cartier to explore the New World so the French could claim that kind of wealth.

FIRST VOYAGE TO THE NEW WORLD: Cartier left France in April 1534, with two ships and 61 men. They crossed the Atlantic in 20 days. The crew landed on Newfoundland. They explored the Strait of Belle Isle and raised a cross at Saint- Servan.

Sailing south, the ships headed for what is now Prince Edward Island. From there, they traveled north to Chaleur Bay. They met a friendly tribe of natives, the Micmacs, and traded with them.

Cartier continued sailing north, to what is now Gaspe Bay. There, they raised another cross and claimed the land for France. The ceremony troubled the local natives, who were Huron Indians from Stadacona (now the city of Quebec). They were in the area

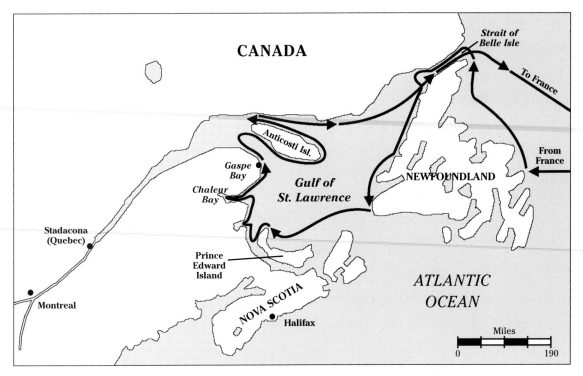

Cartier's first voyage, 1534.

fishing, and they witnessed the ceremony. The local chief, named Donnaconna, let Cartier know that the land belonged to his people.

Cartier eased the tensions with the Huron. He persuaded Donnaconna to send his two sons, Taignoagny and Domagaya, back to France with him. Donnaconna agreed. Cartier headed back into the Gulf of St. Lawrence, then navigated the strait around Anticosti Island. The ships then set sail for France, reaching home in September.

SECOND VOYAGE: In May 1535 Cartier went to sea again, this time with three ships and 120 men. They landed in Newfoundland 50 days later. In August, he reached a bay he named for Saint Lawrence. Later mapmakers named a river, a gulf, and a major seaway for the saint.

Cartier reached the mouth of the St. Lawrence River. They sailed along the river to Stadacona, the home of the Hurons. Donnaconna was reunited with his sons. Cartier continued sailing down the river, as far as the Indian city of Hochelaga, where Montreal now stands. They were greeted by 2,000 Indians.

In Hochelaga, Cartier heard about a famous city of great wealth, the Kingdom of Saguenay. It was supposedly down the river, but because of fierce rapids, Cartier couldn't continue. Before leaving, the Huron showed him a mountain, which he named "Mount Royal," or Montreal.

Cartier sailed back to Stadacona. He decided that they would spend the winter there. By mid-November, the ships were frozen in the ice. The winter was long and bitter. Some of the men developed scurvy. That is a disease caused by lack of Vitamin C. The natives

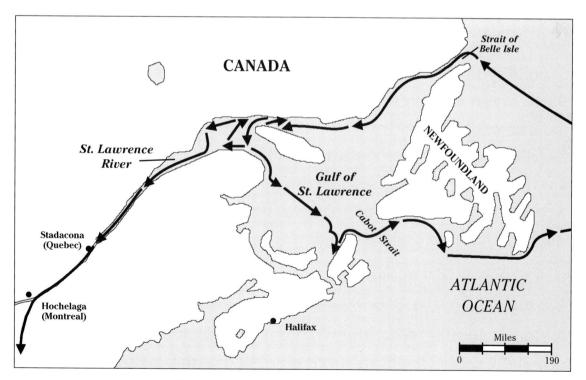

Cartier's second voyage, 1535-1536.

were able to help the Frenchmen, showing them how to brew a tea from cedar trees that stopped the disease.

Throughout the winter, the Huron entertained the French with more tales of Saguenay. When spring came, Cartier decided to force Donnaconna, his sons, and other Hurons to return to France with him. He wanted them to "relate to the King the marvels he had seen in the western lands."

On the return voyage, Cartier discovered the Cabot Strait. They reached France in July 1536. Donnaconna proved to be very popular with the French. The king was especially interested in the stories of Saguenay.

THIRD VOYAGE: Cartier's next voyage took place in 1541. King Francis wanted him to found a French colony. He chose Cartier as the chief navigator, but not as the leader of the voyage. That job went to Jean-Francois de la Rocque de Roberval.

In May 1541, Cartier left France with five ships and 1,500 people. They carried enough food for two years. By that time, all but one member of the Huron tribe who had been forced to go to France had died. When Cartier met the new Huron chief, Agona, he told him only of the death of Donnaconna. Of the others, he said that they "had remained in France where they were living as great lords. They had married and had no desire to return to their country."

The colonists founded their settlement at a place called Charlesbourg Royal, near Stadacona. They searched for Saguenay, but found nothing. What they thought were diamonds and gold turned out to be worthless fool's gold. When they returned to Charlesbourg Royal, they found it in chaos. The settlement had

Cartier and the Grande Hermine, *one of the ships from his voyage of 1535-1536.*

been attacked and some of the colonists were killed, probably by angry Huron Indians.

Cartier and the remaining settlers headed back to France in 1542. In Newfoundland, they met Roberval's ship. He demanded that Cartier return to the settlement. Cartier disobeyed, slipping out at night for home.

Cartier returned to France and never went to sea again. He was never punished for not following orders. Roberval went on to Charlesbourg Royal. But within a year, he realized that the settlement was a failure. All the crew returned to France.

Cartier retired to his estate in Saint-Malo. He wrote a book about his adventures that was published in 1545. He died on his estate in 1557, at the age of 66.

HIS DISCOVERY: At a time when Spain and Portugal were the major powers in world exploration, Cartier made major discoveries for France. The French later became the leading colonial power in the area he explored.

WORLD WIDE WEB SITES:

http://www.civilization.ca/vmnf/explor/carti_e2.html
http://www.mariner.org/age/cartier.html
http://www.win.tue.nl/~engels/discovery/cartier.html

Samuel de Champlain
1567? - 1635
French Explorer of Canada and the Upper Northeastern United States
Founder of Quebec and "The Father of New France"

SAMUEL DE CHAMPLAIN WAS BORN about 1567 in Brouage (broo-AZH), France. His last name is pronounced "sham-PLAIN." His parents were Antoine and Marguerite Champlain. Antoine was a sea captain.

SAMUEL DE CHAMPLAIN GREW UP on the west coast of France. When he was just a boy, he began sailing with his father. His father taught him how to navigate and make maps. Champlain wrote that he learned "from a very young age the art of navigation, along with a love of the high seas."

When he was a teenager, Champlain joined the army of King Henry IV of France. He fought in the wars between Catholics and Protestants that were raging in France at that time.

FIRST VOYAGE TO THE NEW WORLD: In 1599 Champlain made his first voyage to the **New World**. He would repeat the journey across the Atlantic an amazing 22 times in his life.

On this first voyage, Champlain sailed as part of a Spanish crew. For two years, the crew explored Puerto Rico, Mexico, Columbia, Bermuda, and Panama. In Panama, he suggested that the Spanish build a canal linking the Atlantic and Pacific Oceans. That idea, the Panama Canal, would become a reality 300 years later.

When Champlain returned to France, he wrote about his travels, illustrated with his own maps. King Henry IV was delighted with his work. He appointed Champlain his royal geographer. He also wanted Champlain to travel back to the New World.

The king had several goals in mind. He wanted Champlain to discover the **Northwest Passage**. From the early 1500s, many people believed that a passage from Europe to Asia existed through what is now Canada. They sought a sea route linking the Atlantic and Pacific Oceans through the islands of the Canadian Arctic. That would be a shorter route to the riches of China, and not require sailing around the South American continent.

The King also knew of the gold and silver discovered by Spanish and Portuguese explorers. He wanted Champlain to explore the **New World** for a French claim to that kind of wealth.

FIRST VOYAGE FOR FRANCE: In 1603, Champlain traveled to what is now Canada on an expedition paid for by French businessmen. They wanted to expand their fur trading business in the area.

NEW FRANCE: At that time, the area made up of what are now the St. Lawrence River valley, Newfoundland, and Nova Scotia were called "**New France**." They had been named that on a map drawn by the brother of **Giovanni da Verrazzano** after his earlier explorations in 1525. As the French expanded their settlements, the term New France grew to refer to much of the Great Lakes region.

Champlain traveled up the St. Lawrence River. It had first been navigated by **Jacques Cartier** in 1535. They traveled as far as the Indian settlement Hochelaga (now Montreal). His Indian guides told him of huge bodies of water to the west. The Indians were probably describing the Great Lakes.

Champlain continued down the St. Lawrence River west of the settlement. When he reached rapids, he had to stop. Then he had an idea.

The ships the French explorers used were large and difficult to handle. Champlain decided to use Indian canoes to travel on the rapids. When they hit a spot of rough water, the explorers took their canoes out of the water and carried them overland. When they reached calmer waters, they put the canoes back in the water and continued their journey. That is the origin of the word "portage," and it is still used today. It means carrying boats or

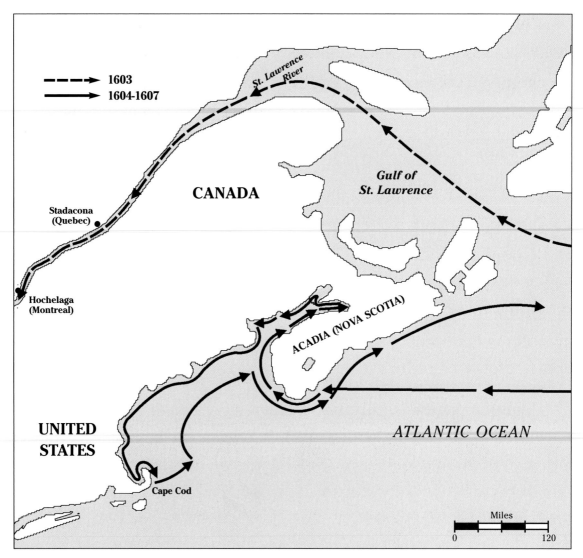

Champlain's expeditions of 1603 and 1604-1607.

goods between two rivers or bodies of water. Champlain returned to France in 1603, but was soon planning another voyage.

SECOND VOYAGE: In 1604 Champlain returned to the **New World**. This time he sailed to what is now the U.S. He traveled with a group of people who hoped to found a settlement. The settlers found a site and began to build a permanent home in what is now Nova Scotia. They called it Acadia.

116

Champlain continued to explore the New World. He journeyed down the east coast of what are now Maine and Massachusetts as far as Cape Cod. He created detailed maps of the area. Meanwhile, the settlers in Acadia faced three harsh winters, and many died. Champlain returned to France in 1607.

VOYAGE OF 1608: Champlain returned to the New World once again in 1608. He sailed down the St. Lawrence River to the Indian settlement called Stadacona. There, in July 1608, he founded the

Champlain and Etienne Brulé on the French River.

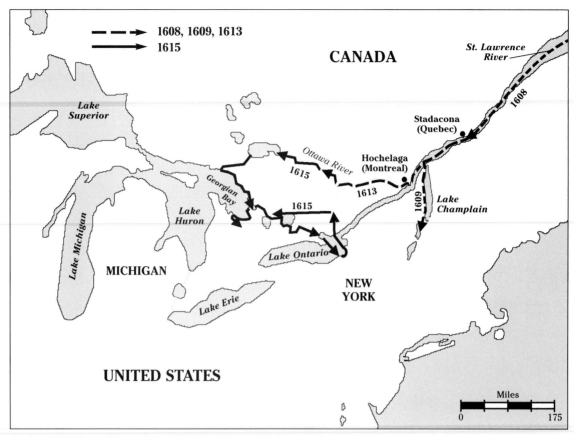

Champain's expeditions of 1608-1616.

city of Quebec. He thought it was an ideal place for fur trade. He also used it as a base for his search for the Northwest Passage.

In 1609, Champlain explored the area south of Quebec and discovered a lake along what is now the border between New York and Vermont. It became known as Lake Champlain. Champlain formed an alliance with the Huron and the Algonquin tribes. Together, they fought the Iroquois. They defeated the Iroquois, but it made the Iroquois enemies of the French for hundreds of years.

MONTREAL: In 1611, Champlain built a trading post at what was then the Indian settlement of Hochelaga. It later became Montreal. While building the fur trade business between the French and the

Indians, Champlain also encouraged exploration. He sent younger explorers, including **Etienne Brulé**, to explore beyond Montreal.

Champlain also began to explore inland from Montreal. He continued past the rapids that had stopped him before. In 1613 he explored the Ottawa River. He'd heard that it ended at a huge body of water. Champlain thought it must be the Northwest Passage. They reached Allumette Island, but not the passage. They returned to Montreal.

LAST VOYAGE OF EXPLORATION: In 1615, Champlain returned to New France. He explored further into the Great Lakes region. He traveled along the Ottawa River as far as Allumette Island, then west into what is now Georgian Bay in Lake Huron. He traveled across the bay, then into what is now Ontario, overland to the shores of Lake Ontario. Once again he joined a battle between the combined Huron and Algonquin tribes and the Iroquois. The Iroquois won the battle, and Champlain was wounded. He spent several months with the Huron recovering.

QUEBEC: Champlain returned to France in 1616. The King wanted him to return to New France to oversee the development of Quebec as a settlement. So he returned to Quebec, where he spent the next years developing the colony.

WAR WITH ENGLAND: By this point, the English had also settled portions of the region. They went to war with France several times over the next 150 years, fighting to control trade and the right to settle the area. In 1629, Champlain was taken prisoner in a skirmish with the English. He was taken to England, where he was

Champain leaving Quebec as a British prisoner, 1629.

imprisoned for three years. Quebec was briefly under English control.

After his release, Champlain returned to Quebec. The colony had returned to the French in 1633. He lived there until his death in December 1635. At the time of his death, the colony had 150 people. It would grow to become one of the greatest cities in Canada.

SAMUEL DE CHAMPLAIN'S HOME AND FAMILY:

Champlain married a young woman named Helene Bouelle in 1610, on one of his visits home. She stayed in France until 1620, then joined her husband in Quebec.

HIS DISCOVERY: Champlain was one of the most important French explorers and a major colonial leader. He founded the city of Quebec and gained the name "Father of New France."

WORLD WIDE WEB SITES:

http://www.civilization.ca/vmnf/explor/champ_e2.html
http://www.mariner.org/age/biohist.html

William Clark
1770 - 1838
American Explorer
Co-Leader of the Lewis and Clark Expedition

WILLIAM CLARK WAS BORN on August 1, 1770, in Caroline County, Virginia. He was the ninth of ten children. All of his brothers fought in the Revolutionary War. One of them, George Rogers Clark, was a famous commander.

WILLIAM CLARK GREW UP first in Virginia, then in Kentucky. His family moved to the area near Louisville when he was still a boy. He had very little formal education, but learned to read, write, and how to live in the wilderness.

BECOMING A SOLDIER: Like his brothers, Clark joined the army as a young man of 19. He was in the army for several years. In 1795, a young man named **Meriwether Lewis** came under his command. Eight years later, Lewis was chosen by President Thomas Jefferson to lead a major expedition to the West.

Jefferson had great plans for the new nation. He wanted to finance an expedition to the far western portion of the continent. Like so many before him, Jefferson wanted to find the **Northwest Passage**. He wanted to find a waterway that connected the known rivers of the west and that led to the Pacific. He wanted the U.S. to lay claim to the natural resources of the West, including possible trade routes. He knew of the travels of **Alexander Mackenzie**. In fact, he and Lewis read Mackenzie's book on his travels in the Canadian northwest with great interest. Jefferson had also seen the maps of **George Vancouver**. He wanted the United States—not the English, Spanish, or French—to claim the West.

Jefferson asked Congress to fund an expedition to explore the West. He had Lewis put together a budget, which came to $2,500, for the exploration. Congress approved the project.

THE LOUISIANA PURCHASE: While he was planning the expedition, Jefferson was also organizing the purchase of a vast amount of territory from France. It was called the Louisiana Purchase. The territory ranged from the Mississippi River to the Rocky Mountains, and from the Canadian border to Texas. It cost the U.S. $15 million, about three cents an acre. With the Louisiana Purchase, the U.S. doubled in size.

THE LEWIS AND CLARK EXPEDITION: Jefferson chose Lewis to put together an expedition to explore the American West. He was clear

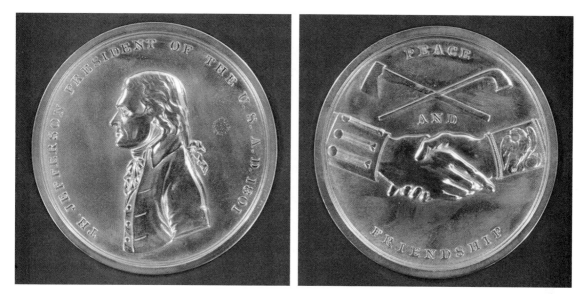

Peace Medal (left) depicting President Thomas Jefferson, and (right) depicting a pair of shaking hands and a peace pipe, given by Lewis and Clark to the Indian tribes they met on their expedition.

about what he expected of the expedition. They were to follow the Missouri River out of St. Louis, looking for a waterway to the Pacific Ocean. They knew the Missouri would lead them to a mountain range—the Rockies. They thought it would be similar in size and scope to the Appalachians. They also knew another river system, the Columbia, flowed into the Pacific on the west coast. Jefferson wanted to find a waterway that connected the two river systems.

The new American government also needed to know all about the western lands. They needed maps, with information about rivers, mountains, and terrain. They needed to know about the plants, animals, and opportunities for trade and settlement. They also needed to know about the many Indian tribes in the vast area. What were they like? Were they peaceful or warlike? And how would they feel about their new leader, Jefferson?

Lewis needed a co-commander. He needed a man with experience as a military leader, and experience in the wilderness. He wanted someone with fine mapmaking skills. Lewis wrote to his old friend and fellow officer William Clark. He told Clark of the planned expedition and asked if he'd like to join. Clark wrote back and said he'd be delighted to accept the offer.

In July 1803, Lewis went to Pittsburgh to pick up the keelboat built for the journey. It was a big boat—55 feet long. They would use it and two smaller boats, called "pirogues," for the trip. Lewis took the keelboat down the Ohio River and up the Mississippi to St. Louis, Missouri, the point of departure for the expedition. In St. Louis, Lewis and Clark put together their company.

The Corps of Discovery: Lewis and Clark hired men to join them in a group they called the "Corps of Discovery." When they began the journey, the Corps numbered 33 men. They came from many different backgrounds. Some were traders, some were soldiers. Another member of the Corps was Clark's African-American slave, York.

Departure — May 14, 1804: The Corps of Discovery left St. Louis on May 14, 1804. Lewis recorded in his journal that they "proceeded on under a gentle breeze up the Missouri." The boats were traveling upstream, against the current. Sometimes they could sail the boats. But when there was no wind, they had to row them, use poles to push them, and even tow them with ropes from the shore.

In August 1804, Lewis held a meeting with Indian chiefs near what is now Omaha, Nebraska. He gave the Indians gifts, including "Peace Medals." These were medals with a picture of President Jefferson on one side, and a pair of shaking hands and a "peace pipe" on the other. He told the Indians of their new "father" (Jefferson). This "head chief of the United States" would protect them, Lewis said.

Frontispiece   Page.220.

A Canoe striking on a Tree,

Lewis and Clark expedition.

Later that month, a member of the Corps named Sgt. Charles Floyd died, probably of appendicitis. He was the only member to die during the expedition. The remaining crew continued up the Missouri, meeting new Indian tribes, some friendly, some hostile.

Fort Mandan: In October 1804, as winter neared, they stopped near what is now Bismarck, North Dakota. There, near the camps of the Mandan and Hidatsa tribes, they made their winter camp.

The men built a triangular-shaped fort, which they named "Fort Mandan" for the local Indian tribe. During the next five months, they hunted and made tools. They had brought the materials to make a forge, and they made tools to trade with the Indians for food.

Sacagawea: Among the Indians they met was a young woman of the Shoshone tribe named **Sacagawea** (sah-CAH-guh-wee-ah). She had been kidnapped when she was just 12 years old in a raid against her people, from her home in what is now Idaho. She had later been sold to a French-Canadian trader named Toussaint Charbonneau. She lived with Charbonneau as one of his two Indian "wives." Sacagawea was never Charbonneau's legal wife. Instead, she was truly a slave.

When Sacagawea met Lewis and Clark, she was about 17 years old and pregnant with her first child. Because she and Charbonneau spoke several Indian languages, they would be valuable as translators. The Corps would also be traveling through Shoshone land, and Sacagawea could help them as a guide. So Lewis and Clark hired Sacagawea and Charbonneau. In February 1805, Sacagawea gave birth to a son, Jean Baptiste Charbonneau. Lewis helped to deliver the baby.

Starting Off Again—April 1805: When the Corps left Fort Mandan in April 1805, Sacagawea went with them, along with Charbonneau and their son. They traveled in the pirogues and six canoes. Lewis sent the keelboat back down the river to St. Louis. It was too large to navigate the river well. In the boat were journals, maps, and plant and animal specimens for Jefferson.

The Corps crossed into Montana. They saw huge herds of buffalo, elk, and deer. They also saw a Grizzly bear for the first time. One chased a crewman up a tree.

During a storm, the boat holding the maps and journals nearly capsized. Sacagawea calmly saved the precious documents. Soon the Corps saw the immense Rocky Mountains.

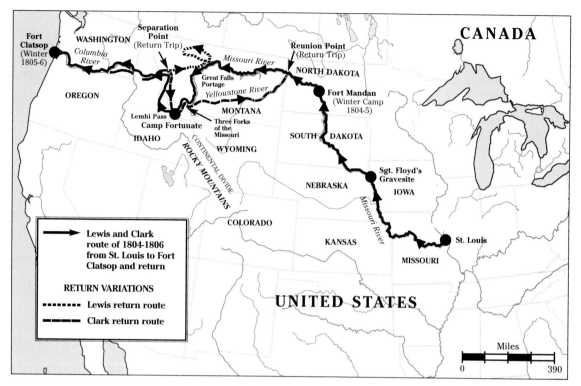

The Lewis and Clark expedition, 1804-1806.

A Fork in the River: The men reached a point where the Missouri divided into a northern and a southern route, or "fork." They chose the southern path, and they soon reached waterfalls. Lewis knew the path was the right one, because the Indians had told him to expect the waterfalls. They were near what is now Great Falls, Montana.

A Long Portage: The boats could not travel over waterfalls, so the crew had to make a long, difficult portage. That is, they had to carry their boats overland. They actually built wheels out of cottonwood, which they attached to the boats. But the 18-mile trip still took them three weeks. Finally, they reached a point in the river where they could put the boats back in the water.

Three Forks of the Missouri: The next major landmark they came to was a place where the Missouri divided into three forks. They named them for three famous Americans. They named one the "Madison," in honor of the Secretary of State (and later President) James Madison. Another was named the "Gallatin," for Secretary of the Treasury Albert Gallatin. And one they named for their President and sponsor, Jefferson. They followed the Jefferson west.

The Continental Divide: In August 1805, Lewis and Clark reached the Continental Divide. That is a point at the crest of the Rocky Mountains where rivers flow either eastward, toward the Mississippi River, or westward, toward the Pacific Ocean.

As Lewis walked to the top of the ridge, he expected to see plains on the other side that led to the Columbia River and the ocean. Instead, he saw the Bitterroot Range of the Rockies. Their hopes to find the Northwest Passage were dashed. The Rockies were so much more vast, in size and scope, than they had ever imagined. Their route would be longer, and harder.

Sacagawea Reunited with her People: Continuing down the other side of the divide, Sacagawea began to recognize the land. She knew she was close to her home. Lewis decided to scout ahead and meet the Shoshone. He met several Shoshone women, then several men. He led them back to the crew, and to everyone's astonishment, Sacagawea recognized an old friend. It was a wonderful reunion. But the greatest surprise came when she recognized her brother, Cameahwait, now the chief. When she saw him, "she jumped up, ran, and embraced him," wrote Lewis. She "threw her blanket over him and cried profusely."

They named their camp, near the Lemhi Pass, "Camp Fortunate." Lewis and Clark traded with the Shoshone for horses.

Captains Lewis & Clark holding a Council with the Indians Page 17

Lewis and Clark expedition.

They knew that their canoes would be of no use in going over the mountains. They would now begin the overland part of their journey. They hired a Shoshone guide named Old Toby. Then they began the difficult crossing of the Bitterroot Mountains.

They crossed from what is now Montana into Idaho. The weather was fierce, and they were near starvation. Once over the mountains, they met members of the Nez Perce tribe. This friendly group gave them food and shelter.

The crew left their horses with the Nez Perce, built new canoes, and proceeded on the Clearwater River. In October, they reached the Snake River, and from that, the Columbia. The river is fierce, with many rapids and waterfalls. Once again, they had to make difficult portages.

The Pacific Ocean: In November 1805, they reached the Pacific Ocean. Clark wrote in his journal of the "great joy in camp" as they reached "this great Pacific Ocean" they had "been so long anxious to see." They had traveled over 4,000 miles in 554 days.

The Corps spent the next four months on the Pacific coast, near what is now Astoria, Oregon. They built a fort, named Fort Clatsop after a local tribe. They hunted and fished, and built a salt-making camp. With salt, they could preserve meat and fish for the journey home.

During the journey, Clark served as the expedition's mapmaker. He started maps at the beginning of the journey, and he added material along the way. He made **compass** readings, measured distances with surveying equipment, and made detailed readings at major landmarks. His maps sometimes contained mistakes, but they were the first maps ever made of the vast area of the new American West.

The Journey Home: In March 1806, the Corps began the journey home. They canoed back up the Columbia, finally reaching the Nez Perce. They got their horses back, and headed back across the Bitterroots. But their path was blocked with snow and ice. After the snow melted, they made their way across the mountains.

The Corps Divides: In July 1806, the Corps separated into two groups. Lewis wanted to explore possible northern routes that could be used by later settlers. He took a group north into the Marias River region. There, near the Canadian border, they had a brief battle with a group of Blackfeet Indians. The groups exchanged gunfire, and two Indians were killed. They were the only Indian deaths of the expedition.

Clark chose a southern route. His group crossed the Rockies, then took the Jefferson River as far as the Three Forks they had passed earlier. The Clark group divided again, and he explored the Yellowstone River region. Clark named an unusual sandstone formation for Sacagawea's son. He called it "Pompy," his nickname for Jean Baptiste. He also wrote his name and the date on the rock. It can still be found, near Billings, Montana.

All the groups came together where the Yellowstone and the Missouri Rivers meet, in August 1806. Lewis had been wounded in a hunting accident, but he was mending.

Sacagawea Leaves: The Corps reached Fort Mandan on August 17, 1806. Sacagawea left the group and remained in the area with Charbonneau and her son.

THE HEROES' RETURN: On September 23, 1806, the Corps of Discovery returned to St. Louis to a heroes' welcome. They had been given up for dead, and all America rejoiced at their return. They had traveled more than 8,000 miles in their two-year journey.

After their triumphant return to St. Louis, Lewis and Clark continued on to Washington with journals, maps, and natural specimens.

LIFE AFTER THE EXPEDITION: Both Lewis and Clark were treated as American heroes. Each received 1,600 acres of land and $1,200. After Lewis died in 1809, Clark saw to it that their journals and maps were published. *The History of the Expedition Under the Command of Captains Lewis and Clark* appeared in 1814.

In March 1807, Jefferson made Clark Brigadier General of Militia and Indian Agent for Upper Louisiana Territory. He became Governor of the Missouri Territory in 1813. He served in that job for seven years.

Because of his background and experience in dealing with Indian tribes, he was named Superintendent of Indian Affairs in 1822. He served in that job until his death on September 1, 1838.

York: York had served Clark faithfully throughout the expedition. When they returned, he wanted his freedom. Clark didn't grant York his freedom for 10 years. Finally, around 1816, York became a free man. He went into the freight business in Kentucky. York died around 1832.

WILLIAM CLARK'S HOME AND FAMILY: Clark married Julia Hancock in 1808. They had one son, Meriwether Lewis Clark. Clark also adopted Sacagawea's two children, Jean Baptiste and Lisette, after she died in 1812.

HIS DISCOVERY: As part of the Lewis and Clark Expedition, Clark is considered one of the most important American explorers. His skills as a leader and mapmaker made him an invaluable member of the Corps. He is also remembered for his work with the Indian tribes, who believed he treated them with great fairness.

WORLD WIDE WEB SITES:

http://www.lewisandclark.org/
http://www.lewisandclarkeducationcenter.com/
http://www.loc.gov/exhibits/lewisandclark/lewisandclark.html
http://www.nps.gov/lecl/
http://nwrel.org/teachlewisandclark/home.html
http://www.pbs.org/lewisandclark/

Christopher Columbus
1451? - 1506
Italian Explorer Who Was the First European
to Discover the New World
Opened North and South America to European
Exploration and Colonization

CHRISTOPHER COLUMBUS WAS BORN in Genoa, Italy. Many facts
about this famous explorer are not known, including exactly when
he was born. Most historians think it was in 1451. His name is written as "Cristoforo Colombo" in Italian, the language of the country
he was born in. It is written as "Cristobal Colon" in Spanish, the

language of the country who sponsored his voyages of exploration. He is known to us as "Christopher Columbus," the English form of his name.

Columbus's father, Domenico Colombo, was a wool worker and merchant. His mother, Susanna Fontanarossa, was a homemaker. Columbus had a brother, Bartholomew.

CHRISTOPHER COLUMBUS GREW UP in Genoa, helping his father in his wool business. Little is known for sure about Columbus's education. He knew Italian, Spanish, and Latin. He also had to learn mathematics and astronomy to become a navigator. He'd read the maps of **Ptolemy** (TOLL-eh-mee.). The writings of **Marco Polo** had also inspired the young man who would become the most famous explorer in history.

GOING TO SEA: Columbus claimed that he had gone to sea at the age of 14. As in much of Columbus's life, it is hard to know what is true and what is legend. Part of the legend says that he was shipwrecked off the coast of Portugal. His ship had been in a battle, and he had to swim to shore.

Columbus lived in Portugal for the next several years. He sailed on Portuguese ships for about 10 years, from around 1475 to 1485. He sailed to England and Ireland. He sailed around the Mediterranean, and to the islands along the west coast of Africa.

In 1479, Columbus met and married Dona Felipa Perestrello e Moniz. She was a widow from a prominent Portuguese family. The couple lived on the Madeira Islands, off the coast of Africa. They had one son, Diego. Dona Felipa died shortly after Diego's birth.

The title page of History of the United States, Vol. I, *showing Columbus holding a sword and banner, with soldiers, priest, and Indian woman kneeling before him.*

Columbus and Diego moved to Lisbon, Portugal. Around this time, Columbus began to plan for the journeys that would make him famous.

Portugal was a powerful nation that controlled the sea routes to the East. Under **Prince Henry the Navigator**, men like **Bartholomew Dias** explored the west coast of Africa. They found a sea way around southern Africa so that Portugal could trade with Asian countries. China, India, and other Asian nations had many goods — silk, spices, precious metals, and foods — highly valued in Europe. Trade was a way to make a country rich.

Columbus was convinced that he could sail *west*, across the Atlantic Ocean, and reach Asia. What he didn't know was that two continents — North America and South America — stood in the way.

Columbus presented his idea to King John of Portugal. He was Henry the Navigator's nephew and supported Portugal's sea expeditions. But after the success of Dias and others, King John wasn't interested in Columbus's plan. He was content to use the route around Africa to reach Asia.

Columbus left Portugal for Spain. It was in Spain that Columbus finally found the support he was looking for.

FERDINAND AND ISABELLA: Ferdinand and Isabella were the King and Queen of Spain. Columbus went to their court and outlined his plan. He asked them to provide the money for his journey to the "Indies." People often called the lands of Asia the "Indies," taking the name from the country of India.

It took Columbus several years, but finally, in 1492, Ferdinand and Isabella agreed to fund his voyage. They provided most of the

Columbus kneeling before Queen Isabella and King Ferdinand of Spain.

money for his ships and crew. They also agreed that Columbus would be called "Admiral of the Ocean Seas." He would be governor of all the land he discovered, and he would receive 10% of all the wealth he brought back. Ferdinand and Isabella, and Columbus, too, were devout Christians. So as part of his mission he agreed to spread the word of Christianity to all the people he met on his journey.

It was a journey that would truly change the world, but not in the way anyone could have imagined in 1492.

FIRST VOYAGE: On August 2, 1492, Columbus set off from Palos, Spain with a fleet of three ships and a crew of 90 men. The three ships were the *Santa Maria,* the *Pinta,* and the *Niña.* Columbus was the captain of the *Santa Maria.* It was a large ship, called a nao in

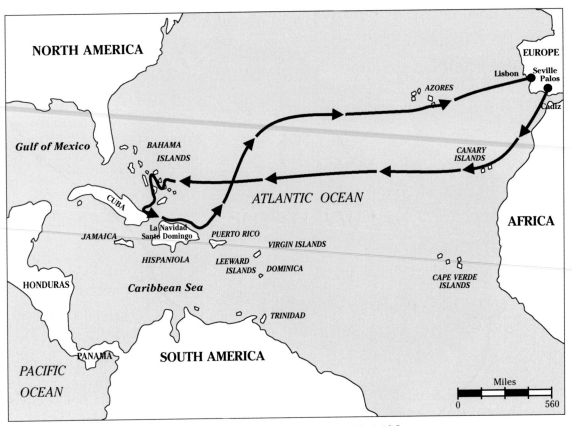

Columbus's first voyage, 1492-1493.

Spanish. The *Pinta* and the *Niña* were **caravels.** The caravels were smaller and easier to navigate, but the *Santa Maria* could hold more cargo.

Columbus sailed south to the Canary Islands off the coast of Africa. He waited for good sailing weather. Then, they departed to the west to cross the Atlantic Ocean. He was able to take advantage of the "trade winds." Those are winds that blow in a westerly direction in that part of the ocean.

Columbus the Navigator: Columbus was considered one of the finest navigators of his time. He piloted his ships using a method called **"dead reckoning."** Dead reckoning requires careful measuring of distance and speed. The navigator measured the course and distance. To measure the course, the navigator used a **compass**. To measure distance, he kept track of time and the speed of the ship.

It is hard to imagine how they measured time and speed, because they didn't have our modern inventions. There were no speedometers to measure speed. Instead, a ship's speed was measured by throwing overboard a log attached to a line of rope with knots at specific distances between them. The sailors would count how many knots would pass by in the time it took the sands to empty from an hourglass. They used an hourglass because there were no clocks that could measure time accurately.

Columbus had predicted that it would take 21 days to reach the Indies. He also calculated that the trip would cover about 2,600 miles.

Even though we say that Columbus "discovered America," he never got to the continental United States. Instead, his journeys took him to several spots in the Caribbean, Central, and South America.

Instead, the trip took 34 days. Many of the sailors were frightened. Although Columbus knew the world was round, many of his crew believed the world was flat. They thought that after so many days at sea, they would soon fall off the edge of the world.

But then, on the 33rd day at sea, branches began to appear in the water. That was a sign that land was near. Finally, on October

12, 1492, shortly after midnight, a sailor named Roderigo de Triana spotted land.

LANDFALL IN THE NEW WORLD: Columbus and his crew went ashore in what is now the Bahamas in the Caribbean. He, of course, thought he'd reached the Indies. He called the land "San Salvador," meaning Holy Savior. He placed a cross, a symbol of Christianity, on the island. Today, no one knows exactly where Columbus and his crew landed. Most historians believe it was on Watling Island in the Bahamas.

The native people of the island were of the Arawak tribe. They were friendly with Columbus. He called them "Indians," because he thought he'd reached the Indies. In fact, Columbus remained convinced for the rest of his life that he'd reached the East. He never claimed that he had discovered new lands unknown to Europeans.

Columbus explored other islands in the area. He was in search of gold, too, and headed for what is now Cuba. There, he explored the coast and met the Carib tribe. They were unfriendly and warlike. Columbus took several of them as slaves.

While Columbus was still exploring the islands, one of his ships deserted the expedition. The *Pinta,* captained by Martin Alonso Pinzon, left Columbus's group and headed out looking for gold. He and his crew were gone on their own for several months.

Columbus next reached what he named "Hispaniola," an island that is now Haiti and the Dominican Republic. He met a native chief with gold to trade. Columbus invited several natives to a Christmas

Landing of Christopher Columbus in the New World.

Eve feast aboard the *Santa Maria*. But that night, the ship hit a reef and sank.

Columbus and his crew reached the shore of Hispaniola safely, but their ship was lost. There, on Christmas day of 1492, Columbus decided to build a settlement, which he called "La Navidad." (That means "Christmas" in Spanish.) Columbus left 40 of his men at La Navidad and planned to return to Spain.

In January 1493, Columbus left for Spain aboard the *Niña*. Soon after, they ran into Pinzon and the *Pinta*. They returned to Spain together. But they encountered a bad storm near the Azores Islands. They finally reached Portugal in March 1493. Columbus actually made the first report of his journey to King John, then returned to Spain.

A FAMOUS EXPLORER: Columbus returned to Ferdinand and Isabella in glory. They were delighted with his successes. They wanted to pay for another voyage. Word of Columbus's bravery and accomplishment spread all over Europe. He was a famous explorer.

Columbus brought back many things that Europeans had never seen before. Pineapples, corn, sweet potatoes, and tobacco were exotic items to Europeans. And the Indians he brought back with him, many as slaves, were also unlike any people that Europeans had ever seen.

SECOND VOYAGE: Columbus left Spain for his second voyage in September 1493. This time, he headed a group of 17 ships and a crew of more than 1,400 men. Again, he headed south to the Canary Islands. From there, the expedition headed west across the Atlantic.

They made the crossing in just 21 days. They saw land in November, an island Columbus called "Dominica" in the Caribbean. Columbus went ashore on the island of Guadeloupe. There, he again encountered the warlike Caribs. The Caribs fought with the Spanish, and people were killed on both sides. Columbus again took several Caribs as slaves.

Columbus sailed on, sighting the Leeward Islands, the Virgin Islands, and Puerto Rico. But when he arrived at Hispaniola, he found that the settlement at La Navidad had been destroyed. All the Spanish settlers were dead. No one is sure what happened to them.

Finally, in June 1504, they were rescued. They returned to Spain in November 1504. By this time, Columbus was old and ill. His patron, Queen Isabella, died in late 1504. King Ferdinand called him to his court in 1505. Old as he was, Columbus tried again to raise money for another voyage. But that was not to be.

DEATH: Christopher Columbus died in May 1506, in the Spanish city of Valladolid. At the time of his death, there were many other explorers who had traveled to the **New World**. But in the past 500 years, it is Columbus who has been considered the most important explorer of them all.

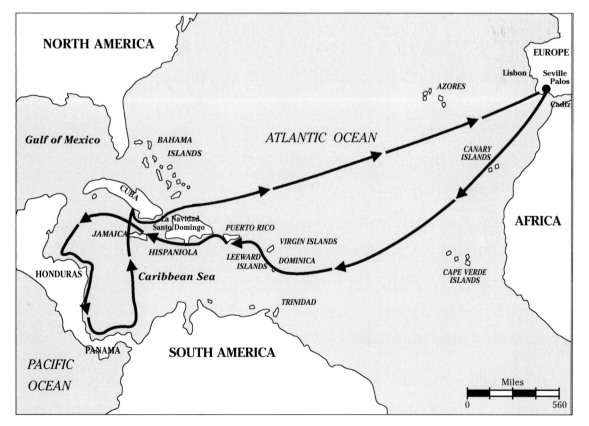

Columbus's fourth voyage, 1502-1504.

WHY IS CHRISTOPHER COLUMBUS SO IMPORTANT? When Columbus left Spain in 1492, most people in the world thought there were only three large land masses: Europe, Asia, and Africa. Although he didn't realize it, it was Columbus who proved that idea wrong.

Even though he thought he'd reached Asia, he'd opened up the **New World** to Europe. More importantly, unlike other explorers who only wanted to trade or travel, Columbus built settlements in the New World. The settlements were created with the intention of having a continuing relationship with the peoples of the New World.

Columbus's explorations, discoveries, and settlements led to enormous changes in the world. These changes brought wealth and the possibilities of a new life in a New World to some individuals. These same changes brought disaster to others.

WHY IS CHRISTOPHER COLUMBUS SO CONTROVERSIAL? Even today, more than 500 years after his first voyage, Columbus is praised by some and condemned by others. His explorations made it possible for Europeans to begin a new life in the colonies of the New World. His discoveries started the migration of Europeans and their ways of life to the New World.

The native peoples of the Caribbean, as well as those of North, South, and Central America had their lives changed forever, too. The Europeans could be brutal and destructive. They fought with and enslaved the native populations. Later explorers, like **Cortes**, conquered native populations and destroyed them.

The Europeans also brought diseases to which the natives had no resistance. Diseases like smallpox and measles were unknown in the New World. These diseases killed entire tribes.

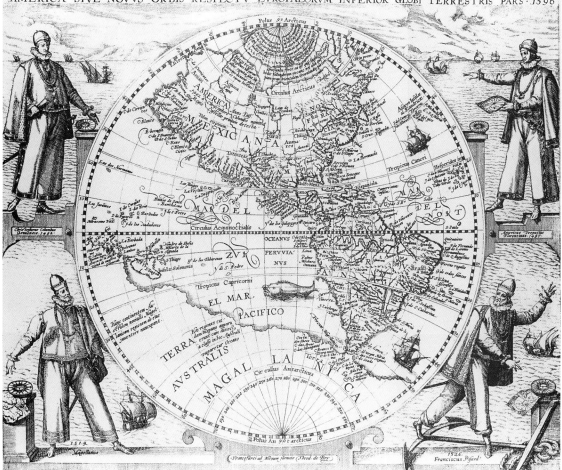

Map of the Americas from 1596 with portraits of Columbus (upper left), Vespucci (upper right), Magellan (lower left), and Pizarro (lower right).

Europeans claimed lands for themselves and their countries. They treated the natural wealth of the lands—the gold especially—as their own. In Columbus's time and later, they forced the Indians to work for them as slaves, and enriched themselves.

While Columbus was not responsible for all of the bad things that happened to the native populations, his discoveries made it possible for Europeans to use and abuse the native populations and their lands. That is why people continue to debate what he did. But regardless of whether he is considered a hero or a villain, Columbus was a brave and able navigator and explorer. He was a man whose actions truly changed the world.

CHRISTOPHER COLUMBUS'S FAMILY: In 1479 Columbus married a widow named Dona Felipa Perestrello e Moniz. They had one son, Diego. Dona Felipa died soon after Diego was born. After Columbus moved to Spain, he had a relationship with a woman named Beatriz Enrique de Arana. She and Columbus had a son named Fernando. She and Columbus never married. Fernando wrote a book about his famous father after Columbus died.

WORLD WIDE WEB SITES:

http://www.mariner.org/age/columbus.html
http://www.loc.gov/exhibits/1492
http://quest.classroom.com/columbus2002/

James Cook

1728 - 1779

**English Explorer, Navigator, and Naval Officer
World Explorer Who Led Three Major Expeditions
Around the Globe, Exploring the South Pacific,
New Zealand, Australia, Many Pacific Islands,
the Canadian Arctic, and Antarctica**

JAMES COOK WAS BORN on October 27, 1728, in Yorkshire, England. His parents were James and Grace Cook. His father didn't own his own farm, but worked on land owned by another man. James was one of nine children. He was a bright child, and his father's employer noticed. He offered to pay for James's education.

JAMES COOK WENT TO SCHOOL at a small village school in Yorkshire. He only attended school until he was 12. Then, he worked on the farm with his father. When he got a job in a general store on the North Sea, he fell in love with ships and sailing.

GOING TO SEA: When he was 18, Cook got a job on a merchant ship. He sailed ships that carried coal between ports in the North Sea. The ships were sturdy, but the North Sea is rough. Cook learned quickly and became an able seaman.

When he was 27, Cook was offered command of his own ship. But he wanted to join the Royal Navy instead. He served in the Navy for the next 23 years.

VOYAGE TO CANADA: Between 1756 and 1763, England and France were at war. During that war, Cook served in Canada. He surveyed areas in what are now Nova Scotia and Quebec. He also made maps of the waterways, and he surveyed the coast of Newfoundland. He developed his navigational skills, and took careful observations of a solar eclipse in 1766.

FIRST VOYAGE OF EXPLORATION: In 1768, Cook was made commander of an expedition to the South Pacific. He was to lead a group of scientists and sailors to observe the planet Venus passing in front of the sun. The best place to watch the eclipse was the Pacific island of Tahiti. He also had a secret mission: to try to find "Terra Australis." That was a legendary island mass in the South Pacific that **Abel Tasman** and others had looked for earlier.

Some scientists thought that a huge southern continent existed. They thought it "balanced" the continents in the north of the globe.

Cook landing on Vanuatu Islands, South Pacific.

Now Cook was chosen to find "Terra Australis." In August 1768, he left England aboard the *Endeavor* with a crew of 94.

Cook sailed southwest across the Atlantic Ocean. He rounded South America at Cape Horn. Sailing up into the Pacific, he reached Tahiti in April 1769. While the scientists prepared for the eclipse, other members gathered plants and animals. On board with Cook was **Joseph Banks**. He was a naturalist who studied living things on all the islands they visited.

Cook explored Tahiti and drew detailed maps of it and other islands. They were among the first accurate charts ever made of Pacific islands. Traveling south and west from Tahiti, they sailed to New Zealand. Cook took the path of a figure-8 in exploring and charting the two islands that make up New Zealand.

153

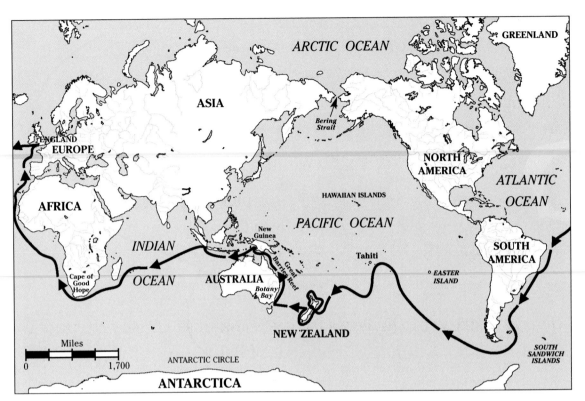

Cook's first voyage of exploration, 1768-1771.

Next, the *Endeavor* headed to Australia. They landed at what they called Botany Bay in April 1770. Cook navigated 2,000 miles of the east coast of Australia. After months exploring the coast, he determined it couldn't be the great legendary land mass.

Then Cook entered the Great Barrier Reef. It was full of coral that could rip the underside of a boat and sink it. Cook made it through most of the way, then the *Endeavor* got caught on the reef. They made it to land on Australia and fixed the ship.

They sailed for England, along the northern coast of Australia. Their route took them across the Indian Ocean, around the southern tip of Africa, and up the West African coast. They reached England in July 1771. Cook had completed his first circumnavigation — voyage around the world.

154

THE END OF SCURVY: Cook was a fine leader who cared about his crew. He made sure that the *Endeavor* carried plenty of fruits and vegetables. Although he had no scientific proof, he thought that a diet with vegetables high in Vitamin C would prevent scurvy. Scurvy was a terrible disease that had caused illness and death on ships since the earliest sea voyages.

Cook made sure the men ate lots of pickled cabbage (sauerkraut), onions, and other foods high in Vitamin C. He also made them bathe and clean the ship every day. His care for his crew saved lives. He didn't lose a single man to scurvy.

When he returned to England, Cook was promoted to commander and met King George III. The success of Banks and the naturalists interested many people. They wanted Cook to continue exploring.

Cook nears Antarctica, 1773.

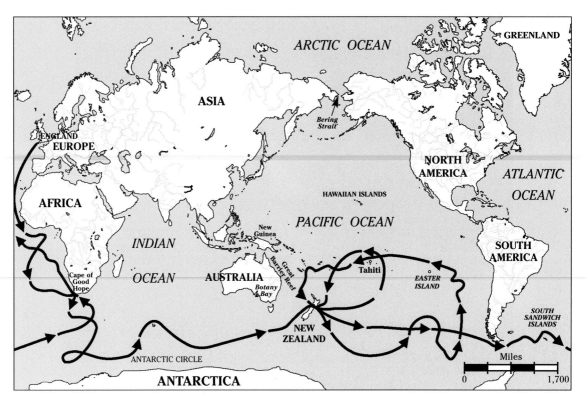

Cook's second voyage, 1772-1775.

This time they would sail to the farthest reaches of the known world. They were going to Antarctica.

SECOND VOYAGE: Cook set sail on his second voyage in July 1772. Aboard the *Resolution*, and accompanied by the *Adventure*, he took a different path. They sailed south from England and down the coast of West Africa. When they reached the tip of South Africa, they continued south.

Soon, they spotted icebergs and what looked like an endless sheet of ice. Cook tried to head further south, but the way was clogged with ice. He traveled north again, then west into the Pacific. He spent many months exploring the ocean and finding many islands. He also visited Tahiti, New Zealand, and Tonga. He went as

156

far east as Easter Island. To the south and east, he discovered New Caledonia, the South Sandwich Islands, and South Georgia Island.

Here and everywhere he traveled, he kept a detailed journal about the people he met. He made notes about how languages and customs were similar in different island groups. Cook was also an excellent navigator. He created accurate charts of the waters he traveled that were used for many years.

Cook returned to England in July 1775. He was made a captain and was greeted as a hero. It wasn't long before he was planning his third voyage.

THIRD VOYAGE: Cook's third and final voyage began in July 1776 (the same month the English colonies in America declared their

Cook in Hawaii.

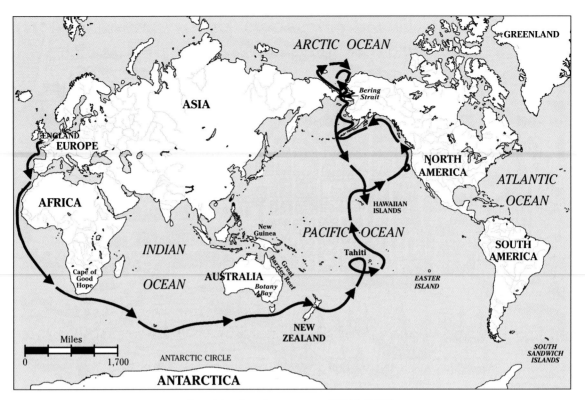

Cook's third voyage, 1776-1779.

independence.) This time, he added his name to those explorers who had searched for the **Northwest Passage.**

From the early 1500s, many people believed that a passage from Europe to Asia existed through what is now Canada. They sought a sea route linking the Atlantic and Pacific Oceans through the islands of the Canadian Arctic.

Cook left England at the head of two ships, the *Resolution* and the *Discovery*, with a combined crew of 182. They headed south along the west coast of Africa, then rounded the tip of Africa.

They sailed across the Indian Ocean and into the Pacific. Cook visited New Zealand and Tahiti. In January 1778, he landed on modern-day Hawaii. He named them the "Sandwich Islands," in honor of the Earl of Sandwich. Cook was fascinated with the people. He was amazed at the Hawaiians' ability to travel great distances in the oceans in their outrigger canoes.

The Hawaiians treated Cook and his crew with friendship. In fact, they thought Cook was a god. After several weeks in Hawaii, Cook and his crew headed north. They reached the coast of what is now Oregon in March 1778. They spent the next few months sailing north along the Pacific coast, past the Aleutian Islands of Alaska. They reached the Bering Strait, the narrow waterway that had been discovered by **Vitus Bering** 50 years earlier.

Cook passed through the strait, then determined it did not lead to a Northwest Passage. He sailed back to Hawaii, landing in

The death of Captain Cook.

January 1779. But when they returned, their relationship with the natives had turned from friendly to hostile.

THE DEATH OF CAPTAIN COOK: In February 1779, Cook's crew was at Kealakekua Bay on the Big Island of Hawaii making repairs to their ship. There were growing problems between the English and the Hawaiians. The Hawaiians had stolen many things from the English ships, including a small boat. Cook decided to confront the problem.

He went to the mainland and took a chief hostage. He told the Hawaiians that he would keep the chief until they returned the boat. A fight broke out, and one of the English sailors fired his gun. The Hawaiians attacked, and Cook and several men were killed in the fight.

The English sailors were devastated by the death of their commander. Cook was buried at sea. The expedition returned to England.

JAMES COOK'S HOME AND FAMILY: Cook married Elizabeth Batts in 1762. They had six children.

HIS DISCOVERY: Cook is considered one of the greatest explorers of all time. He was a brave leader and an excellent navigator. He mapped much of the Pacific Ocean and discovered many islands never before seen by Europeans. His journey to the edge of Antarctica was the farthest southern voyage up to that time.

WORLD WIDE WEB SITES:

http://www.captaincooksociety.com/
http://www.mariner.org/age/cook.html
http://www.win.tue.nl/~engels/discovery/cook.html

Francisco Vázquez de Coronado
1510-1554
Spanish Conquistador Who Explored the Southwest United States

FRANCISCO VÁZQUEZ DE CORONADO WAS BORN in 1510 in Salamanca, Spain. His father was Juan Vázquez Coronado and his mother was Isabel de Lujan. They were both from noble families. Very little is known about Coronado's early life.

TRAVELING TO THE NEW WORLD: When he was 25, Coronado traveled to **New Spain**, to what is now Mexico. He went as an assistant to Viceroy Antonio de Mendoza. He became a member of the city council and was made governor of one of the provinces of

New Spain. The Spanish had enslaved local natives as they took over New Spain. In his early years as governor, Coronado brutally suppressed a slave rebellion.

Alvar Núñez Cabeza de Vaca had explored parts of New Spain in the 1530s. He had heard of the legendary Seven Cities of Cibola (SEE-boh-luh). These cities were supposedly somewhere to the north of New Spain. They supposedly contained gold and treasure. Mendoza was eager to claim that wealth for Spain. He chose Coronado to lead an expedition to the legendary cities.

SEARCHING FOR THE SEVEN CITIES OF CIBOLA: Coronado left the Mexican city of Compostela in April 1540. With him were 1,000 men (many of them slaves), 1,500 horses and mules, and hundreds of cattle, sheep, and pigs.

They traveled north through what is now Mexico and Arizona. They reached the Zuni village of Hawikuh, in modern-day New Mexico. They thought it was one of the Seven Cities, but it was only a small settlement. The Spanish conquered the village. They found no gold, but decided to continue their journey and look for treasure.

Coronado divided his men into several expeditions. One group traveled northwest. They were the first Europeans to see the Grand Canyon. Another traveled east to an Indian settlement called Tiguex. It was along the Rio Grande in New Mexico.

In Tiguex, Coronado met an Indian called El Turco. He told him of the riches of an area called Quivira. Coronado made plans to travel to Quivira, with El Turco as his guide.

EXPLORING THE WEST IN SEARCH OF QUIVIRA: Coronado's men spent the winter of 1540-41 at Tiguex. In April 1541, they traveled

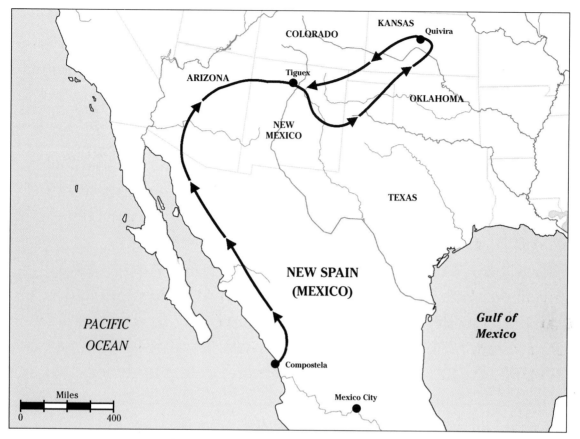

Coronado's expedition of 1540-1542.

east through New Mexico and into Texas. Coronado decided to send part of his group back to Tiguex. With a group of 36 men, he traveled north toward what he thought were the riches of Quivira.

They journeyed through what are now Texas, Oklahoma, and Kansas. Along the way they saw buffalo for the first time. They saw plains Indians who followed the buffalo herd and lived off the meat and skins.

They reached Quivira, in modern-day Kansas, in July 1541. But like Hawikuh, it was nothing more than an Indian settlement. Coronado confronted El Turco. He confessed that he lied about Quivira. Coronado executed him.

163

RETURN TO MEXICO: Coronado returned to Mexico in 1542. Many of his men had died or deserted. Only 100 returned with him. His expedition had ended in failure. Coronado faced an inquiry into his conduct. After a trial, he was cleared of some of the charges. He was fined for other charges. Some sources say he was found guilty of cruelty toward native people and was removed as governor.

Coronado retired to his estate. He died in Mexico City in 1554, at the age of 44.

FRANCISCO VÁZQUEZ DE CORONADO'S HOME AND FAMILY: Coronado's wife was named Beatriz de Estrada. They met and married in Mexico City and had five children.

HIS DISCOVERY: Although he never found gold and riches, Coronado led his expedition farther north than any previous group of European explorers. He expanded the boundaries of Spanish territory into what became the southwest United States. He was also a man capable of great brutality in dealing with the native population. This cruelty is also part of his legacy.

WORLD WIDE WEB SITES:

http://www.nps.gov/coro/pphtml/kids.html
http://www.pbs.org/weta/thewest/people/a_c/coronado.htm
http://www.tsha.utexas.edu/handbook/online/articles/view/CC/
  upcpt.html

Hernando Cortes

1485 - 1547
Spanish Conquistador and Explorer Who Conquered Mexico

HERNANDO CORTES was born in 1485 in Medellin, Spain. His name is also spelled Hernan Cortez. His parents were Martin Cortes and Catalina Pizarro Altamarino.

A record of Cortes's youth calls him "very intelligent and clever in everything he did." He was also, according to the record, ruthless and argumentative, a "source of trouble to his parents."

Cortes was sent away to school when he was 14. He studied law for a few years. Then, he decided he'd had enough of school. He'd heard of the triumphs of **Christopher Columbus**. He wanted to become an explorer.

VOYAGE TO THE NEW WORLD: Cortes sailed to the **New World** in 1504, at the age of 19. He landed on the Spanish colony of Hispaniola (now Haiti and the Dominican Republic). He became a farmer and a city official.

CUBA: In 1511, Cortes sailed with Diego Velazquez on an expedition to Cuba. There, they conquered the local native tribes. Cortes was named mayor of the settlement city of Santiago. He lived in Cuba for several years.

Velazquez saw that Cortes was a popular mayor, but he didn't really trust him. In 1518, he offered Cortes the opportunity to take an expedition to Mexico. Then, he took back the offer. But Cortes wanted to lead the expedition. Without Velazquez's knowledge or permission, he sailed from Cuba in November 1518.

VOYAGE TO MEXICO: Cortes sailed with nearly 1,000 soldiers, 16 horses, and weapons on an expedition that would change Mexico forever.

Cortes sailed for the Yucatan peninsula and landed on the island of Cozumel.

He fought and conquered the local natives. Here and elsewhere, he forced the Indians to convert to Christianity. If they refused, they were killed. The natives were astonished at the Spaniards for more than their powerful army. They had brought horses with them, an animal they'd never seen before.

Cortes's ships in the harbor of Santiago, Cuba.

Cortes then traveled along the coast of Mexico, where he founded a settlement he called Vera Cruz. After landing, Cortes did an amazing thing. He burned his ships. He made it impossible for his soldiers to desert. They had to pledge to fight with him, no matter what the consequences.

THE AZTECS: The Indians he saw on the mainland were Aztecs. The Aztecs had formed an empire that stretched over much of Mexico. They had a highly developed civilization. They grew plenty of food, using irrigation systems, and had a system of trade and taxes.

The Aztecs could be cruel and brutal people. They conquered other tribes and enslaved people. They also practiced a religion that called for human sacrifice to their gods. Part of that religion would help Cortes as he conquered Mexico.

CONQUERING THE AZTECS: The Aztec religion had a legend about a god named Quetzalcoatl (ket-SAHL-kuh-WAHT-el). According to the legend, he had been banished from the empire. The legend foretold that he would return one day to reclaim his place. Quetzalcoatl was described as tall, blond, and bearded. The description fit Cortes.

When the Aztecs first saw Cortes, they reported back to their ruler, Montezuma. He thought Cortes might be Quetzalcoatl. Montezuma sent gifts to Cortes, including gold.

Meanwhile, Cortes was planning to conquer the Aztec empire. He started out toward their major city, Tenochtitlan (the-nock-TEE-tlan). It was where Mexico City is today. Along the way, Cortes fought and defeated the local natives. Some of these Indians were more hostile to the Aztecs than to Cortes. They helped him in his attack on the Aztec empire.

Cortes entered the city and went to Montezuma's palace. He threatened to take Montezuma prisoner unless the Aztec leader turned the empire over to him. Montezuma agreed.

But Cortes was in trouble. Velazquez had sent an army to remove him from power. Cortes fought the Spanish army, under the command of Panfilo Narvaez, and won. He then had Narvaez's soldiers fight with him against the Aztecs. They returned to Tenochtitlan and found the Aztecs in revolt. Cortes led his men in a bloody and costly battle. He lost the fight, half his men, and most of the gold and

Cortes meets Montezuma.

treasure he'd gathered. Retreating to an area outside the city, he planned his next battle.

He attacked Tenochtitlan again, this time conquering it and destroying most of the city. On the ruins of the ancient Aztec capital, Cortes built his capital, Mexico City. He destroyed Aztec temples and replaced them with Christian churches. The Aztecs disappeared, along with their way of life and their civilization.

NEW EXPEDITIONS FOR SPAIN: The King of Spain, Charles V, named Cortes the head of the colony's government and army. Cortes sponsored expeditions to expand the territory of **New Spain**. He sent explorers to what is now Guatemala and Honduras.

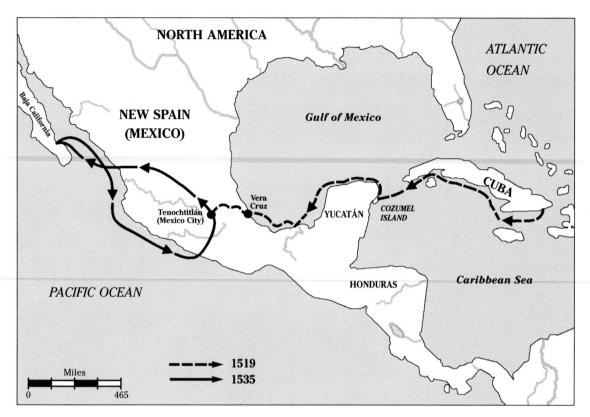

Cortes's expeditions in Mexico, 1519 and 1535.

Cortes himself went to Honduras when the man he had sent to explore it declared himself the independent ruler. The journey took several years, and by the time he returned to Mexico City, there was conflict among the ruling Spaniards. Cortes still had his enemies. Velazquez and others continued to plot against him, both in Spain and in the **New World**.

RETURN TO SPAIN: Cortes wrote a series of letters to the king to explain what he had done and to declare his loyalty. In 1528, he returned to Spain to meet with the king. He was treated as a great hero by the Spanish people.

But the king did not name him governor of New Spain. He appointed another leader, Mendoza, who outranked Cortes.

RETURN TO NEW SPAIN AND TO EXPLORATION: Cortes returned to New Spain and began to explore again. In 1535, he traveled to what is now Baja California. As the years went by, Cortes became old and ill. He returned to Spain, where he died in 1547. He is buried in Mexico City.

HERNANDO CORTES'S HOME AND FAMILY: Cortes was married twice. His first wife, named Catalina, died while he was in Mexico. His second wife was named Juana de Zuniga. Cortes had two sons, Martin and Luis.

A FIGURE OF CONTROVERSY: Cortes has inspired debate for 400 years. He was praised in his homeland as the man who expanded the wealth and lands of Spain. But at what cost? Cortes was a brave military leader, but his brutality led to the end of an entire civilization. The Aztecs, too, were harsh rulers capable of great cruelty, but by what right did Cortes conquer and annihilate them? People have argued about Cortes for hundreds of years, and they will certainly continue to do so.

HIS DISCOVERY: Despite the controversy Cortes has inspired, his conquests changed history. When he defeated the Aztecs, he brought about the Spanish control of Mexico and Central America. The history of the area changed forever with his conquest. The cultures of Mexico and the Central American countries are now a blend of the native and Spanish influences that began with Cortes.

WORLD WIDE WEB SITE:

http://www.rice.edu/armadillo/Projects/cortez.html

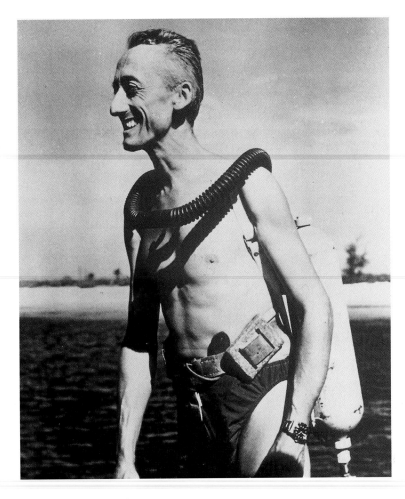

Jacques Cousteau
1910 - 1997
French Ocean Explorer, Film Producer, and Inventor

JACQUES COUSTEAU WAS BORN on June 11, 1910, near Bordeaux, France. His name is pronounced "zhahk koos-TOE." His parents were Daniel and Elizabeth Cousteau. Daniel was a lawyer and Elizabeth was a homemaker. Jacques had an older brother named Pierre.

JACQUES COUSTEAU GREW UP in many different places. His father's work took the family around the world. When he was eight, the family moved to New York for his father's job. They moved back to Paris two years later, but still continued to travel often.

Even when he was little, Cousteau loved the sea. "When I was four or five years old, I loved touching water," he recalled. "Water fascinated me. First floating ships, then me floating, and stones not floating."

He started inventing when he was just a boy, too. He built a model crane when he was 11. At 13, he designed a car that ran on batteries. He got a camera at 15 and started making movies. It was something he would do for the rest of his life.

JACQUES COUSTEAU WENT TO SCHOOL at schools in New York and France. He was very bright, but not very interested in school. He was expelled from one high school for bad behavior. Finally, when he entered the French Naval College, he was studying what he loved. He did very well. He graduated from the Naval College in 1933.

THE NAVY: As a young Navy seaman, Cousteau sailed around the world. He planned to become a Navy pilot, but a serious car accident ended that dream. Instead, he worked on Navy ships at sea for several years. He also began his lifelong career as a diver. He started to experiment with a breathing device that would let a diver stay underwater for long periods of time.

When World War II broke out in 1939, France came under control of the German Nazis. Cousteau was part of the "Underground." That was a group of people within France who fought to defeat the Nazis. In 1945, Germany was defeated, and Cousteau received several awards for bravery.

Cousteau looks out from a two-man underwater observation chamber, 1959.

Even during the war, Cousteau continued to dive and invent. He became an expert undersea diver and made underwater films. He also came up with one of the major inventions in undersea exploration.

SCUBA: Cousteau was still trying to find a way for divers to breathe underwater. In 1943, he and a French engineer developed equipment now used worldwide: SCUBA. SCUBA stands for "self-contained underwater breathing apparatus." It was manufactured under the name "Aqualung."

This ground-breaking invention contained tanks of oxygen connected to a breathing device. It allowed divers to stay under-water for hours.

Cousteau's inventions didn't stop with SCUBA. He also developed ways to use a television camera underwater. He even created an underwater research colony. The Conshelf Program was a laboratory under the sea, where scientists lived and worked for months at a time.

In 1946, Cousteau bought the *Calypso*. He converted the boat into a floating exploration ship. It had a diving platform and an underwater observation chamber. And it became famous to viewers around the world. Cousteau began a series of journeys on the *Calypso*, which he captured on film. On his many expeditions he explored the world's oceans and the plants and animals living there. Combining his devotion to the oceans and to filmmaking, Cousteau produced several award-winning films. He also wrote several best-selling books about his adventures.

Cousteau became the head of several important scientific groups. Through these, he developed research programs for scientists. He also started the Cousteau Society. It is a group devoted to the study and protection of the environment.

"THE UNDERSEA WORLD OF JACQUES COUSTEAU": In 1968, Cousteau brought the ocean world to television viewers all over the globe. That year, the first show in his series "The Undersea World of Jacques Cousteau" was broadcast. Using his skill as a filmmaker and his knowledge of ocean life, Cousteau brought the beauty and mystery of the seas to millions. Through the series, he also made people aware of the dangers of pollution.

Cousteau continued his travels, filmmaking, and writing until his death on June 25, 1997. He was 86 years old.

JACQUES COUSTEAU'S HOME AND FAMILY: Cousteau married his wife, Simone, in 1937. They had two sons, Jean-Michel and Philippe. Working with his father, Philippe became a diver and moviemaker. Sadly, he died in a plane crash in 1979.

HIS DISCOVERY: Cousteau was the first great ocean explorer. Using equipment he invented, he made discoveries that changed the way we think about the undersea world. He brought that world alive to millions in his films. Through them, he presented the beauty and wonder of ocean life, while alerting the world to the dangers of undersea pollution. At his death, the chairman of the National Geographic Society, Gilbert Grosvenor, said, "The ocean environment has lost its greatest champion."

WORLD WIDE WEB SITES:

http://www.cousteausociety.org
http://marine.rutgers.edu/pt/home.htm

D. VASCO DE GAMA.

Vasco da Gama
1460? - 1524
Portuguese Explorer
First European to Sail Around Africa to India

VASCO DA GAMA WAS BORN around 1460 in the Portuguese city of Sines. Very little is known about his early life. His father was named Estevao da Gama, and he had at least one brother, Paulo. As a youth, Da Gama learned to sail and learned enough about mathematics to become a navigator.

IN THE SERVICE OF THE KING OF PORTUGAL: In 1492, King John II of Portugal sent Da Gama to fight sea battles against the French. The French were robbing Portuguese ships.

At this time, Portugal was becoming a major sea power. Da Gama continued the search for a sea route around Africa planned by **Prince Henry the Navigator.** Prince Henry wanted to find a route by water instead of by land to reach Asia. Portugal would use the sea route to trade goods with Asian countries. He also wanted to spread Christianity to Africa and the Middle East.

In 1487, **Bartholomew Dias** sailed as far as the Cape of Good Hope. Now the new king, Manuel, wanted Da Gama to sail all the way to India.

FIRST VOYAGE: In July 1497, Da Gama left Portugal with four ships and 170 men. One of the ships was captained by his brother, Paulo. They sailed south, far off the coast of Africa. They were out of sight of land for many days. Finally, in November, they rounded the Cape of Good Hope, which Dias had discovered.

The expedition continued up the east coast of Africa. They stopped at the cities of Mozambique, Mombassa, and Malindi. These cities were major trading ports under Muslim control. Fighting broke out between Da Gama's men and the Muslim rulers. Portugal wanted to control at least a portion of the trade coming from India. The Muslim rulers wanted to hold on to their control of trade.

Da Gama had a fierce temper and could treat his enemies with great cruelty. He bombarded one port, and took prisoners who were tortured and forced to reveal information.

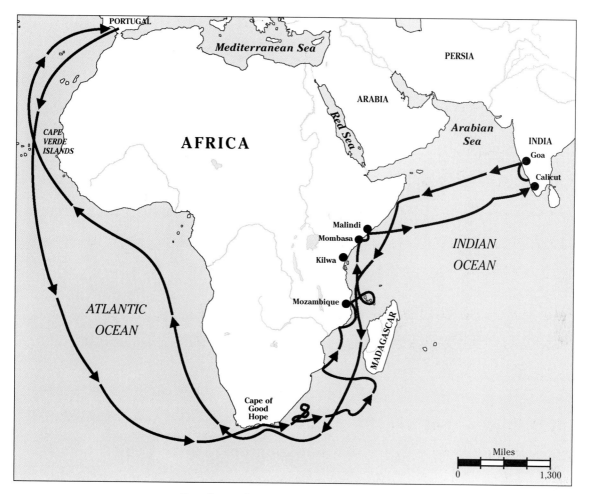

Da Gama's voyages of 1497-1499.
(Two later voyages followed a similar route.)

The expedition left the coast of Africa and headed for India. They landed on the west coast of India, called the Malabar Coast, in May 1498. Da Gama met with the ruler of the main port city of Calicut. Calicut was ruled by Hindu leaders, and the trade was controlled by Muslims.

Da Gama was not warmly welcomed by the ruler. He had brought gifts from King Manuel of Portugal that the ruler thought were rather cheap. He had also heard how Da Gama had treated the Muslims in Africa.

179

Da Gama landing near Calicut, India.

So Da Gama left Calicut in August 1498 with only a sample of spices and gems. The trip back to Portugal was difficult. Many of the men were ill. More than half of the crew died before they reached home. Among the dead was Da Gama's brother Paulo. He died just before they reached Portugal, in September 1499.

Da Gama was welcomed home as a hero. The king wanted missions to go to India again, and soon. He sent **Pedro Alvarez Cabral** to India in 1500. In Calicut, Cabral had trouble with the Muslims and the Indians. Fighting broke out, and many Muslims and Indians lost their lives.

SECOND VOYAGE: Da Gama sailed again for India in February 1502. The king wanted him to firmly establish Portugal's control of trade. Da Gama headed an expedition of 20 ships, many of them war ships.

Da Gama engaged in battles with Muslims and Indians during this voyage. In one instance, he captured a boat carrying 300 Muslims — men, women, and children — returning from a religious journey. He burned the boat, killing everyone on board.

In Calicut, he demanded that the ruler banish all Muslims from the city. He murdered 38 Hindu fisherman to show the Indians what he could do. Da Gama sailed for Portugal in February 1503 and reached home in October.

Over the next 20 years, Da Gama lived a comfortable life as a Portuguese naval hero. He was named a count and adviser of the king.

THIRD VOYAGE: Da Gama's last voyage took place in 1524. The new king, John III, asked him to go back to India. There were problems with the Portuguese trade business there. Da Gama left Portugal in April 1524 with 14 ships. He arrived in India in September. He became ill, and died in December 1524, at the age of around 64.

VASCO DA GAMA'S HOME AND FAMILY: Da Gama married a woman named Caterina sometime around 1500. They had six sons.

HIS DISCOVERY: Da Gama is remembered as the explorer who helped Portugal become a world trading power. Although his tactics were often barbaric and cruel, he was considered a hero to the Portuguese.

WORLD WIDE WEB SITES:

http://www.mariner.org/age/dagama.html
http://www.ucalgary.ca/applied_history/tutor/eurvoya/vasco.html

Charles Darwin

1809 - 1882
English Scientist and Explorer
Developed the Theory of Evolution

CHARLES DARWIN WAS BORN on February 12, 1809, in Shrewsbury, England. His parents were Robert and Susannah Darwin. Robert was a doctor and Susannah was a homemaker. Charles had three older sisters and an older brother. His mother died when he was eight.

CHARLES DARWIN WENT TO SCHOOL at the Shrewsbury School from the age of eight until the age of 16. Darwin didn't like school. He said "school to me was simply a blank." He liked animals, and he liked to collect sea shells and birds' eggs.

At 16, he went to Edinburgh University in Scotland. There, he studied medicine. But he didn't like it, especially watching operations. He didn't want to be a doctor. So he went to Cambridge University. There, he studied to be a minister. But he didn't like that very much, either.

What Darwin loved to do was study plant and animal life. He loved to roam the fields and woods and collect plants, animals, and rocks. One of his teachers at Cambridge, John Henslow, understood him. After Darwin graduated in 1831, Henslow arranged for Darwin to work as a naturalist on an expedition.

Darwin was to sail aboard the *Beagle*, captained by Robert Fitzroy. The goal of the voyage was to map the waters and coasts of South America, then sail around the world. As the ship's naturalist, Darwin would explore the plant and animal life of the lands they visited. It was a voyage that would change Darwin — and the world of science.

SAILING ABOARD THE *BEAGLE*: Darwin left England in December 1831 aboard the *Beagle*. They stopped first in the Cape Verde Islands. Then they sailed on for South America. While the crew charted the waterways, Darwin went ashore and explored.

The *Beagle* stopped in Brazil, Uruguay, Argentina, Chile, the Galapagos Islands, and Australia. Everywhere they stopped, Darwin studied the variety of plants and animals. He took specimens and studied them. He collected fossils, too, and examined rocks and mountains.

In Brazil, Darwin saw more kinds of plants and animals than he'd ever seen in England. He collected hundreds of beetles. Even though he was often seasick on ship, on land he was vigorous and curious. He crammed his trunks with specimens.

In Argentina, Darwin collected fossils that startled him. They looked like large mammals that still existed on Earth. Why did one species die out? How was the modern animal related to its ancient ancestors? And how ancient were the fossils?

In Chile, Darwin witnessed an earthquake. In the Andes, he examined volcanoes that had just erupted. He found fossil shells in the mountains. How did sea shells get to the top of mountains? When had these upheavals of land happened? How had they changed the landscape?

THE GALAPAGOS ISLANDS: Darwin reached the Galapagos Islands, off the coast of Ecuador, in 1835. He spent only five weeks in the Galapagos, but what he found gave him information he would ponder his entire life.

Darwin was amazed at how species of animals—from tortoises to finches—varied so much, in such a small area. Tortoises had different shells, depending on where they lived. Some iguanas had adapted to live on land, others to live in water. Finches had different kinds of beaks, depending on where they lived. The animals seemed to vary depending on the geography and the food available.

Darwin saw that the animals varied widely in key ways. They were large or small, and had certain physical features, depending

Darwin's expedition, 1831-1836.

on where they lived and what they ate. Why was that? Did animals change to adapt to where they lived? How did that happen?

From South America, the ship traveled to Australia. There, Darwin studied how coral reefs are formed. Darwin finally returned to England in 1836. The voyage of the *Beagle* was supposed to take two years. Instead, it had taken five.

Back in England, Darwin mulled over his findings. All of the information he had collected — about animals, plants, and geology — puzzled and fascinated him. He began to develop theories based on his findings.

At that time, many people believed that the world was only about 6,000 years old. They believed that all animals, plants, as well as the mountains and oceans, had been created at the same time, 6,000 years ago. They believed that all living creatures had not changed since their creation. For them, the Bible story of Creation was the truth. But what Darwin found on his journey challenged these beliefs.

THEORY OF EVOLUTION: For Darwin, the Earth and its creatures were constantly changing, or evolving. His observations led him to create a theory of evolution to explain nature.

From his experience in South America, Darwin determined that the Earth itself was constantly changing. Over long periods of time, eruptions and earthquakes transformed the Earth. That way, sea shells that were once on the ocean floor became part of a mountain surface.

Darwin thought that animals, too, had changed over many years. From his examination of fossils, Darwin determined that certain animals had become extinct. They were related to modern animals, but somehow they had died off.

On the Galapagos and elsewhere, Darwin had been struck by the wide variety of species of animals. From these observations, he developed another important theory. He saw that animals had to compete for food, space, and habitat. Those animals that had the greatest chance to succeed were those that could adapt, or change, to suit their environment.

Over time, the most successful species would survive. Those that were less successful would die out. Darwin called this theory "natural selection." It was ground-breaking. It also directly challenged what most people believed.

FAMOUS — AND CONTROVERSIAL — WRITINGS: Beginning in the 1840s, Darwin wrote down his theories. But he didn't want to publish them. He knew that what he was writing was controversial. It challenged people's religious beliefs. It also challenged scientific theories.

Darwin was not the first to develop theories of evolution. In fact, the naturalist **Alfred Russel Wallace** had come up with many of the same ideas. Finally, after many years, Darwin's and Wallace's ideas were presented to scientists. And in 1859, Darwin finally published a book about his scientific findings, *Origin of Species*. As he had feared, they were challenged and condemned by some.

But as scientists read the work, they became convinced that Darwin's theories were true. He had started a revolution in science. Over the years Darwin's findings have become widely accepted, and he is the most famous scientist associated with evolution.

There are some groups that continue to oppose his theories, but most modern evolutionary theory is based on his work.

CHARLES DARWIN'S HOME AND FAMILY: Darwin married his cousin, Emma Wedgewood, in 1839. They had eight children. Three of his sons, Francis, George, and Horace, became scientists. Darwin was in poor health most of his adult life and died in 1882. Some scientists believe he suffered from a disease he'd gotten from an insect bite on his journey.

HIS DISCOVERY: Darwin's ground-breaking theories of evolution changed the way we view our world. His discoveries, inspired by his explorations to South America, have made him one of the most important scientific thinkers in history.

WORLD WIDE WEB SITE:

http://web.clas.ufl.edu/users/rhatch/05-DARWIN-PAGE.html

Alexandra David-Neel
1868 - 1969
French Explorer of Asia
First European Woman to Enter Lhasa, Tibet

ALEXANDRA DAVID-NEEL WAS BORN on October 24, 1868, in Paris, France. She came from a wealthy family who tried to be strict with their only daughter. Yet from a very young age, Alexandra loved to roam, alone.

ALEXANDRA DAVID-NEEL GREW UP first in France, and then in Belgium. Her family moved to Belgium when she was six. Alexandra went to the local schools and was a good student. She especially liked philosophy and religion.

Most of all David-Neel loved to travel. When she was just 15, she traveled by herself to England. She returned when she ran out of money. On this and other journeys, the free-spirited David-Neel didn't tell her parents where she was going or when she'd be back. They worried about her, but there was little they could do to change their daughter's headstrong ways.

When she was 18, David-Neel left Belgium on her bicycle. Without telling her parents, she headed for Spain. She enjoyed herself thoroughly. When she returned home, she decided to go to college.

David-Neel studied religion, philosophy, and languages in Paris. She was especially fascinated by Asian religions. She also became an excellent singer, and performed in operas.

The fearless David-Neel also continued to travel. In 1890, a relative left her money, and she used it to travel to India. She loved India, and spent a year there. She learned more about the religions of India and the mysterious country of Tibet.

ALEXANDRA DAVID-NEEL'S HOME AND FAMILY: In 1904, Alexandra David met Philippe Neel, a railway engineer. They fell in love and married. But David-Neel was not a conventional wife, and her husband understood. So she continued to travel.

A JOURNEY OF 14 YEARS: David-Neel left Europe for Asia in 1911. She told her husband she'd be back in 18 months. Instead, she was gone for 14 years. She first visited India, where she studied language and religion. She traveled north to the small state of Sikkim, in the Himalaya Mountains. She studied Buddhism at ancient monasteries.

The photograph shows David-Neel and Aphur Youngden. The commemorative stone in the picture was placed at the David-Neel museum by the Dalai Lama. The inscription is in French. It reads: "To the memory of Alexandra David-Neel, explorer of Tibet, and to her adopted son, the Lama Youngden."

She also met a young monk named Aphur Youngden. They traveled and studied together, and David-Neel later adopted him. Life was incredibly difficult. The land is a harsh, snow-covered plateau, surrounded by the highest mountains in the world. But David-Neel loved it. Cold and hunger never dimmed her love of exploring and learning.

David-Neel next traveled into southern Tibet. That ancient country, virtually unknown to the outside world, had always fascinated her. But she and Youngden were eventually thrown out by the British, who controlled the Indian-Tibet border.

David-Neel and Youngden next visited Japan, which she found boring after her mountain adventures. She longed for Tibet. "I am 'homesick' for a land that is not mine," she wrote her husband. "I am haunted by the steppes, the solitude, the everlasting snow and the great blue sky."

TIBET: Heading for Tibet, they traveled through Korea and China. They traveled the deserts and studied at the Tibetan Buddhist monastery at Kumbum. There, David-Neel thought up a plan to get into Lhasa. Lhasa is the capital of Tibet, and the home of the Dalai Lama, the spiritual leader of Tibetan Buddhism. It was also closed to all foreigners.

LHASA: But Alexandra David-Neel wasn't about to let that stop her. She smeared grease on her skin to darken it, and dressed as a poor peasant. She achieved her goal, entering Lhasa and visiting many local monasteries. She was the first European woman ever to enter the remote holy city. Finally, in 1925, after 14 years of exploring, David-Neel returned home.

LATER LIFE: Alexandra David-Neel became a world-famous explorer. She was honored by geographic societies and wrote best-selling books. She took one more trip to Asia, in 1937, visiting China and Tibet. She lived and worked out of her home in the French town of Digne. She built a meditation center there, Samten Dzong, now a museum. She died on September 8, 1969, at the age of 100.

HER DISCOVERY: David-Neel was the first European woman ever to visit Lhasa, Tibet. Her travel books brought the remote lands and religions of Asia to life for readers all over the world.

WORLD WIDE WEB SITE:

http://www.alexandra-david-neel.org/

HERHANDO DE SOTO:
Estremeño: uno de los descubridores y conquistadores del Perú: recorrió toda la Florida y venció a sus naturales invencibles hasta entonces: murió en su expedic.ª el año de 1543. á los 42. de su edad

Hernando de Soto

1496? - 1542

Spanish Conquistador Who Explored the
Southeastern United States
First European to Discover the Mississippi River

HERNANDO DE SOTO WAS BORN between 1496 and 1500 in Jerez de los Caballeros, Spain. His parents were members of the nobility. Very little is known about his early life. Some sources say his parents wanted him to be a lawyer. But de Soto wanted to go to the **New World** and seek his fortune.

VOYAGE TO THE NEW WORLD: In 1514, de Soto set out for the Spanish territory of **New Spain** with an expedition led by Pedro Arias Davila. He reached Panama, where he fought in battles that won the area for Spain. He was rewarded with gold and Indian slaves.

WITH PIZARRO: In 1531, de Soto joined the expedition to Peru led by **Francisco Pizarro**. De Soto had heard of the great wealth of an Indian culture that turned out to be the Incas. He was the first Spaniard to make contact with the Inca emperor, Atahuallpa. Pizarro captured and killed the emperor and conquered the Incas. De Soto shared in the huge wealth the Spanish took from the conquered Incas.

RETURN TO SPAIN: De Soto returned to Spain a wealthy man in 1536. But he wanted to go back to the New World. He asked the King of Spain if he could lead a new expedition. The King granted his wish. He sent de Soto back as the Governor of Cuba. He also gave de Soto the right to conquer and claim the land north of Cuba. The King commanded de Soto to treat the Indians kindly. He told him to take the land without "death and robbery of the Indians." But that was not to be.

EXPEDITION TO FLORIDA: In April 1538, de Soto led an expedition of nine ships, 600 men, 250 horses, and supplies to set up colonies. One of the strangest—and most frightening—items of cargo were attack dogs. De Soto used these dogs to attack and kill any natives who would not follow his orders.

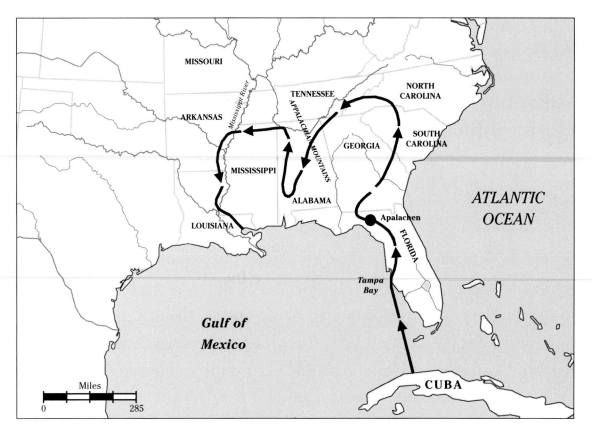

De Soto's expedition of 1538-1542.

EXPLORING THE SOUTHEAST U.S.: The expedition stopped first at Cuba. Then, on May 30, 1538, they landed in what is now Tampa Bay, Florida. They traveled north, fighting skirmishes with local Indian tribes. In one of these battles, they found a Spaniard, Juan Ortiz, who had been lost during the earlier expedition of Panfilo de Narvaez. Ortiz had been living with the Indians for several years. He traveled with de Soto, acting as a translator.

Traveling north, de Soto reached the Indian village of Apalachen. There, and elsewhere in his journey of conquest, he treated the natives with great cruelty. He took Indians hostage and treated them as slaves. When any disobeyed him, he had them killed.

De Soto was in search of treasure. He heard from the Indians of a city that supposedly contained great amounts of gold. He headed north, through what is now Georgia, in search of the city. He found a settlement, but no gold. De Soto was treated well by the ruling queen. She gave him freshwater pearls. De Soto took her prisoner.

De Soto led his soldiers north, through modern-day South and North Carolina. Still, they found no gold. Turning to the west, they continued on their journey across the Appalachian Mountains. They ranged through modern-day Tennessee and Alabama. They didn't find gold, but they did find fierce Indians ready to fight.

Near what is now Mobile, Alabama, de Soto and his men battled a group of Indians. When the fighting was over, many Indians and Spanish were dead or wounded.

De Soto headed northwest through Alabama then west through Mississippi. They fought hostile Indians throughout their journey.

DISCOVERING THE MISSISSIPPI RIVER: On May 21, 1541, de Soto and his men became the first Europeans to see the Mississippi River. They were south of what is now Memphis, Tennessee.

Crossing the great river, they continued west and south, through what is now Arkansas and Louisiana. They headed back up the Mississippi River, but de Soto was ill. He died in May 1542. He was buried in the river. By this point, there were only 300 men left from the original 600 who had started the expedition.

De Soto's men continued under the command of Luis de Moscoso. First, he led them over land, trying to reach New Spain and safety. Finally, in 1543, Moscoso led them down the Mississippi and on to Mexico.

The burial of De Soto.

But that was not the end of the effect of the de Soto expedition. Although they didn't know it, the Spaniards carried deadly diseases, like smallpox, that the Indians had no resistance to. Entire native populations were wiped out in the areas where de Soto's men had traveled. When Europeans went to the area later, many of the tribes de Soto had seen had vanished.

HERNANDO DE SOTO'S HOME AND FAMILY: De Soto married Isabella de Bobadilla in 1536. They had no children.

HIS DISCOVERY: De Soto didn't find gold or other wealth in the **New World**. He didn't establish colonies, either. Many of the native tribes he came in contact with didn't survive. They were wiped out by the Spanish soldiers or by disease. Still, de Soto is considered important as the first European to explore large tracts of what became the United States. He is also remembered as the first European to discover the Mississippi.

De Soto was a man capable of terrible cruelty. He often treated the native people with vicious brutality. Why he did what he did is still discussed by historians and students.

WORLD WIDE WEB SITES:

http://www.floridahistory.com/inset44.html
http://www.nps.gov/deso/index.html
http://www.rice.edu/armadillo/Projects/desoto.html

Bartholomew Dias
1450? - 1500
Portuguese Navigator Who Led the First European Expedition to the Cape of Good Hope

BARTHOLOMEW DIAS WAS BORN in Portugal around 1450. (His name is also spelled "Bartolomeu Diaz.") Very little is known about the early life of Dias. Some people believe he was from a family of sailors and explorers.

THE PORTUGUESE EXPLORERS: Dias continued the search for a sea route around Africa that **Prince Henry the Navigator** first planned.

King John, Henry's nephew, was king of Portugal when Dias became a sailor. King John wanted to continue Henry's quest to find a route by water instead of by land to reach Asia. They would use the sea route to trade goods with Asian countries. At that time, no European had sailed far enough south along the coast of Africa to discover if it was possible to go around Africa to reach Asia.

FIRST EXPEDITION: Dias went on his first expedition in 1481. He sailed down the coast of West Africa as far as what is now Ghana.

DISCOVERING THE CAPE OF GOOD HOPE: Dias's next expedition was the one for which he is best known. In 1487, King John sent Dias to sail down the west coast of Africa, to its southernmost point. Dias commanded a crew of three ships. These ships were **caravels**, which could carry large cargoes and handle rough weather at sea.

It took Dias four months to make the journey south. Along the way, he passed the markers of earlier explorers. He had gone further south than any previous Europeans.

As they sailed south, the explorers faced a fierce storm. In January 1488, the storm forced them to sail out of sight of land. Dias didn't know it, but he had rounded the southern tip of Africa in the storm. He only realized what he had done when he had to turn north to reach land.

Dias landed at what is now Mossel Bay. There, they met angry African tribes who attacked them. Dias's ships continued eastward along the coast, but his crew was ready to return home. They convinced him to turn back.

It was on the return journey that Dias first saw the Cape of Good Hope, the southern tip of Africa. He called it the "Cape of Storms,"

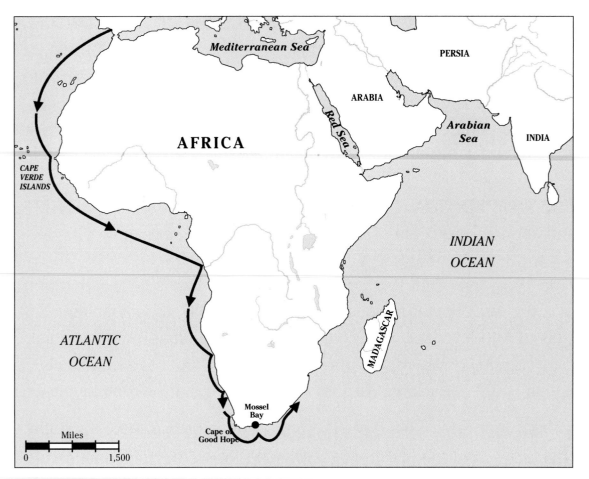

Dias's voyage of 1487.

because it was a storm that had brought them there. Later, King John renamed it the Cape of Good Hope. He hoped that Portugal would now have a trade route to the west, and that Portugal would grow rich through trade with Asia.

Dias returned to Portugal in 1488. As he returned, another explorer, **Christopher Columbus**, was talking to King John about his own plans. Columbus also wanted to reach Asia. But he planned to sail west, not south around Africa. He wanted King John to sponsor him. But since Dias had been successful in discovering the sea route to the east, King John wasn't interested in funding Columbus.

In 1494, Dias helped prepare the boats for **Vasco da Gama's** voyage to the east. Then, in 1497, he sailed as part of Da Gama's fleet as far as Cape Verde. There, Dias set up a trading post. Da Gama continued around the Cape of Good Hope and on to India.

FINAL VOYAGE: In 1500 Dias accompanied **Pedro Alvarez Cabral** on an expedition to India. But Dias never reached Asia. They had headed south from Cape Verde when the trade winds blew them far off course. They reached the shores of the **New World**—Brazil. They were probably the first Europeans to land on the Brazilian coast.

They set out again for the coast of West Africa. Just off shore from the Cape of Good Hope, the ships ran into a terrible storm. Dias's ship sunk, and he died at sea.

HIS DISCOVERY: Dias never achieved the fame of Vasco da Gama or Christopher Columbus. Still, his importance to the history of discovery is great. He was the first European to navigate around the Cape of Good Hope, opening up the sea route to Asia for the Portuguese. And he was part of the first European expedition to reach Brazil.

BARTHOLOMEW DIAS'S HOME AND FAMILY: Very little is known about Dias's family. He had at least one son, named Antonio. His grandson, Paulo, founded the first European city in southern Africa, Luanda, in Angola.

WORLD WIDE WEB SITE:

http://www.mariner.org/age/

Sir Francis Drake
1540? - 1596
English Navigator and Explorer
Second Person to Circumnavigate the World

SIR FRANCIS DRAKE WAS BORN around 1540 in Devonshire, England. His parents were farmers. His father's name was Edmund; his mother's first name is not known. Edmund was also a Protestant preacher. Francis was the eldest of 12 boys born in the Drake family.

EARLY LIFE: When Francis was young, his family was driven from their home during an uprising by English Catholics. They were forced to move to Kent, where they lived in an abandoned ship. All of his life, Drake was a devout Protestant. He hated Catholics, and that fueled his later attacks on Spanish ships sailing for the Catholic king of Spain.

GOING TO SEA: At about the age of 13, Drake first went to sea. He sailed on a small trading ship that traveled in the North Sea. He learned his navigating skills in some of the roughest waters in the world. When the captain of the boat died, he left the ship to Drake.

SAILING TO THE NEW WORLD: When he was 23, Drake sold the boat and started sailing with a relative, John Hawkins. He made his first crossing to the **New World** with Hawkins. They commanded the first English ship to bring African slaves to the New World.

A PIRATE: Over the next several years Drake made a name for himself as a pirate in the service of Queen Elizabeth I. He was actually given royal permission to be a "privateer," as pirates were called.

This was a time when Spain and Portugal were the major sea powers. They controlled sea routes around Africa and to the East, as well as to North America. They used merchant ships to bring back riches from these far lands. Pirate ships like Drake's attacked and stole cargo from merchant ships.

RAIDING SPANISH SHIPS: Drake became famous for looting Spanish ships loaded with silver and gold from the New World. He would take the treasure back and give a portion to England, keeping

Drake's fleet at Santo Domingo Harbor.

a measure for himself. The Spanish were always on the lookout for the English ships, and often fought the pirates.

In 1572, Drake sailed for Panama with two small ships. He wanted to capture a Spanish settlement there. He and his men raided a town and came away with plenty of gold. Drake traveled inland until he reached a spot where he could see the Pacific Ocean. He prayed that he be allowed "to sail once in an English ship in that sea." His prayers would be answered in a few years.

When he returned to England, Queen Elizabeth had just signed a peace treaty with Spain. So he waited for several years, serving in the Queen's service. Then, in 1577, he began the voyage that would make him a famous navigator.

CIRCUMNAVIGATING THE WORLD: Drake began his three-year voyage to sail around the world in December 1577. He was the first man since **Ferdinand Magellan** to attempt a circumnavigation. Drake had the full backing of the Queen. He met her just before he sailed. She told him she wanted revenge on the Spanish King. He vowed to do all he could.

Drake left England with five ships and 164 sailors. He sailed the *Pelican*, which he later renamed the *Golden Hind*. At first the men

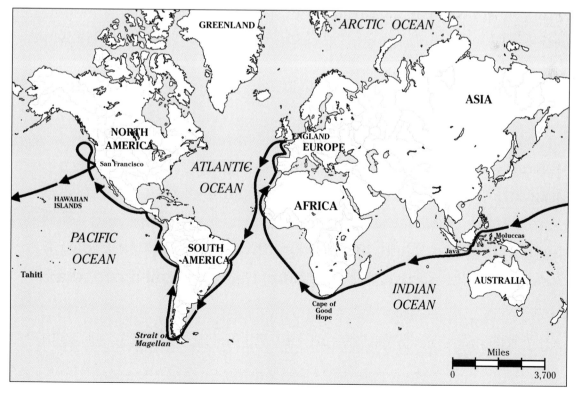

Drake's circumnavigation route, 1577-1580.

were told they were sailing to the Mediterranean. Only later did they learn their true destination.

The fleet sailed across the Atlantic. Drake feared that the ships would become separated. He destroyed two ships, moving all the men and provisions to the other boats. Then one of the ships sunk, and another turned back for England.

It was Drake's ship alone that sailed through the Strait of Magellan. He made an important discovery there. Magellan had thought that Tierra del Fuego was part of a southern continent. Drake discovered it was a group of islands.

Sailing along the west coast of South America, Drake attacked and looted Spanish settlements. He captured ships loaded with gold, silver, and gems. He sailed farther north than any previous explorer. He was the first European explorer to sight what would become the west coasts of the United States and Canada. He went ashore near San Francisco and claimed the land for England. He called it "New Albion."

Drake set out across the Pacific Ocean. He used charts he'd stolen from Spanish ships. He reached the Spice Islands (the Moluccas). There, he loaded tons of valuable cloves onto the *Golden Hind*. The ship sailed on past Java in Indonesia and across the Indian Ocean. Then, he sailed south and around the Cape of Good Hope. He was the first Englishman ever to sail those waters.

In September 1580, Drake sailed into Plymouth, England, in triumph. He was only the second man ever to circumnavigate the globe. And since Magellan had died on his mission, he was the first to sail around the world and survive.

Drake defeating the Spanish Armada.

REWARDED BY THE QUEEN: Queen Elizabeth dined aboard the *Golden Hind.* She made Drake a knight. After that, he was known as Sir Francis Drake.

In 1581, Drake was made mayor of Plymouth. He served in that post for several years. By 1585, the Queen called on him again to defend England against the Spanish.

ATTACKING SPANISH SHIPS: From 1585 to 1587, Drake and his fleet attacked and looted Spanish settlements in the Cape Verde Islands and Santo Domingo (now Haiti). He also attacked and destroyed ships in Spain.

THE DEFEAT OF THE SPANISH ARMADA: In 1588, Drake fought in the major sea battle of the era. It was between England and the Spanish fleet, or "Armada." He was second in command during the battles. Fighting in the English Channel, Drake's fleet destroyed many ships, and the Spanish Armada was defeated.

Drake became a great hero. His feats were celebrated in songs and poems. He continued to sail for England and his Queen.

THE DEATH OF SIR FRANCIS DRAKE: In 1596, while on a mission to Panama, Drake died of a fever. He was buried at sea. He was about 54 years old.

SIR FRANCIS DRAKE'S HOME AND FAMILY: Drake was married twice. He married his first wife, Mary Newman, around 1565. She died in 1583. He married Elizabeth Sydenham in 1585. He had no children.

HIS DISCOVERY: Drake is remembered as a bold and able navigator, and one of the finest seamen of all time. He was only the second man to circumnavigate the globe. His exploration in California led the English to send colonists to the **New World** in the 1600s. While the Spanish called him "the master thief of the unknown world," he was a great hero of Queen Elizabeth's England.

WORLD WIDE WEB SITES:

http://www.mariner.org/age/drake.html
http://www.mcn.org/2/oseeler/drake.htm

Sylvia Earle

1935 -
American Marine Botanist and Oceanographer
Explorer of the Oceans

SYLVIA EARLE WAS BORN on August 30, 1935, in Gibbstown, New Jersey. Her parents were Lewis and Alice Earle. Lewis was an electrician and Alice was a nurse before she had children. Sylvia has two brothers, Lewis and Evan.

SYLVIA EARLE GREW UP in New Jersey and Florida. When she was three, her family moved to a farm near Camden, New Jersey. Sylvia loved it. Her parents introduced Sylvia and her brothers to the wonders of nature.

"My parents used to bring frogs for my brothers and me to get to know. But we were very carefully told always to put them back in the pond. Or to allow a caterpillar to gently walk across you hand, and not to disturb them, because you might get stung by some of their bristles. I learned very early on that if you show respect for other creatures, they won't go out of their way to harm you."

Even as a small child, Sylvia loved to watch the creatures of the forest — squirrels, fish, and frogs — for hours. She loved to wander and think about the natural world around her. Like the scientist she would become, she "made observations and kept notebooks. Nobody had to tell me to do those things — I just did them."

When Earle was 12, her family moved to Clearwater, Florida, on the Gulf of Mexico. Their house was right on the water. "My back yard became the Gulf of Mexico," she recalls. She loved it.

"I had the pleasure of getting acquainted with salt marshes, and sea grass beds." There, she watched the "sea horses and sea urchins, and great crabs with long, spindly legs that were absolutely fascinating. You never knew what you were going to find just walking around in these squishy, but beautiful clear water areas."

SYLVIA EARLE WENT TO SCHOOL at the local public schools. She always did well in school, and she loved it, too. "I just felt this joy of discovery," she says. "I was like a big sponge, absorbing as much as I could. And I enjoyed succeeding. I liked it when I could get my mind around the math problems."

Earle examines a fish reference chart during a dive off the Florida Keys, 1997.

Earle also loved reading the encyclopedia. "It was like a discovery. You never knew what new things you were going to find on every page."

Earle graduated from high school at 16 and went off to college. She studied at St. Petersburg Junior College, Florida State University, and Duke University. She knew by then that she wanted to be a scientist. She wanted to study the plants of the ocean.

DECIDING TO BE A SCIENTIST: Earle studied botany, which is the study of the lives of plants. Her special area of study is marine plants, plants that grow in sea water. She remembers that one of her college professors, Harold Humm, "introduced me to the beauty and interest and common good sense of looking at plants."

THE IMPORTANCE OF MARINE PLANTS: "By knowing the plants, you get some feel for how the whole system works," says Earle. "Plants provide shelter, whether it's underwater or above. They provide food. They provide energy that supplies a whole interacting system."

Earle studied to become a marine botanist. While she was studying, she also got married and had children. Over the next several years, she earned her bachelor's, masters, and doctorate in the study of marine plants. Her specialty within the field is the study of algae (pronounced al-gee).

BECOMING AN EXPERT ON MARINE PLANTS: During the 1960s, Earle traveled all over the world to study marine plants. She became a leading expert on ocean plant life, especially the algae of the Gulf of Mexico.

In 1970, she joined a group of women scientists who lived in an underwater structure on the ocean floor for two weeks. Called "Tektite II," the structure was like an underwater hotel. Tektite II was off the Virgin Islands in the Carribean. It had air, water, and living and study areas for the scientists.

The scientists ate, slept, and worked in the area. Earle spent most of her time out in the ocean waters. There, she identified 153 plants. Twenty-six of them had never been seen before in the area.

The Tektite mission made Earle famous. She and the other scientists met the President and had parades in their honor. Earle used her fame to focus attention on the importance of ocean research.

THE "JIM DIVE": In 1979, Earle made a solo dive off the coast of Hawaii. She dove down 1,250 feet. That was the deepest dive any-one had ever made. She wore a special suit called a "Jim Suit" for its maker, Jim Jarrat. It provided oxygen and special protection from water pressure that can harm a diver.

EXPLORING THE OCEAN FLOOR: With the "Jim Suit," Earle could dive deeper and longer than anyone had before. She explored the ocean floor and discovered plants no human had ever seen. When the American astronaut **Neil Armstrong** landed on the moon in 1969, he had planted an American flag on the surface. Sylvia Earle did the same thing on the ocean floor off Hawaii. She planted an American flag in the ocean. She wanted to emphasize that ocean exploration was every bit as important—and exciting—as space.

HELPING TO SAVE THE OCEANS: Earle knew from her studies that the pollution that affects the air also hurts the oceans. She wrote

articles for magazines like *National Geographic*. She told readers about the beauty of ocean life and the dangers of pollution.

Earle also continued to study the oceans of the world. In the 1970s, she explored the Pacific and Indian Oceans. She followed migrating whales from Hawaii to Australia and Alaska.

In the 1980s, Earle started a business called Deep Ocean Engineering. The company builds undersea vehicles. They help scientists reach ocean depths never before researched.

Now in her late-60s, Earle still loves her work. For her, there are endless questions about the oceans and the life they hold. "There are plants growing where people didn't expect to find plants. That leads to a whole host of questions. Why is this so? Why do they occur here? Why don't they occur somewhere else? Who eats them?"

Earle claims that "it could take ten lifetimes" to explore and learn all there is to know about the oceans. She urges young people to join her in her exploration of the beauty and mystery of the world's waters.

SYLVIA EARLE'S HOME AND FAMILY: Sylvia Earle has been married three times. Her first husband was named Jack Taylor. They had two children, Elizabeth and John, who are grown now. Earle and Taylor divorced in 1967.

Earle's second husband was named Giles Mead. They had one daughter, Gale. Earle married Graham Hawkes in 1986. They divorced in 1990, but they still work together and are friends.

She still loves to dive. In all, she has spent some 6,000 hours in the water. That's equal to an entire year of her life. "Underwater, every spoonful of water is filled with life," she says. That life will inspire her for years to come.

HER DISCOVERY: Earle, along with **Robert Ballard** and **Jacques Cousteau**, brought the importance and excitement of undersea exploration to the world. "People are under the impression that the planet is fully explored. That we've been to all the forests and climbed all the mountains. But in fact many of the forests have yet to be seen for the first time. They just happen to be underwater. We're still explorers. Perhaps the greatest era is just beginning."

WORLD WIDE WEB SITE:

http://www.achievement.org/autodoc/page/ear0bio-1

Erik the Red

950 A.D.? - 1000 A.D.?
Norwegian Viking Explorer Who Founded the First European Settlement on Greenland

ERIK THE RED WAS BORN in Jaeren, Norway, around the year 950 A.D. The exact date is not known. His full name was Erik Thorvaldson (TUR-vahld-suhn). He was called "Erik the Red" because of his flaming red hair. His first name is also spelled "Eirik."

When Erik was about 10, he and his father, Thorvald (TUR-vahl), were forced to leave Norway because Thorvald had fought and killed someone. They moved to Iceland, which had been settled by Norwegian **Vikings.** They looked for land to farm, finally settling on the northwest coast. Erik's father died several years later.

ERIK THE RED'S HOME AND FAMILY: After his father's death, Erik married a girl named Thjodhild. She was from Haukadal in southern Iceland, and the couple moved there to farm. Erik had three sons, Thorvald, Thorstein, and Leif, and a daughter, Freydis. **Leif Erickson** would go on to become a famous explorer.

A VIOLENT TEMPER AND BANISHMENT: It seems that Erik had inherited his father's temper. He became involved in a bloody family feud and killed two men. He was forced to leave Haukadal. Erik moved with his family to an island on the west coast of Iceland.

But Erik became involved in a feud again, and again he committed murder. He was banished from Iceland for three years.

FOUNDING A COLONY ON GREENLAND: Around 982, Erik set out westward from Iceland in a **longship**. He'd heard about a land to the west that a Norwegian named Gunnbjorn Ulfsson had sighted around 900. In a journey of several days, Erik landed on what he later called "Greenland."

Greenland is actually the largest island in the world. Erik the Red and the Vikings were not the first people to live on the island. Inuit (or Eskimo) peoples from what is now Canada had reached it several hundred years before. But by the time Erik reached Greenland, they were not living there.

Erik's first glimpse of Greenland showed it to be a cold and icy land. The eastern coast was rocky. Walls of ice rose from the sea. A huge icecap could be seen inland.

Erik turned his ship southward hoping to find a place to go ashore. He rounded a big cape and then sailed north. As he sailed up the western coast, he found a very different landscape. He could still see the enormous icecap, but he could see fjords similar to those in Norway. These inlets led to green, grassy meadows with plains of short grass. There were birds everywhere, the waters were filled with fish, and caribou roamed the grasslands.

Erik and his crew spent the first winter on a small island that he named Eriksey (after himself). The following year they built huts of sod where they lived during the winter. In the summer, they explored the new land. They looked for places that would be good for farming and ports for ships. By the time his three-year

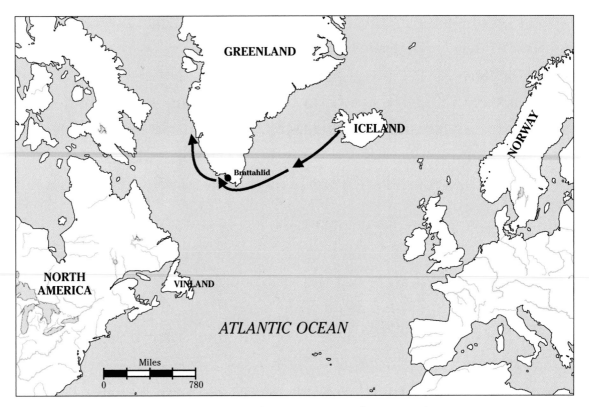

Erik the Red's 982 voyage to Greenland.

exile was over, Erik and his men had scouted about 1,000 miles of coastline.

Erik returned to Iceland triumphant about the new land he had found. He wanted to lead a party of Icelanders back to settle the new land. But he thought that people would be more excited if the island had an attractive name. So he called it "Greenland." Many Icelanders were interested. The soil on Iceland was growing thin, and a few years earlier many people had died in a terrible famine. That made many of them willing to risk crossing the ocean for the promise of a better life in a new, uncrowded land.

In the summer of 986, Erik the Red and his family left Iceland leading a fleet of 25 ships. The ships they sailed were not the

longships used by the Vikings. Instead of speed, these travelers needed space and stability. They needed to bring livestock and tools to their new land. To carry all they needed, they sailed in **knorrs**. Knorrs were big, broad-beamed merchant ships that were ideal for carrying people and cargo across ocean waters.

But this time, the voyage was difficult. Of the 25 ships that started the journey, only 14 made it to Greenland. Some of the others were lost in a storm, and some had to turn back to Iceland.

With a group numbering about 400, Erik began the settlement of Greenland. Following his directions, the settlers spread out along the coast, staying mostly in the southern region.

Over the years, the settlers of Greenland developed farming and trading as ways of making a living. They began to trade furs, hides, woolens, and dairy products with Iceland and Norway.

Erik became a leader of the hearty community. He built a big farm at Brattahlid. He lived there with his family for about 14 years, dying around 1000. And he raised a son who would become the most famous Viking explorer, **Leif Erikson**. In the 1960s, a team of archeologists found the remnants of Erik's farm, at Brattahlid.

ICELANDIC SAGAS: Much of what we know of Erik the Red and his famous son comes to us from Icelandic sagas. Two of these, "The Saga of Erik the Red" and "The Greenlander's Saga," tell about Erik and his famous offspring. These tales of the rulers and famous people of Norway were passed down as myths and eventually written down in the late 1100s and early 1200s. Historians believe that the tales are full of exaggeration, making their characters more legendary than real. But they still offer a glimpse into what life was like during the Viking Age.

HIS DISCOVERY: Erik the Red is remembered as a bold explorer and the man who founded the first European settlement in Greenland.

WORLD WIDE WEB SITES:

http://collections.ic.gc.ca/vikings
http://mnc.net/norway/ericson.htm
http://www.iceland.org/leifur.html
http://odin.dep.no/odin/engelsk/norway/history

Leif Erikson
b. 980? d.1020?
Icelandic Norwegian Viking Explorer
First European to Reach North America

LEIF ERIKSON WAS BORN around 980 in Iceland. His father was the famous Norwegian **Viking** explorer **Erik the Red**. His mother was named Thjodhild. He was the eldest of four children. He had two brothers, Thorstein and Thorvald, and a sister, Freydis. His last name is also spelled Eriksson and Eirikson. Following the custom of his time, his last name was taken from his father's first name. So "Erikson" means "Son of Erik."

LEIF ERIKSON GREW UP in Greenland. His father had been banished from Iceland for killing several people. During his exile, Erik started a Norwegian colony on Greenland. Later, he became the leader of the colonists. Their home was the center of social and political life on the island.

Erikson grew up learning to farm and to sail. He became an excellent sailor. When he was about 20, he sailed to Norway. He didn't stop at Iceland, like most sailors. Instead, he became one of the first people ever to cross the Atlantic directly from Greenland. At that time, the Vikings had no **compasses** or other navigational tools. They sailed by the sun and stars. It took great courage—and skill—to sail the ocean. And Erikson had that courage and skill, as well as the curiosity of an explorer.

HEARING OF THE NEW WORLD: When Erikson returned to Greenland, he heard a tale that roused that curiosity. A man named Bjarni (BYAHD-nee) had been blown off course on his first voyage to Greenland from Iceland. By accident, he had discovered strange new lands.

The first place Bjarni and his men reached was heavily forested and hilly. Bjarni knew it wasn't Greenland, so he set sail again. Two days later, they sighted land again. This time, the shore was flat and wooded. Knowing he wasn't in Greenland, Bjarni set off again. Three days later, they sighted land for the third time. This time it was an island that was mountainous and covered with glaciers. But Bjarni knew he still hadn't reached Greenland.

Erikson on a Viking longship.

Finally, after four more days of hard sailing, Bjarni sighted land once more. At last, they had reached Greenland. When Erikson heard the stories of the lands Bjarni had seen but not explored he was determined to go to the new lands himself. Although he was barely 21 years old, he had been sailing since he was a boy. Like his father, Erikson was adventurous and curious. He could not understand how Bjarni could have seen tempting new lands and not gone ashore.

LEIF ERIKSON'S VOYAGE TO THE NEW WORLD: Erikson began making preparations for his journey. He found 35 sailors who wanted to go with him. He visited Bjarni and asked him for directions to the new lands. He also bought Bjarni's ship.

Next, Erikson asked his father, Erik the Red, to go with him. At first Erik said no; he was too old for the journey. He was comfortably settled at Brattahlid, the family farm. But his son convinced him to go.

On a summer morning, Erik, Leif, and the sailors started down to the beach on horseback. Suddenly, Erik's horse stumbled over a rock. He was thrown to the ground and injured his foot. Seeing it as a bad omen, Erik declared he would not go. Erikson and the others left without the old Viking.

THE JOURNEY OF DISCOVERY: Erikson was quite capable of leading the expedition himself. He was a skilled navigator and had a lot of experience sailing the North Atlantic. The men going with him were more than willing to trust him as their leader.

So around the year 1000, Leif Erikson and 35 men set out to find the land Bjarni had seen to the west. Steering the ship by the sun during the day and the stars by night, the explorers followed Bjarni's route. Within days, they sighted land.

Erikson and a few men went ashore in a small boat. The new land was not very inviting. Mountains covered with glaciers rose to the sky. A narrow strip of land between the mountains and the sea was covered with flat, grey stones. Erikson decided to leave. He called the place Helleland, meaning "land of flat stones."

The crew now headed southwest. The next land they came to looked more promising. It was flat and wooded and had miles of white sand beaches. The Vikings had never seen anything like it before. Once again they went ashore and explored. Erikson named this place Markland, meaning "wooded land."

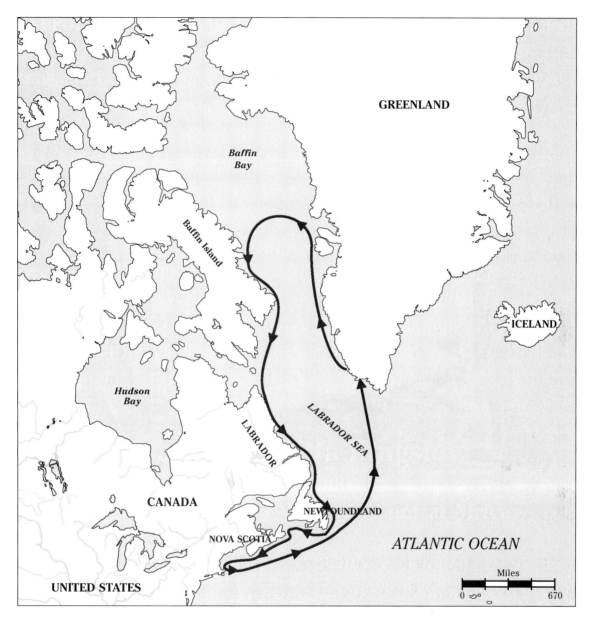

Leif Erikson's possible route from Greenland to the New World, c. 1000.

Since he knew Bjarni had sighted land three times, Erikson set sail again. After about two days of sailing they came to a small island and a larger landmass to the south. Landing on the island, the men found the grass wet with dew. They tasted it with their fingers and thought it was the sweetest thing they'd ever tasted. Now they were excited to get to the mainland.

229

Rowing ashore in their small boat, the men found a peaceful and beautiful land. Rivers and lakes were full of fish, the forest had lumber for building and wood for fuel, meadows invited grazing livestock.

He and his men decided to stay for the winter and built permanent huts of wood. One day one of the men came back to camp with a great discovery — grapes. Grapes did not grow in Greenland or Iceland. Wine made from grapes was a great delicacy. Erikson named the land Vinland, meaning "vine land" or "wine land."

Erikson and his men set to work. Not only were they busy exploring the countryside, they were also cutting trees for timber and harvesting grapes to take home. When spring came, Erikson and his men sailed for home. Just off the coast of Greenland, they came upon a shipwreck. They rescued the crew and took them safely to shore. For his heroic deed, and also for his discovery of Vinland, Erikson was known ever after as "Leif the Lucky."

RETURN TO GREENLAND: Erikson never returned to the beautiful land he had explored. His father, Erik the Red, died a year after his return. Erikson took over the farm at Brattahlid. Two years later, his brother Thorvald borrowed the ship and sailed to Vinland. He was hoping to establish a settlement there. But Thorvald and his men battled a tribe of Native Americans, and Thorvald was killed. He is thought to be the first European buried in the **New World**.

For years, historians have argued about just where Erikson and his men landed on their journey. Today, it is generally believed that what he called Helleland is Baffin Island, which lies 300 miles west of Greenland in the Canadian Arctic. Many think that Markland is Labrador, 600 miles south of Baffin Island.

Erikson aboard ship.

Vinland is probably the northern tip of the Newfoundland, although its actual location is still debated. Some historians think it could be further north in Canada; others think it could be far south along the coast of what is now the U.S. Archeologists have found what they believe to be Viking ruins in an area of Newfoundland called L'Anse aux Meadows. There's no way of knowing if they are the remains of Erikson's settlement, but the clues are fascinating.

HIS DISCOVERY: Regardless of where they landed, Erikson and his men had reached North America, a continent then unknown to the Europeans. And in doing so, Leif Erikson and the Vikings explored the **New World** nearly 500 years before **Christopher Columbus**, who is often called the first European to discover America.

231

Leif Erikson died around 1020. In his short life, he accomplished many things. His life as a Viking explorer has captured the imagination of people all over the world for hundreds of years. In 2000, many groups held celebrations to mark the 1000th anniversary of his journey. Some reenacted his trip, in specially made Viking ships. And in the U.S., October 9 is celebrated as Leif Erikson Day, to honor and remember this brave explorer.

ICELANDIC SAGAS: Much of what we know of Leif Erikson and Erik the Red comes to us from "sagas," or Norwegian folk tales. Two of these, "The Saga of Erik the Red" and "The Greenlander's Saga," tell about Leif and Erik. These tales of the rulers and famous people of Norway were originally passed down as legends. They weren't written down until the late 1100s and early 1200s. Historians believe that the tales are full of exaggeration, making their characters more legendary than real. But they still offer a glimpse into what life was like during the Viking Age.

WORLD WIDE WEB SITES:

http://collections.ic.gc.ca/vikings
http://www.iceland.org/leifur.html
http://odin.dep.no/odin/engelsk/norway/history
http://www.nlc-bnc.ca/history/24/h24-1210-e.html
http://www.viking1000.org/

Faxian

374?-462?
Chinese Buddhist Monk Who Traveled to India and Asia

FAXIAN WAS BORN in the Chinese province of Shansi in the late 300s. His name is also spelled "Fa-hsien." His name means "splendor of religious law."

Very little is known about Faxian's early life. He was raised at a Buddhist monastery, where he studied with the monks. He became a monk when he was about 20. Around the age of 25, he made a remarkable journey, for which he became well-known.

Faxian traveled to India on a religious pilgrimage. At that time, people in China knew very little about India. He wanted to learn more about Buddhism. The religion is based on the teachings of the Buddha, who lived around 500 B.C. in India. Faxian wanted to read the Buddha's teachings in their original language. They were written in Sanskrit, one of the oldest languages in the world. He also wanted to visit the most important and sacred sites of Buddhism.

Faxian began his journey in 399. He traveled across the deserts of Central Asia. It was a hard journey. Faxian described it as an area of "scorching winds," where there were no birds or animals.

Next he had to cross treacherous mountains. When he finally came to India in 402, he visited many Buddhist shrines and monasteries. He spent many years studying ancient Buddhist texts with scholars. He took several of these with him when he returned home.

In 413, Faxian traveled back to China by sea. He first stopped in the island nation of Ceylon (now Sri Lanka.) From there, he sailed for home. But the journey was very difficult. The ship faced a storm that nearly destroyed it. They reached an island that was probably modern-day Java, in Indonesia. Taking another ship, Faxian again sailed for home. That ship was blown off course by a storm. Finally, in 414, Faxian reached China.

He went to a Buddhist monastery in Nanjing. There, he spent many years translating the Buddha's teaching into Chinese. He also wrote a fascinating book about his journeys, *The Travels of Faxian*.

HIS DISCOVERY: Faxian's book was read for centuries. It was the first book to relate a journey overland from China to India. Faxian also recorded the way of life of the people he visited. His accounts gave the people of his and later times an idea of what travel, religion, and life was like in a very different culture. For information on another Chinese Buddhist traveler, see **Hsuan Tsang**.

WORLD WIDE WEB SITES:

http://acc6.its.brooklyn.cuny.edu/~phalsall/texts/faxian.html
http://faculty.washinton.edu/dwaugh/CA/texts/faxian.html

Matthew Flinders
1774 - 1814
English Explorer and Navigator
First European to Circumnavigate Australia

MATTHEW FLINDERS WAS BORN on March 16, 1774, in Lincoln-shire, England. His father was a surgeon and his mother was a homemaker.

MATTHEW FLINDERS WENT TO SCHOOL at the local church school then to Horbling Grammar School. As a boy, he read *Robinson Crusoe,* an English novel about a young man shipwrecked on an island. That made him want to become an explorer.

JOINING THE NAVY: Flinders left school at 15 and joined the Royal Navy. In his early years with the Navy, he sailed to the South Pacific. He became known as an excellent navigator.

AUSTRALIA: In 1798, Flinders sailed to Australia on a mission to navigate and chart the New South Wales area. He and George Bass, the ship's doctor, sailed around what is now Tasmania. They proved it was an island, and not part of Australia. The waterway that separates Tasmania from Australia was named for Bass. An island off Tasmania was named for Flinders.

In 1800 Flinders returned to England. He was eager to return to Australia. Through the help of **Joseph Banks**, he was able to get the government to back his next expedition. Now his goal was to circumnavigate Australia—to sail completely around it.

CIRCUMNAVIGATING AUSTRALIA: Flinders left England in July 1801, commanding the *Investigator* with a crew of 90. On board was **John Franklin**, who would later head an expedition to find the **Northwest Passage.**

The crew arrived at Cape Leeuwin on the southwest coast of Australia in December 1801. From there, Flinders surveyed the southern coast. He reached Sydney, on the southeast coast of Australia, in early 1802. He sailed north from there and navigated the entire east coast of Australia. Heading west, he surveyed the Gulf of Carpentaria, then the north coast. He continued south to where they had first landed, then east again. He reached Sydney again, in June 1803.

Flinders had circumnavigated Australia. By sailing around it, he proved Australia was a separate island, not part of a larger land mass. He was the first European to circumnavigate Australia.

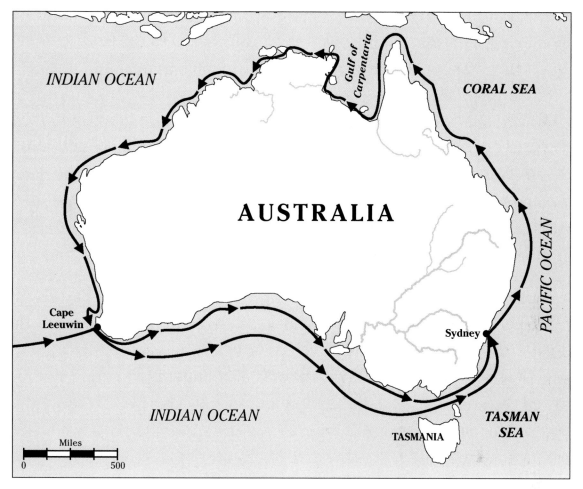

Flinders's circumnavigation, 1801-1803.

Along the way, Flinders and his crew met with other adventures. He had brought a naturalist on board named Robert Brown. Brown found hundreds of new plants and animals and took many samples back with him. Flinders named many of the bays, islands, and other parts of the landscape. He named some for the crew and for places in England. He named an island "Kangaroo Island" because so many of those strange and exotic animals lived on it.

The crew faced tragedy, too. The men needed fresh meat and water, so a few men set out in a small boat to search the mainland. The boat sank and they all died.

Flinders headed back to England in August 1803. But his ship ran aground on the Great Barrier Reef, an area full of underwater coral. He took a canoe back to Sydney, and started for home again.

CAPTURED BY THE FRENCH: In late 1803, Flinders sailed from Sydney aboard the *Cumberland*. But the ship was damaged, and he had to land on the island of Mauritius for repairs. The island, in the Indian Ocean near Madagascar, was under French control. Flinders didn't know it, but England and France were at war. He was captured and accused of being a spy. He was imprisoned for six and a half years.

When Flinders was finally released in 1810, he was in poor health. He spent his remaining years writing a book about his adventures, *A Voyage to Terra Australis*. But Flinders wouldn't live to see the success of his book. He died on July 19, 1814, the day it was published, at the age of 40.

MATTHEW FLINDERS'S HOME AND FAMILY: Flinders married Ann Chapelle in 1801. Soon after their marriage, Flinders set out for Australia. The couple didn't see each other for nine years. After his return to England in 1810, they had a daughter, Anne.

HIS DISCOVERY: Flinders is remembered as an excellent navigator and as the first European explorer to circumnavigate Australia.

WORLD WIDE WEB SITES:

http://members.ozemail.com.au/~fliranre/mflinders.htm
http://www.slnsw.gov.au/flinders/

John Franklin
1786 - 1847
English Officer and Explorer
Searched for the Northwest Passage

JOHN FRANKLIN WAS BORN on April 16, 1786, in Lincolnshire, England. He was the youngest of nine children.

John's father wanted him to be a minister. But from a very young age, John wanted to be a sailor. After attending elementary school, he joined the Royal Navy. He was just 14 years old.

VOYAGE TO AUSTRALIA WITH FLINDERS: In 1801, shortly after entering the Navy, Franklin joined an expedition to Australia. Under the command of **Matthew Flinders**, Franklin became part of the first European crew to circumnavigate Australia.

SEA BATTLES: When Franklin returned to Europe in 1803, England and France were at war. He sailed on ships that fought in the famous battles of Trafalgar (1805) and New Orleans (1814).

VOYAGE OF 1818: In the Navy, Franklin learned to survey and chart the waters. He used these skills in 1818 when he accompanied David Buchan to the Arctic. They were looking for the **North Pole**, which they didn't find. But it was valuable experience for Franklin.

OVERLAND JOURNEY IN THE ARCTIC, 1819-1822: The next year, Franklin commanded an expedition to the Canadian Arctic. Their goal was to find the **Northwest Passage**. From the early 1500s, many people believed that a passage from Europe to Asia existed through what is now Canada. They sought a route linking the Atlantic and Pacific Oceans through the islands of the Canadian Arctic.

Franklin's path on this expedition was over land, rather than water. He started on the west coast of Hudson Bay and traveled northwest across Canada to the Arctic Ocean. He traveled by way of the Coppermine River and surveyed parts of the coast of north-central Canada. When he returned to England, he wrote a book about his travels.

SECOND OVERLAND JOURNEY, 1825-1827: In 1825, Franklin was back in the Canadian Arctic. This time, he started at the mouth of the Mackenzie River and explored westward. He mapped some 1,200 miles of the northern coast of what is now the Yukon Territory in Canada and part of Alaska. On his return to England, he once again wrote about his explorations.

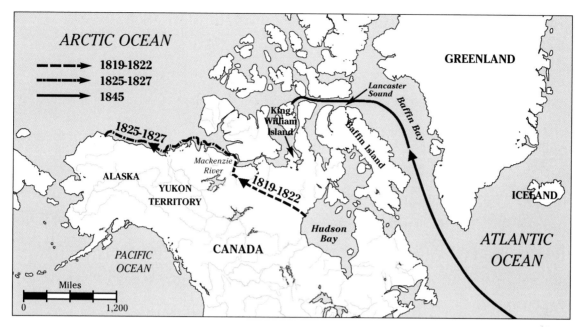

Franklin's expeditions of 1819-1822, 1825-1827, and 1845.

GOVERNOR OF TASMANIA: In 1836, Franklin became the governor of Tasmania (then called Van Diemen's Land), an island south of Australia. He served in that job for seven years. He helped to establish schools and founded a college before he returned in England in 1843.

THE FATEFUL VOYAGE OF 1845: In 1845, Franklin began one of the most famous expeditions in the history of exploration. With two ships, the *Erebus* and the *Terror*, and a crew of 128, he set off to find the Northwest Passage. The ships had been used by **James Clark Ross** on his Antarctic expedition, and they could withstand polar ice. Franklin took food and supplies to last for three years.

They left England on May 19, 1845. They were last seen by a whaling ship as they passed Baffin Island and entered Lancaster Sound on July 26 of that year.

No word of the expedition reached England in 1846 or 1847. By 1848, Franklin's wife and colleagues began to worry. Over the next 12 years, more than 40 rescue crews were sent out to find Franklin and his men. One expedition was headed by Ross, who returned without finding a trace of his former colleague.

The government sent rescue teams, and Franklin's wife did, too. In 1851, a crew discovered Franklin's camp on Beechy Island, including several graves. In 1854, local Inuit told explorer John Rae that white men had been seen four years earlier near King William Island. The Inuit said they had later found the men's bodies near the Great Fish River.

An 1855 rescue effort followed the Great Fish River and found clothing and other things that belonged to Franklin's crew. And in 1859, an expedition led by Francis McClintock found skeletons and a written record of the expedition on King William Island. It was dated April 1848. The entry, signed by Franklin's officers, stated that the ships had become frozen in the ice in 1846. Franklin had died on June 11, 1847. By April 1848, 24 men had died. The men had decided to abandon the boats and walk south, hoping to find a way home. The note ended: "start on to-morrow 26 April 1848 for Back's Fish River."

From the evidence gathered from the rescue missions, historians have pieced together what probably happened to Franklin. They believe that the remaining crew, weary and starving, headed south and died along the way. Skeletons were found 230 miles from the site where the men abandoned their boats.

THE MYSTERY OF THE FRANKLIN EXPEDITION: What happened to the members of the Franklin expedition remains unknown. Even now, more than 150 years Franklin's death, historians still search for answers. The ultimate fate of Franklin's expedition remains one of the great mysteries of exploration. It is a story that continues to challenge historians and fascinate the world.

JOHN FRANKLIN'S HOME AND FAMILY: Franklin married Eleanor Porden in 1823. She died in 1825. Three years after her death Franklin married Jane Griffin. Jane Franklin sponsored the rescue voyage that recovered important information on the fate of her husband's expedition.

HIS DISCOVERY: Franklin is remembered as a brave leader whose many accomplishments are shadowed by his fateful final voyage.

WORLD WIDE WEB SITES:

http://www.ekkane.org/Biographies/BioFranklin.htm
http://www.netscapades.com/franklintrail/franklin.htm
http://www.ric.edu/rpotter/SJFranklin.html

Simon Fraser

1776 - 1862
Canadian Explorer Who Searched for the
Northwest Passage
Fraser River is Named for Him

SIMON FRASER WAS BORN on May 20, 1776, in Mapleton, New York. His parents were Simon and Isabella Fraser. They had emigrated from Scotland to North America in 1773. Simon had two older brothers, William and Angus.

Fraser's parents were Loyalists. That means that during the American Revolution, they remained loyal to the English. During the

244

war, Fraser's father fought on the side of the English. He was captured during a battle and put in jail, where he died in 1779. In 1784, Fraser's mother moved the family to Canada.

SIMON FRASER GREW UP first in New York, then in Canada. In 1790, he went to live with his uncle, John Fraser, a judge in Montreal. Fraser went to school there, then joined two cousins in the fur trade.

BECOMING A FUR TRADER: In 1792, Fraser started to work for the North West Company of Montreal. That was a major trading company in Canada. He moved to the wilderness outpost of Athabasca in what is now Alberta. **Alexander Mackenzie** had worked there 10 years before.

Fraser helped expand the company west of the Rockies. In what is now British Columbia, he helped build several forts, including Fort McLeod, Fort St. James, and Fort Fraser. He also began trading with local Indians.

THE NORTHWEST PASSAGE: In 1808, Fraser became part of the historical search for the **Northwest Passage**. From the early 1500s, many people believed that a passage from Europe to Asia existed through what is now Canada. They sought a water route linking the Atlantic and Pacific Oceans. For 400 years, explorers sought — and died — looking for the Northwest Passage.

The North West Company wanted Fraser to find a water route to the Pacific. They told him to explore a river they thought was the Columbia to its outlet in the Pacific Ocean. Alexander Mackenzie had found a river and overland route in 1793. The company wanted Fraser to find an all-water route, suitable for boats and trading.

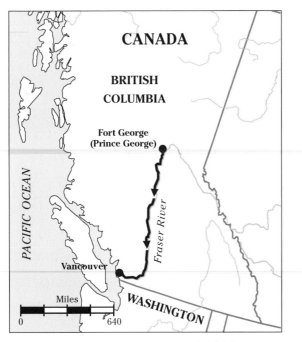

Fraser's expedition of 1808.

JOURNEY TO THE SEA: On May 28, 1808, Fraser and 23 men set out in canoes from Fort George (now Prince George, British Columbia). He took a river route that he thought was the Columbia. He knew the river was rough and full of rapids.

Over 36 days, Fraser and his men traced the 520 miles of the river. It was one of the most difficult journeys in the history of Canadian exploration. They couldn't make portages—take their canoes out of the water and carry them over land. The rapids were surrounded by high cliffs, and not passable on foot.

Instead, they navigated the river south then west, finally reaching the ocean near modern-day Vancouver. Along the way they encountered hostile Indians. They were often in fear for their lives. But Fraser kept the group together. They headed back upstream and reached Fort George on August 6, 1808.

Fraser thought his mission was a failure. The route he'd taken could never be used for trade, because the water was too rough. When he reached Vancouver, he took measurements that showed him he'd never reached the Columbia, which is further south.

Yet his journey had proved him to be a hardy and brave explorer. Years later, his fellow Canadian explorer **David Thompson** named the river he'd so ably navigated the Fraser, in his honor.

LIFE AFTER EXPLORATION: Fraser returned to work for the North West Company. In 1818, he moved to St. Andrews West, in Ontario. He started a mill there.

SIMON FRASER'S HOME AND FAMILY: Fraser married Catherine MacDonell in 1820. They had nine children. Fraser died in 1862, at the age of 86.

HIS DISCOVERY: Fraser is remembered for his brave leadership on the river journey of 1808. The river that now bears his name in British Columbia is a further monument to the explorer.

WORLD WIDE WEB SITES:

http://www.sfu.ca/archives/sf-explorer.html
http://www.nlc-bnc.ca/2/24/h24-1640-e.html

John Charles Frémont
1813 - 1890
American Soldier, Explorer, and Politician
Explored and Mapped the American West

JOHN CHARLES FRÉMONT WAS BORN on January 21, 1813, in Savannah, Georgia. His parents were Charles and Ann Frémont. His father died when he was five. The family then moved to Charleston, South Carolina.

JOHN CHARLES FRÉMONT WENT TO SCHOOL in Charleston. He attended Charleston College, but was expelled in 1831 for poor attendance. He had done well in math, however, and got a job teaching math.

JOINING THE ARMY: Frémont joined the Army's surveying team in 1835. In 1838, he signed up for an expedition led by Joseph Nicollet to map the upper Mississippi and Missouri Rivers. In 1841 Frémont led an expedition to the Des Moines River in Iowa. He surveyed it for Nicollet.

1842 EXPEDITION: In 1842, Frémont led an expedition into the Oregon Territory. He mapped part of what later became the Oregon Trail, which was followed by many later settlers. He climbed the second highest mountain in the Wind River range in Wyoming. (It is now named for him.) The expedition's scout was the colorful **Kit Carson**. Along his journeys, Frémont noted the places where Americans could build homes, forts, or railroads. He thought it was his destiny to lead the expansion of the young nation.

1843 EXPEDITION: Frémont went back to the West in 1843. That year, he completed mapping the Oregon Trail all the way to the mouth of the Columbia River in modern-day Oregon. Frémont once again enlisted Carson, and they were also accompanied by famed mountain man Tom Fitzpatrick. On the return trip, the group headed south, then east, crossing the Sierra Nevada Mountains in winter.

A POPULAR EXPLORER: Back east, Frémont published books about his travels, which were largely written by his wife, Jessie. They were colorful and exciting tales, and the American public loved them. Frémont became a national hero, called "The Pathfinder." His books inspired thousands to consider settling in the West.

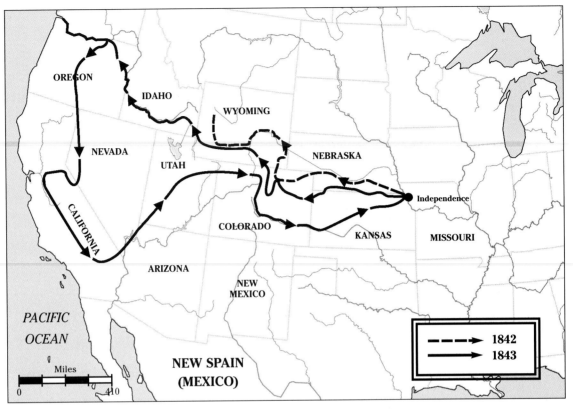

Frémont's expeditions of 1842 and 1843.

1845 EXPEDITION: In 1845, Frémont began his last major expedition. At that time, California was under Mexican control. Frémont went to California with the goal of turning the area into U.S. territory. He encouraged Americans of the region to rebel against the Mexican authorities. He led a group of Americans in the Sonoma area, who declared themselves citizens of the independent Bear Flag Republic. In 1846, Mexico declared war on the U.S. Frémont was made the head of a California battalion. The Mexicans surrendered within months. Frémont was then appointed the military governor of California.

Frémont was ambitious and stubborn. Sometimes his high opinion of himself got in the way of his success. After he'd been appointed military governor, he refused to follow the orders of the general in charge. He wound up being court-martialed (tried and sentenced in a military court). He was later pardoned by President James Polk, but Frémont refused the pardon and resigned from the Army.

THE GOLD RUSH: In 1848, gold was discovered on Frémont's land in California. He became a millionaire. He lived in California for the next several years, then started a career in politics.

POLITICAL CAREER: In 1850, Frémont was elected to serve as the first Senator from California. Frémont detested slavery. He joined the Republican Party, inspired by their anti-slavery beliefs. In 1856, he became the first Republican candidate for President. He lost to

Frémont in a political poster from his Presidential campaign of 1856.

James Buchanan. He didn't run again in 1860, when the nomination went to Abraham Lincoln.

When the Civil War broke out in 1861, Frémont joined the Union Army. He served as the commander of the Western Department. But once again Frémont refused to obey orders. He was removed from command by Lincoln. After the war, Frémont lost most of his money in bad investments. Near poverty, he once again took political office in 1878. He was named the Governor of the Arizona territory, and served in that job until 1883. He died on July 13, 1890, in New York City.

JOHN CHARLES FRÉMONT'S HOME AND FAMILY: Frémont married Jessie Benton in 1841. She was the daughter of Thomas Hart Benton, a U.S. Senator and a firm believer in expansion in the West. He was a strong supporter of Frémont's explorations.

HIS DISCOVERIES: Frémont's books about his expeditions made him hugely popular with the American public. His stories were full of the possibilities of life in the West, and they drew thousands of people to settle in the western U.S. He was an ambitious, complicated man. Bad decisions cost him his career, but he remained a legendary figure to many Americans.

WORLD WIDE WEB SITES:

http://historytogo.utah.gov/jcfrémont.html
http://www.sfu.ca/~fremont/jcfremont.html

Martin Frobisher
1540? - 1594
English Explorer of the Canadian Arctic
Searched for the Northwest Passage

MARTIN FROBISHER WAS BORN around 1540 in Yorkshire, England. Very little is known about his life until he was 13 years old.

At the age of 13, Frobisher went to sea for the first time. He sailed on a voyage to West Africa. It was a risky adventure, and most of the crew died. Frobisher went back to Africa again when he was 14. This time, he was captured, first by Africans, then by the Portuguese, who finally released him.

A PIRATE: At that time, some sailors also made their living as pirates, and Frobisher was one of them. In England, pirates were not always condemned by Queen Elizabeth. This was the time when Spain and Portugal were the major sea powers. They controlled sea routes around Africa and to the East, as well as to North America. Pirate ships would attack and steal cargo from merchant ships. Frobisher made a living as a pirate, or "privateer," as they were also called, for many years.

IN THE SERVICE OF QUEEN ELIZABETH: In 1571, Queen Elizabeth gave Frobisher command of his own ship. His pirate days were over. Now he served the Queen.

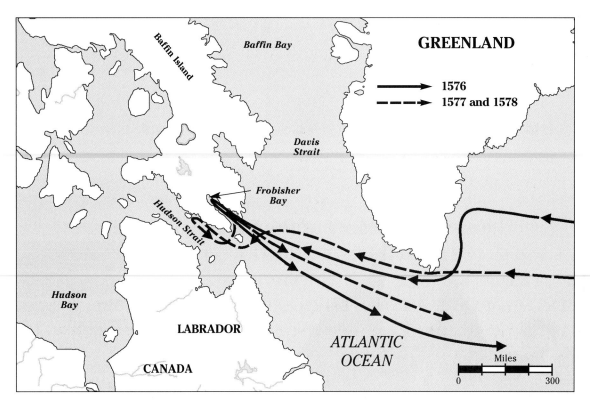

Frobisher's voyages of 1576, 1577, and 1578.

Queen Elizabeth wanted to build the power and wealth of England. She wanted her country to explore and find the riches that filled the treasuries of Spain and Portugal. She wanted Frobisher to search for the **Northwest Passage**. Through it, England would have access to the wealth of Asia.

THE NORTHWEST PASSAGE: From the 1500s, many people believed that a passage from Europe to Asia existed through what is now Canada. They sought a sea route linking the Atlantic and Pacific Oceans through the islands of the Canadian Arctic. Many of these explorers were English. During the 1500s, Spain and Portugal controlled the sea routes closer to the equator. England wanted to find a route they could control and use for trade. For 400 years, explorers sought—and died—looking for the Northwest Passage.

Among the early explorers who searched for the passage were **Jacques Cartier** and **John Cabot.** Frobisher was to follow in their footsteps.

FIRST VOYAGE TO THE NEW WORLD: Frobisher sailed from London, England, on June 7, 1576. Queen Elizabeth waved to them from a palace window as they departed.

This first expedition was made up of three small ships. They faced storms and ice on the six-week crossing. As they sailed from England to Iceland and on to Greenland, one ship sank, and one had to return to England. Frobisher sailed on with a crew of just 18. They reached a large bay, on what is now Baffin Island. They thought they had found the Northwest Passage. It is now Frobisher Bay.

Frobisher went ashore on Baffin Island and met the natives. They were members of the Inuit tribe. The English traded with the Inuit. The crew went on land and brought back flowers, grasses, and a piece of black ore with flecks of gold.

On a journey around one of the smaller islands, five of Frobisher's men became lost in a small boat. He thought they might have been kidnapped by the Inuit. Frobisher kidnapped an Inuit in return and tried to trade hostages. But his men were never found. Frobisher decided to return to England, taking the kidnapped Inuit.

The Inuit captive died soon after reaching England. The black ore with the gold flecks fascinated some of the investors. They thought it contained gold. This finding set off a "gold rush" to the Canadian Arctic. A group called the Cathay Company financed Frobisher's second voyage to the **New World**. Among the investors was the Queen. The Northwest Passage was forgotten. Now the race was on to find gold.

An illustration of Inuit life from a book on Frobisher's 1577 voyage.

SECOND VOYAGE: Frobisher left England in May 1577 with three ships and a crew of 100, many of them miners. They landed on Baffin Island in July. They spent the summer mining black ore, digging up 200 tons of it. After a skirmish with the Inuit, Frobisher took hostages: a man, a woman, and a child. He returned to England in 1577 with them and the ore.

Queen Elizabeth named the land Frobisher had found "Meta Incognita," which means "the unknown goal" in Latin. The Inuit captives were displayed in England. They died within one month.

THIRD VOYAGE: Even before the ore had been tested to see if it contained gold, Frobisher's backers were planning another voyage. It was a huge expedition, with 15 ships and more than 400 men. They left England in late May 1578, and followed the same route as the 1577 voyage. The passage had been difficult, and the ships battled storms and ice. One ship sank, and another returned to England.

The men mined more than 1,000 tons of ore. They set up mines on Countess of Warwick's Island (now Kodlunarn Island) and Mount Warwick. Frobisher was also supposed to set up an English colony, but he could not. The ship that had sunk contained the building materials and supplies for the colony.

The crew did build a small stone house on Kodlunarn Island. They furnished it with mirrors, bells, whistles, and toys. They left it

Remains of the mine and house Frobsisher built in 1578 on Kodlunarn Island.

for the Inuit to discover, with baked bread in the oven. (Hundreds of years later, the remains of the mine and the house were found by archeologists.)

Frobisher returned to England in the fall of 1578. One ship was lost on the way, but the rest reached England safely. The ore was unloaded in England, and the investors waited for it to be tested for gold.

FOOL'S GOLD: Much to their shock, Frobisher and the investors learned that the ore was "fool's gold." It was worthless. The Cathay Company investors lost their money. Frobisher was disgraced.

In his last years, Frobisher returned to the life of a pirate. He also fought in the famous battle in which England defeated the Spanish Armada. He died from wounds suffered in a battle against Spain in 1594.

HIS DISCOVERY: Although Frobisher never discovered the Northwest Passage or gold in the **New World**, his voyages inspired English explorers and colonists. Over the next several hundred years, English people came to Canada to live, and many more explorers sought the Northwest Passage.

WORLD WIDE WEB SITES:

http://www.civilization.ca/hist/frobisher/fr57601e.html
http://collections.ic.gc.ca/arctic/explore/frobishe.htm

Yuri Gagarin

1934 - 1968
Russian Cosmonaut
First Person to Travel in Space

YURI GAGARIN WAS BORN on March 9, 1934, in the village of Klushino, near Moscow, Russia. His parents were farmers. Yuri was the third of four children. When he was growing up, Russia was part of the Soviet Union.

YURI GAGARIN GREW UP during World War II (1939-1945). During the war, the Soviet Union was invaded by Germany. German soldiers attacked Gagarin's village in 1941. They threw his family out of their home. Throughout the war, the family lived in a dugout in the earth. When the war was over, they moved to the city of Gzhatsk.

YURI GAGARIN WENT TO SCHOOL after the war ended. He attended public school for six years. Then, he went to school for technical training. He learned to be a metal worker and got a job in a foundry.

BECOMING A PILOT: From the time he was a boy, Gagarin wanted to fly. In his teens, he'd seen a plane make a forced landing near his home. "We boys all wanted to be brave and handsome pilots," he remembered.

While working at the foundry, Gagarin joined a flying club. He became a pilot, and he was very good. When he was 21, he joined the Air Force. He attended the Soviet Air Force Academy and graduated with honors in 1957. He flew missions as a military fighter pilot.

BECOMING A COSMONAUT: In 1959, Gagarin was chosen to be a "cosmonaut." That is the Russian term for an astronaut. He was part of the first group ever trained to fly in space. He received two years of training to prepare himself, physically and mentally, for the demands of space flight.

THE COLD WAR: When Gagarin became a cosmonaut, the Soviet Union and the U.S. were locked in what was called the "Cold War." After World War II, the Soviet Union and the U.S. became the two strongest nations in the world. They represented two very different political systems. The U.S. was a democracy; the Soviet Union was a Communist country. The two "superpowers" also had powerful nuclear weapons. The relationship between the two nations was very important. For more than 40 years, the hostilities between these two nations affected world politics.

***SPUTNIK* AND THE SPACE RACE:** On October 4, 1957, the Soviets launched the very first satellite, *Sputnik 1*. It was the beginning of the Space Age, and of the Space Race between the Soviets and the U.S.

Because of its military importance, the Space Race between the U.S. and the Soviet Union was always about much more than exploration. The Space Race was also about domination. Each country was afraid that the other would develop the weapons and technology to dominate them. The U.S. was astonished at the success of *Sputnik*. U.S. military leaders had no idea that the Soviets had the technology to launch a satellite. And the same technology that could launch a satellite could launch a missile. But *Sputnik* wasn't the only tremendous "first" for the Soviet space program.

FIRST PERSON IN SPACE: On April 12, 1961, Yuri Gagarin became the first person to leave Earth and travel in space. Aboard the space capsule *Vostok 1*, he orbited the Earth once. He reached an altitude of 188 miles, traveling at 18,000 miles an hour. His flight lasted 108 minutes.

Gagarin didn't pilot his capsule. Instead, the capsule was controlled by a computer on Earth that communicated to the capsule by radio. When his space capsule reentered the Earth's atmosphere, Gagarin parachuted to the ground. He landed safely in western Russia.

Gagarin later described the astonishing beauty of the Earth from space. "I could clearly see the outlines of continents, islands,

Gagarin meeting U.S. astronauts and officials. To his left are astronaut James McDivitt and U.S. Vice President Hubert Humphrey. To his right are French President Georges Pompidou and astronaut Edward White.

and rivers. The horizon presents a sight of unusual beauty. A delicate blue halo surrounds the Earth, merging with the blackness of space in which the stars are bright and clear."

LIFE AFTER HIS FAMOUS FLIGHT: Despite the continued hostilities between the U.S. and the Soviets, Gagarin became a hero to people all over the world. He met the astronauts of *Gemini 4*, Edward White and James McDivitt, and Vice President Hubert Humphrey in 1965.

Although he trained for a second mission, Gagarin never flew in space again. He worked for several years as a test pilot, experimenting with new Soviet aircraft. On March 27, 1968, Gagarin was killed in a crash of a new Soviet fighter plane, a MIG-15. He was 34 years old.

YURI GAGARIN'S HOME AND FAMILY: Gagarin married Valentina Goryacheva in November 1957. They had two daughters, Yelena and Galya.

HIS DISCOVERY: Gagarin, called "The Columbus of the Cosmos," will always be remembered as the first person to travel in space. In the 1970s, a crater on the moon was named in his honor. In July 1971, the *Apollo 15* crew placed a plaque on the moon listing the people who had died during the early years of the space program. Among those names is Yuri Gagarin.

WORLD WIDE WEB SITES:

http://starchild.gsfc.nasa.gov/docs/StarChild/shadow/whos_who_
  level2/gagarin.html
http://www.kosmonaut.se/gagarin
http://www.pbs.org/redfiles/rao/gallery/gagarin

John Glenn
1921 -
American Astronaut and Politician
First American to Orbit the Earth

JOHN GLENN WAS BORN on July 18, 1921, in Cambridge, Ohio. His full name is John Herschel Glenn Jr. His parents were John and Clara Glenn. His father was a railroad conductor who also ran a plumbing and heating business. His mother was a homemaker. John has one sister, Jean.

JOHN GLENN GREW UP first in Cambridge, then in New Concord, Ohio, where the family moved when he was two. John's family was very close. His parents raised their children to be honest, hardworking, and devoted to country, church, and family.

JOHN GLENN WENT TO SCHOOL at the local public schools in New Concord. He always did well in school, and he loved sports. In high school, he played football, basketball, and tennis. He also played in the band and acted in plays. During the summers, he worked as a lifeguard and washed cars.

Glenn graduated from New Concord High School in 1939. (It was later renamed "John Glenn High School.") He went on to Muskingum College, in New Concord. But his college education was interrupted by World War II.

WORLD WAR II: World War II took place between 1939 and 1945 in Europe, Africa, and the Far East. In the war, Germany, Italy, and Japan made up the "Axis" powers. They fought against the "Allies"—the U.S., England, France, and the Soviet Union.

Glenn left college in 1942 and joined the Naval Aviation Cadet Program. He trained to be a fighter pilot. He joined the Marines in 1943 and began flying bombing missions in the Pacific. When the war was over, he decided to stay in the Marines.

Glenn continued to fly and also became a Marine flight instructor. When the Korean War began in 1950, he once again flew combat missions. When the war ended in 1953, he became part of one of the top flying groups in U.S. history.

BECOMING A TEST PILOT: Glenn became a test pilot in the mid-1950s, matching skills with some of the best pilots in the country.

The original seven Mercury astronauts. Front row, left to right, are Walter M. Schirra Jr., Donald K. Slayton, John H. Glenn, Jr. and M. Scott Carpenter. Back row, from left to right, are Alan B. Shepard, Gus Grissom, and L. Gordon Cooper, Jr.

They flew some of the newest, fastest, and most advanced aircraft in the world. Many would go on to become the first astronauts.

BECOMING AN ASTRONAUT: In 1959, Glenn was chosen as an astronaut for the Mercury program. Mercury was run by **NASA** (the National Aeronautics and Space Administration). It was the first manned space program in the U.S. Together with the six other Mercury astronauts, including **Alan Shepard**, Glenn trained for the physical and technical demands of space flight.

THE SPACE RACE: When Glenn became an astronaut, the Soviet Union and the U.S. were locked in what was called the "Cold War." After World War II, the Soviet Union and the U.S. became the two strongest nations in the world. They represented two very different political systems. The U.S. was a democracy; the Soviet Union was a Communist country. The two "superpowers" also had powerful nuclear weapons. The relationship between the two nations was very important. For more than 40 years, the hostilities between these two nations affected world politics.

***SPUTNIK* AND THE SPACE RACE:** On October 4, 1957, the Soviets launched the very first satellite, *Sputnik 1*. It was the beginning of the Space Age and the Space Race.

Because of its military importance, the Space Race between the U.S. and the Soviet Union was always about much more than exploration. The Space Race was also about domination. Each country was afraid that the other would develop the weapons and technology to dominate them. The U.S. was astonished at the success of *Sputnik*. U.S. military leaders had no idea that the Soviets had the technology to launch a satellite. And the same technology that could launch a satellite could launch a missile. But *Sputnik* wasn't the only tremendous "first" for the Soviet space program.

YURI GAGARIN: On April 12, 1961, Soviet cosmonaut **Yuri Gagarin** became the first person to travel in space. Aboard the space capsule *Vostok 1*, he orbited the Earth once. He reached an altitude of 188 miles, traveling at 18,000 miles an hour. His flight lasted 108 minutes.

Once again, the Americans had been beaten by the Soviets.

ALAN SHEPARD: The U.S. entry into the space race came just three weeks later. **Alan Shepard** blasted into space on the morning of May 5, 1961. His flight carried him 116 miles into space and lasted 15 minutes. After traveling 302 miles, his capsule fell into the Atlantic Ocean.

THE FLIGHT OF *FRIENDSHIP 7:* Glenn followed Shepard eight months later. On February 20, 1962, he became the first American to orbit the Earth. Aboard his capsule, the *Friendship 7*, Glenn blasted off from Cape Canaveral and circled the Earth three times. He traveled 81,000 miles in five hours.

A television camera broadcast Glenn's historic journey back to an eager audience on Earth. When his capsule left the Earth's atmosphere, Glenn felt the weightlessness of zero gravity. "Zero-G and I feel fine," he told the world. From his window he saw three sunsets and the vast expanse of stars. He described their beauty to the listeners back on the planet.

Glenn splashed down in the Atlantic. He returned to the U.S. an international hero. He was eager to return to space, but that was not to happen for a long time. President John F. Kennedy thought Glenn was too valuable as a national hero. At that time, space travel wasn't very safe. Fearing for his safety, Kennedy refused to allow Glenn to take part in any future flights. Glenn was bitterly disappointed.

Glenn climbs into his Friendship 7 *space capsule at Cape Canaveral, Florida, February 20, 1962.*

LEAVING THE SPACE PROGRAM: When it became clear that he wouldn't be allowed to fly again, Glenn left the space program. In 1964, he moved back to Ohio and became a businessman.

A LIFE IN POLITICS: After a successful career in business, Glenn decided to run for political office. He was elected to the U.S. Senate from Ohio in 1974. He served until 1998. In his final years in the Senate, Glenn got the chance to go into space again.

Glenn served on a Senate committee on aging. He noted similarities between the effects of aging and the effects of space travel. He

Glenn, 1998.

applied to NASA to study the connection in space. He had to pass tough physical and mental tests, which he did. Once again, Glenn was a NASA astronaut.

BACK INTO SPACE: On October 29, 1998, at age 77, John Glenn became the oldest person to travel in space. For nine days, he traveled aboard the **space shuttle** *Discovery*. He went as part of a scientific mission to conduct space-based research on aging. The differences between his 1962 flight and his 1998 flight were astounding. The crew numbered 7, and the space shuttle was more than 10 times the size of *Friendship 7*. Several of the crew members were scientists doing complicated experiments in astrophysics and medicine. They traveled 3.6 million miles, orbiting the Earth 134 times. Glenn returned to Earth on November 7, delighted with his final mission in space.

RETIREMENT: Glenn left the Senate in January 1999 and returned to Ohio. He's currently heading a program at Ohio State University. It's called the John Glenn Institute for Public Service and Public Policy. The program encourages young people to study politics and consider careers in public service.

JOHN GLENN'S HOME AND FAMILY: Glenn married Annie Castor, his high school sweetheart, in 1943. They have two children, David and Lyn.

HIS DISCOVERY: Glenn is remembered as the first American to orbit the Earth, and as the oldest astronaut to fly in space.

WORLD WIDE WEB SITES:

http://www.grc.nasa.gov/WWW/PAO/html/johnglen.htm
http://jsc.nasa.gov/Bios/htmlbios/glenn-j.html
http://www.glenninstitute.org/glenn/index.asap
http://pbs.org/kcet/johnglenn/

Hanno

c. 500 B.C.
Carthaginian Explorer and Trader
Explored the West Coast of Africa

EARLY LIFE: No one is exactly sure when Hanno was born or when he died. He lived in the city of Carthage near what is now Tunis, along the north African coast. Carthage was a city founded by the **Phoenicians** several hundred years before Hanno was born.

THE TRAVELS OF HANNO: About 500 B.C., Hanno led a group of people from Carthage through the Strait of Gibraltar. That is a narrow passage that connects the Mediterranean Sea with the Atlantic Ocean. From there, Hanno's group traveled down the west coast of Africa. The group was large. According to a report he wrote, there were 30,000 men and women, in 60 boats, on the journey. Along the way, they stopped at several places.

In his report, Hanno said they founded a city that modern historians think is in modern-day Morocco. They built an altar to the sea god Poseidon at a place called Soloeis. They also founded settlements at places they named Carian Fort, Gutta, Acra, Melitta, and Arambys. Historians believe that Hanno traveled as far south as modern-day Sierra Leone.

Hanno described the differences in the landscape as he and his group explored the coast. He wrote about deserts, wild marshes, plains, rivers, and many wild beasts. They encountered elephants, crocodiles, and hippos. Hanno described what was probably an erupting volcano. He and his group called it "Chariot of the Gods." He also commented on the people they met, some friendly, some hostile and threatening.

According to Hanno, when the group ran low on supplies, they returned to Carthage. Historians think that the Carthaginians continued to trade with the people of the African settlements for many years.

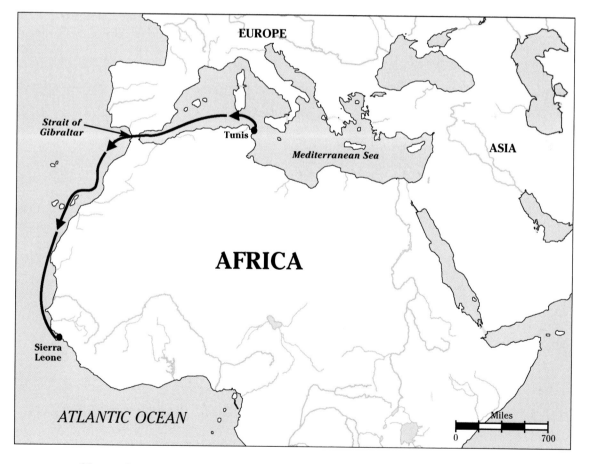

Hanno's possible route from modern-day Tunis to Sierra Leone.

273

HIS DISCOVERY: Modern historians aren't sure that everything in Hanno's report is correct. Some of the geographical information is confusing, and some of it may be untrue. Also, Hanno may have exaggerated the size of his group. One recent source notes that 30,000 people wouldn't have fit in 60 boats of that era. But regardless, Hanno's report was read for hundreds of years. It remains an important document that tells about the travels of one of the earliest explorers.

WORLD WIDE WEB SITE:

http://www.mariner.org/age/hanno.html

Sven Anders Hedin
1865 - 1952
Swedish Explorer and Geographer of Central Asia

SVEN ANDERS HEDIN WAS BORN on February 19, 1865, in Stockholm, Sweden. His parents were Ludwig and Anna Hedin. Ludwig was the Chief Architect of Stockholm.

AN EARLY LOVE OF EXPLORATION: As a young boy, Hedin loved to hear tales of brave explorers. Two favorites were **David Livingstone** and **Adolf Erik Nordenskiöld**. He decided early on that he would be an explorer, too. "Happy is the boy who discovers the bent of his life work during childhood. That indeed was my good fortune," Hedin wrote.

SVEN ANDERS HEDIN went to school in Stockholm and was a good student. When he was 20, he got his first chance to travel. He journeyed through Russia to the city of Baku, Azerbaijan, where he tutored the son of a Swedish family. Over the next year, he traveled to Persia (now Iran) and Turkey. He learned several languages, including Persian and Tatar.

Hedin returned to Sweden and went to college. He attended universities in Sweden and Germany. He also wrote the first of some 35 books about his travels and explorations. When he was 25, he traveled back to the Middle East.

TRAVELING IN THE MIDDLE EAST AND ASIA: In 1890, Hedin went to Iran, where he worked as an interpreter for the Swedish government. From Iran, he traveled to Uzbekistan, Turkestan, and into eastern China.

EXPEDITION OF 1893-1897: In 1893, Hedin took his third trip to Asia. He traveled east through Russia, crossing the Pamir Mountains. Like **Marco Polo** and other explorers before him, he crossed the treacherous Taklamakan Desert. He discovered the remains of ancient civilizations, buried in the sand. Crossing through Tibet, he reached the Chinese city of Beijing in 1897. On his return to Sweden, he published more popular books.

EXPEDITION OF 1899-1902: In 1899, Hedin set out for Asia again. This time, he traveled the Tarim River, visiting places along the ancient **Silk Road.** He visited Tibet again, and drew maps of the country. He traveled home through India.

EXPEDITION OF 1906-1908: Hedin headed out to Asia again in 1906. He traveled east through Iran, into India and north into Tibet. Hedin claimed to have explored and mapped a section of the Himalaya Mountains not before discovered. Later explorers questioned those claims. He also claimed to have found the sources of India's two major rivers, the Indus and the Ganges. That claim, too, was never proved to be true.

In World War I, Hedin sided with the Germans in their war against France, England, Russia, and the U.S. This made him very unpopular throughout the world. Even so, he was able to find money for another expedition.

EXPEDITION OF 1926-1935: On his final expedition, Hedin traveled across China, discovering more sites of ancient civilizations. He traveled through Mongolia, and was briefly held captive by a rebel warlord.

After returning to Europe, Hedin again got involved in politics. He supported Nazi Germany in World War II, and was once again a very unpopular figure in the eyes of the world. He died in Sweden at the age of 87.

HIS DISCOVERY: Hedin is remembered for his explorations and mapping of large sections of Asia.

WORLD WIDE WEB SITE:

http://www.kirjasto.sci.fi/shedin.html

Louis Hennepin

1626 - 1701
French Missionary and Explorer
Explored the Great Lakes Region with La Salle

LOUIS HENNEPIN WAS BORN in Ath, Belgium, in 1626. Very little is known about his early life.

Hennepin studied religion and became a priest. He was sent to the Atlantic coast of France to serve. There, he often heard tales from travelers who had been in the **New World**. He wanted to see it for himself.

TRAVELING TO NEW FRANCE: In 1675, Hennepin got his wish. He was sent to the settlement of Quebec in **New France** (now Canada) as a missionary with **Rene-Robert Cavelier, Sieur de La Salle**. He stayed in Quebec for one year.

In 1678, he joined La Salle's expedition to travel from Lake Ontario to Lake Erie. They saw Niagara Falls. Later, Hennepin became the first European to write about them.

La Salle built a new fort, near Niagara Falls. He also built a merchant ship, the *Griffin*. It was the first merchant ship to sail the Great Lakes. La Salle hoped to use the ship to trade furs. In 1678, La Salle, Hennepin, and their crew sailed on the *Griffin* through Lakes Erie, St. Clair, Huron, and Michigan, ending at the southern end of Lake Michigan. They loaded the boat with goods and sent it back to Niagara. Sadly, the ship and all its cargo was lost along the way.

Hennipin's first sight of Niagara Falls, 1678.

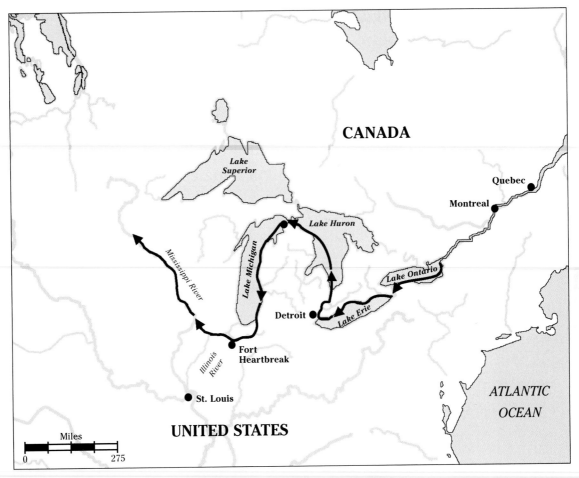

Hennipin's voyages, 1678-1680.

La Salle wanted to reach the legendary Mississippi. Hennepin joined him on his journey. They traveled along the Illinois River to the site of modern-day Peoria, Illinois. They built a fort, called Fort Heartbreak, in 1680. When La Salle returned to Canada for supplies, Hennepin explored the upper Mississippi. (In his later writings, Hennepin claimed to have traveled the length of the Mississippi, but most historians think that is not true.)

In April 1680, Hennepin and his crew were captured by Sioux Indians. Hennepin traveled with his Indian captors. He saw the waterfalls in Minneapolis, Minnesota, and named them for his patron saint, St. Anthony. A French trader named Daniel Greysolon finally rescued Hennepin in July 1680.

Hennepin returned to Quebec, then back to France. In France, he wrote a book about his travels. Most historians think he made up a good deal of the book, but it was successful. Hennepin died in Rome around 1701.

HIS DISCOVERY: Hennepin is remembered for his travels with La Salle, especially through the Great Lakes. Although his book on his travels probably contains exaggerations, it provides a glimpse into what life was like in the wilderness in the late 1600s.

WORLD WIDE WEB SITES:

http://www.civilization.ca/vmnf/explor/henn_e2.html
http://www.win.tue.nl/~engels/discovery/index.html

Silva Pinx!   Wooding Sculp!

Prince Henry the Navigator
1394 - 1460
Portuguese Prince Who Founded a
School to Train Explorers
Started the European Age of Exploration

PRINCE HENRY THE NAVIGATOR WAS BORN on March 4, 1394, in Oporto, Portugal. He was the third son of King John I and Queen Philippa of Portugal. Henry had two brothers, Duarte and Fernando.

GROWING UP: Prince Henry grew up at a time when Europeans knew little about Africa. When he was 21, Henry led a group of soldiers in battle and captured the city of Ceuta in Morocco, across the Strait of Gibraltar from the southern tip of Spain. Prince Henry was fascinated by Africa. Returning to Portugal, he decided he wanted to fund explorations of the West African coast.

FOR GOD AND GOLD: Prince Henry had several goals in mind when he became a sponsor for exploration. He was a devout Catholic and wanted to bring Christianity to the people of Africa. One of his particular goals was to convert Muslims. He also wanted to find a mythical man known as "Prester John." Prester John was supposedly a rich Christian king who lived in the east. The legend of Prester John is often mentioned in accounts of the Age of Exploration.

Henry also wanted Portugal to take part in the profitable trade going on in Africa. He had heard that gold was plentiful along the trade routes across the Sahara Desert. He also wanted to find a sea route around Africa to reach Asia by water instead of by land.

A "SCHOOL FOR EXPLORERS": Using his own money, Prince Henry started a center for explorers in Sagres, in southern Portugal. Here, men came to learn about geography, mapmaking, ship building, and navigation.

Prince Henry began the first systematic approach to exploration. He sent out expeditions that explored the coast of West Africa. Each group would go a little further than the previous one, bringing back information for the next expedition.

"MONSTERS": Prince Henry had to assure the explorers that they wouldn't be in danger. At that time, nothing was known about the coast of Africa. Some people believed that the waters near the equator were boiling hot and full of sea monsters. Some believed the Earth was flat. If they sailed to the south, they believed they would fall off the edge of the Earth. Only after the first explorers returned unharmed did they lose their fear.

FIRST EXPEDITIONS: Prince Henry's first explorers left Portugal in 1419. The first expedition went as far the islands of Madeira and Porto Santo in the Atlantic Ocean off the coast of Morocco. In 1434 the explorer Gil Eannes reached Cape Bojador in what is now the Western Sahara. It was the southernmost point any European had reached to that date. Later voyages reached the Azores Islands to the west of Portugal. Another reached as far south as the Cape Verde Islands and the modern country of Sierra Leone. By 1460, Prince Henry's explorers had traveled some 1,500 miles along the coast of Africa.

THE SLAVE TRADE: While Prince Henry's expeditions are important to the history of discovery, they also brought a shameful legacy to the Age of Exploration.

Henry's men also brought back Africans as slaves to Portugal. This was the beginning of the Portuguese slave trade. The explorers raided the coastal villages, and traded with both Arabic and African slave traders. In the name of exploration, the Portuguese and others helped to build the slave trade.

DEATH: Prince Henry died in 1460 at the age of 66. He had never married or had children. Instead, he devoted his life to directing and funding his explorations.

HIS DISCOVERY: Although Prince Henry himself did not become an explorer, he funded the explorations of others. Some of those who explored in his name were Alvise de Cadamosto, Gil Eannes, and Pedro de Sintra.

In 1487, 27 years after Henry's death, Portuguese explorer **Bartholomew Dias** rounded the southern tip of Africa. He and his fellow Portuguese sailors had learned from what Henry had begun.

WORLD WIDE WEB SITE:

http://www.mariner.org/age/princehenry.html

Matthew Henson
1866 - 1955
African-American Explorer
Traveled to the North Pole with Robert E. Peary

MATTHEW HENSON WAS BORN on August 8, 1866, in Maryland. His parents were sharecroppers. They both died when he was young.

STARTING TO WORK: When he was 12, Henson walked from Washington, D.C., to Baltimore, Maryland, to find work. He was hired as a cabin boy on the ship *Katie Hines.* Captain Childs was the ship's commander. Over the next several years, he took over

Henson's education. He taught him how to sail, as well as math, geography, and other subjects.

MEETING PEARY: Henson returned to Washington around 1883. He was working in a men's store when he met **Robert E. Peary**. Peary was working for the Navy and planning a trip to Nicaragua. He hired Peary to be his servant, and the two left for Central America.

Peary was impressed with Henson. He told him of his plans for exploration. Henson was eager to explore, too. When Peary went on an expedition to Greenland in 1891, Henson went with him.

GREENLAND: Over the next 23 years, Peary and Henson returned to Greenland many times. In 1891, they explored the northeastern portion. They took a sledge as far as Independence Fjord to examine and map the coastline. Henson was an able navigator and dogsledder, and an excellent mechanic and carpenter.

LEARNING FROM THE INUIT: Peary and Henson met Inuit tribes and learned how they survived in the Arctic. From them, they learned the proper clothing to wear to protect against the cold. Using all of this information, Peary set his mind on his ultimate goal: the **North Pole**.

THE RACE FOR THE POLES: By the end of the 19th century, most of the surface of the planet had been explored. What remained were the North and South Polar regions. Explorers from many countries competed against one another to locate and claim the North Pole and South Pole. Crews from the U.S., Russia, Norway, England, Germany, and other nations were locked in a race to be the first to reach either pole.

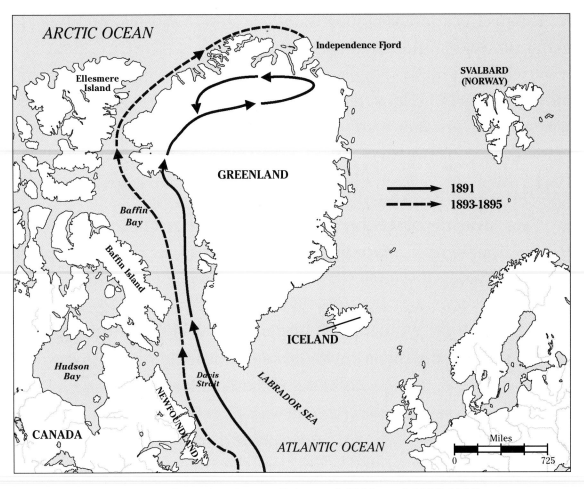

Henson's Greenland expeditions of 1891 and 1893-1895.

THE 1893-1895 EXPEDITION: Peary and Henson first attempted to reach the North Pole in 1893. That year, they traveled to northern Greenland and tried to reach the Pole. But bad weather stopped them. Throughout the next 15 years, Peary and Henson continued to attempt to reach the Pole.

THE 1905 EXPEDITION: Peary had a special boat built that could stand the ice. Aboard the *Roosevelt,* he and Henson again headed for the Pole on July 16, 1905. But the ship became stuck in the ice. The crew had to return home. They were determined to try again.

REACHING THE NORTH POLE: Their next attempt was a success. On March 1, 1909, the crew set out again from Ellesmere Island. The original team included 19 sledges and 24 men. Then, on April 6, 1909, Peary, Henson, and five Inuit reached what they thought was the North Pole. They carefully measured their location. They were confident they were the first people to reach the North Pole. They planted an American flag at the site.

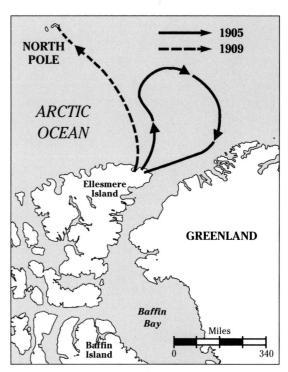

Henson's North Pole expeditions of 1905 and 1909.

COOK AND CONTROVERSY: Peary and his crew returned to the U.S. in triumph. "We have planted the Stars and Stripes on the North Pole," he claimed. But his glory was short lived. Just before Peary made his announcement, another explorer, Dr. Frederick Cook, claimed that he had been the first to reach the Pole, in April 1908.

Peary challenged Cook's claim, as did other experts. The National Geographic Society examined all the evidence—the men's journals, maps, and calculations. They determined that Peary, not Cook, had been the first to reach the North Pole.

LIFE AFTER THE NORTH POLE EXPEDITIONS: Henson and Peary both retired from exploring after their final expedition. Henson wrote a book about his experiences. In 1913, President Taft appointed him to a job in the U.S. Customs office. He served in that job until his retirement.

Henson received many awards for his accomplishments. In 1937, he was elected to the Explorers Club of New York. He received awards from the Geographic Society of Chicago and the U.S. Department of Defense. In 1954 he was honored by President Dwight D. Eisenhower for his role in the discovery of the North Pole. A glacier in Greenland was named for him, and he received several honorary degrees. Henson died in New York City on March 9, 1955.

MATTHEW HENSON'S HOME AND FAMILY: Henson was married twice. His first marriage, to Eva Flint, ended in divorce. His second wife was named Lucy Jane Ross.

HIS DISCOVERY: Peary always claimed that Henson was the most valuable member of his crew. "Henson must go all the way," he said about his attempts to reach the Pole. "I can't make it there without him." Henson is buried next to Peary in Arlington National Cemetery. On his gravestone is this quote: "The lure of the Arctic is tugging at my heart. To me the trail is calling. The old trail. The trail that is always new."

WORLD WIDE WEB SITES:

http://matthewhenson.com/
http://www.unmuseum.mus.pa.us/henson.htm

Herodotus
484 B.C.? to 420 B.C.?
Greek Historian, Geographer, and Traveler
"The Father of History"

HERODOTUS WAS BORN in the city of Halicarnassus (hal-i-kahr-NAS-uhs), in what is now western Turkey. His name is pronounced "huh-RAHD-uht-uhs." Very little is known about Herodotus's early life. Historians believe he came from a wealthy family and was well-educated.

During Herodotus's youth, a dictator came to power. Herodotus left home and began to travel. He probably journeyed in the Aegean Islands, now part of Greece. He returned to his homeland and helped to defeat the tyrant. But instead of settling down, Herodotus set out again.

THE TRAVELS OF HERODOTUS: Herodotus traveled over more area than any Greek of his time. He explored what is now modern Greece, Turkey, the Middle East, North Africa, and Egypt. It is thought that he traveled some 1,600 miles north to south, and 1,700 miles east to west.

Most importantly, Herodotus studied the cultures he visited. He learned the history of the areas from the people who lived there. He gathered information about their ways of life, their religions, and their governments. Then he wrote about them.

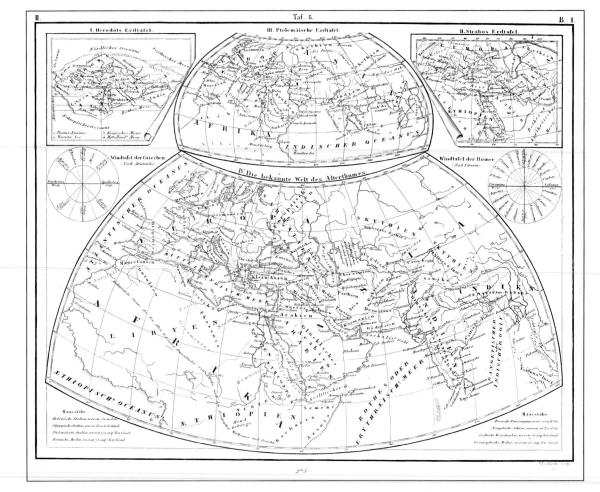

Ancient maps of the world, including those of Herodotus.

HIS DISCOVERY: Herodotus wanted to learn as much as he could about the people of different lands. He is best known for his histories of the wars between the Persians and the Greeks of the ancient era. But they are more than the histories of wars. In his histories Herodotus talked about what the people of those areas believed. He included myths, legends, and fantastic stories in his history. For this reason, his works are important for what they tell us about how people in the ancient world actually lived.

Herodotus was also one of the important geographers of his time. He kept notes about the seas, rivers, and other geographical features he visited. Then he made educated guesses about the world. For example, he tried to figure out if Africa was part of the continent of Asia. Traveling to Egypt, he tried to find the source of the Nile river. He was also the first geographer to determine that the Caspian Sea was an inland sea, not part of an ocean.

Herodotus lived the last years of his life in a Greek colony in modern-day Italy. Historians believe that he died there around 420 B.C.

WORLD WIDE WEB SITE:

http://www.herodotuswebsite.co.uk

Hsuan Tsang
600 - 664
Chinese Monk Who Traveled to Asia and India

HSUAN TSANG WAS BORN into a family of scholars in 600. Very little is known about his early life. His name is pronounced "shoe-an zang." It is also spelled Xuan Zang. In Chinese, a person's last name appears first, so the last name of this early explorer was Hsuan.

Hsuan's older brother was a Buddhist monk. Hsuan went to school in a Buddhist monastery and became a monk when he was about 21. He was an excellent student. He was especially interested in Buddhist philosophy.

Hsuan wanted to learn more about his faith. He wanted to travel to India, where Buddhism began, to study. The religion is based on the teachings of the Buddha, who lived around 500 B.C. in India.

Hsuan wanted to read the Buddha's teachings in their original language. They were written in Sanskrit, one of the oldest languages in the world. He also wanted to visit the most important and sacred sites of Buddhism.

In 629, Hsuan set out for India. He traveled west from Chang-an. He journeyed as far as modern-day Uzbekistan, then turned south. He traveled through Afghanistan and across the Hindu Kush mountains.

The way was full of danger and adventure. Hsuan was captured by pirates who almost killed him. When a fierce storm came up, they were frightened, and let him go.

Finally, in 633, Hsuan reached India. He sailed down the Ganges River and visited many Buddhist holy sites. He studied with great Buddhist scholars. And he collected a vast amount of material to translate from Sanskrit to Chinese.

Hsuan returned to China in 645. He had traveled 40,000 miles. Hsuan was greeted as a hero. The emperor was eager to hear about all the people and places he had seen.

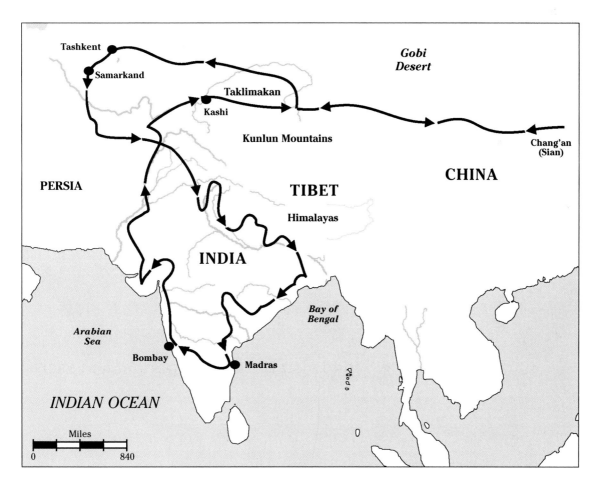

Hsuan Tsang's voyages from 629-645.

HIS DISCOVERY: Hsuan wrote about his travels in a book read for generations. He provided a vivid and colorful report of people, places, and ways of life unknown to the Chinese.

Hsuan spent the rest of his life translating the Buddhist texts he'd brought from India. When he died in 664, he was mourned throughout China.

WORLD WIDE WEB SITE:

http://www.silk-road.com/artl/hsuantsang.shtml

Henry Hudson
1565? - 1611
English Navigator and Explorer
Explored the Arctic Ocean and North American Coast
First European to Sail the Hudson River and
Enter Hudson Bay

HENRY HUDSON WAS BORN around 1565 in England. Nothing is known about his early life. He is known for his four voyages seeking a passage to the East through the Arctic Ocean.

FIRST VOYAGE: In 1607, Hudson was hired by the Moscovy Company, a trading company in England. He was to try to find a **Northeast Passage** from Europe to Asia.

Hudson Coat of Arms.

In the 1500s and 1600s, Portugal and Spain controlled the sea routes from Europe to the riches of the East. Other countries, especially England and the Netherlands, wanted to find a sea route to Asia by a northern route across the Arctic Ocean. Early explorers like **Sebastian Cabot** of England and **Willem Barents** of the Netherlands traveled north from Europe, then east, exploring the Russian coast of the Arctic looking for the passage.

Hudson was an excellent navigator. He knew that in the summer the sun shone on the **North Pole** almost 24 hours a day. He thought that if he sailed during the spring and summer, he would find the North Pole free of ice and find the passage.

Hudson left England in April 1607 with his son, John, and 10 other sailors. Their ship, the *Hopewell,* sailed north until they reached the polar ice pack north of Norway. They traveled east, then were stopped by ice. They returned home.

SECOND VOYAGE: In 1608, the Muscovy Company sent Hudson on another expedition to discover the Northeast Passage. Aboard the *Hopewell,* he traveled north. Once again he was stopped by ice. His crew threatened to mutiny. Hudson headed back to England.

THIRD VOYAGE: Hudson sailed again in 1609, this time for the Dutch East India Company. They were a trading company based in

Holland. They, too, wanted Hudson to find the Northeast Passage. Hudson sailed from Holland aboard the *Half Moon* in April 1609. His crew was made up of English and Dutch sailors. When they reached the Arctic waters, they ran into terrible storms.

Hudson turned the ship around. But he didn't head back to Holland. Instead, he headed west across the Atlantic. He told the

Hudson's ship the Half Moon.

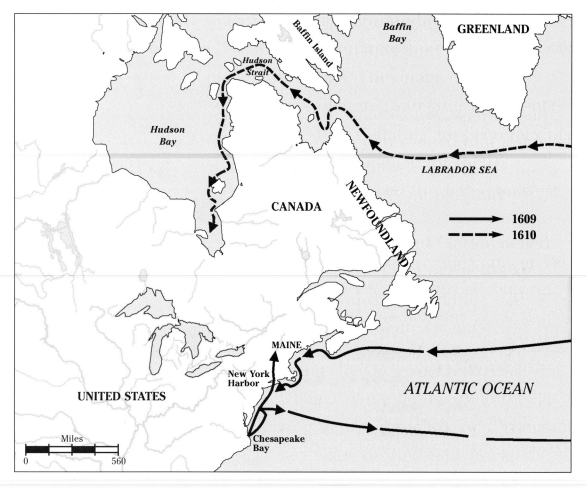

Hudson's voyages of 1609 and 1610.

crew they were going to seek the **Northwest Passage.** Like the Northeast Passage, the Northwest Passage was a long hoped-for link to the East, through the waters of the Canadian Arctic.

The ship reached the Atlantic coast of what is now Maine. They headed south as far as Chesapeake Bay. Heading north again, they entered New York Harbor, which had been discovered by **Giovanni da Verrazzano** in 1524. Hudson and his crew traded with the local Indians.

Hudson thought that the harbor was an entrance to the Northwest Passage. After sailing along the river that flowed north

300

from the harbor, he realized it was not the passage. He reached as far north as what is now Albany, New York, then turned back.

Years later, the river he navigated was named the Hudson River after him. The area he explored became New Amsterdam, then New York. Many Dutch settlers came to the region over the next hundred years. It became one of the most successful settlements in the **New World**.

Hudson headed home for Europe, stopping first in England. The English government ordered him to stay there. After hearing the tales of his third voyage, they wanted him to sail only for England.

FOURTH VOYAGE: Hudson's fourth and final voyage was sponsored by English businessmen. He and his crew, including his son, left England on the *Discovery* in April 1610. They sailed northwest, heading for Newfoundland. They sailed around the northern tip of Newfoundland and through what is now called the Hudson Strait. Hudson thought it must be the entry to the Northwest Passage.

Instead, they entered what is now called Hudson Bay. They sailed south, ending up in the southern part of the bay. They sailed for weeks, not knowing where they were. The crew became frightened. They thought that Hudson had gone mad.

They were forced to face a terrible winter in the bay. They almost died of cold and starvation. In the spring, the crew wanted to head for home. But Hudson wanted to continue west.

MUTINY: Several members of Hudson's crew staged a mutiny, taking command of the *Discovery*. They set Hudson, his son, and a few loyal sailors to drift in a small boat. That was in June 1611. None of them were ever seen again.

Hudson set to drift in Hudson Bay with his son and others.

The *Discovery* sailed back to England. The members of the crew who had staged the mutiny were dead by the time they reached home. None of the other crew members was punished in the case.

HIS DISCOVERY: Hudson never found the Northeast or the Northwest Passages. But he led four voyages that expanded the knowledge of the known world. His crews traveled further north than any previous expedition. He navigated the Hudson River, the Hudson Strait, and Hudson Bay. All of these are named for him. And his travel to what became New York led to the Dutch settlement of one of the most prosperous and important areas of the **New World**.

WORLD WIDE WEB SITES:

http://www.ianchadwick.com/hudson
http://www.mariner.org/age/hudson.html
http://www.newnetherland.org/
http://www.pbs.org/wnet/newyork/laic/episode1/topic1/e1_t1_
  s1-hh.html

Alexander von Humboldt
1769 - 1859
German Scientist and Explorer
Explored South America, Mexico, and the United States

ALEXANDER VON HUMBOLDT WAS BORN on September 14, 1769, in Berlin, in what is now Germany. His father was an army officer and his mother was a homemaker. Alexander had one brother, Wilhelm. His father died when he was nine.

ALEXANDER VON HUMBOLDT WENT TO SCHOOL at home until he was college-age. He and his brother studied languages, mathematics, and history with tutors. At first, Alexander wasn't a very good student. But in college he found a subject that fascinated him: plants.

Humboldt studied botany (plant life) at the University of Gottingen. He later studied geology—the study of rocks and the Earth—at the Freiburg School of Mines. He found two subjects that he loved. He spent his days studying geology in the mines, attending classes, and hunting for plant specimens.

FIRST JOBS: In 1792 Humboldt started working for the mining department of the government. He organized the mining of gold, copper, and other minerals.

BECOMING A SCIENTIFIC EXPLORER: In 1797, Humboldt left mining behind. He wanted to be a scientific explorer, and he wanted to explore South America. At that time, most of the continent was under Spanish control. Humboldt met with representatives of the Spanish government and got permission to explore.

Humboldt's mother had died and left him a large fortune. Using his own money, he put together an expedition to South America. His traveling companion was a French botanist named Aime Bonpland. They left Europe in 1799 for a five-year adventure in South America.

EXPLORING SOUTH AMERICA—THE ORINOCO RIVER: The two explorers started in Caracas, Venezuela. They headed south to the Apure River. Traveling by canoe, they took the Apure to the Orinoco. As they traveled, Humboldt made observations about the

305

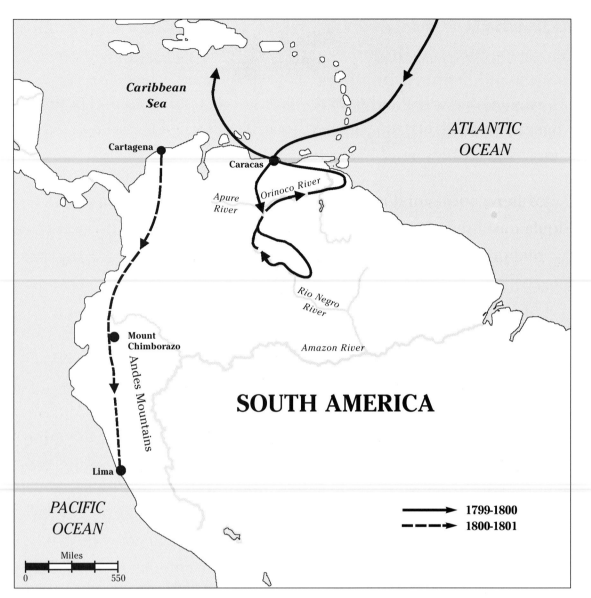

Humboldt's expeditions, 1799-1800 and 1800-1801.

Orinoco River. He studied how it was connected to the Amazon River through a natural canal system.

Traveling through the rain forests was difficult. Despite the heat and humidity, the two explorers learned much about the plants, animals, and land. They also visited tribes as they traveled. Humboldt kept a journal of close observations of people, places, and plants.

They traveled 1,700 miles on the Orinoco, and Humboldt mapped it. He also collected live birds and monkeys to take back to Europe.

At the end of his river journey, Humboldt visited Cuba. From there, he and Bonpland planned their next adventure. In 1800, they headed for the Andes Mountains.

THE ANDES: Starting in Cartagena, Colombia, the two explorers traveled through the Andes, stopping to observe the changing terrain and plant life. Humboldt studied the volcanoes in the area, and took careful notes. Later, his findings changed scientists' understanding of volcanoes.

The notes from Humboldt's travels also helped geographers create some of the first maps of South America. Humboldt also climbed some of the highest mountains in the world, including Mt. Chimborazo in Ecuador. He didn't reach the summit, but he climbed to 19,000 feet. It was a mountain-climbing record that wasn't broken for another 30 years.

Humboldt traveled as far as the Pacific Ocean in Lima, Peru. There, he noted a cold current that ran off the coast. That discovery led to the current being named for him. Humboldt was treated as an honored guest and famous explorer by the people of South America.

MEXICO: In 1803, Humboldt and Bonpland set out for Mexico. They spent the next year studying the people, plants, and geography. Everywhere he went, Humboldt made detailed notes on the weather. They are some of the first detailed weather data recorded. He also made one of the first maps of Mexico. He shared that map with President Thomas Jefferson.

MEETING THOMAS JEFFERSON: In May 1804, Humboldt visited the United States. He was greeted by President Thomas Jefferson. Humboldt's visit came as **Lewis and Clark** were making their famous explorations in the West. Humboldt and Jefferson became great friends.

RETURN TO EUROPE: Humboldt left the U.S. in June 1804. He lived in Paris for the next 23 years. There, he wrote about his journeys and explorations in a 30-volume collection. He knew many of the leading scientists of the day, and he shared his findings with them. He also sponsored young scientists in their studies.

In 1827, Humboldt returned to Berlin. He had spent all of his money, and he served his last years in the service of the King. He was the prince's tutor, and he served in the court.

In 1829, Humboldt visited mines in Russia and Siberia for the Czar. Back in Berlin, he continued his studies. In his last years he continued his scientific explorations into fields as varied as geography, geology, botany, and the Earth's magnetic fields. He wrote about his findings in a five-volume work of science for general readers. The work was a bestseller for many years.

Alexander von Humboldt died at the age of 90 in 1859. His long and active life had been devoted to science and exploration. At his death, another scientist said, "no individual scholar could hope any longer to master the world's knowledge about the Earth."

HIS DISCOVERY: One of the world's greatest scientists, **Charles Darwin**, called Humboldt: "the greatest scientific traveler who ever lived." For his discoveries in South America, and for his broad range of interests and scientific findings, Humboldt is considered one of the great men of his age.

WORLD WIDE WEB SITES:

http://www.humboldt.edu/~german/Alex/ALEX1.HTM
http://www.win.tue.nl/~engels/discovery/

Ibn Battuta

1304 - 1368?
"The Traveler of Islam"
Moroccan Who Visited All of the Muslim Nations
of His Era and Wrote One of the Most Famous
Travel Books of All Time

IBN BATTUTA WAS BORN on February 24, 1304, in Tangier, Morocco. He had a very long name: Abu 'abd Allan Muhammad Ibn 'abd Allah Al-lawatic At-tanji Ibn Battuta. He is referred to as Ibn Battuta (EE-bin bah-TOO-tah).

Ibn Battuta was raised in a family with many relatives who were judges. He also studied the law and later became a judge himself.

FIRST JOURNEY: Ibn Battuta was a Muslim, a follower of the religion called Islam. One of the most important requirements of Islam is that believers should make a trip to Mecca. That is a city in modern-day Saudi Arabia where Muhammad, the founder of Islam, was born. So Ibn Battuta prepared for his pilgrimage to Mecca, called a hajj.

In 1325, when he was 21, Ibn Battuta left Tangier for Mecca. He was sad to leave his family, but he was eager to travel. He journeyed east across the coast of North Africa. At first he traveled alone, then joined a caravan. Because so many people in North Africa were Muslim, there were often caravans going to Mecca.

The journey took Ibn Battuta through the ancient cities of Algiers, Tunis, Alexandria, and Cairo. Travel was often dangerous. Along the way, the group was attacked by robbers on camels. But it offered rewards, too. Another rule of Islam is to give to charity. Muslim pilgrims on their way to Mecca were treated with generosity. Wherever he traveled in the Muslim world, Ibn Battuta met people who gave him food, clothing, shelter, and more.

Ibn Battuta traveled south from Cairo along the Nile. He was unable to cross over the Red Sea to Saudi Arabia, so he returned north. He then traveled up into what is now Syria and Israel, then south to Mecca. He also visited the sacred city of Medina, where Muhammad is buried.

During breaks in his journeys, Ibn Battuta stopped in centers of Islamic learning to study. In this way, he gained a legal education, and became a judge. Through a combination of performing duties as an Islamic judge, as well as the generous charity of the people he met, Ibn Battuta made his living.

THE LOVE OF TRAVEL: After this first hajj, Ibn Battuta didn't return home. He loved to travel, and decided to continue on. He wanted to visit as many places as he could, and to "never travel any road a second time." Over the course of 29 years, he traveled some 75,000 miles.

After his first visit to Mecca, Ibn Battuta traveled to the Middle East. There, he explored what are now Iran, Iraq, and Azerbaijan. In 1330, he decided to visit Africa. He traveled as far as modern-day Tanzania. He returned to Mecca, following the coast of the Arabian Peninsula, visiting ports on the Persian Gulf.

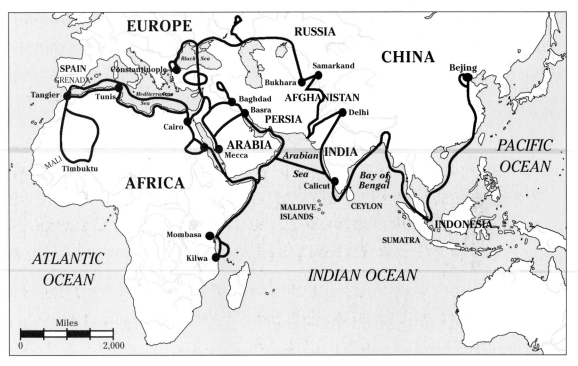

Ibn Battuta's journeys, 1325-1353.

TO INDIA: Next, Ibn Battuta decided to travel to India. His route took him through Egypt, Syria, Turkey, and further north. He reached as far north as the northern coast of the Black Sea. From there, he journeyed west to Constantinople.

Heading east, Ibn Battuta traveled to what is now Russia. He journeyed north along the Volga River, as far as modern-day Volgograd. Heading back south, he visited the ancient cities of Samarkand and Bukhara. Journeying south through Afghanistan, he crossed the forbidding Hindu Kush mountains.

Ibn Battuta finally reached the Indian city of Delhi. He spent several years there. He worked as a judge for a fierce sultan. Even though he was well-treated, Ibn Battuta knew that the sultan could be willful. He could praise someone one day, then condemn him to death the next.

The sultan asked Ibn Battuta to visit the emperor of China as his representative. He accepted, and he began another long journey. From Delhi he traveled south down the coast of India by boat. Along the way, his boat was attacked by pirates, then shipwrecked. All the gifts sent by the sultan for the Chinese rulers were lost.

Ibn Battuta went on to Ceylon (now Sri Lanka). He still wanted to get to China. He traveled by boat along the coast of the Bay of Bengal, stopping in Indonesia at Sumatra. From there, he sailed north to China. At last, in 1346, he reached the city of Beijing.

Then, Ibn Battuta headed home. It took him three years, but he returned to Morocco in 1349.

FINAL VOYAGES: Ibn Battuta journeyed out again in 1350. This time he traveled north to the Muslim area of southern Spain, Grenada. In 1352, he went on his last journey. He traveled to the African kingdom of Mali. In 1353, after traveling for 28 years and 75,000 miles, Ibn Battuta came home to stay.

WRITING THE "TRAVELS": Ibn Battuta was summoned to the court of the Sultan of Morocco. The Sultan delighted in his stories. He wanted them written down, so Ibn Battuta began telling his stories to a writer named Ibn Juzayy. The author wrote down his tales. They became a famous book, *The Travels of Ibn Battuta.*

It is on the basis of these tales that Ibn Battuta is known to us. They tell a rich tale of a man who had spent most of his life traveling and learning about the world. Ibn Battuta commented on the way people thought, how they lived, and what they believed in. He described people, places, and things with wisdom and wit. Some scholars say he exaggerated, and the little bits of poetry added by Ibn Juzayy also make the work fanciful at times.

But Ibn Battuta's book is a valuable record of a world now vanished. Over the years, his book was translated into many languages. It brought him fame as one of the greatest travelers of the Middle Ages.

MARRIAGE AND FAMILY: Like many Muslims of his time, Ibn Battuta had several wives and many children. In his travel book, he refers to marrying and divorcing many woman, but then doesn't discuss them again. He also had slaves that were given to him during his travels.

After completing the "Travels," Ibn Battuta became a judge. He died around 1368, and was buried in the town of his birth, Tangier.

HIS DISCOVERY: Ibn Battuta is remembered as the author of one of the most famous travel books ever written. He brought to life a world generally unknown to people of the Middle Ages.

WORLD WIDE WEB SITE:

http://nisus.sfusd.k12.ca.us/schwww/sch618/Ibn_Battuta/
 Ibn_Battuta_Rihla.html

Mae Jemison
1956-
American Scientist and Doctor
First African-American Woman to Travel in Space

MAE JEMISON WAS BORN October 17, 1956, in Decatur, Alabama. Her parents are Charlie and Dorothy Jemison. Mae's dad is a maintenance supervisor and her mom is a teacher. Mae has a sister, Ada, and a brother, Charles.

MAE JEMISON GREW UP in Chicago, where her family moved when she was four. Growing up, she had lots of friends and activities. She liked dance and sports and also loved to read and draw.

EARLY INTEREST IN SPACE: Jemison always knew she wanted to be an astronaut. She remembers watching the early space missions on TV. She knew she'd be a part of it.

"It was something I knew I wanted to do," she says. "I read lots of books about space. I don't remember the time I said, 'I want to be an astronaut'. It's just always been there."

"When I was about five or six years old, I used to look at the stars with my uncle. He would tell me they were just like the sun except they were millions of miles away. That was why they were so small. I have always been interested in astronomy and what goes on in the world. So I guess you could say I've been interested in space travel ever since I can remember."

MAE JEMISON WENT TO SCHOOL at the public schools in Chicago. The name of her grade school was Alexander Dumas Elementary School. She says she wasn't a straight-A student, although she did very well. "Maybe the reason I didn't get straight As was that I did stuff because I enjoyed it."

Jemison went on to high school at Morgan Park High. She did very well in math and science. She also enjoyed dancing and cheer-leading. Jemison graduated a year early, at age 16, and went on to college.

Jemison attended Stanford University in California. She studied both engineering and African studies and graduated in 1977. Then, she went to medical school at Cornell University, getting her degree in 1981. As a medical student, she traveled to Kenya and Thailand and provided medical care to people there.

MAE JEMISON'S FIRST JOBS: After her travels, Jemison knew she wanted to help out in poor countries. She joined the Peace Corps in

1983. That is a group that sends U.S. citizens to countries around the world to help out in many ways. Peace Corps volunteers use their skills to help people grow food, build homes, or fight disease. Jemison worked as a doctor in the African countries of Liberia (lie-BEER-ee-ah) and Sierra Leone (see-ER-uh lee-OHN) as a Peace Corps member.

Jemison holding miniature space shuttle.

BECOMING AN ASTRONAUT:

After two years in the Peace Corps, Jemison came back to the U.S. and began to work as a doctor. She was working in Los Angeles when she decided to apply to **NASA** — the National Aeronautics and Space Administration. NASA plans all the U.S. space missions and hires astronauts.

Jemison knew it might be tough to get into the space program. She was one of 2,000 people who applied to be an astronaut. Still, she wanted to fulfill her childhood dream.

In June 1987, she finally got the call she had been waiting for. She had been chosen to be an astronaut! She studied many different things to get ready to be an astronaut. She learned how to fly an airplane. She also used her training in medicine and engineering to understand how the body responds to space travel. As a scientist, she prepared for experiments in space.

Jemison with the crew of the Endeavor.
Front row, left to right, Jerome Apt and Curtis Brown; back row, N. Jan Davis,
Mark C. Lee, Robert Gibson, Jemison, and Mamoru Mohri.

BLAST OFF: It was five years before Jemison actually went into space. On September 12, 1992, Jemison and a crew of six blasted off. She spent eight days orbiting the Earth. While in space she studied motion sickness and took part in an experiment hatching frog eggs. These little tadpoles became the first creatures to develop in space.

After her space flight, Jemison became famous all over the world. She was the first black woman ever to be an astronaut. Children wrote to her from all over. In Detroit, a school was named for her. The Mae C. Jemison Academy is a grade school that specializes in math and science.

In 1993, Jemison left NASA. She started her own company, The Jemison Group. Her company brings medical help and money to poor countries around the world. She also runs a science camp for kids 12 to 16. "The whole idea of understanding the world around you is important to everyone," she says.

Jemison continues to work to bring new technology and scientific advances to people all around the world. At her science camp, students work together to answer tough questions that affect all of us. Some of their topics have included "How Many People Can the Earth Hold" and "What to Do with All This Garbage."

MAE JEMISON'S HOME AND FAMILY: Jemison is single and lives in Houston, Texas. She has a cat named Sneeze that she got while working in Africa. She still has a lot of hobbies, including reading and dancing. She also likes to travel and she loves art. She still draws and takes photographs, and she collects African art.

HER DISCOVERY: Jemison is remembered as the first African-American women to travel in space. She is also known for her commitment to science, and to getting young people and other African-Americans involved in science.

WORLD WIDE WEB SITES:

http://starchild.gsfc.nasa.gov/docs/StarChild/whos_who_level2/
    jemison.html
http://www.princeton.edu/~mcbrown/display/jemison.html
http://www.quest.arc.nasa.gov/women/TODTWD/jemison.bio.html

Louis Jolliet

1645-1700
French Explorer and Cartographer
Explored the Mississippi River with Jacques Marquette

LOUIS JOLLIET WAS BORN in 1645 in Quebec in what is now
Canada. When he was born, it was called **"New France."** His last
name is pronounced "zho-lee-ET." It is also spelled "Joliet." His
parents were Jean Jolliet and Marie d'Abancourt. He had two
brothers named Adrien and Zacharie. Jolliet was the first important
European explorer born in the **New World**.

LOUIS JOLLIET WENT TO SCHOOL at a Catholic school in
Quebec. As a young man, he loved music and learned to play

several instruments. Jolliet studied to be a Jesuit priest, but he never became one. He left Quebec in 1667 and traveled to France. There, he studied cartography (mapmaking).

RETURNING TO CANADA: In 1668, Jolliet returned to Canada and became a fur trader. He traded goods throughout French Canada and what is now Michigan for several years.

MEETING JACQUES MARQUETTE: Jacques Marquette was a Catholic missionary from France. He had lived and taught among the Indians of Quebec and Michigan for several years when, around 1671, he met Jolliet.

By this time, Jolliet and Marquette had heard from the Indians about a great river that ran south. It was the Mississippi River. The French wanted to explore it. They thought it might lead them to the Pacific Ocean. If it did, it would be an important trade route for them.

In 1673, Jolliet and Marquette got permission to explore the Mississippi. Jolliet would explore for the benefit of the people of New France. Marquette would teach religion to the native peoples they met.

EXPLORING THE MISSISSIPPI: Jolliet and Marquette left St. Ignace in May 1674. They had a crew of five, with two canoes. They traveled west along the northern coast of Lake Michigan, stopping at Green Bay, Wisconsin. They traveled west from there on the Fox River. Then they followed the Wisconsin River to the Mississippi. Along the way, they met the Illinois tribe. They were very friendly to the French explorers. They even gave them a peace pipe for their journey.

Marquette and Jolliet entered the Mississippi on June 17, 1674. They were the first French explorers ever to reach it. They followed

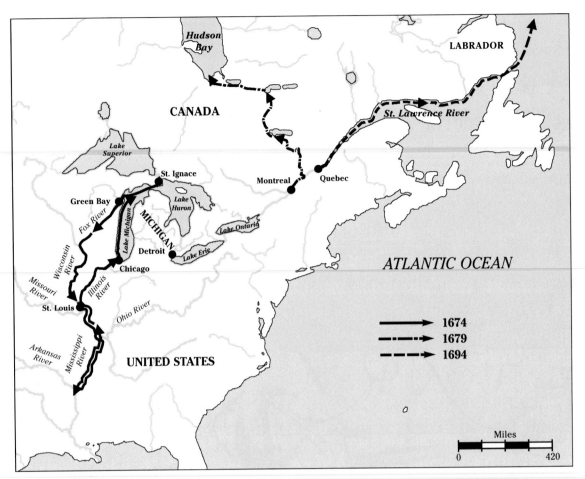

Jolliet's voyage with Marquette in 1674; Voyages of 1679 and 1694.

the river south, noting where other powerful rivers, like the Missouri and the Ohio, entered. They hoped that they had found the route to the west. They thought they would reach the Pacific by continuing to the west.

But it soon became clear that the river traveled south. They realized they would reach the Gulf of Mexico if they continued in that direction.

They went only as far south as the Arkansas River. They knew they had reached the area under Spanish control. As Marquette wrote later, they feared falling "into the hands of the Spaniards."

322

If that happened, no one would ever know of their important discoveries.

Marquette and Jolliet headed north in July 1674. They traveled up the Mississippi, fighting a strong current. Then they took the Illinois River further north. They took the Chicago River to Lake Michigan, and on to Green Bay. Marquette died soon after their return, in 1675.

FATHER JOLIET AND MARQUETTE DESCENDING THE MISSISSIPPI.

Jolliet settled in Quebec and became a trader once again. He was also given land, including Anticosti Island in the St. Lawrence River. In 1679, the French became concerned about the English traders trying to take over their territory. They hired Jolliet to spy on the British traders in the Hudson Bay area. He traveled to the area and reported back to the French authorities.

EXPLORING LABRADOR: In 1694, Jolliet led an expedition to Labrador. The crew of 18 traveled north through the Strait of Belle Isle and Eskimo Bay. They traded with the local Indians, and Jolliet made notes and measurements for maps. They returned to Quebec when the weather became too cold.

Jolliet continued to trade and to make maps of the regions he'd explored. In 1697, he was named a professor of mapmaking at the College of Quebec. He died in 1700, possibly while traveling to his land in the St. Lawrence.

LOUIS JOLLIET'S HOME AND FAMILY: Jolliet married a woman named Claire-Francoise Bissot after his return from the Mississippi. He became a leading figure in the Quebec colony. One source says he played the organ at the cathedral there.

HIS DISCOVERY: Jolliet's expedition to the Mississippi paved the way for French exploration in the Mississippi Valley.

WORLD WIDE WEB SITES:

http://www.civilization.ca/vmnf/explor/jolli_e2.html
http://www.win.tue.nl/~engels/discovery/jolmar.html

Mary Henrietta Kingsley
1862 - 1900
English Explorer of West and Central Africa

MARY HENRIETTA KINGSLEY WAS BORN on October 13, 1862, in London, England. Her father was a doctor. She had one brother, Charles.

MARY HENRIETTA KINGSLEY WENT TO SCHOOL at home, where she was taught by her father. She had no formal schooling and very little contact with people.

The family moved to Cambridge, England, in 1886. Both of her parents were quite ill, and they both died in 1892. After their deaths, Kingsley decided she would travel.

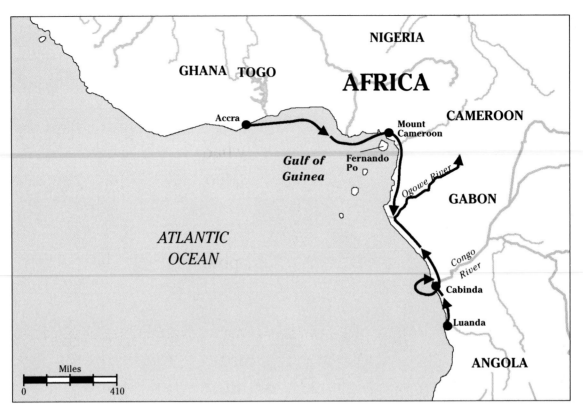

Kingsley's expeditions 1893-1895.

FIRST TRIP TO AFRICA: Kingsley's father had been working on a book about West African religions and law when he died. She decided she would continue his research. She went to West Africa in August 1893. She landed first in Luanda (now in Angola). She traveled north, to what is now Cabinda, at the mouth of the Congo River (now the Zaire). She traveled as far north as the island of Fernando Po. Throughout her trip, she gathered beetles and fish. When she returned to England in 1894, she gave the specimens to the British Museum.

RETURN TO AFRICA: Kingsley returned to Africa in late 1894. This time, her travels took her to Accra (in modern Ghana), then to Calabar (in modern Nigeria). She went on the Ogowe River in

Gabon. She traveled up the river as far as she could by boat. Then she took a canoe further inland. She visited the Fang people, taking notes on their religion and culture. She also collected more insects, plants, and fish for the British Museum.

On her return down the river, Kingsley had several extraordinary experiences. She fought a crocodile and a leopard, fell into spear traps, and saw a gorilla. At that time, few Europeans had ever encountered a gorilla. She later wrote about seeing the gorilla travel through the bush. "It is a graceful, powerful, superbly perfect hand-trapeze performance."

Kingsley traveled back toward the African coast. She climbed the 13,428-foot Mount Cameroon. She was the first woman to climb it. It is still an active volcano, and the highest peak in West Africa.

When she returned to England in 1895, Kingsley wrote a book about her experiences. She also began to lecture on her travels. She captivated audiences with her adventures. Her travels brought important findings in science, too. She brought back specimens of fish that had never been known to European scientists.

Kingsley's first book, *Travels in West Africa*, was such a success that she wrote another, *West African Studies*. She passionately believed that African people and cultures were threatened by out-side forces. She was especially critical of European missionaries, whom, she felt, were out to destroy the native way of life. Instead, she defended the original tribal religions of the West Africans.

FINAL TRIP: Kingsley journeyed to Africa one more time. She went to South Africa, where the Boer War was raging. She served as a nurse to soldiers, and in doing that, she caught typhoid fever and died on June 3, 1900. She was only 38 years old.

HER DISCOVERY: Kingsley was an important explorer who contributed scientific and cultural discoveries. She believed that the cultures and religions of the African people deserved respect. Her books and lectures shed light on a world little known to 19th-century Europeans.

WORLD WIDE WEB SITE:

http://africanhistory.about.com/library/weekly/aa01102a.htm

Rene-Robert Cavelier, Sieur de La Salle

1643 - 1687
French Explorer of the Mississippi River
Claimed the Mississippi River Region for France,
Named it "Louisiana"

RENE-ROBERT CAVELIER, SIEUR DE LA SALLE WAS BORN on November 22, 1643, in Rouen, France. His name when he was born was Rene-Robert Cavelier. His parents were Catherine and Jean Cavelier. The "Sieur" portion of his name was added later, by King Louis XIV of France. "Sieur" is a title, meaning "Lord." "La Salle" was the name of the family estate in France. He is known as "La Salle."

La Salle went to school at a Catholic school. He studied to be a Jesuit priest. But when he was about 20, he decided he'd rather be an explorer.

NEW FRANCE: La Salle left France in 1666. He sailed to Montreal, Canada, which was part of **New France** at that time. He was given land and became a farmer and fur trader.

La Salle was very successful, but he was still eager to explore. Like earlier French colonists, he had heard of a great waterway inland from Montreal. It was the Mississippi River. The French wanted to explore it. They thought it might lead them to the Pacific Ocean. If it did, it would be an important trade route for them.

VOYAGE OF 1669: La Salle began his first explorations in 1669. He sold his land and set out to explore what is now Ohio. He followed the Ohio River, hoping it would lead him east to the Pacific. His crew included eight canoes, trading goods, and several priests.

He didn't reach the Mississippi on that expedition. In 1673, **Louis Jolliet** and **Jacques Marquette** led the first expedition down the Mississippi.

FRONTENAC: In 1673, Frontenac, the governor of **New France**, sent La Salle to the north shore of Lake Ontario. There, near modern-day Kingston, Ontario, he met with the local Indians, the Iroquois. Frontenac wanted to protect the French fur trade in the area. The Indians agreed to allow the French to build a fort to protect their interests.

MEETING KING LOUIS: In 1677, La Salle returned to France to meet with King Louis XIV. He wanted the King to allow him to explore

The building of the Griffin.

"the western parts of New France." He also wanted to build forts and control part of the fur trade. King Louis agreed, but La Salle had to raise the money for the expedition himself.

La Salle sailed back to New France. With him on the journey was **Louis Hennepin**, a priest who would explore with him. Also on the journey was an Italian soldier named Tonty. He became La Salle's friend and fellow explorer.

La Salle and his comrades built a new fort, near Niagara Falls. He also built a merchant ship, the *Griffin*. It was the first merchant ship in the Great Lakes. La Salle hoped to use the *Griffin* to trade

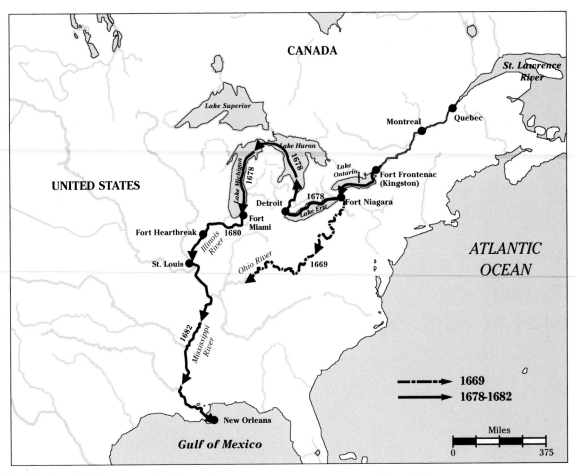

La Salle's voyages of 1669 and 1678-1682.

furs. In 1678, La Salle, Hennepin, and Tonty sailed on the *Griffin* through Lakes Erie, St. Clair, Huron, and Michigan, ending at the southern end of Lake Michigan. They loaded the boat with goods and sent it back to Niagara Falls. Sadly, the ship and all its cargo were lost along the way.

La Salle built another fort, Fort Miami, near modern-day St. Joseph, Michigan. Now he began his quest to find the Mississippi.

THE MISSISSIPPI: La Salle and his crew of 23 Frenchmen and 18 Indians set out in 1680. They traveled down the Kankakee and

Illinois Rivers. They built another fort, Fort Heartbreak, near what is now Peoria, Illinois.

But the expedition faced many problems. Part of the crew, including Hennepin, was captured by Indians while exploring a branch of the Illinois River. Fort Heartbreak was also destroyed.

La Salle was determined to follow the Mississippi to its end. Finally, in April 1682, La Salle and Tonty reached the Gulf of Mexico.

CLAIMING LOUISIANA FOR FRANCE: La Salle held a ceremony in which he claimed the entire area—one half of North America—for France. He named it "Louisiana" in honor of his King.

La Salle traveled back up the Mississippi. He built a new fort, called "St. Louis." He asked the leaders of New France for help to build a settlement. But the new governor refused.

RETURN TO FRANCE:
La Salle returned to France. He met with King Louis and asked him to reverse the governor's decision. King Louis did, and he also agreed to La Salle's plan to build a permanent French settlement at the mouth of the Mississippi. The expedition had another purpose: to try to take lands claimed by Spain.

The Griffin.

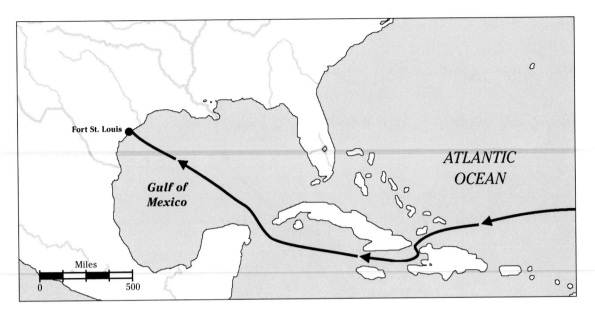

La Salle's voyage of 1684.

FINAL VOYAGE: La Salle returned to the **New World** as head of a huge expedition. In August 1684, he led 300 colonists, on four ships, from France to the Gulf of Mexico. There, they were to find the entrance to the Mississippi and build a colony.

This final voyage of La Salle was a disaster. One ship was sunk by the Spanish, and the other three sailed past the entrance to the Mississippi. La Salle landed on the coast of what is now Texas in 1685. They were in the Matagorda Bay, 500 miles west of the Mississippi. One of the three remaining ships ran aground. The commander of another ship sailed back to France.

The remaining ship, under La Salle's command, tried to find the Mississippi. That ship, too, was wrecked on the coast of Texas. The remaining colonists built a fort, Fort St. Louis. They suffered from hunger and illness, and many died. They were later attacked by hostile Indian tribes.

In January 1687, La Salle took a party of 17 men and headed north. Three months later, La Salle was killed by his own men, near Navasota, Texas.

HIS DISCOVERY: La Salle is a controversial figure in the history of exploration. He had great goals, but he had trouble achieving them. His life and last expedition ended in tragedy and failure.

Yet La Salle is remembered for navigating the length of the Mississippi and for claiming Louisiana for the French. That led to French control of the Mississippi Valley for many years.

WORLD WIDE WEB SITES:

http://www.civilization.ca/vmnf/explor/lasal_e2.html
http://www.sec.state.la.us/archives/lasalle/lasalle-b.htm

Leo Africanus
1485? - 1554?
Arab Traveler Who Explored Africa South of the Sahara Desert

LEO AFRICANUS WAS BORN around 1485 in Grenada, Spain. He came from a Muslim Arabic family. "Leo Africanus" is the name he was given as an adult. His name when he was born was al-Hassan ibn Muhammad al-Wizaz al-Fasi. He was called "al-Fasi." His ancestors had come to Grenada from Morocco. They were called "Moors," because of their Moroccan background.

King Ferdinand and Queen Isabella were the rulers of Spain when Leo Africanus was young. In 1492, they conquered Grenada and added it to Spain. Ferdinand and Isabella were Christians, and they wanted Spain to be only for Christians. Many Muslims and Jews had been living in Spain for centuries. But the rulers demanded that they either convert to Christianity or leave the country.

So in 1492, the Muslims and Jews who would not convert were banished from Spain. Among the Muslims who were forced to leave was the family of al-Fasi. They moved to Morocco, to the city of Fez. There, al-Fasi studied law and Islam.

THE LIFE OF A TRAVELER: After he completed school, al-Fasi began to travel. Many of his travels were for his work as a merchant and diplomat. His journeys took him across the Mediterranean to the Middle East and Turkey. He also traveled across North Africa to Egypt, and south of the Sahara Desert to Mali and Niger. He visited the legendary city of Timbuktu.

CAPTURED BY PIRATES: In 1518, while sailing on the Mediterranean, al-Fasi was captured by pirates. They took him to the Pope in Rome. There, he was presented as a slave to Pope Leo X. The Pope was astonished by his intelligence and learning. He freed him. He also gave him the name by which we know him, Leo Africanus.

The Pope named him "Leo," after himself, and "Africanus," meaning "from Africa" in Latin. Leo Africanus decided to convert to Christianity.

A POPULAR SCHOLAR: Leo Africanus became a popular scholar in Rome. He taught languages and wrote books. The most famous book he wrote was about his journeys throughout Africa and the Middle East.

THE HISTORY AND DESCRIPTION OF AFRICA: In *The History and Description of Africa,* Leo Africanus described a world unknown to most Europeans. He had traveled to Africa south of the Sahara Desert. He explored the ancient cities of Gao and Timbuktu. He described all of these places in his book.

HIS DISCOVERY: Leo Africanus's vivid descriptions of the people and cultures of Africa amazed the Europeans of his time. He described the way the people dressed, the architecture of their homes, and the way that they lived. It offered many Europeans their first glimpse into the world of Africa. His book was one of the main sources of information on Africa for several hundred years.

Leo Africanus moved back to what is now Tunisia in his later years. He died in the city of Tunis around 1550. He died before his book was published, and he never knew how famous it became.

WORLD WIDE WEB SITE:

http://www.wsu.edu:8080/~wldciv/world_civ_reader/world_civ_reader_2/leo_africanus.html

Meriwether Lewis

1774 - 1809
American Explorer
Co-Leader of the Lewis and Clark Expedition

MERIWETHER LEWIS WAS BORN on August 18, 1774, in Albemarle County, Virginia. His parents were William Lewis and Lucy Meriwether Lewis. He was the second of three children. He had an older sister named Jane and a younger brother named Reuben.

William Lewis was a wealthy landowner whose large plantation was worked by slaves. Lucy was a homemaker known for caring for the local folk with herbal medicines. Meriwether grew up near the plantation of Thomas Jefferson. Jefferson, a family friend, became the third President of the United States.

Meriwether Lewis didn't have a chance to know his father. In 1775, William Lewis enlisted in the army fighting the Revolutionary War. In 1779, he died of pneumonia after his horse drowned in a raging flood. In 1780, his mother married Captain John Marks. Meriwether soon had two more siblings, John and Mary.

MERIWETHER LEWIS GREW UP loving to roam the Virginia countryside. He was curious and active, and he loved to explore. When he was around eight years old, he moved to Georgia. It was his first real adventure, and he loved it.

Meriwether helped move the family, with livestock and all personal things, the many miles to Georgia. Every day they walked, hunted, and fished. At night they set up camp. Meriwether soon showed his talent for hunting, fishing, and finding his way in the wilderness. He didn't wear shoes, even in winter. He hunted in the snow in his bare feet.

Lewis lived in Georgia for about four years. In addition to learning the ways of the wilderness, he learned to recognize different kinds of plants from his mother. Many of these were the ones she used to make medicines.

MERIWETHER LEWIS WENT TO SCHOOL for the first time when he was 13. He had learned to read and write in Georgia, but at 13 he returned to Virginia for formal schooling.

Over the next several years, Lewis studied with tutors. He took courses in Latin, math, science, and English. He also loved reading about explorers. **Captain James Cook** was a special favorite.

Lewis's schooling ended in 1792, when he was 18. Captain Marks, his mother's second husband, had died. His mother wanted to return to Virginia, and Lewis took charge of moving her and all the household back. They settled at the family estate, Locust Hill, which he had inherited from his father.

During the next two years, Lewis ran the plantation. He oversaw the farming and other daily activities. He also still loved to roam.

BECOMING A SOLDIER: In 1794, Lewis joined the army. He spent six years in the service, becoming a captain in 1800. His life as a soldier allowed him the freedom to travel in what was still wilderness at the time. In 1795 he served briefly in the company of **William Clark**. Clark would later join Lewis to lead the most important American expedition ever assembled.

SECRETARY TO PRESIDENT THOMAS JEFFERSON: Thomas Jefferson was elected President in 1800, and he asked Lewis to become his private secretary. Over the next three years, Lewis lived at the White House with Jefferson.

Jefferson had great plans for the new nation. He wanted to finance an expedition to the far western portion of the continent. Like so many before him, Jefferson wanted to find the **Northwest Passage**. He wanted to find a waterway that connected the known rivers of the West and that led to the Pacific. He wanted the U.S. to lay claim to the natural resources of the West, including possible trade routes. He knew of the travels of **Alexander Mackenzie**. In fact, he and Lewis read Mackenzie's book on his travels in the Canadian northwest with great interest. Jefferson had also seen the maps of **George Vancouver**. He wanted the United States — not England, Spain, or France — to claim the West.

Frontispiece   Page.220.

A Canoe striking on a Tree,

Lewis and Clark expedition.

Jefferson asked Congress to fund an expedition to explore the West. He had Lewis put together a budget, which came to $2,500, for the exploration. Congress approved the project.

THE LOUISIANA PURCHASE: While he was planning the expedition, Jefferson was also organizing the purchase of a vast amount of territory from France. It was called the Louisiana Purchase. The territory ranged from the Mississippi River to the Rocky Mountains, and from the Canadian border to Texas. It cost the U.S. $15 million, about three cents an acre. The Louisiana Purchase doubled the size of the U.S.

THE LEWIS AND CLARK EXPEDITION: Jefferson chose Lewis to put together an expedition to explore the American West. He was clear about what he expected of the expedition. They were to follow the Missouri River out of St. Louis, looking for a waterway to the Pacific Ocean. They knew the Missouri would lead them to a mountain range — the Rockies. They thought it would be similar in size and scope to the Appalachians. They also knew another river system, the Columbia, flowed into the Pacific on the west coast. Jefferson wanted to find a waterway that connected the two river systems.

The new American government also needed to know all about the western lands. They needed maps, with information about rivers, mountains, and terrain. They needed to know about the plants, animals, and opportunities for trade and settlement. They also needed to know about the many Indian tribes in the vast area. What were they like? Were they peaceful or warlike? And how would they feel about their new leader, Jefferson?

Preparation: Lewis began to prepare for his expedition in the spring of 1803. He studied botany, medicine, and navigation. All these skills, as well as his leadership ability, would be crucial to the success of the expedition.

Also crucial to his success was his choice of a co-commander. He wrote to his old friend and fellow officer William Clark. He told Clark of the planned expedition and asked if he'd like to join. Clark wrote back and said he'd be delighted to accept the offer.

In July 1803, Lewis went to Pittsburgh to pick up the keelboat built for the journey. It was a big boat — 55 feet long. They would use it, and two smaller boats, called "pirogues," for the trip. Lewis took the keelboat down the Ohio River and up the Mississippi to St. Louis, Missouri, the point of departure for the expedition. There, he put together his company and supplies.

The Corps of Discovery: In St. Louis, Lewis and Clark hired men to join them in a group they called the "Corps of Discovery." When they began the journey, the Corps numbered 33 men. They came from many different backgrounds. Some were traders, some were soldiers. Another member of the group was Seaman, Lewis's Newfoundland dog.

Departure — May 14, 1804: The Corps of Discovery left St. Louis on May 14, 1804. Lewis recorded in his journal that they "proceeded on under a gentle breeze up the Missouri." The boats were traveling upstream, against the current. Sometimes they could sail the boats. But when there was no wind, they had to row them, use poles to push them, and even tow them with ropes from the shore.

In August 1804, Lewis held a meeting with Indian chiefs near what is now Omaha, Nebraska. He gave the Indians gifts, including "Peace Medals." These were medals with a picture of President Jefferson on one side, and a pair of shaking hands and a "peace pipe" on the other. He told the Indians of their new "father" (Jefferson). This "head chief of the United States" would protect them, Lewis said.

Later that month, a member of the Corps named Sgt. Charles Floyd died, probably of appendicitis. He was the only member to die during the expedition. The remaining crew continued up the Missouri, meeting new Indian tribes, some friendly, some hostile. As they traveled, Lewis kept a journal with detailed observations of people, plants, and animals.

Fort Mandan: In October 1804, as winter neared, they stopped near what is now Bismarck, North Dakota. There, near the camps of the Mandan and Hidatsa tribes, they made their winter camp.

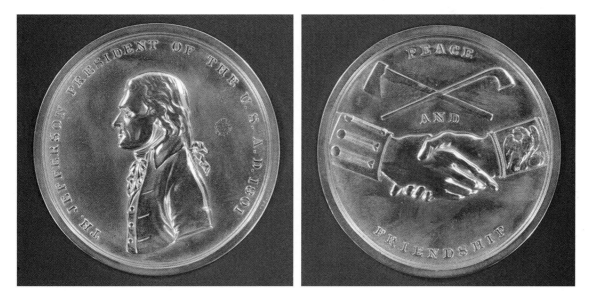

Peace Medal (left) depicting President Thomas Jefferson, and (right) depicting a pair of shaking hands and a peace pipe, given by Lewis and Clark to the Indian tribes they met on their expedition.

The men built a triangular-shaped fort, which they named "Fort Mandan" for the local Indian tribe. During the next five months, they hunted and made tools. They had brought the materials to make a forge, and they made tools to trade with the Indians for food.

Sacagawea: Among the Indians they met was a young woman of the Shoshone tribe named **Sacagawea** (sah-CAH-guh-wee-ah). She had been kidnapped when she was just 12 years old in a raid against her people, from her home in what is now Idaho. She had later been sold to a French-Canadian trader named Toussaint Charbonneau. She now lived with Charbonneau as one of his two Indian "wives." Sacagawea was never Charbonneau's legal wife. Instead, she was really a slave.

When Sacagawea met Lewis and Clark, she was about 17 years old and pregnant with her first child. Because she and Charbonneau spoke several Indian languages, they were valuable to the expedition as translators. The Corps would also be traveling through Shoshone land, and Sacagawea could help them as a guide. So Lewis and Clark hired Sacagawea and Charbonneau. In February 1805, Sacagawea gave birth to a son, Jean Baptiste Charbonneau. Lewis helped in delivering the baby.

Starting Off Again—April 1805: When the Corps left Fort Mandan in April 1805, Sacagawea went with them, along with Charbonneau and their infant son. They traveled in the pirogues and six canoes. Lewis sent the keelboat back down the river to St. Louis. It was too large to navigate the river well. In the boat were journals, maps, and plant and animal specimens for Jefferson.

Lewis was in high spirits as they left Fort Mandan. "This little fleet altho' not quite so respectable as those of Columbus or Capt. Cook, were still viewed by us with as much pleasure as those deservedly famed adventurers ever beheld theirs," he wrote. "We were now about to penetrate a country at least two thousand miles in width, on which the foot of civilized man had never trodden." He wrote about how long he'd dreamed of the moment. He called it "among the most happy of my life."

The Corps crossed into Montana. They saw huge herds of buffalo, elk, and deer. They also saw a Grizzly bear for the first time. One chased a crewman up a tree.

During a storm, the boat holding the maps and journals nearly capsized. Sacagawea calmly saved the precious documents. Soon the Corps saw the immense Rocky Mountains.

A Fork in the River: The men reached a point where the Missouri divided into a northern and a southern route, or "fork." They chose

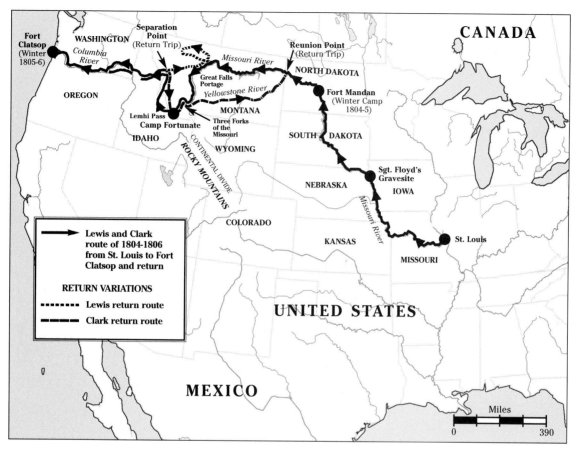

The Lewis and Clark expedition, 1804-1806.

the southern path, and they soon reached waterfalls. Lewis knew the path was the right one, because the Indians had told him to expect the waterfalls. They were near what is now Great Falls, Montana.

A Long Portage: The boats could not travel over waterfalls, so the crew had to make a long, difficult portage. That is, they had to carry their boats overland. They actually built wheels out of cottonwood, which they attached to the boats. But the 18-mile trip still took them three weeks. Finally, they reached a point in the river where they could put the boats back in the water.

Three Forks of the Missouri: The next major landmark they came to was a place where the Missouri divided into three forks. They named them for three famous Americans. They named one the "Madison," in honor of the Secretary of State (and later President) James Madison. Another was named the "Gallatin," for Secretary of the Treasury Albert Gallatin. And one they named for their President and sponsor, Jefferson. They followed the Jefferson west.

The Continental Divide: In August 1805, Lewis and Clark reached the Continental Divide. That is a point at the crest of the Rocky Mountains where rivers flow either eastward, toward the Mississippi River, or westward, toward the Pacific Ocean.

As Lewis walked to the top of the ridge, he expected to see plains on the other side that led to the Columbia River and the ocean. Instead, he saw the Bitterroot Range of the Rockies. Their hopes to find the Northwest Passage were dashed. The Rockies were much more vast, in size and scope, than they had ever imagined. Their route would be longer, and harder.

Sacagawea Reunited with her People: Continuing down the other side of the divide, Sacagawea began to recognize the land. She knew she was close to her home. Lewis decided to scout ahead and meet the Shoshone. He met several Shoshone women, then several men. He led them back to the crew, and to everyone's astonishment, Sacagawea recognized an old friend. It was a wonderful reunion. But the greatest surprise came when she recognized her brother, Cameahwait, now the chief. When she saw him, "she jumped up, ran, and embraced him," wrote Lewis. She "threw her blanket over him and cried profusely."

Captains Lewis & Clark holding a Council with the Indians   Page 17

Lewis and Clark expedition.

They named their camp, near the Lemhi Pass, "Camp Fortunate." Lewis and Clark traded with the Shoshone for horses. They knew that their canoes would be of no use in going over the mountains. They would now begin the overland part of their journey. They hired a Shoshone guide named Old Toby. Then they began the difficult crossing of the Bitterroot Mountains.

They crossed from what is now Montana into Idaho. The weather was fierce, and they were near starvation. Once over the mountains, they met members of the Nez Perce tribe. This friendly group gave them food and shelter.

The crew left their horses with the Nez Perce, built new canoes, and proceeded on the Clearwater River. In October, they reached the Snake River, and from that, the Columbia. The river was fierce, with many rapids and waterfalls. Once again, they had to make difficult portages.

The Pacific Ocean: In November 1805, they reached the Pacific Ocean. Clark wrote in his journal of the "great joy in camp" as they reached "this great Pacific Ocean" they had "been so long anxious to see." They had traveled over 4,000 miles in 554 days.

The Corps spent the next four months on the Pacific coast, near what is now Astoria, Oregon. They built a fort, named Fort Clatsop after a local tribe. They hunted and fished, and built a salt-making camp. With salt, they could preserve meat and fish for the long trip east.

The Journey Home: In March 1806, the Corps began the journey home. They canoed back up the Columbia, finally reaching the Nez Perce. They got their horses back, and tried to cross the Bitterroots. But their path was blocked with snow and ice. They waited until the snow melted, then made their way across the mountains.

The Corps Divides: In July 1806, the Corps separated into two groups. Lewis wanted to explore possible northern routes that could be used by later settlers. He took a group north into the Marias River region. There, near the Canadian border, they had a brief battle with a group of Blackfeet Indians. The groups exchanged gunfire, and two Indians were killed. They were the only Indian deaths of the expedition.

Clark chose a southern route. His group crossed the Rockies, then took the Jefferson River as far as Three Forks. The Clark group divided again, and he explored the Yellowstone River region. Clark named an unusual sandstone formation for Sacagawea's son. He called it "Pompy," his nickname for Jean Baptiste. He also wrote his name and the date on the rock. It can still be found, near Billings, Montana.

All the groups came together where the Yellowstone and the Missouri Rivers meet, in August 1806. Lewis had been wounded in a hunting accident, but he was mending.

Sacagawea Leaves: The Corps reached Fort Mandan on August 17, 1806. Sacagawea left the group and remained in the area with Charbonneau and her son.

THE HEROES' RETURN: On September 23, 1806, the Corps of Discovery returned to St. Louis to a heroes' welcome. They had been given up for dead, and all America rejoiced at their return. They had traveled more than 8,000 miles in their two-year journey.

After their triumphant return to St. Louis, Lewis wrote his report to Jefferson. He knew the President would be disappointed to learn there was no Northwest Passage. But he was confident that the route they had forged could be used for later explorers and settlers. "In obedience to your orders we have penetrated the continent of North America to the Pacific Ocean," he wrote. "And sufficiently explored the interior of the country to affirm with confidence that we have discovered the most practicable route which does exist across the continent by means of navigable branches of the Missouri and Columbia Rivers." His journals brimmed with detailed reports of plants, animals, and close observations of the Indian tribes they'd met. They provided information used by generations.

LIFE AFTER THE EXPEDITION: Lewis returned to the Washington area, where he lived for several years. He worked on his journals, which he planned to publish. He received his payment for leading the expedition, which included 1,600 acres of land and $1,200. But he was restless and unhappy.

In 1807, Jefferson appointed Lewis to be Governor of the Upper Louisiana Territory. But this active, vigorous explorer wasn't made for a job in government. He soon had problems, both professional and personal. He wasn't an effective governor, and he began to drink heavily. Jefferson and Clark both knew him well. They knew that he could become depressed, and they worried about their friend.

DEATH: In October 1809, Lewis was traveling along the Natchez Trace in Tennessee. He stopped at an inn. On October 11, 1809, Lewis died of gunshot wounds. Most historians believe he died by his own hand. It was a tragic end to a life of accomplishment and promise.

HIS DISCOVERY: Lewis is remembered as one of the most important explorers of the American West. His expedition opened up the land to settlement, paving the way for the expansion of the country to the shores of the Pacific. Jefferson had once described him as a man of "courage undaunted," and he is remembered for his wholehearted devotion to the expedition that bears his name.

WORLD WIDE WEB SITES:

http://www.lewisandclark.org/
http://www.lewisandclarkeducationcenter.com/
http://www.loc.gov/exhibits/lewisandclark/lewisandclark.html
http://www.nps.gov/lecl/
http://nwrel.org/teachlewisandclark/home.html
http://www.pbs.org/lewisandclark/

David Livingstone
1813 - 1873
Scottish Missionary and Explorer of Africa
Discovered Victoria Falls and Many African Landmarks
Rescued by Henry Stanley in 1871

DAVID LIVINGSTONE WAS BORN on March 19, 1813, in Blantyre, Scotland, near the large city of Glasgow. His family was very poor. He was one of seven children, and the family lived in a one-room apartment. It was next to the local cotton mill, where his father worked. David and his siblings started to work there, too, while they were still children.

GOING TO WORK AT THE AGE OF TEN: When he was ten years old, Livingstone went to work at the cotton mill. He worked 14 hours a day, from 6 a.m to 8 p.m.

After 14 hours of work, at 8 p.m. at night, Livingstone went to night school with the other mill children. Most of the children slept, but David was determined to get an education. He stayed up late and studied almost every night.

BECOMING A MISSIONARY: Livingstone's parents were both devout Christians. By the 1830s, Livingstone was planning to become a medical missionary. He wanted to travel to other countries and teach his religious beliefs. He studied religion and went to medical school in Glasgow in the winter, and worked in the mill in the summer.

Livingstone had hoped to become a missionary in China. But by 1839, China was fighting a war. He heard a lecture by Robert Moffat, a Christian missionary who worked in southern Africa. Livingstone decided to become a missionary to Africa.

GOING TO AFRICA: Livingstone arrived in Cape Town, South Africa, in March 1841. He went first to Robert Moffat's mission at Kuruman. But Livingstone wanted to go to Central Africa. He wanted to meet other tribes, to learn their languages, and to teach them about Christianity.

Livingstone also loved to explore. He traveled deep into Central Africa. In 1842, he traveled into the Kalahari Desert (in modern-day

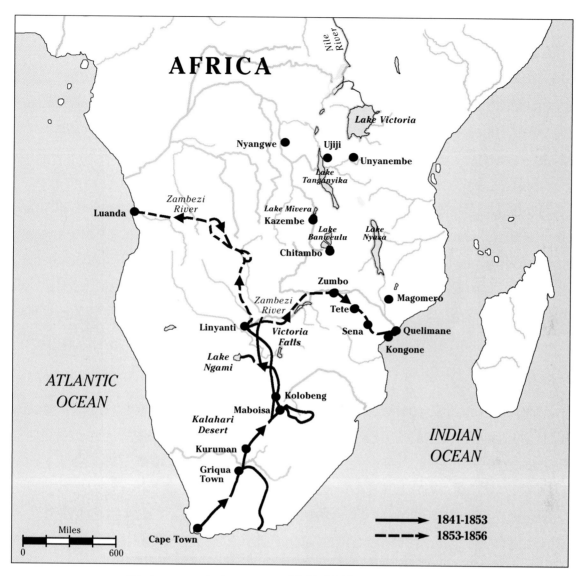

Livingstone's journeys, 1841-1853 and 1853-1856.

Botswana). He was the first European ever to reach that far north into Africa. In 1844, Livingstone was attacked by a lion. The lion mauled his shoulder, and he never had full use of it again.

But the experience didn't stop him. He continued to explore, and find areas to build missions. He met many African tribes. He learned their languages and customs. He valued their traditions and way of life.

DAVID LIVINGSTONE'S HOME AND FAMILY: In 1845, Livingstone was back in Kuruman. He fell in love with Moffat's daughter, Mary. She shared his passion for religion and exploration. They were married in 1845, and for the next several years traveled together in Africa. They soon had four children, and they, too, traveled with their parents.

LAKE NGAMI: The Livingstones set up several missions near what is now the border region of South Africa and Botswana. Livingstone made trips north of the Kalahari Desert. In August 1849, he became the first European to discover Lake Ngami, in what is now north-west Botswana. The discovery won Livingstone fame in England. He received a cash prize from the Royal Geographical Society of London. The Society continued to support his expeditions for years.

In 1852, Livingstone sent his wife and children back to Scotland so the children could go to school.

THE AFRICAN SLAVE TRADE: Even though slavery had supposedly been abolished in Africa, Portuguese slave traders still kidnapped and sold Africans. Livingstone hated slavery. He was devoted to ending it.

Livingstone set out to find a river route from the interior to the Atlantic coast that could be used for trade. He wanted it to be "the highway to the interior." If Africans could buy and sell goods among themselves and to the world, they could weaken the power of the slave trade. In 1853, Livingstone made the famous statement: "I shall open up a path into the interior, or perish."

A RIVER ROUTE TO THE OCEAN: Livingstone and a small crew set out in November 1853 from Linyanti. Traveling northwest,

Livingstone discovered the Zambezi River. They finally reached the Atlantic coast at what is now Luanda, Angola, in May 1854. On his journey Livingstone caught several illnesses, including malaria and rheumatic fever. Even though he was weak from illness, he took notes on the people, animals, plants, and lands he traveled through.

VICTORIA FALLS: On November 17, 1855, while returning south, Livingstone discovered what the natives called "Mosi-oa-tunya," or "the smoke that thunders." He renamed it Victoria Falls. He continued eastward to the east coast of Africa. Livingstone reached the city of Quelimane (in modern-day Mozambique) in May 1856. He had traveled more than 4,300 miles across the continent.

A FAMOUS EXPLORER: In 1856, Livingstone returned to England a hero. He wrote a popular book about his experiences. He gave lectures, which were later published and also a great success.

RETURN TO AFRICA: In May 1858, Livingstone returned to Africa. The English government sponsored his new expedition, which was to explore the Zambezi. The expedition had a further goal: "the extinction of the slave-trade."

But the expedition faced tragedy. Livingstone's wife Mary was part of the crew. She became ill and died in 1862. Several other crew members also became ill and died. Others quarreled with Livingstone and left the expedition. There were also navigation problems on the Zambezi. The expedition had been given a steamboat, which was too big to navigate the river easily. It had to be replaced with smaller craft.

Despite the tragedies, problems, and personal loss, Livingstone pressed on. He discovered Lake Nyasa (now called Lake Malawi).

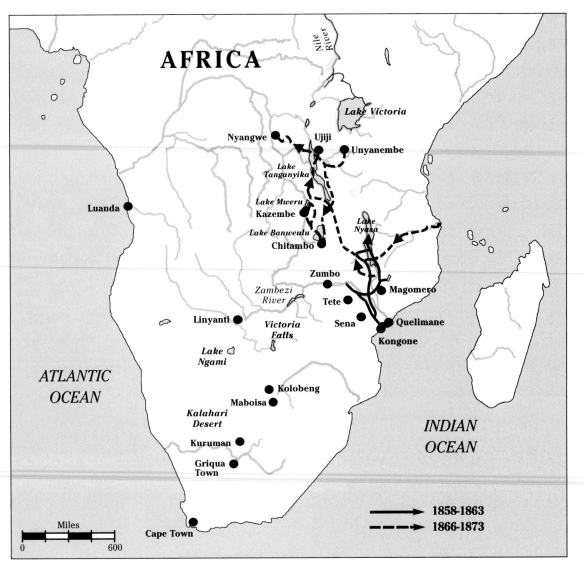

Livingstone's journeys, 1858-1863 and 1866-1873.

He found that the southern portion of the lake was a center for the slave trade. Furious, he began to free slaves and set up missions for them. Portuguese slave traders in turn destroyed his missions and killed the freed slaves.

In 1863, Livingstone was recalled to England. He returned there in 1864. Once again, he wrote a successful book on his expedition. Continuing his fight against the slave trade, he met with tradesmen and businessmen, encouraging them to go to Africa and teach skills to Africans. He gave a series of lectures in which he fiercely condemned slavery.

FINAL AFRICAN EXPEDITION: In 1866, Livingstone returned to Africa. This time, his expedition was funded by the Royal Geographical Society. The goal was to find the source of the Nile River—the point where the great river began.

John Hanning Speke and **Richard Francis Burton** had searched for the Nile's source earlier. Speke thought he'd found it, but his claim wasn't accepted by everyone.

Livingstone started out from the east coast of Africa. He and his small crew headed inland to Lake Nyasa. From there, they headed north. Once again, Livingstone had problems with his men. Some deserted, and one stole his medical supplies.

The remaining crew headed north to Lake Tanganyika. On the way, Livingstone discovered Lake Mweru and Lake Banweulu. He finally reached Lake Tanganyika in 1869. He continued northwest, reaching Nyangwe (now in the Congo) in March 1871. It was the farthest point inland in Africa yet reached by a European.

HENRY STANLEY AND THE RESCUE OF LIVINGSTONE: By this point, Livingstone had been gone for five years. People around the world were worried that the famous explorer might have died. The *New York Herald* sent a journalist, **Henry Morton Stanley**, to find him.

On October 23, 1871, Stanley found Livingstone in the city of Ujiji. Stanley spoke the famous line: "Dr. Livingstone, I presume." Although Livingstone wasn't lost, he was in dire need of food, medicine, and companionship. Stanley gave him all those things. The two became great friends.

Stanley wanted Livingstone to return with him to Europe. But Livingstone refused. He felt he hadn't completed his African mission. David Livingstone died before he was able to accomplish any more. On May 1, 1873, he was found dead at his camp in Chitambo, in modern-day Zambia. His heart was buried under a tree. His body was taken back to England where he was buried in Westminster Abbey in London. The day of his funeral was a national day of mourning in England.

HIS DISCOVERY: By the time of his death, Livingstone had explored more of Africa than any other European. He discovered several important landmarks, including Lake Ngami and Victoria Falls.

Livingstone made Westerners aware of the horrors of the slave trade that still existed in Africa. He was a man true to his religious beliefs, which included a deep hatred of slavery and an equally deep respect for the African people he met. His famous books included geographical information that was used for years by historians and others.

WORLD WIDE WEB SITES:

http://atschool.eduweb.co.uk/blantyre/living/comm.html
http://www.biggar-net.co.uk/livingstone/history1.htm

Alexander Mackenzie

1764 - 1820
Scottish Explorer
First European to Reach the Pacific Ocean Over Land

ALEXANDER MACKENZIE WAS BORN in 1764 in Scotland. Very little is known about his young life.

Mackenzie moved to Canada when he was a boy. He grew up in Montreal and started to work in the fur trade when he was 15. In 1788, he became head of a trading post in Fort Chipewyan, on Lake Athabasca, in modern-day Alberta. The following year, he began a bold expedition to find the **Northwest Passage**.

THE NORTHWEST PASSAGE: From the early 1500s, many people believed that a passage from Europe to Asia existed through what is now Canada. They sought a sea route linking the Atlantic and Pacific Oceans through the islands of the Canadian Arctic. For 400 years, explorers sought — and died — looking for the Northwest Passage. Among the early explorers who searched for the passage were **Jacques Cartier, Martin Frobisher,** and **Henry Hudson.**

JOURNEY TO THE ARCTIC: Mackenzie thought that he could reach the Pacific using river routes across Canada. He started out in June 1789 with a small group, including Indian guides. They took the Peace River north to the Slave River. From there, they canoed across the Great Slave Lake. At the lake's far western tip, they found a mighty river. It would take them 1,100 miles, all the way to the Beaufort Sea, and into the Arctic Ocean.

Mackenzie was disheartened that he hadn't found the passage. He called the great river they'd traveled "Disappointment River." But later, the river they had taken to the sea, and the bay that opens into the Beaufort, were named for the Scottish explorer.

Mackenzie returned to Fort Chipewyan and made plans. He was determined to try to find the Northwest Passage. He knew he had to learn more about navigation, so he traveled to England to study. He spent the next year learning the most recent techniques. Then, he returned to Fort Chipewyan.

JOURNEY TO THE PACIFIC: Mackenzie's next journey took place in May 1793. He and a crew of nine headed west along the Peace River. They took it all the way to the Rocky Mountains, where the river became rapids. From the Peace River, they took the Parsnip River, following it past the Continental Divide. (That is the point along the

Alexander Mackenzie and his explorations.

The Mackenzie River.

Rocky Mountains where rivers flow either east toward the Atlantic or west toward the Pacific from the height of the range.)

When they reached the Fraser River, Mackenzie decided they would continue on foot. He traveled a route that took him over the Rainbow Mountains and down the Bella Coola River. They reached the Pacific in July 1793, at what is now Dean Channel, British Columbia.

At a spot near Dean Channel, Mackenzie wrote a message on a rock. It read: "Alexander Mackenzie, from Canada, by land, the twenty-second of July, one thousand, seven hundred, and ninety-three." He was the first European to make an overland crossing to the Pacific north of Mexico.

Several years after his journey, Mackenzie returned to England. He was knighted by the King. He spent his later years writing about his explorations. Mackenzie returned to Scotland, where he died in 1820.

HIS DISCOVERY: For his discovery of the Mackenzie River, and for his overland journey to the Pacific, Mackenzie is an honored explorer. After his books were published, the world learned of the bold discoveries of the Scottish explorer. One interested reader of Mackenzie's work was Thomas Jefferson. When he became President, Jefferson sponsored another great overland journey, that of **Lewis and Clark.**

WORLD WIDE WEB SITES:

http://www.lafete.org/new/v_ger/ex/alexE.htm
http://www.nlc-bnc.ca/2/6/h6-221-e.html

Ferdinand Magellan
1480? - 1521
Portuguese Navigator and Explorer
Led First Expedition to Circumnavigate the World

FERDINAND MAGELLAN WAS BORN around 1480 in Portugal. His father was Rui de Magalhaes and his mother was Alda de Mesquita. His father served in the court of King John II of Portugal.

Magellan grew up as a page at the court of Queen Leonor of Portugal. When he was seven, he started school. By the age of 15 he had studied math, geography, and mapmaking. It was the perfect background for a young navigator.

At this time, Portugal was a major sea power. Since the time of **Prince Henry the Navigator**, several Portuguese navigators, including **Bartholomew Dias** and **Vasco de Gama**, had established sea routes to the East. They traveled south around the tip of Africa, then headed north and east. Using these routes, Portuguese traders brought gold, spices, and other goods from Asia to Europe.

FIRST VOYAGE: It was along this route that Magellan took his first voyage. In 1505, when he was about 15, he sailed from Portugal to India. The expedition was led by Francisco de Almeida. The purpose of the voyage was to strengthen Portuguese trade in India.

They reached the west coast of India and landed at Cannanore. There, Magellan fought in a battle and was wounded. The expedition moved on to Africa. Trade on the east coast of Africa was controlled by Arab merchants. The Portuguese attacked and took over several of their ports.

Magellan sailed back to India. In 1509, he was once again wounded in combat. That same year, Magellan sailed for Malacca, an empire in what is now Malaysia. There, he fought in battles again.

In 1510 Magellan was given command of his own ship. He returned to Malacca. There, Magellan supposedly bought a boy slave who was 13 years old. From there, he may have visited the spice-rich Moluccas. He also sailed to the Philippine Islands.

In 1512, Magellan returned to Portugal. He spent several more years in the military and fought in Morocco. In 1516 he went to King Manuel. He wanted to sail to the west, and he wanted more money for himself and his voyage. The king refused.

Magellan discovering the Strait.

SAILING FOR SPAIN: Magellan went to the court of King Charles V of Spain. He told the king of his idea to travel west, like **Christopher Columbus**, to reach the Moluccas and the riches of the East. He wanted to sail across the Atlantic and circle the continent at its southern tip. The plan was bold, but Magellan knew he could do it. The king agreed to his plan.

Magellan sailed from Spain in September 1519. The expedition included five ships, more than 270 men, and two years' worth of supplies. The ships were named *Trinidad, San Antonio, Concepcion, Victoria,* and *Santiago.* Magellan captained one of the ships. The others were commanded by men chosen by the king, not by Magellan.

MUTINY: They sailed south to the Canary Islands, then southwest across the Atlantic. During the crossing, one of the captains, Juan de Cartagena, led a mutiny (rebellion). He tried to take control of the expedition from Magellan. Magellan fought back and regained control. He arrested Cartagena and put him in the ship's jail.

They reached what is now Rio de Janeiro in Brazil in December. Then, they sailed south to what is now Argentina. Magellan saw the entrance of what is now the Rio de Plata. He explored it, looking in vain for a way to reach the Pacific.

A WINTER IN PATAGONIA: Magellan continued down the coast of South America. Winter was coming, and he decided to have his expedition wait out the severe weather on land. That winter, the men were the first Europeans to see penguins. The local natives visited them. Magellan noted that the animal skins they wore on their feet looked like paws. He called them "Patagonians," from the Spanish word for "paws." That area is still called Patagonia.

But Magellan faced mutiny again. In April 1520, Gaspar de Quesada led a rebellion against Magellan. The majority of the crew defended their leader, and the mutiny didn't succeed. Magellan had Quesada executed. Cartagena, who had aided Quesada, was put ashore.

That would not be the end of Magellan's troubles with his crew. The expedition started off again in October 1520. Magellan sent the *San Antonio* down the coast in search of a pathway to the Pacific. But the ship took another route: home to Spain. Then the *Santiago* ran aground. Magellan was down to three ships.

THE STRAIT OF MAGELLAN: At last, Magellan reached the passage to the Pacific. He entered what he called the Strait of Saints (now the Strait of Magellan) in late October. At night, they saw fires on the land. Magellan called it "Tierra del Fuego," which means "land of fire" in Spanish.

THE PACIFIC OCEAN: It took them more than one month to make the passage. Finally, on November 27, 1520, they entered the calm waters of the Pacific Ocean. Magellan named it, too, for the Spanish word for "peaceful."

A LONG JOURNEY ACROSS THE PACIFIC: Magellan led his ships to the north, along the coast of what is now Chile, then out to sea. He had no idea how large the Pacific was. He thought he would

The Victoria.

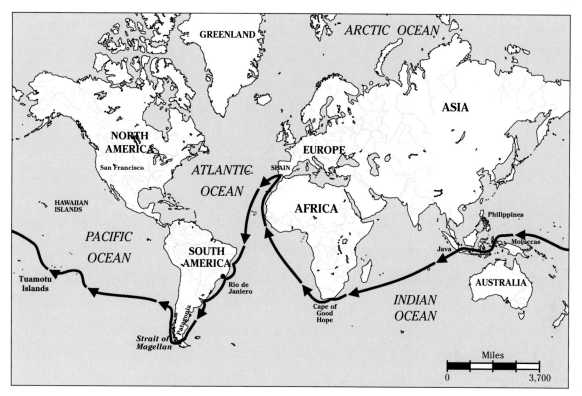

Magellan's circumnavigation route, 1519-1522.

reach the Moluccas in about one month. Instead, it took five months. The crew ran out of food and water. The men began to die of starvation. Some had scurvy, an illness brought on by lack of Vitamin C.

At last, they saw an island. They had reached the Tuamotu Islands. They found food and water. Traveling on, they reached Guam, in the Mariana Islands. From there, they sailed to what are now the Philippine Islands. They had traveled more than 13,000 miles.

ARRIVING IN THE PHILIPPINES: Magellan and his crew visited several islands in the Philippines. On the island of Cebu, they met with the native leader. Magellan convinced him to swear allegiance

371

to the Spanish king and to accept Christianity. Next, he traveled to the Phillipine island of Mactan to try to persuade more tribal leaders. When they refused to accept his demands, Magellan attacked.

THE LAST BATTLE OF MAGELLAN: In the battle, Magellan was severely wounded. He died on April 27, 1521, without reaching the Moluccas. New leaders were appointed to the expedition, but they were killed in another skirmish with natives.

The crew next came under the command of Juan Sebastian Elcano and Gonzalo de Espinosa. They took one ship each, Elcano took the *Victoria,* and Espinosa the *Trinidad.* Because the crew was so small, they didn't need the third ship, so it was burned.

CONTINUING THE QUEST TO CIRCLE THE GLOBE: The two ships sailed for the Moluccas, finally reaching them in November 1521. There, taking a load of spices, they planned to sail for home. Elcano sailed west, following the path across the Indian Ocean and around the Cape of Good Hope, as Magellan had planned. Espinosa's ship needed repairs, and once they were done, he planned to sail east, back across the Pacific.

Elcano finally returned to Spain on September 8, 1522, having "circumnavigated," or circled the earth. It had taken nearly three years to complete the journey. Of the original crew of 270, only 18 survived. Luckily for history, one of the survivors was a man named Antonio Pigafetta. He kept a journal of the journey that is still used today to study the expedition.

Elcano received both riches and glory for completing the journey. He was given a globe on which was written, "The First One to Circle Me."

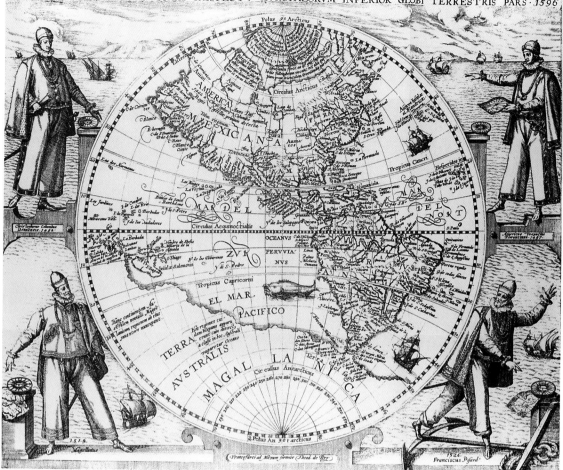

Map of the Americas from 1596 with portraits of Columbus (upper left), Vespucci (upper right), Magellan (lower left), and Pizarro (lower right).

Espinosa's ship never returned to Spain. He and his crew were captured by Portuguese traders and Espinosa was imprisoned. He finally returned to Spain many years later, by land, not sea.

FERDINAND MAGELLAN'S HOME AND FAMILY: In 1517, before his famous voyage, Magellan married Beatriz Barbosa. They had one son, Rodrigo.

HIS DISCOVERY: Although he never lived to complete his mission, Magellan is renowned as the leader of the first expedition to circumnavigate the Earth. It is considered one of the most important achievements in the history of exploration.

WORLD WIDE WEB SITES:

http://campus.northpark.edu/history/WebChron/WestEurope/
  Magellan.CP.html
http://www.mariner.org/age/magellan.html

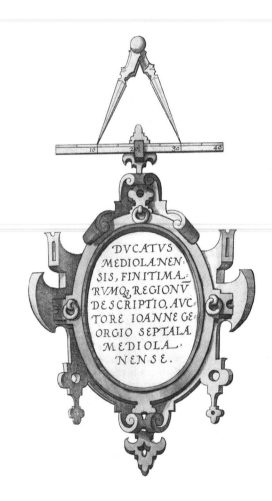

Jacques Marquette
1637 - 1675
French Missionary and Explorer
Explored the Mississippi River with Louis Jolliet

JACQUES MARQUETTE WAS BORN on June 10, 1637, in Laon, France. When he was 17, he decided to become a Catholic priest. He wanted to be a missionary and to "set out for foreign lands."

As an adult he wrote that "I wanted to explore since my earliest childhood." He studied to be a Jesuit priest.

GOING TO THE NEW WORLD: When he finished college, Marquette was sent to a Catholic mission in Quebec. It was a settlement in **New France** (now Canada) founded by **Samuel de Champlain**. He arrived in September 1666.

Marquette went to the French-Canadian city of Three Rivers and began to study the languages of the local Indians. Like his country-man **Etienne Brulé**, Marquette learned the local Indian languages. But he wanted to teach them religion, not trade with them.

In May 1668, Marquette left Quebec for Sault Sainte Marie, in what is now Michigan. There, he founded the first European settlements in Michigan. He taught the Christian faith to the Ottawa Indians. In 1669, Marquette traveled to the western part of Lake Superior. He founded a mission there, called Pointe du Saint-Esprit. Here, he also met Indians from the Illinois tribe. In 1671, Marquette traveled back to Michigan and founded another settlement in St. Ignace. From the Ottawa, Marquette learned of a great river that ran south. It was the Mississippi.

MEETING JOLLIET: Louis Jolliet (zho-lee-ET) was a French explorer who had been hired by the leaders of New France to find the Mississippi. The French thought it might lead them to the Pacific Ocean. If it did, it would be an important trade route for them.

Marquette and Jolliet met sometime around 1671. In 1673, Jolliet got permission for the two of them to explore the Mississippi. Jolliet would explore for the benefit of the people of New France. Marquette would teach religion to the native peoples they met.

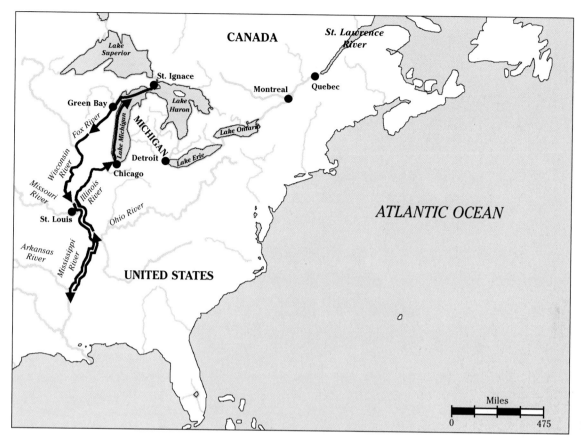

Marquette's voyage with Jolliet in 1674.

EXPLORING THE MISSISSIPPI: Jolliet and Marquette left St. Ignace in May 1674. They had a crew of five, with two canoes. They traveled west along the northern coast of Lake Michigan, stopping at what is now Green Bay, Wisconsin. They traveled southwest from there on the Fox River. Then they followed the Wisconsin River to the Mississippi. Along the way, they met the Illinois tribe. They were very friendly to the French explorers. They even gave them a peace pipe for their journey.

Marquette and Jolliet entered the great river on June 17, 1674. They were the first French explorers ever to reach it. They followed the river south, noting where other powerful rivers, like the Missouri and the Ohio, joined it. They hoped that they had found the route

377

FATHER JOLIET AND MARQUETTE DESCENDING THE MISSISSIPPI.

to the west. They thought they would reach the Pacific by continuing to the west.

But it soon became clear that the river ran south. They realized they would reach the Gulf of Mexico if they continued in that direction.

They went only as far south as the point where the Mississippi meets the Arkansas River. They knew they had reached the area under Spanish control. As Marquette wrote later, they feared falling "into the hands of the Spaniards." If that happened, no one would ever know of their important discoveries.

Marquette and Jolliet headed north in July. They traveled up the Mississippi, fighting a strong current. Then they took the Illinois River further north, then took the Chicago River to Lake Michigan, and on to Green Bay.

Marquette left Green Bay in October 1674 to found a mission for the Illinois. In April 1675, he preached to a large gathering of Indians along the Illinois River. But he was ill and needed to return to St. Ignace. Marquette died on his journey home, at the age of 38, near what is now Ludington, Michigan. He is buried in St. Ignace.

HIS DISCOVERY: Marquette was a deeply religious man who was also a brave explorer. With Jolliet, he paved the way for French exploration along the Mississippi.

WORLD WIDE WEB SITE:

http://www.win.tue.nl/~engels/discovery/jolmar.html

Fridtjof Nansen
1861 - 1930
Norwegian Arctic Explorer, Scientist, and Statesman

FRIDTJOF NANSEN WAS BORN on October 10, 1861, near Oslo, Norway. His first name is pronounced "FRICH-awf." He was from a wealthy family. His parents stressed the importance of hard work and service to others.

FRIDTJOF NANSEN GREW UP in the family home near a great forest. From an early age, he loved to be outdoors. He was a fine athlete and won a national cross-country skiing championship 12 years in a row. He was also an excellent speed skater. When he was 18, he held the world record for the one-mile race.

FRIDTJOF NANSEN WENT TO SCHOOL in Oslo, where he attended the university. He did well in many subjects, including math and physics. But he settled on zoology — the study of animals — for his college major. He graduated in 1882.

When he was 21, Nansen traveled to the Arctic Ocean on a sealing boat. His job was to make scientific observations. He approached his work with an exacting, curious mind. He made careful measurements of the movements of wind, water, and ice. He noted that there was driftwood in the Arctic near Greenland. Where had it come from? Nansen began to develop a theory. He thought the wood came from Siberia and had floated across the **North Pole** on an ocean current to reach the Canadian Arctic waters. It was a theory he would test later, in his famous voyage on the *Fram.*

FIRST JOBS: When Nansen returned to Norway, he became head of the natural history collection at the Bergen Museum. He worked in that job for six years. He also continued his study of zoology. And he began to plan his first major expedition: exploring Greenland. The interior of the vast island nation had never been explored.

EXPLORING GREENLAND: Nansen's plan was to land on Greenland's forbidding east coast, then travel east to west. It had never been done before, because the east coast was full of dangerous icebergs and moving pack ice. Nansen had a hard time finding money for the trip and convincing people that his plan would work.

He eventually found funding, and in June 1888, after months of careful planning, he set out for Greenland. The expedition included

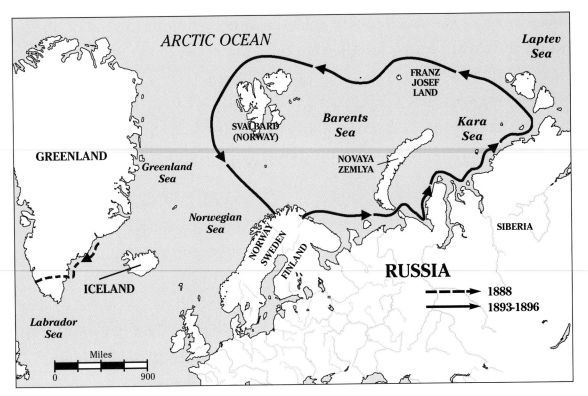

*Nansen's Greenland expedition, 1888, and the
route of the* Fram *expedition, 1893-1896*

six men. They reached Greenland on July 17. They left their large ship for small ones and began to row for land. But fierce winds and strong currents blew them 300 miles to the south. They finally reached the shore, then faced the mountain range along Greenland's eastern coast. Despite storms and temperatures up to 45 degrees below zero, they explored Greenland, on skis, from east to west. In crossing the country, they'd made an important discovery: Greenland is covered by a continuous ice sheet.

They spent the winter on the west coast of Greenland, where Nansen met local Inuit people and learned their language. They returned to Norway in 1889. To his surprise, Nansen learned that he'd become a famous explorer.

VOYAGE OF THE *FRAM*, 1893-1896: Nansen was soon planning his next expedition. The wreckage of an American ship, the *Jeannette*, that had sunk off the coast of Siberia had been found in Greenland. This fired Nansen's imagination and scientific curiosity about the movements of Arctic Ocean currents. He developed a theory: the currents moved in a westerly direction, from Siberia to Greenland.

He also developed a plan to test that theory. He would build a ship that, when frozen in the Arctic ice, would float with the currents across the ocean.

Nansen's plan was simple, but bold. He spent three years preparing for his voyage. He called his ship the *Fram*, which means "forward" in Norwegian. The boat's hull was rounded in shape, so that when it became frozen in the ice, it would be lifted, not crushed by the pressure. The interior was a comfortable, homey space for the crew, for they were to spend years on their journey. Also onboard were scientific instruments for the study of weather, currents, and animals.

The *Fram* left Norway in June 1893, with Nansen, a crew of 12, and enough food and fuel for six years. They traveled east along the coast of Siberia, then north. They reached the pack ice on September 20, and the *Fram* became frozen in. It began its slow drift across the ice.

The boat withstood the pressure of the ice, but her progress was slow. It appeared that the ship would not follow a course to take it to the North Pole. So Nansen decided to try to reach the Pole using skis and sleds. On March 14, 1895, he and one companion left the *Fram* with skis, kayaks, and dog sleds. They faced terrible storms and huge floes of ice. They were forced to turn back before reaching the Pole, but they traveled closer than anyone prior to that point.

They headed back toward Franz Josef Land and reached one of its small islands. They built a cabin of ice and rocks that would be their home for nine months. They hunted polar bears for food and fuel. When spring came, they headed south, where they met a British exploration team. They traveled with them back to Norway.

There, they rejoined the crew of the *Fram*. The ship had drifted as far Svalbard and was sailing home after completing her three-year journey in the Arctic.

Nansen and the crew of the *Fram* reached Oslo on September 9, 1896, to world-wide fame. Nansen wrote a popular history of his travels that was a bestseller all over the world. But his triumph wasn't just as an explorer. He and his men had gathered information on weather, ice, currents, geology, and the Earth's magnetic fields. They had also discovered that there was no large land mass, like Greenland, on the Siberian side of the Arctic. They had also discovered that the Arctic Ocean was thousands of feet deep.

RETURN TO TEACHING: In 1897, Nansen became a professor of zoology at the University of Oslo. He also began the study of oceanography, which was a new science at that time. Nansen traveled to the Arctic on a number of scientific missions during the early years of the 20th century. He also made plans for further polar exploration, but that was not to be. Instead, he devoted his last years to helping victims of war, poverty, and starvation.

LEAGUE OF NATIONS: In 1914, World War I began. In the war, Great Britain, France, Russia, and the U.S. went to war against Germany and Austria. Millions of people died in the war, which finally ended in 1918.

After the war, the League of Nations was formed. It was an international organization like the modern United Nations, created to help resolve conflicts and promote peace. Nansen was the representative for Norway. At that time, nearly 500,000 Germans had been living for years near starvation in Russian prison camps. Nansen arranged for their safe return to Germany.

SAVING MILLIONS FROM STARVATION: In 1921, Nansen helped raise funds to keep millions of Russians from starving during a time of famine. The following year he helped millions of refugees who had fled their countries during war. Nansen created a system that gave identification papers to these homeless people. The papers allowed them to find jobs and places to live.

THE NOBEL PEACE PRIZE: Nansen received the Nobel Peace Prize in 1922, for his humanitarian work. He gave the prize money to international relief agencies. He continued his work with refugees until his death in 1930.

FRIDTJOF NANSEN'S HOME AND FAMILY: Nansen's wife was named Eva Sars. They had a daughter, Liv.

HIS DISCOVERY: Nansen is remembered for his exploration of Greenland and his journey across the Arctic in the *Fram*. He was also a great humanitarian whose work on behalf of war refugees saved millions of lives.

WORLD WIDE WEB SITES:

http://www.fni.no/christ.htm
http://www.mnc.net/norway/Nansen.htm

Adolf Erik Nordenskiöld
1832 - 1901
Finnish-Born Swedish Explorer and Scientist
First to Navigate the Northeast Passage

ADOLF ERIK NORDENSKIÖLD WAS BORN on November 18, 1832, in Helsinki, Finland. His last name is pronounced "NORD-en-shold." His parents were Nils and Sofia Nordenskiöld. Nils was a geologist and mining specialist.

ADOLF ERIK NORDENSKIÖLD WENT TO SCHOOL at home for several years, then to a school in Porvoo, Finland. While still a teenager, he went on geological trips with his father to the Ural Mountains in Russia.

Nordenskiöld went to the University of Helsinki, where he studied chemistry and geology. He received his bachelor's, master's, and doctoral degrees from the University. After college, he began working as a geologist.

MOVING TO SWEDEN: In 1857, Nordenskiöld moved to Sweden. He didn't agree with the Finnish government, which at that time was under Russian control. Nordenskiöld settled in Stockholm. He became head of the department of minerals at the Swedish Royal Museum. He also began his career as an explorer.

FIRST ARCTIC EXPEDITIONS: Over the next 25 years, Nordenskiöld made many expeditions to the Arctic. In 1858 and 1861, he went to the Arctic island of Spitsbergen with geologist Otto Torell. Spitsbergen, part of the Svalbard Islands, is in the Arctic Ocean north of Norway. It was discovered by **Willem Barents** in 1596.

Nordenskiöld and Torell wanted to measure the way the Earth curved in the Arctic. Nordenskiöld went back to the Arctic in 1864 and 1868 to continue his study. On the 1868 expedition, he tried to reach the **North Pole**. He didn't reach the Pole, but he did reach a position farther north than anyone before.

In 1870, Nordenskiöld set out for Greenland. He explored inland and studied the ice formations. Next, he tried once again to reach the North Pole, this time with reindeer-drawn sledges (heavy sleds). But they became caught in the ice, and he returned without reaching the Pole.

THE NORTHEAST PASSAGE: Nordenskiöld next turned his attention to finding the **Northeast Passage**. It had been a passion of explorers since the 1500s, when Portugal controlled the sea routes from Europe to the riches of the East. For hundreds of years, explorers had traveled north from Europe, then journeyed east across the Arctic coast of Russia and Siberia looking for the passage.

After hundreds of years of failed attempts, Nordenskiöld took up the challenge. He made two voyages to the Arctic waters along the coast of Siberia in 1875 and 1876. On July 21, 1878, he sailed aboard the steamship *Vega* from Tromso, Norway. He stayed close to the coast of northern Scandinavia, Russia, and Siberia, wending his way eastward. At the end of September 1878, the ship was frozen in the ice near the Bering Strait.

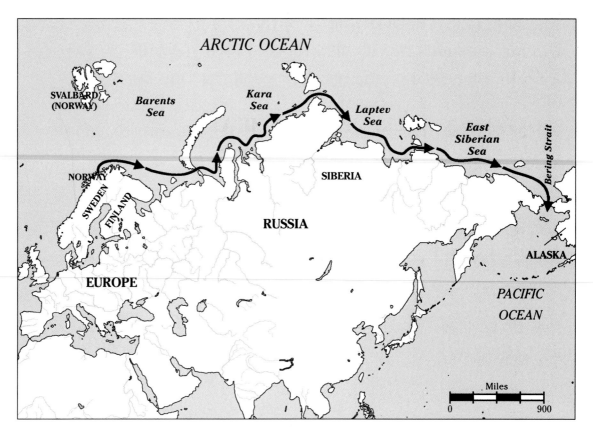

Nordenskiöld's expedition to navigate the Northeast Passage, 1878-1879.

In July 1879, the *Vega* became free of the ice and continued on its journey. Nordenskiöld sailed through the Bering Strait and reached Alaska on July 22, 1879. The *Vega* became the first ship ever to navigate the Northeast Passage. They returned homeward sailing down the coast of Siberia and China and around India. They sailed through the Arabian Sea, the Red Sea, and through the Suez Canal. Nordenskiöld reached Sweden on April 24, 1880. The route Nordenskiöld charted became widely used for shipping in the 20th century.

Nordenskiöld went on one more expedition, to Greenland, in 1883. He then retired from exploration. He wrote bestselling books about his adventures, served as head of the Swedish Academy, and

began to collect and study historic maps. When he died on August 12, 1901, his collection contained more than 24,000 maps, from the 1400s to the 1900s.

ADOLF ERIK NORDENSKIÖLD'S HOME AND FAMILY:
Nordenskiöld married Anna Maria Mannerheim in 1863. They had four children.

HIS DISCOVERY: Nordenskiöld is remembered as the first explorer to successfully navigate the Northeast Passage. His accomplishments inspired later Arctic explorers, including **Fridjof Nansen** and **Robert Peary.**

WORLD WIDE WEB SITES:

http://kirjasto.sci.fi/aenord.htm
http://www.win.tue.nl/~engels/discovery/index/html

Francisco de Orellana
1511? - 1546
Spanish Explorer Who Was the First European to Navigate the Amazon River

FRANCISCO DE ORELLANA WAS BORN in Trujillo, Spain, around 1511. His last name is pronounced "oh-ray-YAH-nah." Very little is known about his early life. It is known that he was related to **Francisco Pizarro.**

When he was around 16 years old, Orellana went to the Spanish colony in **New Spain**. No one is sure exactly where he landed, but most think it was Panama. There, he joined Pizarro's expedition to Peru.

CONQUERING THE INCAS WITH PIZARRO: Orellana fought with Pizarro's soldiers as they conquered the Incas in 1531. After that, he lived for a while in the port city of Portoviejo in what is now Ecuador.

THE SEARCH FOR EL DORADO: As had many explorers before him, Orellana had heard tales of a city of incredible riches called El Dorado. With Pizarros's half-brother Gonzalo, he set out from Quito to find the legendary city in 1541. Their route took them east across the Andes Mountains. What we know of the expedition is based on the diary of a monk named Carvajal, who traveled with Orellana.

The expedition went badly. They never found El Dorado or any treasure, and they nearly starved. In late 1541, Orellana left Gonzalo Pizarro and sailed down the Napo River in search of food. He took a group of 50 men.

They traveled for months, never finding enough food to take back to the main camp. According to Carvajal's diary, they were "chewing our boots and belts." In 1542, Orellana decided to continue downstream. Why he chose to do that, rather than returning to Gonzalo Pizarro, has puzzled historians for centuries. Did he abandon Pizarro, or could he not navigate the fierce current upstream? Whatever the reason, it led to his discovery of the Amazon River.

Orellana's expedition of 1541-1542.

DISCOVERING THE AMAZON: Following the Napo, Orellana's expedition reached what is now the Amazon River in May 1542. The Indians called it the Maranon. Orellana named it "Rio Negro," which means "Black River."

Orellana sailed east for three months along the Amazon. They were the first Europeans to make the journey. They traveled more than 3,000 miles, facing the fierce heat and strange animals of the tropical rain forest. They also met friendly and hostile Indian tribes.

HOW DID THE AMAZON GET ITS NAME? As they traveled the Amazon, they heard legends of a tribe of women warriors. To Orellana, the women sounded like the "Amazons" of Greek myth, who were also a race of female warriors. Based on the legends, the great river became known as the Amazon.

Orellana's expedition reached the mouth of the Amazon, on the Atlantic coast, in August 1542. They continued north along the coast as far as modern-day Venezuela. They finally reached Trinidad and prepared to sail for home.

RETURN TO SPAIN: Orellana returned to Spain in 1543. In 1544, the King of Spain made him the governor of the lands he had explored. Orellana was eager to return to the Amazon.

BACK TO THE NEW WORLD: Orellana's expedition left Spain in May 1545. The crossing was difficult. It took seven months to reach Brazil, and one ship was lost along the way. The expedition reached the Amazon, but Orellana lost more ships and crew. He became ill and died in Brazil in 1546.

HIS DISCOVERY: Orellana is remembered as the first European to navigate the Amazon.

WORLD WIDE WEB SITES:

http://www.win.tue.nl/~engels/discovery/orellana.html
http://www.pbs.org/conquistadors/orellana/

Mungo Park
1771 - 1806
Scottish Explorer of the Niger River in Africa

MUNGO PARK WAS BORN in Selkirk, Scotland, on September 10, 1771. His parents were farmers. Very little is known about his early life.

Park went to college at the University of Edinburgh and became a surgeon. In 1792, he became the doctor on a merchant ship headed for Indonesia. He traveled in Sumatra and studied the plants and animals.

FIRST VOYAGE OF EXPLORATION: Park wrote about his findings, and they impressed another explorer, **Joseph Banks**. Banks was head of a society that funded exploration. He chose Park to explore the Niger River in Africa.

The Niger is the third largest river in Africa. Banks and other scientists wanted to know which way the Niger flowed. They could then use it to continue to explore or to use as a trade route.

Park left England in June 1795 and began his journey. Once he got to Africa, he started at the mouth of the Gambia River. He traveled 200 miles to the east, but became very sick. After recovering, he continued his journey.

CAPTURED: Park met many different African tribes on his journey. Some were friendly and some were hostile. Twice robbers took all

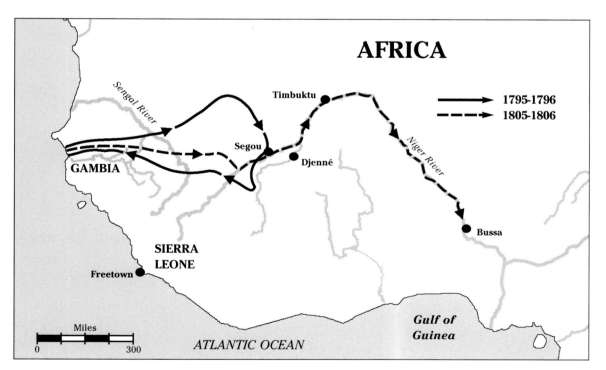

Park's West Africa expeditions, 1795-1796 and 1805-1806.

his belongings. And when he met an Arabic trading party, he was captured and imprisoned. He managed to escape, and continued on his quest.

He finally reached the Niger River in what is now Segou, Mali. He followed the river for awhile. He finally determined that it flowed eastward. Then, he decided to head back up the river. But he became sick again. He was cared for by friendly natives and regained his strength.

Park returned to the ocean with the help of a trading caravan. He returned to England in 1797 and wrote a book about his adventures. It was a great success, and Mungo Park became famous.

SECOND VOYAGE: Park returned to the Niger in 1805. The English government sent him on his second voyage, with 40 men. But the expedition faced disaster from the start. Many of the men caught malaria and other diseases and died. The few who remained followed the Niger to the legendary city of Timbuktu. Traveling east, they reached the river village of Bussa. There, sometime around January 1806, Park and his crew were attacked by natives, and all were killed.

HIS DISCOVERY: Park was able to determine that the Niger flowed eastward. He also provided information used by later explorers of Africa.

WORLD WIDE WEB SITES:

http://www.electricscotland.com/history/other/park_mungo.htm
http://www.travelbooks.co.uk/ext/africax.html

William Edward Parry
1790 - 1855
English Navigator and Explorer
Explored the Canadian Arctic

WILLIAM EDWARD PARRY WAS BORN on December 19, 1790, in Bath, England. Very little is known about his life when he was young.

GOING TO SEA: When Parry was just 13 years old, he joined the English Royal Navy. He served in the North Sea during the Napoleonic Wars between England and France. In 1812, he was sent to North America. He remained there during the War of 1812 between the U.S. and England.

THE NORTHWEST PASSAGE: In 1818, Parry joined the centuries-long search for the **Northwest Passage**. From the early 1500s, many people believed that a passage from Europe to Asia existed through what is now Canada. They sought a sea route linking the Atlantic and Pacific Oceans through the islands of the Canadian Arctic. Many of these explorers were English.

JOURNEY TO THE ARCTIC WITH ROSS: Parry's first journey to the Canadian Arctic was under Captain John Ross. Also on board was Ross's nephew, **James Clark Ross**, who accompanied Parry on his later missions. They followed the path of **William Baffin**, who had explored the area 200 years earlier. The expedition headed through the Davis Strait toward what Parry would later name Baffin Bay. But Ross thought the passage was blocked by land. They returned to England.

FIRST EXPEDITION: Back in England, Parry planned his first expedition. He was convinced that a passage existed. Parry left England in May 1819 with two ships, the *Hecla* and the *Griper*. They followed the same path as the Ross expedition, heading along the north shore of Baffin Island into Lancaster Sound.

Parry's expedition reached as far west as Melville Island. But winter was coming, and the water was full of ice. Parry and the crew spent the winter on Melville Island.

It was a long, cold winter, but Parry was a man of great spirit. He encouraged his men to have a good time. They sang, talked, and read through the bitter cold. Parry even composed an opera, *The*

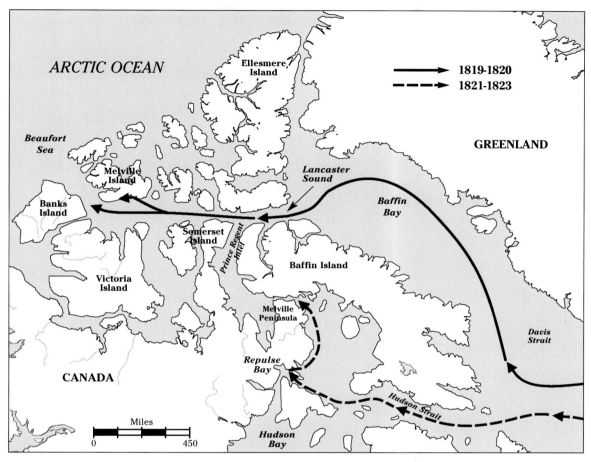

Parry's expeditions of 1819-1820 and 1821-1823.

Northwest Passage. His men responded with loyalty and affection for their leader.

The ships were kept in by ice until August 1820. Finally, the expedition got underway again. They headed west, but because of the ice could only reach as far as an island Parry named Banks Island. They returned to England, reaching home in 1820. Parry was a national hero. He was promoted to Commander.

Although they hadn't discovered the Northwest Passage, the expedition was vitally important. Parry had shown that Lancaster

Sound was in fact a strait, leading to a group of islands almost always surrounded by ice. And on this and all his expeditions, Parry charted waters and lands not then known to Europeans.

SECOND EXPEDITION: Parry was ready and willing to try again to find the passage. In April 1821, he set out from England to try to find a more southern route. He traveled through the Hudson Strait to the west of Baffin Island. He reached Repulse Bay, looking for an inlet that would lead to a passage.

The expedition couldn't find the passage. Once again, the crew wintered in the Arctic. And once again, Parry brought humor and a sense of fun to winter. His crew formed the Royal Arctic Theater. Every two weeks they put on plays. The men also did scientific experiments and kept journals on weather.

That winter, a group of Inuit Indians visited Parry's camp. They told Parry that there was a strait nearby that led west. But when summer came and they tried to find it, the way was blocked with ice. He decided to cross it on foot. Winter set in again. The men spent their second year near what is now Igloolik at the tip of the Melville Peninsula.

The following summer, their way was still blocked by ice. They headed back to England, reaching home in October 1823.

THIRD EXPEDITION: Parry began his third Arctic expedition in 1824. He was once again in search of the Northwest Passage. Once again he sailed with the *Hecla* and the *Fury*. And once again ice held up their journey west. He traveled from Baffin Bay through Lancaster Sound. They wintered in Prince Regent Inlet, on the west coast of Baffin Island.

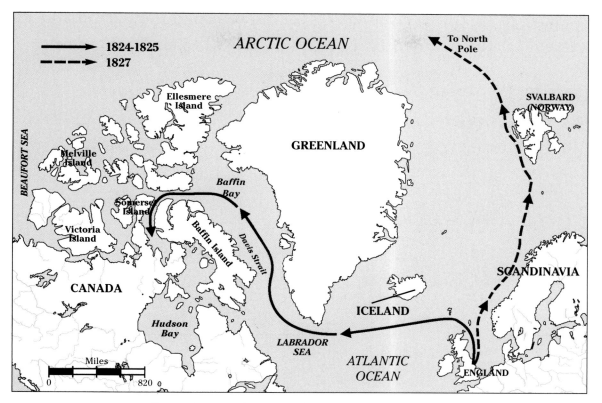

Parry's expeditions of 1824-1825 and 1827.

When summer came, the ice still made the waters impassable. The *Fury* was damaged in the ice. It had to be abandoned, and all the men had to sail on the *Hecla*. The crew returned to England. Later, the food aboard the *Fury* saved James Clark Ross's Arctic expedition from starvation.

FINAL EXPEDITION: Parry made one final voyage to the Arctic. In his last journey, he set out to find the **North Pole**. In 1827, his expedition started out from England north to Spitsbergen Island (part of the Svalbard Islands). They traveled in heavy boats that could also be used as sledges. They never reached the Pole, but they did travel farther north than anyone up to that point.

Parry's exploring days were over. He returned to England and worked for the Navy until his death on July 8, 1855.

HIS DISCOVERY: Parry was an outstanding explorer and leader who is remembered for his attempts to find the Northwest Passage. Although he failed in that goal, Parry learned much about the Canadian Arctic, which helped later explorers.

WORLD WIDE WEB SITES:

http://collections.ic.gc.ca/arctic/explore/parry.htm
http://www.nlc-bnc.ca/2/24/h24-1820-e.html

Robert E. Peary

1856 - 1920
American Arctic Explorer
Claimed to Be the First Person to Reach the North Pole

ROBERT E. PEARY WAS BORN on May 6, 1856, in Cresson, Pennsylvania. His parents were Charles and Mary Peary. Charles died when Robert was three. After his father's death, Robert and his mother moved to Cape Elizabeth, Maine, near Portland.

ROBERT E. PEARY WENT TO SCHOOL at the local public schools. He graduated from Portland High School in 1873 and went on to Bowdoin College. He graduated from college in 1877 with a civil engineering degree.

FIRST JOBS: Peary's first job was as a surveyor in Maine. After two years, he moved to Washington, D.C., to work for a U.S. government mapmaking project. He joined the Navy in 1881. In 1885 he was sent to Nicaragua, where he worked on a plan to build a canal.

FIRST ARCTIC EXPEDITION: In 1886, Peary left the Navy for a brief time to explore Greenland. He and a companion explored inland about 100 miles.

After his return, Peary went back to Washington. There, he hired an African-American assistant, **Matthew Henson**. Henson had spent several years at sea. He was an able assistant in many ways. Peary shared his plans to explore the Arctic. Henson was eager to join Peary on his explorations. They would be companions in Arctic expeditions for many years.

BACK TO GREENLAND: In 1891, Peary and a crew that now included Henson explored northern Greenland. Peary believed that Greenland was an island. He took a sledge (heavy sled) as far as Independence Fjord to examine and map the coastline.

LEARNING FROM THE INUIT: Peary met Inuit tribes and learned how they survived in the Arctic. From them, he learned the proper clothing to wear to protect against the cold. He also learned how to travel by dog sled.

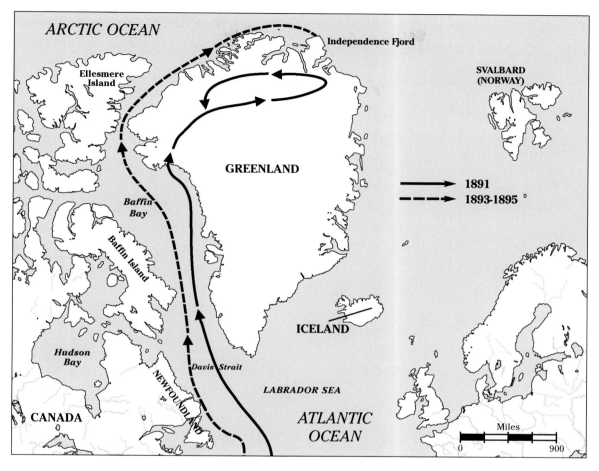

Peary's Greenland expeditions of 1891 and 1893-1895.

Peary developed other methods to explore the Arctic. He set up several base camps and traveled among them. He studied the flow of the Arctic waters, so he could build a ship to withstand the ice. Using all of this information, Peary set his mind on his ultimate goal: the **North Pole**.

THE RACE FOR THE POLES: By the end of the 19th century, most of the surface of the planet had been explored. What remained were the North and South Polar regions. Explorers from many countries competed against one another to locate and claim the North Pole

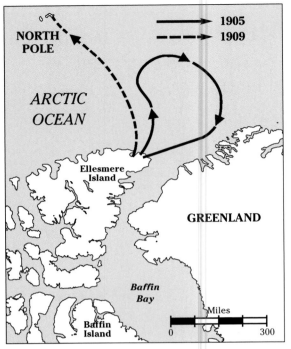

*Peary's North Pole expeditions
of 1905 and 1909.*

and South Pole. Crews from the U.S., Russia, Norway, England, Germany, and other nations were locked in a race to determine who would reach either pole first.

THE 1893-1895 EXPEDITION:

Peary's first attempt to reach the North Pole was in 1893. That year, he traveled to northern Greenland and tried to reach the Pole. But bad weather stopped him. Over the next several years, Peary spent most of his time in Greenland.

He navigated around its northern tip. He proved it was indeed an island, not connected to any land mass at the northern edge of the world.

From 1895 to 1897, Peary discovered meteorites that had fallen to earth. They were valuable for their iron content, so he sent them back to the U.S.

President Theodore Roosevelt was an enthusiastic supporter of Peary. So was the National Geographic Society. They helped him fund the building of a boat, the *Roosevelt,* to use in Arctic exploration.

THE 1905 EXPEDITION: Aboard the *Roosevelt,* Peary headed for the Pole on July 16, 1905. But the ship became stuck in the ice. The crew had to return home. Peary was determined to try again.

REACHING THE NORTH POLE: Peary's next attempt was a success. On March 1, 1909, he set out from Ellesmere Island. His original team included 19 sledges and 24 men. Then, on April 6, 1909, Peary, Henson, and five Inuit reached what they thought was the North Pole. They carefully measured their location. They were confident they were the first people to reach the Pole. They planted an American flag at the site.

COOK AND CONTROVERSY: Peary returned to the U.S. in triumph. "We have planted the Stars and Stripes on the North Pole," he claimed. But his glory was short lived. Another explorer, Dr. Frederick Cook, had just claimed that he had been the first to reach the Pole, in April 1908.

Peary challenged Cook's claim, as did other experts. The National Geographic Society examined all the evidence — the men's journals, maps, and calculations. They determined that Peary, not Cook, had been the first to reach the North Pole.

A FAMOUS EXPLORER: Peary became a national hero. For decades he was honored as the greatest U.S. Arctic explorer. He retired from the Navy in 1911 and lectured and wrote about his discoveries. He died on February 20, 1920.

ROBERT E. PEARY'S HOME AND FAMILY: Peary married Josephine Diebitsch in 1888. She went with Peary on his Arctic expedition of 1891.

HIS DISCOVERY — DID HE REALLY REACH THE POLE? In the 1980s, researchers began to question Peary's claim. Once again, experts investigated his records. This time, they decided that Peary had not reached the true North Pole. Instead, he had reached a point 30 to 60 miles south of it. Today Peary's achievement is still uncertain. But he is remembered for his determination to reach the Pole and to learn all he could about the Arctic.

WORLD WIDE WEB SITES:

http://www.memory.loc.gov/
http://www.pbs.org/wgbh/amex/ice/sfeature/peary.html

Ida Pfeiffer

1797 - 1858
Austrian Traveler and Writer
Traveled Around the World Alone and Wrote
of her Journeys

IDA PFEIFFER WAS BORN on October 14, 1797, in Vienna, Austria. Pfeiffer became her last name when she married. It is pronounced "FIFE-er." Her name at her birth was Ida Reyer.

IDA PFEIFFER GREW UP in a family of five boys. Her father encouraged her to be as active and curious as her brothers. She was tutored at home. From a very early age, she loved to read about explorers and travel. She longed to travel herself.

Ida's father died when she was nine. After his death, Ida's mother insisted she behave and dress "like a girl."

IDA PFEIFFER'S HOME AND FAMILY: When Ida was 22, her mother forced her to marry an older man. He was an attorney named Mark Anton Pfeiffer. They had two sons. Her husband lost his job when the boys were small. Ida taught piano and art to support the family.

Pfeiffer's marriage was very unhappy. When her mother died in 1831, she left Ida a small inheritance. Ida then left her husband and took her sons to Vienna to raise them. By 1842, the boys were grown and on their own. Ida Pfeiffer decided to realize her life-long dream: to travel.

JOURNEY TO THE MIDDLE EAST: Pfeiffer's first journey was to visit the Holy Land (Jerusalem). As she did on all her trips, she traveled alone, and with very little money. She relied on generous strangers to offer her food and places to stay.

Pfeiffer traveled first to Jerusalem and then to Egypt. She traveled by camel across the desert. She visited the Great Pyramid at Giza and the Sphinx. She returned to Europe, visiting Italy along the way. When she got back to Vienna, Pfeiffer wrote a book about her travels, *A Visit to the Holy Land*. It was a smashing success. She made enough money to continue her travels.

JOURNEY TO ICELAND: In 1845 Pfeiffer made her second trip, this time to Iceland and Scandinavia. She traveled by pony cart around Iceland. She wanted to experience life the way it was lived by

Icelanders. She ate what they ate and slept in their small cottages. She collected plants and rocks and brought them back to Vienna. When she returned home, she once again wrote about her travels. And her second book, *Journey to Iceland, and Travels in Sweden and Norway* was a success. But Pfeiffer had even bigger plans. She wanted to travel around the world.

FIRST TRIP AROUND THE WORLD: In 1846, Pfeiffer set off on a two-and-a- half year voyage around the world. She left Europe and landed first in

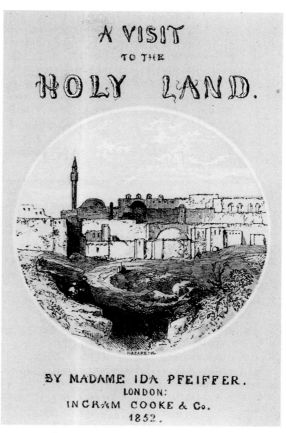

Title page of A Visit to the Holy Land, *1852.*

Brazil. She traveled inland and saw the rainforest and the native Indians. She traveled down the coast and past Tierra del Fuego.

Pfeiffer visited Chile, then set out across the Pacific to Tahiti. From there, she went to China. Next, she went to India, where she hunted for tigers. From Asia, she went to the Middle East. She visited what are now Iraq and Iran. She joined a caravan traveling across the desert, then turned north to visit Russia. In Russia, she was briefly arrested because officials thought she might be a spy.

Pfeiffer often traveled in men's clothes. If she had been discovered to be a woman in some countries, she might have been imprisoned. She carried a small pouch for water, a frying pan,

CAPE HORN.

LONDON: NATHANIEL COOKE,
MILFORD HOUSE, STRAND.

Title page of A Woman's Journey
Round the World, *1854.*

and some bread and rice. That way, she could cook meals if she needed to.

From Russia, Pfeiffer traveled through Turkey, Greece, and Italy. She reached home in November 1848. She had traveled more than 37,000 miles. She immediately began to write about her experiences. And when *A Woman's Journey Round the World* came out in 1850, she became famous.

SECOND TRIP AROUND THE WORLD: In 1851, Pfeiffer announced she was ready to travel around the world again. This time, she was offered free travel by ship and train. She sailed from London to Cape Town, South Africa. From there she headed to Singapore and Borneo. On Borneo, she visited the rainforest and the Dyak tribe. They were rumored to be headhunters, but Pfeiffer found that she liked them.

Her next stop was in Sumatra. There, she visited the Batak tribe, who were supposed to be cannibals. She was the first person ever to visit and report on their lives. Pfeiffer was afraid of them — she was worried she might be eaten! She talked to them, as best she could, in her version of their language. "Why, you don't mean to say you would kill and eat a woman, especially such an old one as I am!

I must be very hard and tough!" she said. The Batak laughed at their guest. She left as their friend.

Pfeiffer traveled next to the United States, where she visited San Francisco. From there, she traveled to Central and South America. She traveled to New Orleans, then up the Mississippi. She visited several American cities before returning to Europe in 1855. Once again, Pfeiffer's report of her journeys, *A Lady's Second Journey Around the World*, was popular with many readers.

FINAL JOURNEY: Pfeiffer took her final trip in 1856. She traveled to Madagascar, but soon found herself in trouble. She was falsely accused of plotting to overthrow the Queen and was imprisoned. After her release, she went to the island of Mauritius to recover. But she had become very ill. When she returned to Vienna, she was very sick. Ida Pfeiffer died on October 28, 1858.

HER DISCOVERY: While not an explorer in the traditional sense, Pfeiffer was the first woman to travel alone to parts of the world rarely seen by Europeans. Her books sold thousands of copies and were translated into many languages. Her vivid descriptions of the people and places she saw were eagerly read by thousands of people.

WORLD WIDE WEB SITE:

http://www.uscolo.edu/history/seminar/pfeiffer.thm

The Phoenicians

The Phoenicians lived in the coastal region of modern-day Lebanon, Syria, and Israel. They were excellent sailors. They were probably among the earliest explorers of the land around the Mediterranean Sea. They were also among the earliest people to explore beyond the Strait of Gibraltar. From there, they traveled south, exploring the west coast of Africa. They also traveled north, exploring along the Atlantic coast of Europe.

The Phoenician culture flourished between about 1100 B.C. and 500 B.C. They built fast ships and became great traders. Their boats were made of cedar and used both sails and oars for power. Their main cities were Sidon and Tyre. They also established colonies all around the Mediterranean. One of their most famous colonies was Carthage, in what is today Tunisia. The early explorer **Hanno** was from Carthage. From those cities, the Phoenicians traded goods from throughout the known world.

The Phoenicians also made goods to sell. They worked with glass and metal, including gold and silver. They also wove cloth. The Phoenicians were famous for a purple dye they used to color cloth.

The Phoenicians also created one of the first alphabets. The Greeks created their alphabet from Phoenician. Later, Greek became the source of the alphabet for English and many other languages.

Around 850 B.C., Phoenician cities were captured by the Assyrians. They were never an independent people again. Over the next 1,000 years, they were ruled by other invading countries, including the Persians, Greeks, and Romans.

Zebulon Pike
1779 - 1813
American Explorer and Soldier
Explored the American West
Pike's Peak in Colorado Is Named for Him

ZEBULON PIKE WAS BORN on January 5, 1779, in Lamberton, New Jersey. His full name was Zebulon Montgomery Pike. His parents were Isabella and Zebulon Pike. His father was an army officer who had fought in the Revolutionary War.

BECOMING A SOLDIER: Pike joined his father's regiment when he was a young man. He was made a lieutenant in 1799.

EXPLORING THE MISSISSIPPI: In 1805, General James Wilkinson chose Pike to lead an expedition to find the "source" of the Mississippi River. (The source of a river is the place where it begins.) His group was made up of 20 soldiers, who traveled 2,000 miles up the Mississippi, on water and on land.

Pike also met with Indian leaders and fur traders along his route. He told them that the area was now under U.S. control, thanks to the Louisiana Purchase.

THE LOUISIANA PURCHASE: In 1803, President Thomas Jefferson organized the purchase of a huge amount of territory from France. It was called the Louisiana Purchase. The territory ranged from the Mississippi River to the Rocky Mountains, and from the Canadian border to Texas. It cost the U.S. $15 million, about three cents an acre. With the Louisiana Purchase, the U.S. doubled in size. The new land was explored by the **Lewis and Clark Expedition.**

Pike's group started their journey in St. Louis, Missouri, in August, 1805. They traveled as far as Leech Lake, Minnesota. Pike thought he had reached the source of the great Mississippi, but he was mistaken. The expedition returned to St. Louis in April, 1806.

EXPEDITION OF 1806-1807: In July 1806, Pike went on his most important expedition. He traveled west out of St. Louis along the Osage River, crossing Missouri and into Kansas. He headed north into southern Nebraska, then south back into Kansas, where he traveled west on the Arkansas River.

PIKE'S PEAK: Pike headed west as far as the area that is now Colorado Springs, Colorado. At the edge of the Rockies, he saw a

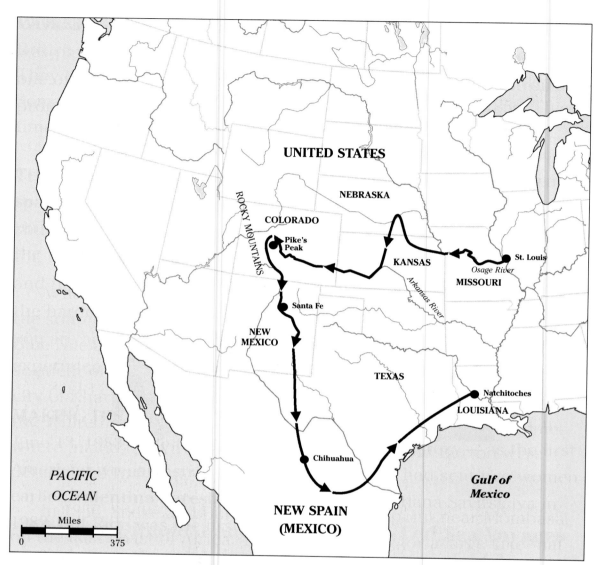

Pike's expedition of 1806-1807.

mountain, which he and two soldiers tried to climb. Pike never reached the summit, but it is now named "Pike's Peak" after him.

INTO SPANISH TERRITORY: From Colorado, Pike headed south. Soon, he was in Spanish territory. He was arrested by Spanish authorities and taken first to Sante Fe (now New Mexico). Later, he was taken to the Mexican city of Chihuahua. He and his men were treated well, but he was suspected of spying, and all his journals were taken from him.

Pike and his men were then taken across Texas and released near the town of Natchitoches, in what is now Louisiana. Back in U.S. territory, he rejoined the army. Several years after he returned, he published a book about his travels. It was a popular source of information for Americans wondering about the Western U.S.

WAS HE A SPY? No one knows for sure whether or not Pike was on a secret mission. For years historians have wondered if he was spying

View of Pike's Peak.

for the U.S. Some have suggested that he may have been working with Aaron Burr, who conspired to set up his own country in the American Southwest. But Pike was never charged or tried for any wrongdoing.

THE WAR OF 1812: Pike served in the War of 1812 between the U.S. and the English. He was killed in a battle outside of what is now Toronto, Canada, on April 27, 1813.

ZEBULON PIKE'S HOME AND FAMILY: Pike married a woman named Clarissa Brown in 1801. They had several children.

HIS DISCOVERY: Pike is noted for his journeys in the West and for climbing what became Pike's Peak. His book on the Western U.S. led many Americans to consider settling west of the Mississippi.

WORLD WIDE WEB SITES:

http://www.tsha.utexas.edu/handbook/online/articles/view/PP/
    fpi19.html
http://www.win.tue.nl/~engels/discovery/index.html

Ille ego qua propria famam virtute paraui
Pizardus patri nothus, ac notißimus Orbi,
Armis namque meis olim ampla Peruuia ceßit,
Omnis vt Hispano, duce me, sit sit subdita sceptro:
Pluraque fecißem numeroso carmine digna,
Indigna si non sublatus morte fuißem.

Francisco Pizarro
1475? - 1541
Spanish Conquistador Who Explored Peru and Ecuador
Conquered the Incas and Colonized Peru

FRANCISCO PIZARRO WAS BORN around 1475 in Trujillo, Spain. He was the son of Gonzalo Pizarro and Francisca Gonzalez. His father was an army captain and his mother was a young peasant girl. They never married.

According to legend, Pizarro grew up in his grandparents' home. He tended the pigs on their farm, and he never went to school.

FIRST VOYAGE TO THE NEW WORLD: In 1502, Pizarro sailed to Hispaniola (now Haiti and the Dominican Republic) with Nicolas de Ovando. Ovando was the governor of Hispaniola.

Around 1510 Pizarro became an explorer. He took part in an expedition to what is now Colombia with Alonso de Ojeda. In 1513, he was with **Vasco Núñez de Balboa** when he reached the Pacific Ocean.

Throughout history, Pizarro has been called a ruthless man. He showed this side in dealing with Balboa. In 1518, Pedrarias, the governor of Panama, sent Pizarro to lure Balboa to him. Pedrarias was jealous of Balboa, and once he had captured him, he had Balboa tried and executed.

Pizarro settled in Panama. He ran a business with two men, a soldier named Diego de Almagro and a priest named Hernando de Luque. They traded cattle, food, and slaves.

VOYAGES TO SOUTH AMERICA: Pizarro had heard tales about a wealthy kingdom along the west coast of South America. He made his first journey there in 1524. It was unsuccessful. He tried again in 1526. He reached as far as what is now Ecuador. He was running low on food and sent for supplies and soldiers.

The governor of Panama refused to send more men. Instead, he sent a ship and told Pizarro to let his men return. According to legend, Pizarro drew a line in the sand. He told those who wanted riches to continue with him. The others could return to Panama and poverty.

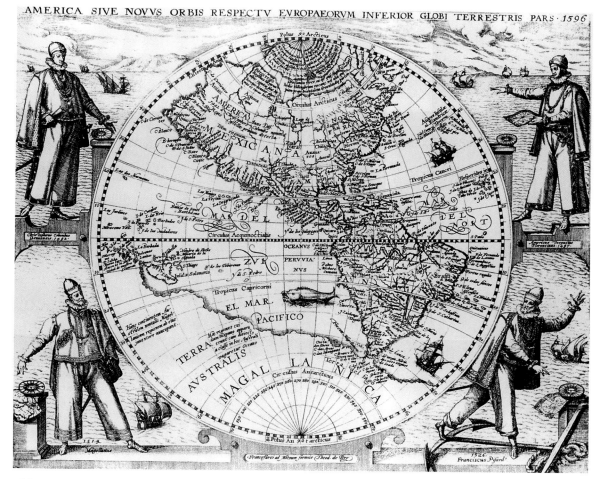

Map of the Americas from 1596 with portraits of Columbus (upper left), Vespucci (upper right), Magellan (lower left), and Pizarro (lower right).

Thirteen of Pizarro's men crossed over the line. They continued with him down the coast. On that journey, they found gold. They also found jewelry and other artifacts of the Incan empire.

THE INCAS: The Incas were a wealthy, advanced civilization that flourished along the west coast of South America for centuries. By the time of Pizarro, the empire stretched from Ecuador to Chile, and included almost 12 million people.

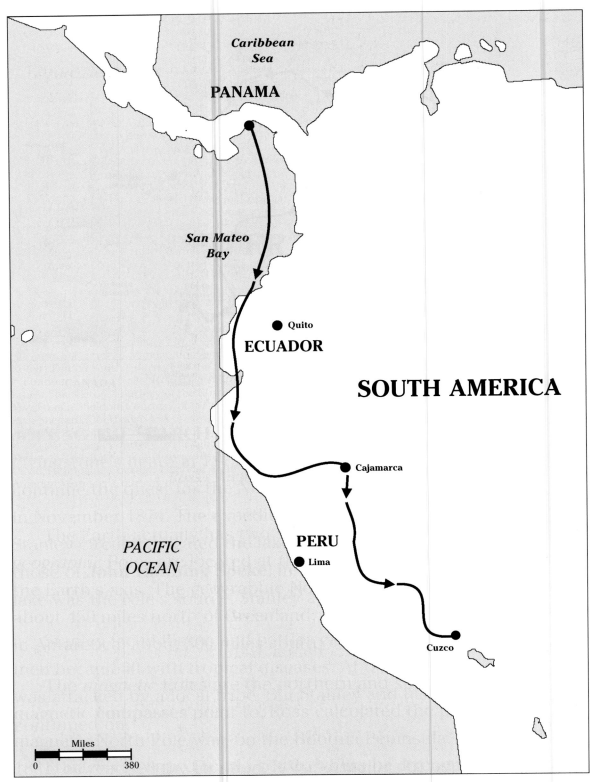

Pizarro's expedition to the Inca Empire, 1531-1533.

RETURNING TO SPAIN: Pizarro needed more money to travel further into South America. He returned to Spain and asked King Charles for backing. He took with him Inca treasures: jewelry, gold, and silver. Charles named Pizarro governor of the province of New Castille. That allowed him to explore and conquer the area reaching 600 miles south of Panama.

JOURNEY TO THE LAND OF THE INCAS: Pizarro left Spain in 1530 for Panama. In 1531, he set out for Peru with one ship, 180 men, and 37 horses. They traveled down the coast of Ecuador, landing near what is now San Mateo Bay. They continued south on foot. With him was **Hernando de Soto.**

Pizarro explored sections of Peru and founded a Spanish settlement. He made contact with local Incas. He sent de Soto to arrange a meeting with the Inca leader.

By the 1530s, the Inca empire had begun to decline. The Inca emperor and many of the rulers had recently died during an epidemic, probably of smallpox. The new emperor, Atahuallpa (aht-uh-WAHL-puh), was living near the city of Cajamarca. With him was an army of 30,000 men.

Pizarro marched into Cajamarca with his small band of men. He invited Atahuallpa to meet him in the city. His soldiers hid while Atahuallpa entered the city with 4,000 unarmed men.

Pizarro sent a priest to Atahuallpa. He demanded that the Inca emperor convert to Christianity and accept Spain as his ruler. Atahuallpa refused, and he and his men were set upon by the Spanish. They killed most of the Incas and captured Atahuallpa.

Atahuallpa pleaded for his life. He promised Pizarro a treasure of silver and gold. When the treasure was delivered — enough to fill

The murder of Pizarro.

a large room from the floor to the ceiling, Pizarro would still not let his captive go. Instead, he had Atahuallpa killed.

The rest of the Inca soldiers outside the city fled. Pizarro continued his journey south, to the Incan city of Cuzco. The Incas surrendered without a fight. By the end of 1533, the mighty Inca empire had been destroyed.

FOUNDING LIMA: Having conquered the Incas, Pizarro founded the city now known as Lima on the Pacific coast. There, he built a palace. He lived there, sponsoring expeditions and strengthening Spanish power in the region.

Pizarro had lived a ruthless and brutal life, and he had many enemies. One of his brothers had murdered his former business partner, Almagro. In 1541, Almagro's son attacked Pizarro in his palace and murdered him.

HIS DISCOVERY: Today Pizarro is remembered as the conqueror of the Incas. He was a brutal man whose destruction of an empire led to great wealth for him and for Spain, at a horrible cost to a native population now lost to history.

WORLD WIDE WEB SITES:

http://askeric.org/Virtual/Lessons/crossroads/sec4/Unit_2
http://www.win.tue.nl~engels/discovery/index.html

Marco Polo

c. 1254 - 1324
Venetian Merchant and Traveler
Explored Eastern, Central, and Southern Asia

MARCO POLO WAS BORN in Venice, in what is now Italy, around 1254. At the time of his birth, Venice was an independent city-state, and Italy was not yet a country.

There are very few facts known about Marco's early life. His father was Niccolo Polo; his mother's name is not known. She died when Marco was a young boy, and he was raised by relatives.

Niccolo Polo was from a family of wealthy merchants. He and his brother Maffeo traveled frequently to trade goods. They left Venice when Marco was just a baby. They didn't return until he was 15 years old.

THE TRAVELS OF NICCOLO AND MAFFEO POLO: In 1255, Niccolo and Maffeo set out for Constantinople (now Istanbul, Turkey). They developed their trading business there, then moved north into what is now Russia.

At that time, most of Asia was under the rule of the Mongols. The lands that make up Russia, China, and most of Asia had been conquered by Genghis Khan, head of the Mongols, around 1220. The Polos traveled to different cities ruled by Mongol lords to trade. In 1265, they decided to visit the head of the Mongols, Kublai Khan.

KUBLAI KHAN: Genghis Khan's grandson, Kublai Khan, was the Mongol leader. The Polos traveled to the city of Cambaluc (now Beijing, China), where he lived. At that time, that part of China was called "Cathay." Kublai Khan liked foreigners. He wanted to learn about their countries.

Kublai Khan asked the Polos to visit the Catholic Pope in Rome. He wanted the Pope to send representatives to his court to exchange ideas on religion. He also wanted the Polos to go to Jerusalem. He had heard about Jesus, and he wanted oil from the lamp at Jesus's tomb.

Niccolo and Maffeo finally returned to Venice in 1269. At the age of about 15, Marco Polo truly met his father for the first time. Because the Pope had just died, Niccolo and Maffeo weren't able to fulfill Kublai Khan's request. But they were eager to return to Cathay.

TRAVELING TO THE EAST: Niccolo wanted to take his son with him on his trip to the East. So in 1271, when he was about 17, Marco left Venice with his father and his Uncle Maffeo. They traveled first to the port city of Acre and on to Jerusalem. There, they got the oil from Jesus's tomb and letters from the new Pope to present to the Khan. From Jerusalem, they traveled through what is now Turkey, Iraq, and Iran to the port of Hormuz on the Persian Gulf. They had hoped to travel to Cathay by boat. But the ships they saw weren't sturdy enough to make the trip. So they decided to go by land.

Traveling along parts of the **Silk Road,** the Polos traveled north and east, across deserts and mountains, on their way to China. The journey was long and hard. They traveled through Iran and entered Afghanistan. They stayed in Afghanistan for about one year. Marco's later book about his travels indicated that he was sick during this time. Historians think he may have had malaria.

When they continued their journey, they traveled across the Pamir Mountains. They crossed the Taklimakan Desert and then the Gobi Desert. It took over a month to cross the Gobi, and they saw no animals at all in the barren wastes. Sometimes Polo would see or hear things that weren't there — mirages. In his later writings, he described them. "It often seems to you that you hear many instruments sounding, especially drums."

They finally reached Cathay, where they visited Kublai Khan at his summer palace in Shangdu, also called "Xanadu" (ZAN-ah-doo). It had taken them three years.

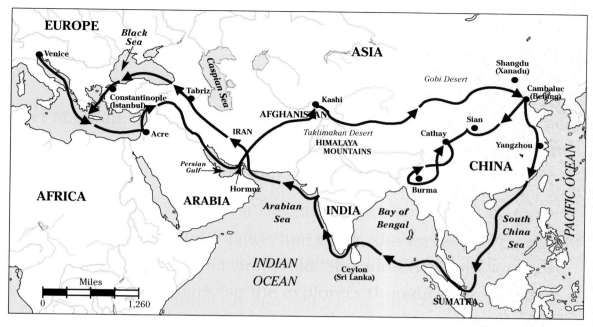

Marco Polo's travels, 1271-1295.

THE COURT OF KUBLAI KHAN: Kublai Khan was delighted with the return of Niccolo and Maffeo. He took a special interest in Marco. Marco could speak several languages. He enjoyed telling the Khan about his journeys and the people and places he had visited.

For more than 15 years, the Polos traveled throughout China for Kublai Khan. Niccolo and Maffeo Polo continued to trade goods. Kublai Khan sent Marco on missions all over his empire. He traveled to places rarely seen by Europeans. He journeyed to India. He visited what are now the countries of Vietnam and Burma. There, he learned about the people and how they lived. Returning to Kublai Kahn, he entertained the ruler with his tales.

Marco was also impressed with the incredible riches of Kublai Kahn. In his book, he talked about the beauty of the palace and grounds. Xanadu had a palace made of marble, with rooms "painted with figures of men and beasts and birds, and with a variety of trees and flowers." The palace was surrounded with a huge park. The Khan had parties for up to 40,000 people.

The Grand Canal also impressed Marco. That is a system of rivers and canals that was started by the Chinese in 500 B.C. It is more than 1,000 miles long and connects the two major waterways of China, the Yangtze and the Yellow Rivers. It is still in use today.

Marco noted Kublai Khan's military feats. Genghis Khan had united the Mongol kingdom. Kublai wanted to expand it. He tried several times to invade Japan, but failed. Marco described what he knew of Japan in his book. It was then completely unknown to Europeans. When they read Polo's book years later, it was their introduction to that island nation.

Marco Polo noted many other fascinating things about China and the kingdom of Kublai Khan. They used coal for fuel, which the Europeans did not yet do. They used paper money instead of coins. They had a mail system that used a series of riders on horses who could travel 250 miles a day to deliver the Khan's letters.

RETURN TO EUROPE: After many years in China, the Polos longed to return to Venice, but Kublai Khan didn't want them to go. Finally, he let them leave. They agreed to accompany a Mongolian princess to Iran for her wedding to the Khan's great-nephew.

The Polos sailed from China in 1291. The traveling group was huge: 14 ships and over 600 people. They sailed south through the South China Sea, stopping in Vietnam, Malaysia, and Sumatra. They spent time in Ceylon (now Sri Lanka), then sailed on along the west coast of India on their way to Hormuz. They took the princess to Iran. There, they learned that the great Kublai Khan had died.

Continuing their travels homeward, the Polos were attacked by bandits. The robbers stole most of their money and other riches. They continued on their journey, finally reaching Venice in 1295. They had been gone for 24 years. Marco, who had left Venice at 17, was now 41 years old.

A famous legend about the Polos' return relates that when they reached Venice, their relatives didn't recognize them. They had been gone so long, their relatives thought they were dead. Only when the Polos showed them the jewels they'd sewn into their clothes did they realize the long-lost travelers had returned.

IMPRISONMENT: Around 1297, Venice went to war with the city of Genoa. Marco Polo fought in a sea battle and was captured. He was imprisoned in Genoa, and over the next year dictated the book that would make him famous.

Polo told his story to a man named Rustichello. Rustichello was a writer of romances, and he used his art to create a vivid retelling of the adventures of Marco Polo.

Polo was released from prison in 1299. He returned to Venice. He married, had a family, and became a successful merchant. But when Rustichello's book on his life appeared, he became one of the most famous men of his time.

THE TRAVELS OF MARCO POLO: Polo begins his famous book with a grand statement.

"Here begins the introduction for this book which is called the description of the world. Lords, Emperors, and Kings, Dukes, and Marquesses, Counts, Knights, and Burgesses, and all people who wish to know the different generations of men and the diversities of

Polo returns from his travels, and his relatives do not recognize him.

the different regions of the world, then take this book and have it read and here you will find all the greatest marvels and the great diversities."

Marco Polo's book appeared in about 1300. It was a tremendous success throughout Europe. It was translated and read in many countries. The people of Europe learned about a world they'd never known before. They learned of peoples and cultures they never new existed. They read about the incredible riches — jewels, gold, and silver.

They also read things that seemed too outrageous to be true. Polo told stories of fantastic animals — like snakes with legs and huge mouths. Most historians think Polo made up some of these tales. It's possible that he got carried away telling his story, or that Rustichello created some of the exaggerations.

It is important to remember that when Polo's book came out, there was no printing press. Rustichello's original copy is lost. The book was copied by hand by many different people. Some of those copiers created scenes of their own, adding things to amuse their readers. Today, there are more than 150 different versions of *The Travels of Marco Polo*.

Despite the questions of what was true and what was imaginary in his tale, Marco Polo's book was a sensation. Its influence continued for centuries. Nearly 200 years after it appeared, a young Italian named **Christopher Columbus** read it as he planned to sail west from Europe in hopes of reaching the riches of India.

MARCO POLO'S HOME AND FAMILY: After his return to Venice, Polo married a woman named Donata. They had three daughters. Polo spent the last years of his life as a successful merchant, like his father.

As Polo was dying, he made a final statement about the truthfulness of his great book. "I did not write half of what I saw," he claimed. Marco Polo died in Venice in 1324.

THE NATURE OF HIS DISCOVERY: Marco Polo is remembered as the most famous traveler of all time. In his lively and entertaining book, he made the world of Asia come alive to the people of Europe. While some of his stories may be exaggerated, Polo gave Europeans a glimpse of people and places they had never known existed. He inspired generations of explorers for hundreds of years.

WORLD WIDE WEB SITES:

http://www.fordham.edu/halsall.source/mpolo.html
http://www.nationalgeographic.com/ngm.0105/feature1/
http://www.silk-road.com/artl/marcopolo.shtml

Juan Ponce de León

1460? - 1521
Spanish Explorer Who Was the First European to Reach Florida
Searched for the "Fountain of Youth"

JUAN PONCE DE LEÓN WAS BORN around 1460 in the Leon area of northern Spain. Very little is known about his early life. He went to military school and became a soldier. Later, he worked at the court of a Spanish prince. That prince became King Ferdinand.

FIRST VOYAGE: Many of the facts of Ponce de León's life are unclear. Some sources say he was a savage conqueror; some say he

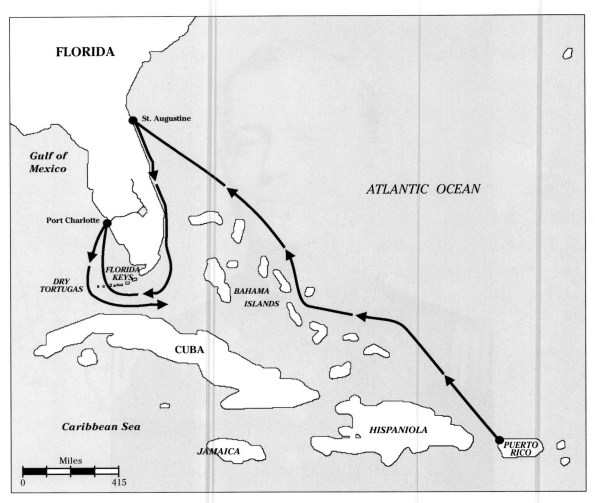

Ponce de León's voyage of 1513.

was nonviolent. Even the date of his first voyage to the **New World** is uncertain. Some sources say he sailed with **Christopher Columbus** on his second voyage in 1493. Others say he reached the New World later.

It is known that Columbus was living on Hispaniola (now the Dominican Republic and Haiti) around 1502. There was a mutiny among the Indians on Haiti, and Ponce de León was sent to end it. Historians disagree about how he handled it. Some say he brutally crushed the rebellion; others say he ended it peacefully.

PUERTO RICO: He left Hispaniola and conquered what is now Puerto Rico around 1508. Ponce de León founded a settlement there, near modern-day San Juan. He was made governor of the island. However, he later lost that title.

DISCOVERY OF FLORIDA: Ponce de León heard about a land of great wealth to the north of Puerto Rico. He received permission to look for the land, which was supposed to have a "fountain of youth." According to legend, the water from this fountain could keep a person young forever.

Ponce de León led an expedition of three ships in March 1513. They sighted land a few weeks later. Historians think that they landed around what is now Saint Augustine. Ponce de León named the place "Florida." It is possible that he named it using the Spanish word for "flowery," or for the Easter celebration, called "Pascua Florida" in Spanish.

Ponce de León went ashore with his men. He didn't know he'd reached the mainland of what would become the United States. He thought he was on an island. They explored the land for several days. Then, they headed south in their ships.

THE GULF STREAM: While sailing south, Ponce de León reached an area where the current changed. They had found the Gulf Stream. That is an ocean current that flows north from the Caribbean, along the coast of North America, and out into the Atlantic. It became an important waterway for ships from the 1500s on. Because of the swiftness of the current, ships could travel faster along the Gulf Stream and shorten the time it took to reach Europe.

View of San Juan Bay, from a fortress supposedly built by Ponce de León.

Ponce de León sailed south around what is now the Florida Keys. He sailed up the Gulf Coast of Florida, perhaps as far as Port Charlotte. Then they turned south again. On their way back to Puerto Rico, they spotted a group of islands. The islands were covered with turtles. Ponce de León named the islands the "Tortugas." That is Spanish for "turtles."

Ponce de León sailed home to Spain in 1514. He was named Governor of Florida. He returned to Puerto Rico and led another expedition to Florida in 1521. They landed on the Gulf Coast. This time, the local natives fought them. Ponce de León was wounded in the battle. He was taken to Cuba, where he died in July 1521.

HIS DISCOVERY: Ponce de León is remembered as the first European to reach Florida and to discover the Gulf Stream, while looking for the "fountain of youth."

WORLD WIDE WEB SITE:

http://www.floridahistory.org/history/ponce1.htm

John Wesley Powell
1834 - 1902
American Scientist and Explorer
Explored the Grand Canyon and the Colorado
and Green Rivers

JOHN WESLEY POWELL WAS BORN on March 24, 1834, in Mount Morris, New York. His parents, Mary and Joseph Powell, had immigrated to the U.S. from England before he was born. They were both passionately anti-slavery. Joseph Powell was a Methodist minister.

John was the fourth of nine children. The family moved often, and John lived on farms in New York, Ohio, Wisconsin, and Illinois. His father was often away from home preaching, and John did a lot of work on the farm.

As a child, Powell loved to explore the natural world around him. He collected plants, rocks, and animal specimens.

JOHN WESLEY POWELL WENT TO SCHOOL at the local public schools where he lived. He later attended Wheaton College in Illinois and Oberlin College in Ohio. At Oberlin, he studied botany (the science of plants) for the first time. He loved it.

DOWN THE MISSISSIPPI, THE OHIO, AND THE ILLINOIS: While still in college, Powell spent summers getting to know three major U.S. rivers. In 1856, he traveled the length of the Mississippi River, alone, in a row boat. The next year, he traveled the length of the Ohio River, and in 1858 the Illinois River. On these expeditions, Powell gathered specimens and studied how the rivers flowed, and how they affected the land around them. He joined the Illinois State Natural History Society and became its specialist in "conchology." That's the study of shells.

In 1860, Powell began teaching school in Hennepin, Illinois. But the Civil War was coming, and Powell spent only a year as a teacher.

THE CIVIL WAR: When the Civil War began in 1861, Powell volunteered and served as a Union officer. At the Battle of Shiloh, he was wounded and lost his right arm. After he recovered, he returned to active duty and served until the end of the war in 1865.

STUDYING AND TEACHING GEOLOGY: After the war, Powell became a professor of geology at Illinois Wesleyan University. He also directed the natural history museum. In his job, he took several field trips to the west. He began to plan a major expedition. He wanted to explore the great Colorado and Green Rivers, and the vast river canyons.

THE EXPEDITION OF 1869 — THE COLORADO RIVER AND THE GRAND CANYON: After several years of planning, Powell began the expedition for which he is best known. He wanted to explore the Colorado River and the Grand Canyon. At that time, little was known about the area, and no one had explored it yet. Powell wanted to understand the route and depth of the Colorado and the terrain of the canyons.

On May 24, 1869, Powell and nine other men left Green River City, Wyoming. They followed the Green River to where it meets the Colorado. Then they followed the Colorado through the Grand Canyon, and on to where it meets the Virgin River, in Arizona.

The crew traveled in four boats that were specially built for the expedition. They carried enough supplies for 10 months. Along with food and tools, the boats carried surveying equipment, because Powell planned to map the region.

The trip was challenging and often dangerous. Over the course of three months, they traveled over 900 miles, passing through some of the roughest water in the American West. They lost the boat that carried most of the food early on in the trip. The conditions were treacherous. They often slept on canyon floors, and they were cold and hungry.

Powell's expedition of 1869.

The crew dwindled to six. One member quit after one month, saying the trip was too dangerous. Three more left just days before the journey was completed. They, too, truly feared for their lives. Sadly, the three were never seen alive again. Most historians think they were killed by a local Indian tribe.

Powell with his crew at the start of the expedition at Green River City, Wyoming.

Powell and his crew finally reached the mouth of the Virgin River, now under Lake Mead, on the Arizona and Nevada border on August 30, 1869. They were the first explorers ever to make the journey by boat.

Powell was greeted as a hero on his return to Illinois. He wanted to go back to the West, so he began a speaking tour, hoping to raise enough money. He related his adventures for audiences all over the county.

Powell also described the awesome beauty of the vast landscape. "The Grand Canyon is a land of song. Mountains of music swell in the rivers, hills of music billow in the creeks, and meadows of music murmur in the rills that ripple over the rocks. Altogether it is a symphony of multitudinous melodies. All this is the music of waters."

Powell retraced his journey in 1871 and 1872. He wanted to carefully map the river and canyons. Based on these findings, he wrote several important books, including *Exploration of the Colorado River of the West and Its Tributaries*. Powell made recommendations to the government about how the West should be developed. He was particularly concerned about the land and water use in the southwest.

THE U. S. GEOLOGICAL SURVEY: In 1881, Powell became head of the U.S. Geological Survey (U.S.G.S.). The U.S.G.S. is the science agency of the U.S. Department of the Interior. It provides information on biology, geology, mapping, and water and land use for the U.S. and the world. Powell oversaw the development of the U.S.G.S. and directed this important government department until 1894.

BUREAU OF ETHNOLOGY: In addition to his geological interests, Powell was fascinated by languages. During his field trips, he visited and recorded the languages of many western Indian tribes. In 1879, Powell became the first director of the U.S. Bureau of Ethnology at the Smithsonian Institution. (Ethnology is the study of language and culture of different peoples.) He wrote studies on over 50 native languages. His work is still used today. Powell continued to run the bureau until his death.

JOHN WESLEY POWELL'S HOME AND FAMILY: Powell married Emma Dean in 1862. They had one child, a daughter named Mary. Powell died of a stroke on September 23, 1902, at the age of 68.

Powell's boats at Marble Canyon, along the Colorado River.

HIS DISCOVERY: Powell is remembered as one of the most important explorers of the American West. His knowledge of science, especially of land and water use, helped guide the development of the West. Lake Powell, on the border of Utah and Arizona, lies along the route he forged through the Colorado River. It is named for this brave and important explorer.

WORLD WIDE WEB SITES:

http://historytogo.utah.gov/jwpowell.html
http://kaibab.org/powell/
http://www.nps.gov/grca/photos/powell/pages/career.htm
http://www.powellmuseum.org
http://www.usgs.gov

Ptolemy

100 A.D.? to 165 A.D.?
Greek Astronomer, Geographer, and Mathematician
Ancient Mapmaker Whose Maps Were Used for
Over 1,000 Years

EARLY LIFE: Almost nothing is known about the life of Ptolemy (TOLL-eh-mee.) Facts about his birth, education, family, and death are not available. But his importance to the history of exploration is great. His maps were used by explorers until the time of **Christopher Columbus.**

Ptolemy was from the Greek city of Alexandria, in Egypt. He is known today for his work in astronomy, math, and mapmaking. He published many books on these subjects. They were translated and used for centuries.

Ptolemy believed that the Earth was the center of the universe, and that it did not move. We know now that the Earth is not the center of the universe. Like the other planets in our solar system, it revolves around the Sun and rotates on its axis. But Ptolemy's theories were accepted for centuries. He also added to the known number of stars. Observing the sky, he counted some 1,022 stars, which he listed in his catalog.

As a geographer, Ptolemy helped develop systems for measuring the Earth. These measurements, called **longitude** and **latitude**, divide the Earth into imaginary lines running north and south, and east and west. The lines each have numbers, so that any spot on the Earth can be located and assigned a numerical point.

Latitude is the name of the horizontal measurement lines on a map or globe. Latitude measures the distance of a place north or south of the equator. In latitude measurement, the equator is 0 degrees, the **North Pole** is 90 degrees north, and the **South Pole** is 90 degrees south. All the places in between have a measurement, in degrees of latitude north or south. These degrees appear on maps as horizontal lines.

Longitude lines are the vertical lines on a map or globe. Longitude measurements divide the Earth into 360 segments. The starting point for longitude, the place that is 0 degrees longitude, is called the "Prime Meridian." The Prime Meridian runs through Greenwich, England. There are 180 degrees running west and 180 degrees running east of the Prime Meridian.

Ptolemy didn't create longitude and latitude. They were concepts that earlier geographers and mathematicians developed. But he made contributions in using them to create maps. First, he figured out a way to create a map that could show the curve of the earth, even when drawn on a flat piece of paper.

Ptolemy made mistakes in his estimates, however. He didn't estimate the circumference, or distance around the Earth, correctly. He thought it was 18,000 miles (instead of about 25,000 miles.) When he created his map of the world, he made Asia too big. He didn't know about the existence of North and South America, or the Pacific Ocean. He thought Asia stretched all the way to the edge of Europe.

HIS DISCOVERY: Ptolemy's maps were used until the early 1500s. His mistakes may have led **Christopher Columbus** and other explorers to believe they'd reached India when in fact they'd discovered the **New World**. But his systems of measurement were extremely important to early explorers, giving them a sense of the shape and size of the Earth.

Pytheas

345 B.C.? to 300 B.C.?
Greek Navigator and Geographer
One of the Earliest Explorers of the North Atlantic Coast
of Europe and the British Isles

EARLY LIFE: Pytheas (PITH-ee-is) came from the Greek colony of Massilia, in what is today southern France. He was probably born sometime around 345 B.C. Very few facts are available about his life. What we know about his remarkable journey is taken from his book, *On the Ocean*. All copies of the book are now lost. His achievements are known today through the work of other historians who wrote about him.

During Pytheas's lifetime, Greece competed with the **Phoenicians** for control of trade in the coastal regions of the Mediterranean Sea. Each group tried to establish colonies to trade goods along the coast.

By the time of Pytheas, the Phoenecians were trading with the people of modern-day Europe and England. They traveled there to trade for tin, silver, and other goods. The Phoenecians even tried to block the Strait of Gibraltar, the channel connecting the Atlantic Ocean and the Mediterranean. But somehow, in about 325 B.C., Pytheas got through.

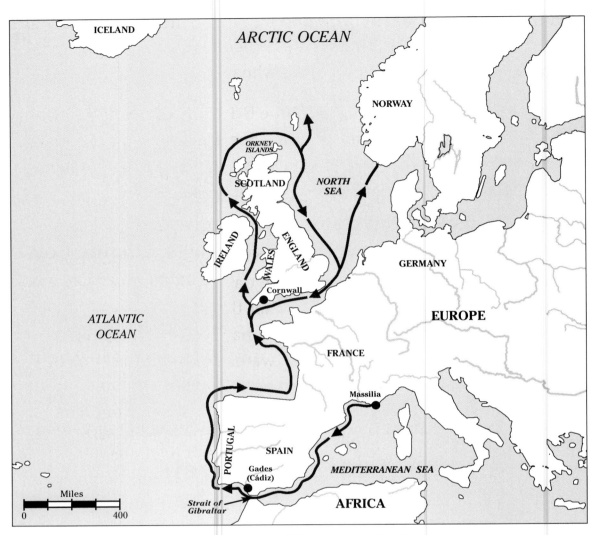

Possible route of Pytheas, c. 325 B.C.

WHAT PYTHEAS DISCOVERED: Pytheas traveled north from the Strait of Gibraltar, along the Atlantic coast of Europe. He stopped in the city of Gades, which is modern-day Cádiz, Spain.

Continuing his journey north, he stopped in what he called Belerium, which is modern-day Cornwall, in England. There, he visited the famous tin mines. Pytheas probably explored parts of Britain on foot. He was a close observer of people and customs. He described the people he met as friendly and very hard-working.

Their climate was cold and forbidding to him, and he noted that life was hard for them. He even described their drinks made from cereal grains, and their way of preparing wheat.

Pytheas next journeyed around the British Isles. He traveled north from Cornwall, through the Irish Sea. He stopped in Scotland, and may also have stopped in the Orkney Islands off the northern tip of Scotland.

The next part of Pytheas's journey is unclear. He said in his writings that he reached a land he called "Thule." It was a six-day journey from Britain. He noted that the days were endless, with the sun never setting. He also observed that the water became "thick." Modern historians believe that Pytheas had reached as far as Norway, or even Iceland. The "thick" water was probably ice floes forming in the cold water of the Arctic.

From Thule, Pytheas traveled south along the east coast of Britain. There, he visited islands off the coast of modern-day Germany. He described abundant amounts amber, which was valued as a trading item.

When Pytheas returned to Massilia, he wrote of his discoveries in *On the Ocean*. A skilled mathematician and geographer, he also included his calculations about the lands and distances he had traveled. He estimated, accurately, that the circumference, or total distance around Britain, was 4,000 miles. He also closely estimated the distance from Massilia to Britain.

Pytheas made other observations, too. He noted that the Pole Star was not at the true **North Pole**. He showed how to determine **latitude** using math. He was one of the first to observe that the tides were somehow linked to the movements of the moon.

Many of his readers didn't believe Pytheas's tales. They had never heard of water filled with ice, or a region where the sun never sets in the summer. But many modern historians consider him to be the first true explorer. If he was indeed the first European to reach Iceland, then he accomplished that feat 1,000 years before the **Vikings**.

HIS DISCOVERY: Today Pytheas is remembered for his remarkable early exploration of the British Isles. He is noted as a courageous and observant explorer.

FOR MORE INFORMATION ABOUT PYTHEAS:
www.mariner.org/age/pytheas.html

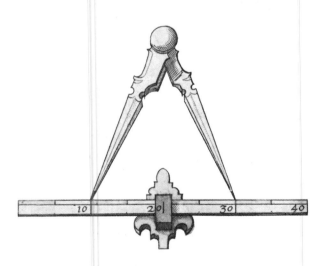

Sir Walter Raleigh

1554? - 1618
English Explorer, Statesman, and Soldier
Founder of the Roanoke Colony and Explorer
of the Orinoco River

SIR WALTER RALEIGH WAS BORN around 1554 in Devonshire, England. He was from a wealthy family. He had a half-brother, Humphrey Gilbert, who was a son from his mother's first marriage.

SIR WALTER RALEIGH.
OB. 1618.
FROM THE ORIGINAL OF ZUCCHERO IN THE COLLECTION OF
THE MOST NOBLE THE MARQUIS OF BATH.

He also had another brother, Carew, and a sister, Margaret. His last name is also spelled Rawleigh and Relegh.

Very little is known about Raleigh's childhood. As a teenager, he fought in the religious wars in France. He was a Protestant at a time of great conflict between Protestants and Catholics in England and Europe.

In 1572, he attended college at Oxford, and later studied law. In 1580 he fought against a group of Irish rebels. That brought him to the attention of Queen Elizabeth.

When Queen Elizabeth came to the throne, she wanted to build the wealth and power of England. This was a time when Spain and Portugal were the major sea powers. They controlled sea routes around Africa and to the East, as well as to North America. They also controlled the riches brought back from these far lands. Pirate ships from England often attacked and stole cargo from their merchant ships.

A FAVORITE OF THE QUEEN: Raleigh became a member of the Queen's court and one of her favorites. He was given licenses to sell cloth and wine and headed mines in Cornwall. Elizabeth also encouraged him and others in their pirating adventures against the Spanish.

His half-brother Humphrey Gilbert was also a favorite. When he died, Raleigh took over Gilbert's claim to create a settlement in the **New World**. Although Raleigh never traveled there himself, he sent three expeditions to the New World.

FOUNDING THE ROANOKE COLONY: Raleigh sent the first expedition in April 1584. They landed near Roanoke Island in what is now North Carolina. They returned to England that September, with pearls, animal skins, and two Indians. Raleigh named the area "Virginia," for Elizabeth, the Virgin Queen.

In 1585, the second expedition tried to establish a site for settlement. They landed in Roanoke in July, with about 100 people who planned to colonize the area. Some colonists explored the area. But they met hostile Indians, and many feared for their safety. **Sir Francis Drake** visited the colony in 1586, and the colonists left Roanoke with him for England.

THE LOST COLONY: Raleigh sent a third expedition in 1587. It contained over 100 settlers, including many families. They were led by a man named John White, the first governor of the colony. When the ships that carried their supplies returned to England, the colonists urged White to go, too. They wanted to make sure that they had someone who would remember them and their needs in England.

White returned to England. When he visited Roanoke in 1590, the colonists had vanished. They were never seen again. What happened to the Roanoke settlement, called "The Lost Colony," is still a mystery.

Even though the colony failed, Raleigh remained a favorite of the Queen. She knighted him in 1585 and made him captain of her guard in 1587. But around 1592, he lost her favor forever.

374   West Indianischer Historien Ander Theil

Raleigh in the New World.

BANISHED TO THE TOWER: Queen Elizabeth never married, and she liked to keep her favorites from marrying, too. Defying the Queen, Raleigh married Elizabeth Throckmorton, in secret, around 1588. She was a lady-in-waiting to the Queen. In 1592, Queen Elizabeth found out. She sent both of them to the Tower of London. That is a famous prison in London, where traitors were kept. Raleigh bought their freedom, and they left the Queen's court.

EXPLORING THE ORINOCO: In 1595, Raleigh led an expedition to the **New World**. He sailed for what is now Venezuela. He was in search of treasure, and for the mythical city of El Dorado. Explorers had been tempted for years by stories of this legendary city, which was supposedly full of gold and silver.

Raleigh sailed up the Orinoco River, but found no vast treasure. He returned to England. In 1596, he sailed with the Earl of Essex on an expedition against the Spanish city of Cadiz.

JAMES I: Queen Elizabeth died in 1603. The next king, James I, was Catholic and wanted to make peace with Spain. He didn't like Raleigh, who was known to be anti-Spanish. Raleigh also had many enemies. They plotted against him, and in 1603 he was accused of trying to overthrow James I.

Raleigh was convicted and sent to the Tower of London again. He spent his time in prison writing a book, *The History of the World*. It was the first of several popular books he published.

Raleigh was released in 1616 and went back to Venezuela. He promised the King he would not do any harm to any Spanish holdings. But when he was ill one of his captains captured and burned a Spanish settlement. His oldest son, Walter, was killed in the attack.

A CHARGE OF TREASON AND DEATH: On his return to England, Raleigh was imprisoned for treason. He was executed in 1618.

SIR WALTER RALEIGH'S HOME AND FAMILY: Raleigh married one of Queen Elizabeth's ladies-in-waiting, Elizabeth Throckmorton. They had two sons, Walter and Carew.

HIS DISCOVERY: Raleigh is remembered for his travels in the name of Queen Elizabeth. As the founder of the Roanoke colony, Raleigh played a major role in establishing English settlements in the **New World**.

WORLD WIDE WEB SITES:

http://www.btinternet.com/~richard.towers/jim/raleigh.html
http://www.fordham.edu/halsall/mod/1595raleigh-guiana.html
http://www.lib.unc.edu/ncc/raleigh.html
http://www.nps.gov/fora/sirwalter.htm

Sally Ride

1951-
American Astronaut and Scientist
First American Woman to Travel in Space

SALLY RIDE WAS BORN on May 26, 1951, in Los Angeles, California. Her full name is Sally Kirsten Ride. Her parents are Dale and Carol Ride. She has one younger sister, Karen.

SALLY RIDE GREW UP in Encino, near Los Angeles. She was an active and curious child. Her parents gave Sally and Karen the freedom to choose activities they loved. "We might have encouraged, but mostly we let them explore," her father said.

Sally loved to play sports with the neighborhood boys. Her sister remembers that "when the boys chose up sides, she was always first." At one point, she wanted to be a professional football player. She was especially good at tennis. She was offered a scholarship to a private school to play on their team.

SALLY RIDE WENT TO SCHOOL at the local public schools until high school. She went to a private school, Westlake School for Girls, where she got an excellent education. She remembers in particular a science teacher who encouraged her abilities. Ride did very well in school and continued to improve at tennis.

By the time she graduated from Westlake in 1968, she was a national champion tennis player. She went to Swarthmore College for just three semesters. Then she decided to drop out and try to become a professional tennis player. But after several months she decided that she wasn't really good enough. She went back to college, this time to Stanford University.

At Stanford, Ride had a double major in physics and English Literature. She was fascinated by the world of science, but also by the beauty of Shakespeare's plays. She completed her bachelor's degree in 1973. Ride stayed on at Stanford to study astrophysics. She received her Master's degree in 1975 and Doctorate in 1978.

APPLYING TO THE SPACE PROGRAM: Ride entered the space program right after graduation. She saw a newspaper ad saying that **NASA** (the National Aeronautics and Space Administration) was looking for scientists to fly in space. She applied, and she was accepted.

Ride aboard the Challenger, *June 1983.*

WORKING FOR NASA: So in 1978, Ride moved to Texas. She was part of a new group of 34 astronaut trainees. And she was one of the first six women ever chosen to be part of the astronaut program.

Ride spent the next four years training at the Johnson Space Center in Houston. She learned how to fly an airplane, and then a **space shuttle**. She studied the communication systems on the shuttle, mastering the role of the CAPCOM, or capsule communicator. She helped to develop a robotic arm that was used to launch and retrieve satellites. Ride recently recalled her training. She said the hardest part was "learning everything that you need so that you are an expert on every detail of the space shuttle and the experiments."

MAKING HISTORY — FIRST AMERICAN WOMAN IN SPACE: On June 18, 1983, Ride flew into space — and into history — as the first American woman astronaut. The Soviet Union had sent two women earlier, **Valentina Tereshkova** in 1963, and Svetlana Savitskaya in 1982. But Ride was the first American woman.

She flew aboard the space shuttle *Challenger* with a crew of five. Her job on the flight was as a mission specialist. On the mission, she conducted experiments and launched satellites. When she returned to Earth on June 24, 1983, Sally Ride was famous.

Ride flew again on October 5, 1984. This time, she was part of a crew of seven. On the mission Dr. Kathryn Sullivan became the first woman to walk in space. Ride conducted experiments and also served as the flight engineer. In that role, she was involved with the launch and re-entry of the shuttle.

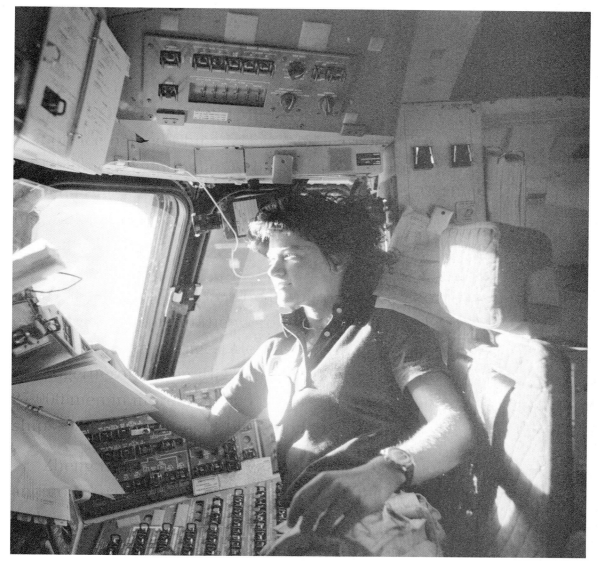

Ride on the Challenger *flight deck, June 1983.*

In June 1985, Ride was chosen to fly on another shuttle mission. But then a tragedy occurred that changed her career, and the space program, for years.

THE *CHALLENGER* CRASH: In January 1986, the *Challenger* crashed after takeoff. All the astronauts on board died. Ride became a member of the commission investigating what happened in the accident. She stopped her training to devote herself to the assignment.

After the *Challenger* accident, there were no space shuttle flights for three years. Ride decided to leave NASA and return to teaching and research. She taught at Stanford, then at the University of California at San Diego. She also became Director of the California Space Institute.

Today, Ride teaches physics and conducts research at the University of California at San Diego. She has also written a children's book about her experience in space, *To Space and Back*.

SALLY RIDE'S HOME AND FAMILY: Ride married Alan Hawley in 1982. They divorced in 1987. They didn't have children. Ride lives and works in San Diego. She is still a spokesperson for the space program and encourages kids to get involved in science and math.

HER DISCOVERY: Ride is remembered as the first American woman to travel in space.

WORLD WIDE WEB SITES:

http://ltp.arc.nasa.gov/space/frontiers/chat_archives/
    ride03-23-99.html
http://starchild.gsfc.nasa.gov/docs/StarChild/shadow.whos_
    who_level2/ride.html
http://www.jsc.nasa.gov/Bios/htmlbios/ride-sk.html

James Clark Ross

1800 - 1862

English Navigator and Explorer of the Arctic and Antarctic
Located the North Magnetic Pole and Discovered the Ross Sea

JAMES CLARK ROSS WAS BORN on April 15, 1800, in London, England. His parents were George and Christina Ross. He went to school at the Chislehurst Academy until he was 11.

JOINING THE NAVY: Ross joined the Royal Navy ten days before his 12th birthday. His uncle, John Ross, was a naval commander and explorer. Young James served with his uncle for several years.

FIRST JOURNEY TO THE ARCTIC: In 1818, Ross joined his uncle and **William Parry** on his first arctic voyage. They were in search of the **Northwest Passage**. From the early 1500s, many people believed that a water passage from Europe to Asia existed through what is now Canada. They sought a sea route linking the Atlantic and Pacific Oceans through the islands of the Canadian Arctic.

Ross's boats entered Baffin Bay and took the water route as far west as Lancaster Sound. On the expedition, Ross discovered "red snow." It was actually snow that had been turned red by microorganisms. The crew mapped the waters of Baffin Bay, finding good resources for whaling ships. The expedition failed to find the passage, but Ross was eager to return to the Arctic. He accompanied Parry on his next four voyages.

ARCTIC VOYAGES WITH PARRY: From 1819 to 1827, Ross accompanied Parry on four expeditions to the Arctic. (See Parry entry for map.) In 1819, their goal was again the Northwest Passage. They traveled through Baffin Bay and Lancaster Sound. They were forced to spend the winter on Melville Island. The ice, even in summer, blocked their path west, so they returned to England.

In 1821, Parry led another expedition in search of the passage. This time they took a more southern route. They took the Hudson Strait, traveling to the west of Baffin Island. They spent two winters in the Arctic. During the expedition, Ross learned about surveying and how to drive a sledge (a heavy sled). He became an excellent naturalist, and discovered a new species of sea gull. But the expedition came to an end in 1823. Again their path was blocked by ice, so they headed back to England.

In 1824, Parry made his final attempt to find the passage. This time, his route took him through Baffin Bay to Prince Regent Inlet. Ross's ship, the *Fury*, became caught in the ice. The ship had to be abandoned, and the crew returned to England on another ship. Years later, Ross's expedition of 1829 would survive using the supplies left on the *Fury*.

SEARCH FOR THE NORTH POLE: Ross accompanied Parry on the aging explorer's final expedition in 1827. In that voyage, they tried to reach the **North Pole** from a group of Arctic islands north of Norway. They traveled in heavy boats that could also be used as sledges. They didn't reach the Pole, but Ross kept the goal in mind.

EXPEDITION OF 1829: Ross and his uncle returned to the Arctic in 1829. Once again, they were looking for the Northwest Passage. They followed Parry's route, reaching as far as Lancaster Sound. They headed south to the Prince Regent Inlet. But they became trapped in the ice.

The group wintered in the Arctic. Ross had become a good dog sledder, and he also spent time exploring by sledge. He got to know the local Inuit people. They gave food and clothes to Ross and his men.

THE NORTH MAGNETIC POLE: Ross took many readings of their position by the stars and by measuring the Earth's magnetic fields. He was looking for the North Magnetic Pole.

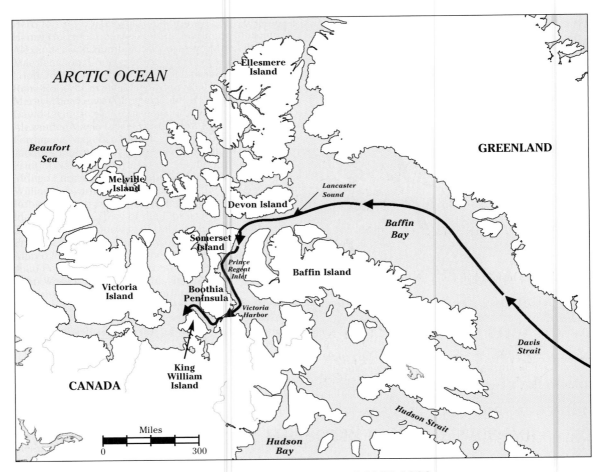

Ross's Arctic expedition of 1829-1833.

The Earth actually has two sets of Poles. The North and South *geographic* Poles are located at the northern and southern end of the Earth's axis. The geographic North Pole lies in the Arctic Ocean, about 450 miles north of Greenland. The geographic **South Pole** lies in Antarctica, about 300 miles south of the Ross Ice Shelf.

The *magnetic* Poles are the northern and southern points that magnetic **compasses** point to. Ross calculated the place where the magnetic North Pole was, on the Boothia Peninsula. On May 31, 1831, he reached the location. It was a major discovery. From that point on, navigators could use the compass with greater accuracy.

Despite his discovery, Ross had other problems. His ship still could not get through the ice. The crew was forced to abandon their ship. They traveled on foot across the ice. They reached the site where Parry's expedition had abandoned the *Fury*. They tried to head for home in small boats, but they couldn't get through. They had to winter in the Arctic again, and many were ill with scurvy. They were finally rescued in 1833 by a whaling crew, who took them back to England. The expedition had taken four years. Many in England had given them up for dead.

FIRST VOYAGE TO ANTARCTICA: In 1839 Ross was chosen to lead an expedition to Antarctica. The goal was to find the magnetic South Pole. In October 1839, the crew left England aboard two ships, the *Erebus* and the *Terror*. (The ships were used later in **John Franklin's** Arctic expedition.) The ships had very thick hulls, to help them take the pressure of the ice. Franklin also made sure the ships were filled with plenty of food, including lots of meat and vegetables to prevent scurvy.

They traveled south and reached Tasmania in August 1840. They immediately started to take magnetic readings. Ross knew that at least two other expeditions, one French and one English, were looking for the Pole, too. Ross's crew left Tasmania in November 1840. The race was on.

The crew sailed south, and on January 1, 1841, they crossed the Antarctic Circle. They forced their way through an ice pack, finally reaching open water. They had reached what would later be named the Ross Sea. Ross continued his search for the Pole.

They sighted land on January 11. Ross named several mountains, calling the region "Victoria Land" for Queen Victoria of England.

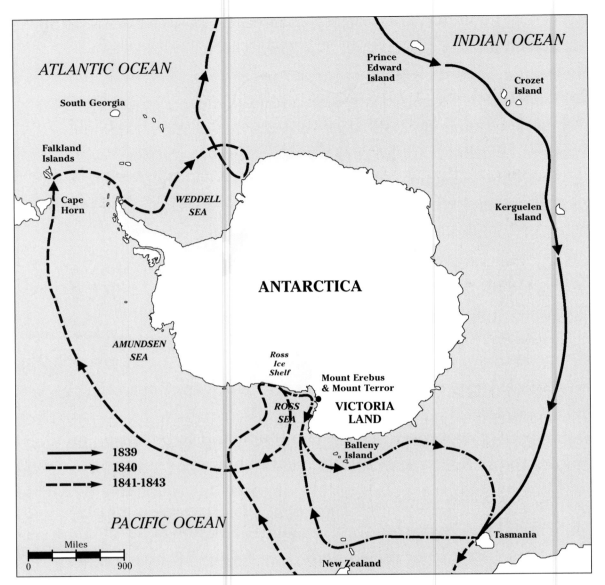

Ross's Antarctic expedition, 1839-1843.

Next, they encountered an active volcano, spewing smoke and flame. It was an incredible sight. Franklin named it Mount Erebus, for his ship. Seeing another volcano, he called it Mount Terror.

But more incredible discoveries were yet to come. Sailing south, they came upon what Ross called "a perpendicular cliff of ice." It was about 150 feet above sea level, "perfectly flat and level at the top." He named it the Victoria Barrier; it was later renamed the Ross Ice Shelf. It is an enormous shelf of ice, as big as the state of Texas.

SECOND VOYAGE TO ANTARCTICA: Ross realized that they wouldn't find the Pole that season. They returned to Tasmania for the winter. They set out for Antarctica again in November 1841. They reached the continent, but the weather was so fierce that the *Erebus* was damaged. They made repairs, but the ice made progress impossible. They decided to sail north to Cape Horn.

On the way, the two ships collided while trying to avoid an iceberg. The *Erebus* was nearly destroyed, but Ross managed to maneuver her back to port. They stayed in Cape Horn for five months.

THIRD VOYAGE TO ANTARCTICA: In December 1842, Ross began his last voyage to Antarctica. He hoped, once again, to find the magnetic South Pole, but it wasn't to be. Once again, they became caught in pack ice. After charting the waters, they sailed for home, reaching England on September 2, 1843. They had been gone for four years.

Back in England, Ross married and settled in the countryside. He came out of retirement in 1848. That year, he once again journeyed to the Arctic, this time to search for John Franklin, who had disappeared. Sadly, Ross returned to England without finding a trace of Franklin. Ross died on April 3, 1862, in Aylesbury, England.

HIS DISCOVERY: Ross is remembered as a brave and capable explorer whose expeditions took him to the Arctic and Antarctic. He discovered the magnetic North Pole and some of the most important sites in Antarctica.

NOTE: There is a British research ship, the *RRS James Clark Ross*, that is assigned to Antarctica. Their web site is the first one listed below. It includes diaries written by the crew about life in Antarctica, and information about their expeditions.

WORLD WIDE WEB SITES:

http://www.antarctica.ac.uk/Living_and_Working/Diaries/RRS_
   James_Clark_Ross/ antarctica
http://www.south-pole.com/p0000081.htm
http://www.theice.org/discovered.html

Sacagawea

c. 1778 - 1812

Shoshone Indian Guide and Translator for the
Lewis and Clark Expedition

SACAGAWEA WAS BORN around 1778 in what is now Idaho. Her name is also spelled "Sacajawea" and "Sacakawea." It is pronounced many different ways, including "sah-CAH-guh-wee-ah," "sack-uh-guh-WAY-uh" and "sack-uh-juh-WAY-uh." She was a member of the Shoshone tribe.

KIDNAPPED: Around 1800, Sacagawea was kidnapped by Hidatsa Indians, who were enemies of the Shoshone. As a prisoner, she was taken to the Hidatsa village near Bismarck, North Dakota. She was later sold as a slave to a French-Canadian trader named Toussaint Charbonneau. Charbonneau claimed that Sacagawea and another young Indian woman were his "wives," but there is no evidence that he ever married them. Instead, Sacagawea served as his slave.

MEETING LEWIS AND CLARK: In 1804, Sacagawea met **Meriwether Lewis** and **William Clark**. She was to become the only woman on the most important American expedition to the West.

THE LEWIS AND CLARK EXPEDITION: In 1803, President Thomas Jefferson had chosen Lewis to put together an expedition to explore the American West. Jefferson was clear about what he expected of the expedition. They were to follow the Missouri River out of St. Louis, looking for a waterway to the Pacific Ocean. They knew the Missouri would lead them to a mountain range — the Rockies. They thought it would be similar in size and scope to the Appalachians. They also knew another river system, the Columbia, flowed into the Pacific on the west coast. Jefferson wanted to find a waterway that connected the two river systems.

The new American government also needed to know all about the western lands. They needed maps, with information about rivers, mountains, and terrain. They needed to know about the plants, animals, and opportunities for trade and settlement. They also needed to know about the many Indian tribes in the vast area. What were they like? Were they peaceful or warlike? And how would they feel about their new leader, Jefferson?

Lewis and Clark named their crew the Corps of Discovery. The 33 men who made up the Corps set out from St. Louis, Missouri, on May 14, 1804.

Fort Mandan: In October 1804, as winter neared, they stopped near what is now Bismarck, North Dakota. There, near the camps of the Mandan and Hidatsa tribes, they made their winter camp. It was there that they met Sacagawea.

When Sacagawea met Lewis and Clark, she was about 17 years old and pregnant with her first child. She and Charbonneau spoke several Indian languages, so the explorers thought they would be valuable as translators. And because the expedition was traveling through Shoshone territory, Sacagawea could help as a guide. So Lewis and Clark hired Sacagawea and Charbonneau. In February 1805, Sacagawea gave birth to a son, Jean Baptiste Charbonneau. Lewis helped in delivering her baby.

Starting Off Again — April 1805: When the Corps left Fort Mandan in April 1805, Sacagawea went with them, along with Charbonneau and her son. They traveled in two boats called pirogues and six canoes. Jean Baptiste traveled strapped to his mother's back during the long, difficult journey. The little boy grew to become a favorite of William Clark, who called the boy "Pompy."

The Corps crossed into Montana. They saw huge herds of buffalo, elk, and deer. They also saw a Grizzly bear for the first time. One chased a crewman up a tree.

During a storm, the boat holding the maps and journals nearly capsized. Sacagawea calmly saved the precious documents. Lewis wrote that she was as brave as any man in handling the near-tragedy.

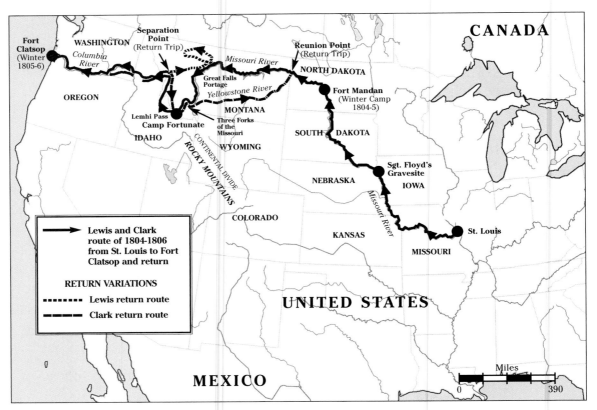

The Lewis and Clark expedition, 1803-1806.

A Fork in the River: The crew reached a point where the Missouri divided into a northern and a southern route, or "fork." They chose the southern path, and they soon reached waterfalls. Lewis knew the path was the right one, because the Indians had told him to expect the waterfalls. They were near what is now Great Falls, Montana.

A Long Portage: The boats could not travel over waterfalls, so the crew had to make a long, difficult portage. That is, they had to carry their boats overland. They actually built wheels out of cottonwood, which they attached to the boats. But the 18-mile trip still took them three weeks. Finally, they reached a point in the river where they could put the boats back in the water.

Three Forks of the Missouri: The next major landmark they came to was a place where the Missouri divided into three forks. They named them for three famous Americans. They named one the "Madison," in honor of the Secretary of State (and later President) James Madison. Another was named the "Gallatin," for Secretary of the Treasury Albert Gallatin. And one they named for their President and sponsor, Jefferson. They followed the Jefferson west.

The Continental Divide: In August 1805, Lewis and Clark reached the Continental Divide. That is a point at the crest of the Rocky Mountains where rivers flow either eastward, toward the Mississippi River, or westward, toward the Pacific Ocean.

As Lewis walked to the top of the ridge, he expected to see on the other side plains leading to the Columbia River and to the ocean. Instead, he saw the Bitterroot Range of the Rockies. Their hopes to find the **Northwest Passage** were dashed. The Rockies were so much more vast, in size and scope, than they had ever imagined. Their route would be longer, and harder.

Sacagawea Reunited with her People: Continuing down the other side of the divide, Sacagawea began to recognize the land. She knew she was close to her home. Lewis decided to scout ahead and meet the Shoshone. He met several Shoshone women, then several men. He led them back to the crew, and to everyone's astonishment, Sacagawea recognized an old friend. It was a wonderful reunion. But the greatest surprise came when she recognized her brother, Cameahwait, now the chief. When she saw him, "she jumped up, ran, and embraced him," wrote Lewis. She "threw her blanket over him and cried profusely."

U.S. Mint Commemorative Coin Cover for Sacagawea Golden Dollar, Jan. 2000.

They named their camp, near the Lemhi Pass, "Camp Fortunate." Lewis and Clark traded with the Shoshone for horses. They knew that their canoes would be of no use in going over the mountains. They began the overland part of their journey. They hired a Shoshone guide named Old Toby. Then they began the difficult crossing over the Bitterroot Mountains.

They crossed from what is now Montana into Idaho. The weather was fierce, and they were near starvation. Once over the mountains, they met members of the Nez Perce tribe. This friendly group gave them food and shelter.

The crew left their horses with the Nez Perce, built new canoes, and proceeded on the Clearwater River. In October, they reached the Snake River, and from that, the Columbia. The river is fierce, with many rapids and waterfalls. Once again, they had to make difficult portages.

The Pacific Ocean: In November 1805, they reached the Pacific Ocean. Clark wrote in his journal of the "great joy in camp" as they reached "this great Pacific Ocean" they had "been so long anxious to see." They had traveled over 4,000 miles in 554 days.

The Corps spent the next four months on the Pacific coast, near what is now Astoria, Oregon. They built a fort, named Fort Clatsop after a local tribe. They hunted and fished, and built a salt-making camp. With salt, they could preserve meat and fish for the journey home.

The crew learned that a dead whale had washed up on shore near their camp. Sacagawea especially wanted to see it. Clark wrote that "she observed that she had traveled a long way with us to see the great waters, and that now that monstrous fish was also to be seen." She saw the whale, and was impressed.

The Journey Home: In March 1806, the Corps began the journey home. They canoed back up the Columbia, finally reaching the Nez Perce. They got their horses back, and headed back across the Bitterroots. But their path was blocked with snow and ice. After the snow melted, they made their way across the mountains.

The Corps Divides: In July 1806, the Corps separated into two groups. Lewis wanted to explore possible northern routes that could be used by later settlers. He took a group north into the Marias River region. There, near the Canadian border, they had a run-in with a group of Blackfeet Indians. The groups exchanged gunfire, and two Indians were killed. They were the only Indian deaths of the expedition.

Clark chose a southern route, and Sacagawea went with him. His group crossed the Rockies, then took the Jefferson River as far as

Statue of Sacagawea near Fort Mandan, North Dakota, where she joined Lewis and Clark.

Three Forks. The Clark group divided again, and he explored the Yellowstone River region. Clark named an unusual sandstone formation "Pompy" for Sacagawea's son. He also wrote his name and the date on the rock. It can still be found, near Billings, Montana.

All the groups came together where the Yellowstone and the Missouri Rivers meet, in August 1806. Lewis had been wounded in a hunting accident, but he was mending.

Sacagawea Leaves: The Corps reached Fort Mandan on August 17, 1806. Sacagawea's part of the expedition was over. As the Corps continued on to St. Louis and a heroes' welcome, she stayed in the area with Charbonneau and her son. Charbonneau was paid $500 and given 300 acres of land for his services to the expedition. Sacagawea received nothing.

Later, Clark wrote to Charbonneau. "Your woman who accompanied you that long dangerous and fatiguing route to the Pacific Ocean and back deserved a greater reward for her attention and services than we had in our power to give her." Sacagawea never knew the importance of her contribution to the Lewis and Clark Expedition.

SACAGAWEA'S HOME AND FAMILY: Several years after Sacagawea returned to the Hidatsa village, she had another child, a girl named Lisette. Sacagawea died in 1812, around the age of 25. Both of her children were adopted by William Clark after her death. Jean Baptiste grew up in St. Louis, where Clark paid for his education. There is no information about what happened to Lisette.

HER DISCOVERY: As a valued member of the Lewis and Clark expedition, Sacagawea is remembered as an excellent translator and brave guide.

Sacagawea has become a legendary figure in American history. Even though no one is exactly sure what she looked like, there are many depictions of her, including statues and a golden dollar with her picture on it. Two hundred years after the Lewis and Clark expedition, Sacagawea continues to inspire and fascinate people of all ages.

WORLD WIDE WEB SITES:

http://www.lewisandclark.org/
http://www.lewisandclarkeducationcenter.com/
http://www.loc.gov/exhibits/lewisandclark/lewisandclark.html
http://www.nps.gov/lecl/
http://nwrel.org/teachlewisandclark/home.html
http://www.pbs.org/lewisandclark/

Robert Falcon Scott

1868 - 1912
English Naval Officer and Explorer of Antarctica

ROBERT FALCON SCOTT WAS BORN on June 6, 1868, in Devonport, England. His parents were John and Hannah Scott. He was the third of five children. He had three sisters, Ettie, Rose, and Katherine, and a brother, Archie. His father owned a brewery.

ROBERT FALCON SCOTT GREW UP in a large, comfortable home. "Con," as he was called, liked to play with his siblings and daydream.

JOINING THE NAVY: When he was 13, Scott joined the Navy. Over the next several years, he rose through the ranks of the Navy. He sailed to many different parts of the world and learned to be a leader of men.

THE RACE FOR THE POLES: By the end of the 19th century, most of the surface of the planet had been explored. What remained were the North and South Polar regions. Explorers from many countries competed against one another to locate and claim the North and South Poles. Crews from the U.S., Russia, Norway, England, Germany, and other nations were locked in a race to determine who would reach either pole first.

FIRST EXPEDITION TO ANTARCTICA, 1901-1904: In 1900, Scott was chosen to lead an expedition to Antarctica. His ship, the *Discovery*, was equipped to withstand the pressure of pack ice. He left England in 1901 and established a base at McMurdo Sound. The expedition was based at the edge of the Ross Ice Shelf. (It had been named for English explorer **James Clark Ross**.)

At that time, almost nothing was known about Antarctica. Part of their purpose was to gather scientific data about the continent. The crew also had to learn to deal with the challenges of the land and weather. The continent spends six months each year in sunlight, and six months in darkness. Winter temperatures reach 128 degrees below zero. Frostbite was a constant threat. Deadly blizzards came up suddenly. The glare of the sun on the ice caused snowblindness. Any exploration was limited to just a few months each year.

Scott expedition at the base of Mount Erebus, Antarctica.

Scott and his crew traveled inland during the Antarctic summer, which begins in December. At that time of year, the light is constant and the storms are generally not as fierce. He used both sleds pulled by dogs and sledges (heavy sleds) pulled by men. When the Antarctic winter came, they secured the ship to the edge of the ice shelf. Soon it was locked in the ice. The men built huts and endured the long and dangerous winter.

Ernest Shackleton accompanied Scott on his first expedition. They explored almost 400 miles inland, heading toward the South Pole. On the return trip to the coast, Shackleton became very ill with scurvy. Many of the sled dogs starved and had to be killed. When they finally reached base camp, Scott sent Shackelton home aboard a supply ship.

The following spring, Scott pressed further into the interior of Antarctica. They never reached the South Pole, but they gathered important information on the land and the weather of Antarctica. The crew mapped the area. They studied glaciers and the local penguins. They returned to England in 1904.

SECOND EXPEDITION TO ANTARCTICA, 1910: In 1910 Scott was again chosen to lead an Antarctic expedition. This time their goal was to be the first men to reach the South Pole.

THE RACE TO THE POLE: Scott and his crew left England in 1910 aboard the *Terra Nova*. After reaching Antarctica, they set up base camp at McMurdo Sound. They set out for the Pole on October 24, 1911. Racing the English crew to the Pole was the Norwegian explorer **Roald Amundsen**.

The expedition had problems from the start. Scott's crew had motorized tractors, ponies, and dogs. The tractors broke down.

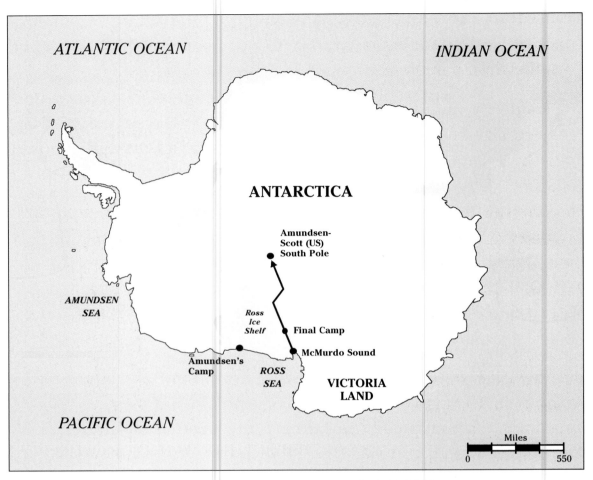

Scott's Antarctic expedition of 1911-1912.

The ponies were unable to move in the ice pack and had to be destroyed. The dogs and many of the crew were also sent back to base camp. The remaining men hauled the sledges themselves as they headed for the Pole. They traveled for 81 days in blinding blizzards and temperatures as low as 45 degrees below zero.

On January 18, 1912, Scott, along with four remaining crewmen, reached the South Pole. But Amundsen had gotten there first. He had left a flag and a tent. Scott wrote in his diary, "The Pole, yes, but under very different circumstances to those expected. But this is an awful place." Disappointed, the five men headed back to camp.

Scott wrote, "Now for the run home and a desperate struggle. I wonder if we can do it!"

Tragically, not one of them returned alive. One crewman, Edgar Evans, died of injuries on February 17. As supplies ran out, another crewman, Lawrence Oates, walked into the blizzard, saying "I am just going outside and may be some time." He was never seen again.

Scott and the two remaining men, Edward Wilson and Henry Bowers, died of starvation and cold on March 29, 1912. They were within 11 miles of their camp. Scott had kept a diary of their final voyage. The diary and the bodies of the three

Scott in Antarctica, January 26, 1911.

crewman were found by a rescue team in November, 1912. The world mourned the loss of the brave explorers.

ROBERT FALCON SCOTT'S HOME AND FAMILY: Scott married a woman named Kathleen Bruce in 1908. They had one son.

HIS DISCOVERY: Scott is remembered for his two expeditions to Antarctica, especially his heroic attempt to reach the South Pole. He is also remembered as a brave leader. One of his last diary entries reads: "Had we lived, I should have had a tale to tell of the hardihood, endurance, and courage of my companions which would have stirred the heart of every Englishman. These rough notes and our dead bodies must tell the tale."

WORLD WIDE WEB SITES:

http://212.219.145.16/south/discovery1.htm
http://ast.leeds.ac.uk/haverah/spaseman/scott.shtml
http://south-pole.com/p0000089.html
http://www.ibiscom.com/scott.htm

Ernest Shackleton
1874 - 1922
Irish-Born English Explorer of Antarctica

ERNEST SHACKLETON WAS BORN on February 15, 1874, in County Kildare, Ireland. His parents were Henry and Henrietta Shackleton. Henry was a farmer and later became a doctor. Henrietta spent her time caring for a lively family of ten children. Ernest was their second child. He had one brother and eight sisters.

ERNEST SHACKLETON GREW UP first in Ireland, then in England. His father moved the family to England in 1884, after he became a doctor. Ernest was an active boy and loved sports. He also loved to read adventure stories. One favorite was *20,000 Leagues under the Sea*. In that adventure classic by Jules Verne, Shackleton pictured himself as the brave Captain Nemo.

ERNEST SHACKLETON WENT TO SCHOOL first at home, where he studied with a tutor. When he was 11, he attended Fir Lodge Preparatory School. At 13, he went on to Dulwich College, which was a high school. Shackleton was never a good student. He was good at sports, but bored in the classroom.

GOING TO SEA: Shackleton left school at 16 and became a sailor on a merchant ship. His first trip took him to South America. It was a long, hard introduction to life at sea. They traveled to Cape Horn, battling winter storms.

It was during this voyage that Shackleton first thought of exploring Antarctica. "I think it came to me during my first voyage. I felt strangely drawn towards the mysterious south. Many a time, even in the midst of all the discomfort, my thoughts would go southward."

Shackleton loved life at sea. Over the next 10 years, he traveled the world. By 1898, he'd worked his way up the ranks to the level of "Master," which allowed him to command a ship. Around this time he had a dream about becoming a polar explorer. "I seemed to vow to myself that some day I would go to the region of ice and snow and go on and on till I came to one of the poles of the earth." The next 20 years of his life were devoted to that dream.

Endurance *crew playing football on the ice.*

THE RACE FOR THE POLES: By the end of the 19th century, most of the surface of the planet had been explored. What remained were the North and South Polar regions. Explorers from many countries competed against one another to locate and claim the North and South Poles. Crews from the U.S., Russia, Norway, England, Germany, and other nations were locked in a race to determine who would reach either pole first.

TO ANTARCTICA WITH SCOTT: In 1901, Shackleton was chosen to accompany **Robert Falcon Scott** on an expedition to Antarctica. Aboard the *Discovery,* they left England in 1901 and established a base camp at McMurdo Sound. The expedition was stationed at the edge of the Ross Ice Shelf. (It had been named for English explorer **James Clark Ross**.)

At that time, almost nothing was known about Antarctica. Part of their purpose was to gather scientific data about the continent. The crew also had to learn to deal with the challenges of the land and weather. The continent spends six months each year in sunlight, and six months in darkness. Winter temperatures reach 128 degrees below zero. Frostbite was a constant threat. Deadly blizzards came up suddenly. The glare of the sun on the ice caused snowblindness. Any exploration was limited to just a few months each year.

With Scott, Shackleton explored almost 400 miles inland, heading toward the South Pole. They didn't reach the Pole, and on the return trip to the coast, Shackleton became very ill with scurvy. Many of the sled dogs starved and had to be killed. When they finally reached base camp, Scott sent Shackleton home aboard a supply ship.

As Shackleton recovered, he vowed to return to Antarctica and try again to reach the South Pole. After several years of planning and finding funding, he returned to Antarctica.

THE *NIMROD* EXPEDITION, 1907-1909: In 1907, Shackleton sailed for Antarctica aboard the *Nimrod*. They landed near McMurdo Sound in early 1908. Over the next year the crew made several major discoveries. They were the first men to climb Mount Erebus and to reach the magnetic South Pole. (The Earth actually has two sets of Poles. The North and South *geographic* Poles are located at the northern and southern end of the Earth's axis. The *magnetic* Poles are the northern and southern points that magnetic compasses point to.)

Endurance *on the ice.*

The crew also had many dangerous scrapes with death. Several of the men fell through the ice and nearly drowned. Once, a sledge almost disappeared over a crevasse. The three men hauling the sledge were nearly dragged down into the icy water. But except for frostbite and injuries, the men stayed healthy.

On October 29, 1908, Shackleton and three men set out for the South Pole. Within 97 miles of the Pole, faced with blizzards and a low food supply, they had to return to camp. Although they were disappointed, they had come closer than any previous expedition. They returned to England in 1909, with Shackleton burning to return and claim the Pole for himself and England.

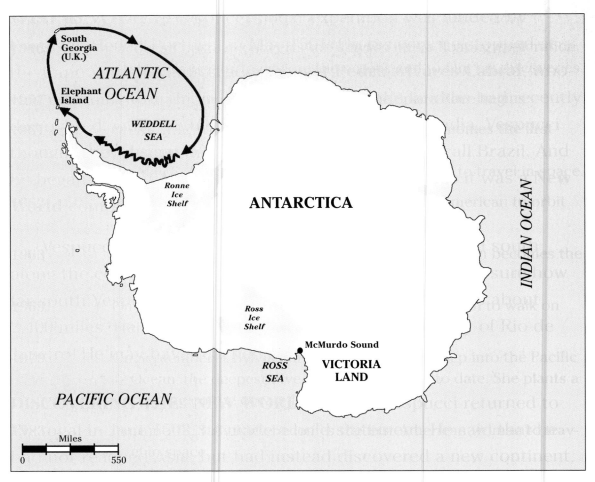

The route of the Endurance *expedition, 1914-1917.*

Two years later that honor went to **Roald Amundsen**, who reached the South Pole on December 14, 1911.

Still full of ambition and curiosity, Shackleton planned another expedition. This time, he would attempt "the first crossing of the Antarctic continent from sea to sea." "Every step will advance geographic science," he claimed. "It will be the greatest polar journey ever attempted." Although Shackleton's expedition of 1914 didn't reach its goal, it is one of the most famous journeys in the history of exploration.

THE *ENDURANCE* EXPEDITION, 1914-1917: In 1914, Shackleton set off for Antarctica. The expedition included two ships, the *Endurance* and the *Aurora.* Shackleton sailed aboard the *Endurance,* with 27 men and 69 sled dogs. They left South Georgia Island in December 1914. While heading for the Weddell Sea, the *Endurance* became stuck in the pack ice.

They could see Antarctica, but they never reached it. The *Endurance* drifted in the ice for ten months. During that time, Shackleton had the men move from the ship to tents. He kept their spirits up by having them play football and exercise the dogs.

But the *Endurance* was doomed. The ship was crushed in the ice and sank. Shackleton and his men saved the small lifeboats from the ship. For five more months the crew was stranded on a floe of drifting ice. Throughout their ordeal, Shackleton told the men they would make it home. He never gave up, and he didn't let them give up.

In a daring attempt to reach the open sea, they rowed across open water for one week, in a blizzard. They reached deserted Elephant Island safely. Shackleton then decided to try to make it to South Georgia for help. He and five others crossed the South Atlantic in winter, in one of the boats. Fighting ocean gales on some of the roughest waters in the world, they reached South Georgia in 16 days. After a three-day hike over the mountains and across a glacier, they reached a whaling station on the island.

Shackleton then found a boat to take them back to Elephant Island, where he rescued every one of his men. Not a life was lost. It was an incredible feat of heroism. They returned to England in 1917.

Shackleton before his final expedition, 1921.

FINAL VOYAGE — THE *QUEST*: Shackleton was in poor health when he attempted his last trip to Antarctica. Aboard the *Quest*, and with many of the *Endurance* crew, he left England in 1921. He never reached Antarctica. Ernest Shackleton died of a heart attack off South Georgia Island. He was 47 years old. His wife decided he should be buried there, in the lands he loved so well.

ERNEST SHACKLETON'S HOME AND FAMILY: Shackleton married Emily Dorman in 1904. They had three children, Raymond, Cecily, and Edward.

HIS DISCOVERY: Shackleton is remembered as an explorer of great determination and a superb leader. Against tremendous odds, he saved the *Endurance* crew, with a combination of strength, will, courage, and optimism. Shackleton's character was described by a member of the *Nimrod* expedition. "For scientific leadership, give me Scott, for swift and efficient travel give me Amundsen. But when you are in a hopeless situation, when you are seeing no way out, get down on your knees and pray for Shackleton."

WORLD WIDE WEB SITES:

http://212.219.145.16/south/nimrod1.htm
http://www.south-pole.com/p0000097.htm

May French Sheldon
1847 - 1936
American Explorer of East Africa

MAY FRENCH SHELDON WAS BORN on May 10, 1847, in Pittsburgh, Pennsylvania. "Sheldon" is her married last name. Her name when she was born was May French. Her father, Joseph French, was an engineer. Her mother, Elizabeth French, was a doctor.

Sheldon went to school in New York and in Europe. She moved to England, where she started a publishing company, Saxon & Company. She wrote several novels and short stories and also sculpted. She married an Englishman, Eli Sheldon, in 1876. He was a publisher and banker.

Sheldon met both **David Livingstone** and **Henry M. Stanley**. She was fascinated by their stories of Africa. She decided she would travel there.

FIRST EXPEDITION: In 1891, May French Sheldon began a trip that would make her famous. She led her own expedition, which she paid for herself, into East Africa. She was independent, and she knew what she wanted to do.

Sheldon wanted "simply to study the native habits and customs free from the influence of civilization." She especially wanted to learn about the lives of African women and children. She faced a lot of criticism from the English press. They called her a "vulgar American" and made fun of her expedition. English government officials in Africa discouraged her.

Sheldon didn't care what they thought. She traveled from Zanzibar into East Africa. Her crew included over 150 African tribesmen who served as guides and porters. She carried food, medicine, and many items, like beads, to use in trade or as gifts. Sheldon carried some peculiar things, too. She brought a ball gown and blonde wig to wear when meeting tribal chiefs.

Sheldon traveled almost 1,000 miles through Tanzania. She circumnavigated Lake Chala and explored Mount Kilimanjaro. She traveled through "primeval forest trees." She fell into ancient piles of leaves, "into which I sank up to my armpits."

She also met more than 35 different tribes. Many had never seen a white woman before. Unlike many Europeans who explored Africa, Sheldon did not consider the tribal people to be inferior. Instead, she declared they were mistreated by "zealots" who tried to impose their way of life on native Africans.

In her later writings, Sheldon described the daily lives of Africans. She wrote about their homes, family rituals, food, and relationships. The African people she met created a name for her: "Bebe Bwana," which means "Woman Master."

When she returned to London, she wrote about her discoveries. Her book, *Sultan to Sultan*, was a great success. For her travels and writings, Sheldon was elected to the Royal Geographical Society. She traveled to the U.S., where she gave a series of popular lectures.

LATER EXPEDITIONS: Sheldon traveled to Africa again in 1894, when she visited the Congo. In 1905, she led her final African expedition, to Liberia. May French Sheldon died in London in 1936.

HER DISCOVERY: Sheldon was one of the first women to explore Africa. She visited tribes never before seen by a European or American. Her reports of the daily lives of the tribal people, particularly of women and children, were important to later studies.

WORLD WIDE WEB SITE:

http://digital.library.upenn.edu/women/eagle/congress/sheldon-may.html

Alan Shepard

1923 - 1998
American Astronaut
First American to Travel in Space

ALAN SHEPARD WAS BORN on November 18, 1923, in East Derry, New Hampshire. His full name was Alan Bartlett Shepard Jr. His parents were Alan and Renza Shepard. He had a sister named Pauline.

ALAN SHEPARD GREW UP on a farm in East Derry, New Hampshire. When he was young, he dreamed of being a pilot. He used to ride his bike to the local airport, where he helped out so he could be near the planes.

ALAN SHEPARD WENT TO SCHOOL at the local public schools. For college, he went to the U.S. Naval Academy. He was a good student and also played several sports. When Shepard graduated from the Academy in 1944, the U.S. was fighting World War II.

WORLD WAR II: World War II took place between 1939 and 1945 in Europe, Africa, and the Far East. In the war, Germany, Italy, and Japan made up the "Axis" powers. They fought against the "Allies" —the U.S., England, France, and the Soviet Union.

THE NAVY: Shepard served aboard the destroyer *Cogswell* from his graduation in 1944 until the war ended in 1945. After the war, he trained to be a pilot.

TEST PILOT: Shepard earned his wings in 1947. He entered the U.S. Navy Test Pilot School in 1950. After graduating, he tested some of the newest, fastest, and most advanced aircraft in the world. His flight training continued at the Naval War College, where he graduated in 1957.

BECOMING AN ASTRONAUT: In 1959, Shepard applied to be one of the first Mercury astronauts. The Mercury program was run by **NASA** (the National Aeronautics and Space Administration). It was the first manned space program in the U.S. It was incredibly tough to get in, and it meant everything to Shepard. "That was competition at its best," he recalled. "Not because of the fame or the recognition that went with it, but because America's best test pilots went through this selection process."

Launch of Freedom 7, *May 5, 1961.*

Shepard was chosen as one of the seven Mercury astronauts. He began two years of intensive physical and technical training. He was then selected as the first American to fly in space. His flight was scheduled for early 1961.

THE COLD WAR: When Shepard became an astronaut, the Soviet Union and the U.S. were locked in what was called the "Cold War." After World War II, the Soviet Union and the U.S. became the two strongest nations in the world. They represented two very different political systems. The U.S. was a democracy; the Soviet Union was a Communist state. The two "superpowers" also had powerful nuclear weapons. The relationship between the two nations was very important. For more than 40 years, the hostilities between these two nations affected world politics.

***SPUTNIK* AND THE SPACE RACE:** On October 4, 1957, the Soviets launched the very first satellite, *Sputnik 1*. It was the beginning of the Space Age, and the Space Race between the U.S. and the Soviets.

Because of its military importance, the Space Race between the U.S. and the Soviet Union was always about much more than exploration. The Space Race was also about domination. Each country was afraid that the other would develop the weapons and technology to dominate them. The U.S. was astonished at the success of *Sputnik*. U.S. military leaders had no idea that the Soviets had the technology to launch a satellite. And the same technology that could launch a satellite could launch a missile. But *Sputnik* wasn't the only tremendous "first" for the Soviet space program.

YURI GAGARIN: On April 12, 1961, the Soviet cosmonaut **Yuri Gagarin** became the first person to leave Earth and travel in space.

Shepard being picked up by a helicopter after splash-down of
Freedom 7, *May 5, 1961.*

Aboard the space capsule *Vostok 1*, he orbited the Earth once. He reached an altitude of 188 miles, traveling at 18,000 miles an hour. His flight lasted 108 minutes.

Shepard's flight was scheduled for May 1961. But in the weeks prior to his flight, there were some significant failures for the U.S. space program. Two test rockets had gone off course on take-off, and had to be shot down. All eyes were on Alan Shepard, hoping for a successful start to the U.S. space program.

THE FLIGHT OF *FREEDOM 7*: Shepard blasted off from Cape Canaveral, Florida, on the morning of May 5, 1961. His space capsule, the *Freedom 7*, rode into space on top of a Redstone rocket. His flight carried him 116 miles into space and lasted 15 minutes. After traveling 302 miles, his capsule fell into the Atlantic Ocean near Bermuda. He was picked up by a helicopter, and Shepard returned to the U.S. a hero.

He met President John F. Kennedy, who awarded him the Medal of Honor. After the success of Shepard's flight, Kennedy stated: "I believe this nation should commit itself to the goal, before the decade is out, of landing a man on the Moon and returning him safely to Earth." Now, the race to the Moon was on.

But Alan Shepard wouldn't go into space for ten more years. He suffered from an inner ear disorder that took years to treat properly. His ear problem threw off his balance and affected his ability to navigate a space craft. Shepard was determined to remain in the space program. He stayed with NASA and served as the Chief of the Astronaut Office. He helped select and train astronauts and planned NASA missions.

Finally, in 1969, Shepard had surgery that corrected his ear problem. In 1971 he returned to active duty. He was chosen to lead the *Apollo 14* mission to the Moon. The Apollo missions began in the 1960s to stage the first landing of a human on the Moon. In July 1969, **Neil Armstrong** realized that amazing feat, becoming the first person to walk on the Moon.

APOLLO 14: On January 31, 1971, Shepard blasted off into space again. With him on the mission were Stuart Roosa and Edgar Mitchell. Shepard and Mitchell landed on the Moon's surface, in the lunar module *Antares,* on February 5. Roosa stayed aboard the main shuttle, orbiting the Moon until the mission was complete.

Shepard on the Moon, January 31, 1971.

WALKING ON THE MOON: As he stepped onto the Moon's surface,
Shepard said, "It's been a long way, but we're here." He and Mitchell
spent nine hours on the surface, collecting soil and rock samples
and doing experiments. Shepard was a golfer, and before they left,
he pulled out a golf club and hit a few balls. One traveled "miles
and miles and miles," reported a delighted Shepard. They returned
to Earth on February 9. Shepard became one of only 12 Americans
to walk on the Moon. And at 47, he was the oldest person ever to
achieve that feat.

RETIREMENT FROM NASA: Shepard retired from NASA in 1974. He headed a construction company in Houston for several years, then became president of the Astronaut Scholarship Foundation. That group raises money for scholarships for students in science and engineering.

ALAN SHEPARD'S HOME AND FAMILY: Shepard married Louise Brewer in 1944. They had three daughters, Julie, Laura, and Alice. Alan Shepard died of leukemia on July 21, 1998, at the age of 74.

HIS DISCOVERY: Shepard is remembered as the first American to travel in space. Throughout his life, he said his proudest accomplishment was being chosen as one of the first Mercury astronauts.

Shepard wasn't comfortable being the center of attention. "During the actual process of flying spacecraft, one doesn't think of oneself as being a hero," he said. "One does it because the challenge is there." Still, in one of his final interviews, he admitted, "maybe I am a piece of history after all."

WORLD WIDE WEB SITES:

http://www.jsc.nasa.gov/Bios/htmlbios/shepard-alan.html
http://www.nasa.gov/shepard.html

John Hanning Speke

1827 - 1864
English Explorer Who Discovered the
Source of the Nile River

JOHN HANNING SPEKE WAS BORN in Devon, England, on May 4, 1827. Very little is known about his young life.

IN INDIA: When he was 17, Speke left home and joined the British Army. He was sent to India, where he served for several years. From India, he traveled to the Himalayas and Tibet.

EXPLORING WITH BURTON: In 1855, Speke joined the famous British explorer **Richard Francis Burton** on an expedition to Africa. They explored what is now Somalia, where Speke was wounded by Somali fighters. Speke and Burton returned to Africa in 1856. This time they were looking for the source of the Nile.

THE NILE: The Nile River is 4,160 miles long — the longest river in the world. People have been fascinated with the great river for centuries. Many people had tried to find its source — the point where the river begins. But by the 19th century no one had found it.

What Speke, Burton, and others were actually looking for was the source of the White Nile. The Nile's two main tributaries are the Blue Nile and The White Nile. The White Nile forms the longest segment of the Nile River system. It connects with the Nile at the city of Khartoum. What Speke wanted to know was exactly where the White began. In his time, explorers knew that it started somewhere inland from the east coast of Africa. He and Burton were determined to find it.

In 1856, Speke and Burton started from a point near Mombasa, on the east coast of Africa. They were looking for a large lake that local legend said was the source of the Nile. They headed inland and explored East Africa. They became the first Europeans to reach Lake Tanganyika, in February 1858.

But then disaster struck. Burton developed malaria, and Speke became blind from a tropical disease. Luckily, Speke's blindness was temporary. He traveled on, north from the city of Tabora, leaving Burton to recover.

On July 30, 1858, Speke reached the great lake he was sure was the source of the Nile. He called it "Lake Victoria" in honor of

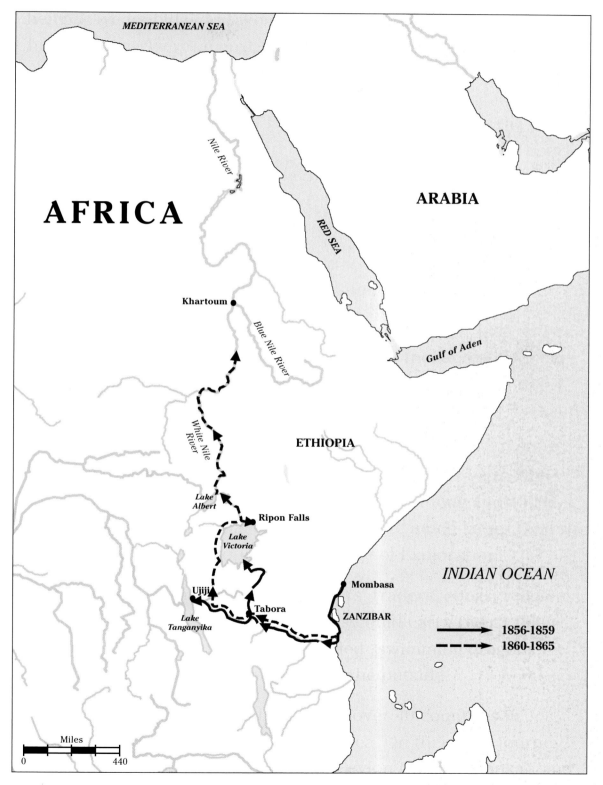

Speke's expedition of 1856-1859 and 1860-1863.

England's Queen. Speke returned to Burton to tell him of his success. But Burton didn't believe him.

Speke returned to England and was greeted by many as a hero. Still, some doubted he had found the Nile's source, especially Burton. The Royal Geographical Society sponsored Speke on another expedition to prove his discovery.

BACK TO AFRICA WITH GRANT: In 1860, Speke returned to Africa, accompanied by explorer James Grant. Together they reached Lake Victoria and mapped parts of it. Then Grant injured his leg and had to recuperate. Speke went on alone and found where the Nile leaves Lake Victoria, at Ripon Falls.

Speke wanted to prove that he'd found the great river's source. He found Grant, who had recovered, and they followed the White Nile north. But the river was blocked by warring local tribes.

They returned to England, where Burton still doubted their discovery. He challenged Speke to a public debate on the issue. But the day before the debate, Speke shot and killed himself in a hunting accident. He was just 37 years old.

HIS DISCOVERY: Later expeditions proved that Speke was right: he had indeed discovered the source of the world's great river. He is remembered for that accomplishment.

WORLD WIDE WEB SITE:

http://www.win.tue.nl/~engels/discovery/index.html

Henry M. Stanley

1841 - 1904
English-American Explorer and Journalist
Explored Central Africa and Rescued David Livingstone

HENRY M. STANLEY WAS BORN on January 28, 1841, in Denbigh, Wales. His name when he was born was John Rowlands. He changed his name to Henry Stanley as an adult. His parents were John Rowlands and Elizabeth Parry. They were never married.

HENRY M. STANLEY GREW UP with relatives, then at St. Asaph Workhouse. At that time in England, poor children without family or money lived and went to school at workhouses.

Stanley was a good student, but a rebellious boy. He hated the workhouse, and he left at age 15. He decided to go to America to seek his fortune. He sailed for New Orleans in 1859.

AMERICA AND A NEW NAME: In New Orleans Stanley worked for a businessman named Henry Stanley. He became very attached to Stanley, and he took the man's name for his own. He also became a U.S. citizen.

In 1861, the Civil War began. Stanley fought on both the Confederate and Union sides, before becoming ill and returning to Wales. After a brief visit, he was back in the U.S. He worked for a time on merchant ships and in the U.S. Navy. In 1867, he began a career as a journalist. It would lead to his fame as an explorer.

THE SEARCH FOR LIVINGSTONE: Stanley worked for the *New York Herald* as a reporter. In 1871, Stanley's editor sent him to find **David Livingstone.**

Livingstone was a famous missionary and explorer from England. He had explored central Africa, discovering several major landmarks, including Victoria Falls. He had also set up Christian missions and tried to destroy the slave trade that still existed in Africa. Livingstone had written several books about his work in Africa. They had made him a world-famous explorer and anti-slavery champion.

In 1866 Livingstone had begun an expedition to find the source of the Nile River. By the time Stanley's editor sent him to Africa, Livingstone had been missing for five years.

A painting of Stanley's African adventure.

Stanley began his search from Zanzibar, on the east coast of Africa. He traveled inland to Lake Tanganyika. On October 23, 1871, the two men met in the city of Ujiji. Stanley spoke the famous line: "Dr. Livingstone, I presume." Although Livingstone wasn't lost, he was in dire need of food, medicine, and companionship. Stanley gave him all those things. The two became great friends.

Stanley wanted Livingstone to return with him to Europe. But Livingstone refused. He felt he hadn't completed his African mission. Stanley returned to England, and Livingstone died in 1873, in what is now Zambia.

Stanley published a book on his experience, *How I Found Livingstone*, in 1872. The work made him a famous explorer, whose name is forever linked to Livingstone's.

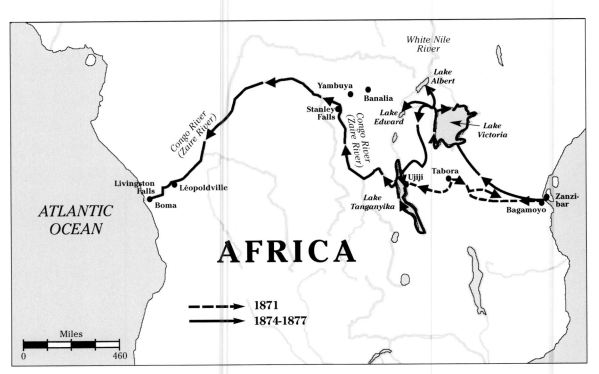

Stanley's expeditions of 1871 and 1874-1877.

JOINING THE SEARCH FOR THE SOURCE OF THE NILE: After Livingstone's death in 1873, Stanley put together an expedition to continue the quest for the Nile's source. He started from Zanzibar in November 1874. The expedition headed inland to Lake Victoria. Stanley circumnavigated the lake. He compared his findings with those of **John Hanning Speke**. In 1858, Speke had claimed that the lake was the Nile's source. Stanley agreed.

Stanley faced illness and battles on his expedition. Many of his men became ill with tropical diseases. At one point, the expedition was attacked by a local tribe. But Stanley and his men escaped and continued on.

Stanley continued to the south, where he circumnavigated Lake Tanganyika. Next, the expedition headed west and picked up the

Congo River, which they followed all the way to the Atlantic Ocean. Along the way, Stanley named a waterfall for Livingstone. The expedition reached the ocean in August 1877, ending a three-year journey.

Stanley's book on his expedition, *Through the Dark Continent*, was published in 1878. It became an international success. By 1879, he was planning another trip to Africa.

EXPLORING THE CONGO: Stanley spent the next five years exploring the Congo River area. He received money for the trip from King Leopold of Belgium. Leopold wanted to make the area a colony. Stanley traveled throughout the region that is now the Democratic Republic of Congo. He met with tribal leaders and developed treaties establishing Belgian settlements. He built roads in the region. This led to his nickname, Bula Matari, which means "Breaker of Rocks." The area became known as the Congo Free State, under Belgian control. A city, Stanleyville, was named for him.

Stanley's book on the expedition was called *The Congo and the Founding of Its Free State*. Published in 1885, it added to his ever-growing fame. In this and all his books, Stanley created vivid portraits of life in Africa. He described the different tribes he met, the exotic foods, the tropical diseases, the landscape. He made Africa come alive for Europeans.

FINAL EXPEDITION: In 1887, Stanley was back in Africa. Once again, he was on a rescue mission. The governor of the Equatorial Province of Egypt (in what is now Sudan) was facing a rebellion. Stanley was chosen to find him and bring him to safety.

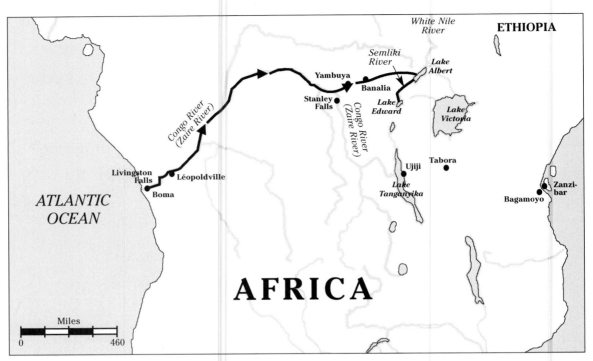

Stanley's expedition of 1887-1889.

Stanley started at Boma in the Congo. He traveled up the Congo River, then overland to Lake Albert. He found the governor, Mehmed Emin Passa, at Lake Albert. But the governor wanted military help, not rescue. Stanley finally convinced him to leave with him. They headed east, back to the Congo River, and to the Atlantic.

Along the way, the Stanley expedition explored the Ruwenzori Mountains and the Semliki River. Stanley made some important discoveries regarding the Nile's source. In locating the Semliki, he discovered how it linked Lake Edward to Lake Albert. Lake Albert flows into the White Nile, which later joins the Nile.

FINAL YEARS: Stanley returned to England in 1889. His book on the expedition, *In Darkest Africa*, came out in 1890. He decided to become an English citizen again in 1892, and he was knighted in 1899. He served in the English Parliament from 1895 to 1900.

HENRY M. STANLEY'S HOME AND FAMILY: Stanley married a woman named Dorothy Tennant in 1890. They had one son, Denzil, whom they adopted. Stanley died after having a stroke on May 10, 1904. He was 63 years old.

HIS DISCOVERIES: Stanley is best known for his rescue of Livingstone. He is also known for his journeys into the interior of Africa, particularly for his explorations of the Congo and other waterways. He is also remembered for his vivid books, which recreated the exotic world of Africa for Western readers.

WORLD WIDE WEB SITES:

http://www.theatlantic.com/issues/96sep/congo/stanley.htm
http://www.win.tue.nl/~engels/discovery/index.html

Abel Janszoon Tasman
1603-1659
Dutch Explorer and Navigator Who Was the First European to Discover Tasmania, New Zealand, the Fiji Islands, and Tonga
Proved Australia Was a Continent

ABEL JANSZOON TASMAN WAS BORN in 1603 in the city of Lutjegast, in the Netherlands. Very little is known about his young life. As a young man, he moved to Indonesia and began a career as a sailor.

THE DUTCH EAST INDIA COMPANY: Around 1632, Tasman joined the Dutch East India Company. It was a very powerful business that controlled much of the trade between Asia and Europe. Tasman headed trading expeditions for them. He traveled throughout Indonesia and to Japan, Southeast Asia, and Taiwan.

FIRST VOYAGE TO THE SOUTH PACIFIC: In 1642, Tasman was chosen to lead an expedition to the South Pacific. At that time, Dutch navigators had explored and sighted the coastline of what we now know as Australia. In 1606 Wiilem Jansz was the first European to see Australia. But at that time, no one knew exactly what it was.

Was it the edge of a huge southern continent, the legendary "Terra Australis"? Was it a group of islands? Tasman's task was to find out. He was also to sail as far to the east as possible. The Dutch knew of the wealth of Chile in South America. They wanted part of the rich trade there.

Tasman left Jakarta, Indonesia, in August 1642. He headed an expedition of two ships and about 100 men. They carried items to trade along the way. They sailed first to Mauritius, an island in the Indian Ocean. From there, they sailed southeast.

TASMANIA: On November 24, they saw land. It was the island we now call Tasmania, after Tasman. He called it Van Diemen's Land, after the governor who had chosen him for the expedition. They went ashore and found food, but no people. They were the only visitors for more than 100 years.

NEW ZEALAND: They continued to sail eastward, passing through what was later called the Tasman Sea. On December 13, they saw land again. It was the South Island of New Zealand. Tasman called it Staten Island. He thought it was part of the great southern land mass. They passed through part of Cook Strait, which separates the two islands that form New Zealand.

Tasman headed northeast. After several weeks, he sighted the Tonga Islands, then the Fiji Islands. He was the first European to see them. His ships traveled west, and over the next months sailed through the Solomon Islands, and along the north coast of New Guinea. They were soon in waters they knew, reaching Indonesia and Jakarta in June 1643.

Without knowing it, Tasman had sailed around the southern portion of Australia. That proved that Australia was not part of a huge southern land mass. Instead, it was a continent, bordered by oceans. It was a very important discovery.

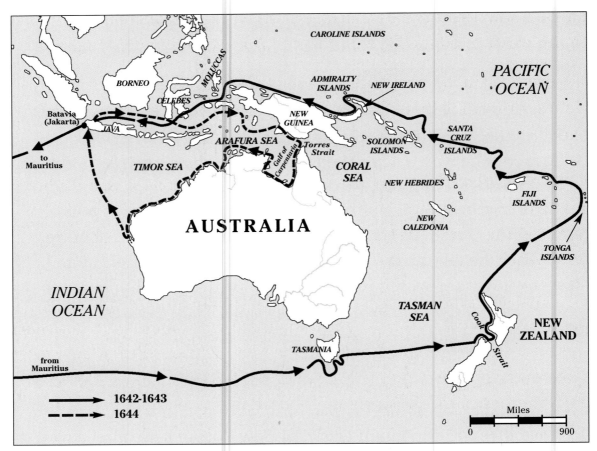

Tasman's expedition, 1642-1644.

Yet Tasman's company was disappointed with his expedition. He hadn't found great wealth or the passage to Chile. But they were willing to finance another journey.

SECOND VOYAGE: In 1644, the Dutch East India Company sent Tasman on another expedition to the South Pacific. He was to sail to the area between New Guinea and the great land mass to the south.

Tasman left Jakarta in February 1644, heading to New Guinea. He sailed into the Torres Strait, which separates Australia and New Guinea. Turning south, Tasman sailed along the coast of the Gulf of

Carpentaria. He continued along the coast of Australia all the way to the western edge of the continent. Then, he headed for Jakarta.

Once again, his employers were disappointed. He had found no riches, or trading possibilities. But Tasman's sailing days were not over.

LAST YEARS AT SEA: Tasman became the commander of a trading ship. He continued to sail for the Dutch. He also fought in a battle between the Dutch and the Spanish in the Philippines in 1648. In his later years, he returned to Jakarta. He died there in 1659.

The Dutch East India Company never made Tasman's findings public. No one is sure why. They might have thought that the lands were not wealthy enough to bother with. Or, perhaps they thought that someday they would explore the region again, and find and keep the riches for themselves.

HIS DISCOVERY: Tasman is remembered for his discovery of Tasmania, New Zealand, Tonga, and the Fiji Islands. And although he didn't know it, he proved that Australia was a separate continent, not part of a great land mass to the south. An island and sea now bear his name in the part of the world he helped to explore.

WORLD WIDE WEB SITE:

http://www.dnzb.govt.nz/dnzb

Valentina Tereshkova

1937 -
Russian Cosmonaut and First Woman to Travel in Space

VALENTINA TERESHKOVA WAS BORN on March 6, 1937, in Maslennikovo, Russia. Her mother worked in a clothing factory and her father was a tractor driver. Valentina was the second of three children. She has an older sister and a younger brother.

VALENTINA TERESHKOVA WENT TO SCHOOL at the age of eight. When she was 16, she left school and started working at a textile plant.

GETTING CHOSEN FOR THE SPACE PROGRAM: Tereshkova loved parachute jumping. It was because she was so good at it that she was chosen for the Soviet space program.

THE COLD WAR: When Tereshkova was growing up, Russia was part of the Soviet Union. The Soviet Union and the U.S. were locked in what was called the "Cold War." After World War II, the Soviet Union and the U.S. became the two strongest nations in the world. They represented two very different political systems. The U.S. was a democracy; the Soviet Union was a Communist state. The two "superpowers" also had powerful nuclear weapons. The relationship between the two nations was very important. For more than 40 years, the hostilities between these two nations affected world politics.

***SPUTNIK* AND THE SPACE RACE:** On October 4, 1957, the Soviets launched the very first satellite, *Sputnik 1*. It was the beginning of the Space Age and the Space Race.

Because of its military importance, the Space Race between the U.S. and the Soviet Union was always about much more than exploration. The Space Race was also about domination. Each country was afraid that the other would develop the weapons and technology to dominate them. The U.S. was astonished at the success of *Sputnik*. U.S. military leaders had no idea that the Soviets had the technology to launch a satellite. And the same technology that could launch a satellite could launch a missile. But *Sputnik* wasn't the only tremendous "first" for the Soviet space program.

YURI GAGARIN: On April 12, 1961, the Soviet cosmonaut **Yuri Gagarin** became the first person to leave Earth and travel in space. Aboard the space capsule *Vostok 1*, he orbited the Earth once. He reached an altitude of 188 miles, traveling at 18,000 miles an hour.

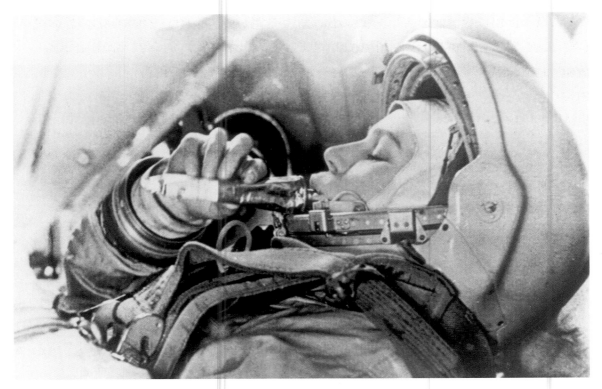

Tereshkova eats food from a tube on her flight into space, June 1963.

His flight lasted 108 minutes. The Soviets had beat the Americans into space. Now they would send the first woman into space.

TRAINING FOR HER FLIGHT IN SPACE: In 1962, Tereshkova was one of four women chosen to be part of the Soviet space program. She had no piloting experience, so she spent the next year training. She learned to pilot the space capsule. She also trained for the physical demands of space travel, like weightlessness, and the changes in gravity that take place during re-entry.

THE FIRST WOMAN IN SPACE: On June 16, 1963, Valentina Tereshkova entered history as the first women to travel into space. She took off aboard the *Vostok 6*. She spent 71 hours in space (just under three days), orbiting the Earth 48 times.

When she returned, she was greeted as a hero. She recently recalled that her first feeling was that "I had done my duty." She also said she was "convinced that men and women could work in space." After she landed, she was "simply overwhelmed with joy that it was all over and behind."

Tereshkova received many awards and was named a Hero of the Soviet Union. She also accepted the United Nations Gold Medal of Peace.

Tereshkova never flew again. She became active in the Communist Party and spoke all over the Soviet Union. She is now head of the Russian Center for International and Scientific Cooperation. She oversees educational programs for business people and students. One program brings students from all over the world to study in Russia.

VALENTINA TERESHKOVA'S HOME AND FAMILY: Tereshkova married another cosmonaut, Andrian Nikolayev. They had one daughter, Elena. Soviet scientists were interested in Elena, because she was the first child born to two astronauts. She was a perfectly normal child, and is now a doctor in Russia. Tereshkova and Nikolayev are now divorced.

HER DISCOVERY: Tereshkova is remembered as the first woman to travel in space. It took the U.S. 20 years to match this achievement. It wasn't until 1983 that **Sally Ride** became the first American woman to travel in space.

WORLD WIDE WEB SITE:

http://starchild.gsfc.nasa.gov/docs/StarChild/whos_who_level2/
 tereshkova.html

David Thompson
1770 - 1857
English Explorer and Geographer
Explored and Mapped the Canadian West

DAVID THOMPSON WAS BORN on April 30, 1770, in London, England. His father died when he was two years old, and David grew up very poor. He was sent to a charity school for boys in London. He was an excellent math student.

MOVING TO CANADA TO WORK FOR THE HUDSON BAY COMPANY: When he was 14, Thompson moved to Canada. He began to work for the Hudson Bay Company, which controlled much of the fur trade. He worked as a clerk for several years, at Churchill on Hudson Bay. He was then sent to work at forts on the Saskatchewan River. Thompson spent the winter of 1787 living with the Peigan Indian tribe. He learned their language and studied their culture.

In 1788, Thompson broke his leg. While he was recuperating, he met a mapmaker who taught him how to survey. Thompson loved the work. "Now I could make of this uncharted land a known quality," he wrote later. "And to this end I kept for 60 years records of all observations of each journey made." Thompson's maps would become the most important early geographic records of Canada.

Although he learned the fur trade, Thompson always preferred exploring to trading. During his years with the Hudson Bay Company, he most enjoyed traveling in the West, exploring, and making maps.

THE NORTH WEST COMPANY: In 1797, Thompson left the Hudson Bay Company. He went to work for their main competitor, the North West Company. That year, he began a survey that covered 4,000 miles of rivers.

Thompson traveled south out of Manitoba down the Assiniboine River to the Missouri River. He reached the area near Bismarck, North Dakota, the home of the Mandan Indians. Just seven years later, **Lewis and Clark** would build Fort Mandan there. He traveled further east and discovered Turtle Lake, one of the headwaters of the Mississippi River.

From there, Thompson headed to Lake Superior, where he surveyed the shoreline. In the late 1790s Thompson moved west,

Thompson in the Athabasca Pass, 1810.

to the edge of the Rocky Mountains. He lived in the town of Rocky Mountain House, in what is now Alberta. He married a local young woman and started a family. Over the next several years, he explored and charted the Red Deer River, the Bow River, and the Peace River.

In 1806 the North West Company asked Thompson to find a trade route through the mountains. Thompson spent several years searching for a pass through the mountains. He eventually chose what is called Howse Pass, near the Columbia River.

MAPPING THE COLUMBIA RIVER: In 1807, Thompson crossed the Rocky Mountains at Howse Pass. There, he built the Kootenay House trading post. Then he set off to map the Columbia River. It took him four years, as he surveyed, established trading posts, and followed the Columbia, including many of its tributaries.

On his journey Thompson discovered the Athabasca Pass, which he took across the Rocky Mountains to the Columbia. The Pass was used by traders for many years. Thompson traveled through what is now British Columbia, Idaho, Montana, and

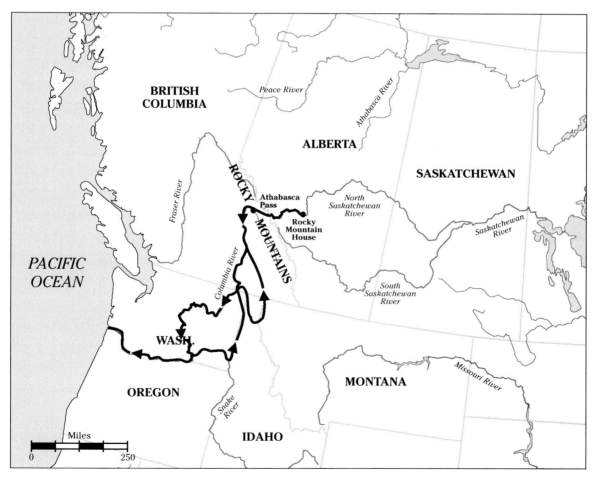

Thompson's expedition to map the Columbia River, 1807-1811.

Washington. He reached the mouth of the Columbia on the Pacific Ocean, on July 15, 1811. He was the first European to explore the great river from beginning to end.

MOVING BACK EAST: In 1812, Thompson retired from exploring. He moved, with his family, to Terrebonne, near Montreal. He spent the next several years completing a detailed map of the area he'd explored. When it was finished, it covered more than 1.5 million square miles. It was so large that it covered an entire wall.

In 1816, Thompson began a ten-year project to survey the boundary between the U.S. and Canada. He completed the project in 1826.

DAVID THOMPSON'S HOME AND FAMILY: Thompson married Charlotte Small in 1800. In 57 years of marriage, they often traveled together, sometimes with their children. They had 13 children, and 10 survived to adulthood. Thompson died on February 10, 1857, in Longeuil, Canada.

HIS DISCOVERY: Thompson's great contributions to mapmaking were not discovered until the 20th century. His maps of the Canadian West became the basis of all later maps. He is now considered one of the greatest Canadian geographers.

WORLD WIDE WEB SITES:

http://www.davidthompsonthings.com/
http://www.lafete.org/new/v_ger/ex/daveE.htm

George Vancouver
1757 - 1798
English Explorer and Navigator
Surveyed the Pacific Coast of North America from
San Francisco to Alaska

GEORGE VANCOUVER WAS BORN on June 22, 1757, in Norfolk, England. Nothing is known about his early life.

GOING TO SEA: When he was just 13 years old, Vancouver joined the English Royal Navy. Ten years later, he served with **Captain James Cook** on his second voyage (1772-1775) and third voyage (1776-1780).

On the third voyage, in 1776, Vancouver traveled with Cook to look for the **Northwest Passage**. The English wanted to find a water route through the islands of the Canadian Arctic. On that voyage, in March 1778, Vancouver became one of the first Europeans to set foot on modern-day British Columbia.

During their voyage to the Sandwich Islands (Hawaii), Cook was killed, and Vancouver was wounded. Vancouver sailed back to England. He next served in the Caribbean for nine years. In 1791, he was chosen to lead an expedition to navigate the Pacific coast of North America. In fulfilling that task, he would also circumnavigate the globe.

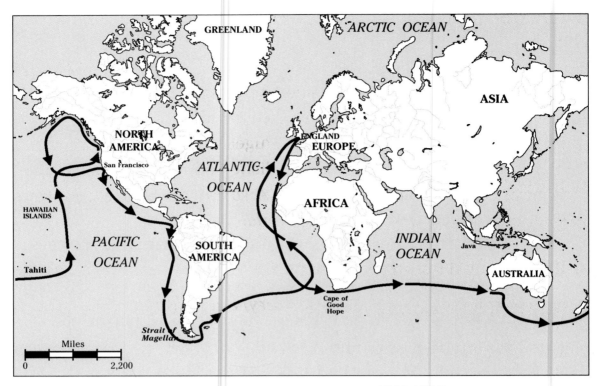

Vancouver's circumnavigation, 1791-1795.

EXPEDITION TO MAP THE PACIFIC COAST: Vancouver left England in April, 1791, with two ships. In a journey that took four years, he traveled south around Africa and across the Indian Ocean. They landed briefly on the southwest coast of Australia. Vancouver surveyed the area. They made additional measurements in Tahiti and Hawaii.

Vancouver reached the area north of San Francisco in April 1792. He began his survey of every inlet and bay north of San Francisco to what is now Vancouver Island. Over the next three years, he mapped the coast as far as Cook Inlet in Alaska.

Vancouver searched for evidence of a water route leading out to the ocean. But after he reached Alaska, he concluded that there was no Northwest Passage. He sailed for home around the tip of

South America, reaching England in October 1795. He died there in 1798.

HIS DISCOVERY: Vancouver is remembered for his thorough and detailed survey of the Pacific Coast. He also named some of the important landmarks he sighted, like Puget Sound and Mount Rainier in Washington. Vancouver published his charts, maps, and account of his explorations in a book, *A Voyage of Discovery to the North Pacific Ocean, and Round the World.*

WORLD WIDE WEB SITE:

http://www.win.tue.nl/~engels/discovery/vancouver.html

Giovanni da Verrazzano

1485? - 1528
Italian Navigator Who Explored for France
First European to Sight New York Harbor and
Narragansett Bay

GIOVANNI DA VERRAZZANO WAS BORN near Florence, Italy, in about 1485. Very little is known about his early life.

SAILING FOR FRANCE: When he was a young man, Verrazzano moved to France. There, he began to work as a sailor. He sailed on merchant ships to the Mediterranean Sea. He was also a pirate, sailing on boats that looted Spanish ships.

In about 1525, Verrazzano was sent on an expedition by King Francis I of France. At that point in history, the Spanish and English had been traveling to and from what they called the "**New World**" for years. Spain had settlements in Florida, Mexico, and the Caribbean. England had trading posts in Newfoundland. King Francis wanted Verrazzano to claim lands for France while searching for a sea route to China.

REACHING THE NEW WORLD: In early 1525, Verrazzano left France with four ships, but only his own, *The Dauphine*, made it to the New World. The ship reached what is now Cape Fear, North Carolina, in March.

Over the next five months, Verrazzano explored the coast of North America from North Carolina to Newfoundland. On board with him was his brother, Girolomo, who was a mapmaker. As they sailed up the coast, the brothers decided that what they were seeing was just a narrow piece of land. They didn't realize that North America was a vast continent, thousands of miles wide. So Girolomo's map of the area shows a narrow land mass, surrounded by two oceans. This mistake was repeated on maps for 100 years.

NEW YORK HARBOR: In April 1525, Verrazzano sailed into what is now New York Harbor. He stayed in the Narrows of the bay, which is now named for him. The Verrazzano Narrows Bridge is also named for him.

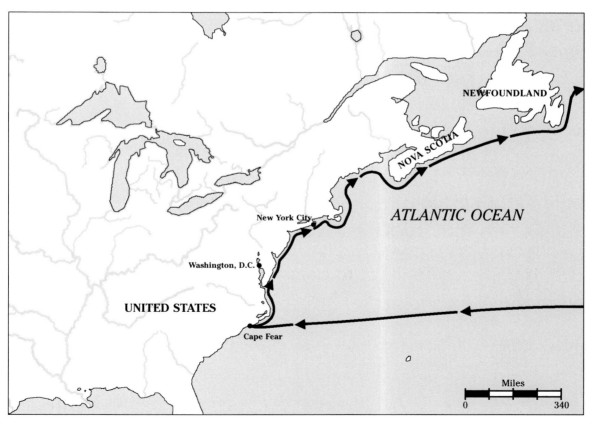

Verrazano's 1525 expedition.

Verrazzano continued sailing north, reaching what is now Rhode Island. He discovered Block Island and Naragansett Bay. He also met the local natives, of the Wampanoug tribe.

Continuing his journey, Verrazzano sailed along the coast of Maine and further north. Some historians believe he reached the coast of Newfoundland. Turning east, he returned to France in July 1525.

SECOND VOYAGE: Verrazzano sailed to the **New World** again in 1527. This time, he landed in Brazil. There, his crew cut down Brazil wood, which was used to dye cloth.

LAST VOYAGE: In 1528, Verrazzano made his final voyage to the New World. Girolomo went with him again, and was present for his terrible death. The ship landed first in Florida, then traveled to islands known as the Lesser Antilles. On one of the islands, probably Guadeloupe, Verrazzano went ashore. He didn't realize it, but the natives were cannibals. They captured, killed, and ate him. His horrified brother and crew couldn't save him. They returned to France and told the story of Verrazzano's last voyage.

HIS DISCOVERY: Verrazzano is remembered as the first European to sight New York Harbor and Narragansett Bay and to explore the Atlantic coast of North America.

WORLD WIDE WEB SITE:

http://www.win.tue.nl/~engels/discovery/index.html

Amerigo Vespucci

1451 - 1512
Italian Explorer
Explored Coast of South America
First to Claim that North and South America
Were Continents
The "Americas" Are Named for Him

AMERIGO VESPUCCI WAS BORN in Florence, Italy, in 1451. His name is pronounced "ah-MER-ah-go ves-POO-chee." He was from a wealthy merchant family. He liked books and maps when he was young. He also liked astronomy.

As a young man, Vespucci worked for the Medici (meh-DEE-chee) family. That was one of the wealthiest, most powerful families in Florence. He worked in their businesses and as a banker for them.

In 1492, he went to Seville, Spain. There, he helped outfit Spanish ships for trips of exploration. Historians think that Vespucci helped supply the voyages of **Christopher Columbus**.

VOYAGES OF EXPLORATION: The record of Vespucci's explorations is a bit unclear. There is a letter, supposedly by Vespucci, that claims he went on his first voyage in 1497. It also states he went on four voyages altogether. But most historians think the letter is a forgery. They believe that Vespucci went on two voyages of discovery.

FIRST VOYAGE: Most historians think Vespucci went on his first voyage in 1499. He sailed with Alonso de Ojeda (oh-HEY-dah) for Spain. Ojeda had been on Columbus's second voyage. At that time, no one knew that Columbus had actually reached a new continent. Columbus himself was convinced he'd reached Asia.

Vespucci sailed from Spain with four ships in May, 1499. He captained one of the ships. After 24 days at sea, they landed in what is now Brazil. Vespucci sailed north along the coast of Brazil. He saw the mouth of the Amazon River and the Orinoco River. Some historians claim that Vespucci was the first European to cross the Equator in the west.

Vespucci then turned north and sailed to the Spanish settlement of Hispaniola (modern-day Haiti and the Dominican Republic). He rejoined Ojeda's other ships, and they sailed back to Spain. Vespucci stopped in the Bahamas and captured 200 natives. He took them back to Spain as slaves. He reached home in June 1500.

Possible route of Vespucci's voyages of 1499-1500 and 1501-1502.

SECOND VOYAGE: Vespucci's next expedition was funded by Portugal. He left Portugal in May 1501. On his way, he stopped at the Cape Verde Islands. There, he met **Pedro Alvares Cabral**, who was returning from India. Cabral described the land he had recently discovered, while on his journey from Portugal to India. Vespucci thought they'd seen the same land—what we now call Brazil. And he began to think that the land was *not* Asia. Perhaps it was a **New World** completely.

Vespucci and his crew sailed on to Brazil. He headed south along the coast of what is now South America. No one is sure how far south Vespucci traveled. Most historians think it was about 2,400 miles. He sailed past the area that is now the city of Rio de Janeiro. He may have reached southern Argentina.

DISCOVERING THE "NEW WORLD": When Vespucci returned to Portugal in June 1502, he made a bold statement. He said that he had not reached Asia, but had instead discovered a new continent, not known to Europeans. He called the continent the "New World."

NAMING THE NEW WORLD FOR AMERIGO: Vespucci wrote a book about his travels that was read all over Europe. In 1507, a German mapmaker named Martin Waldseemueller made a famous map that included the new continent. He named it "America." He said it was for "Amerigo, its discoverer, a man of great ability."

Later, in 1538, the famous mapmaker Gerhardus Mercator named North America and South America for Amerigo Vespucci. So although Columbus is generally considered the "discoverer of America," the continents of the New World bear the name of Amerigo.

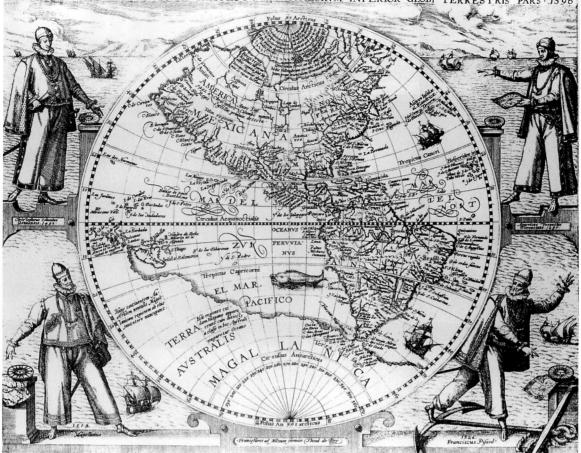

Map of the Americas from 1596 with portraits of Columbus (upper left), Vespucci (upper right), Magellan (lower left), and Pizarro (lower right).

Columbus wasn't angry that the **New World** was named for Vespucci. In fact, they were friends. Columbus called Vespucci "a man of good will."

Vespucci didn't go on any more voyages. He worked for the Spanish government as Pilot Major. In that job, he kept records of all the sea voyages made by the Spanish explorers.

AMERIGO VESPUCCI'S HOME AND FAMILY: Vespucci lived his last years in Seville, Spain. He married a woman named Maria de

Cerezo. They had no children. Amerigo Vespucci died in Seville on February 22, 1512.

HIS DISCOVERY: Vespucci's most important discovery was that the land mass between Europe and Asia was indeed a continent. He was the first to call it the "**New World**." While his individual explorations were not as important as others, the way he thought about the lands he saw *was* new, and very important.

WORLD WIDE WEB SITE:

http://www.mariner.org/age/biohist.html

The Vikings

THE VIKINGS were people who lived in what are now Norway, Sweden, and Denmark. They were a fierce, warlike people. In their swift **longships**, they raided the coastal villages of England, Scotland, Ireland, and France. They also sailed across the seas and down the rivers of Eastern Europe as far as the Middle East.

The Viking longships were long, narrow boats made of oak. The front of the ship was carved with a fierce dragon's head, often painted red and inlaid with gold. The ship used one large, square sail. The longships also had oars, so that a ship could move when there was no wind. They were swift, light, and easy to launch and land.

Those same ships took them sailing across the Atlantic, where they founded colonies in Iceland, Greenland, and Newfoundland. Many historians believe the Vikings were the first European explorers in North America.

The Vikings flourished between about 750 and 1000. This era is called "The Viking Age." Around 750, these fierce and ruthless warriors began raids on what is now England, Scotland, Ireland, and France. The Vikings, or Norseman, as they were called, could be incredibly cruel. They murdered people, destroyed buildings and churches, stole weapons, furs, precious stones, and anything of value. They captured people and made them slaves.

Norseman also attacked and raided ships traveling from Europe to England. Others traveled the rivers of Eastern Europe, moving south through the Black Sea and Caspian Sea. They reached as far south as Baghdad, in modern-day Iraq.

What made the Vikings the fierce, feared people who plundered Europe? No one knows for sure—they didn't keep written records of their conquests. But historians think that they left their homes in search of food and land. The soil of the Scandinavian countries is not rich. So as their population grew, they needed to find food from other places. Also, the Vikings made settlements where their people could move and build their own cities and farms. Some also traded—rather than raided—with the people they encountered.

The Vikings were also among the earliest explorers of the **New World**. In around 870, Norwegian Vikings set out across the North Atlantic and reached Iceland. They became the first permanent settlers. In 986, **Erik the Red** founded the first European settlement on Greenland. His son, **Leif Erikson**, was probably the first European explorer to reach North America. He sailed to a place he called "Vinland." Historians think that Vinland was probably on Newfoundland.

What we do know about the Vikings has come down to us through their sagas. These were tales passed down from generation to generation, finally written down several hundred years after the events they celebrate happened.

Although the Viking era lasted for only about 300 years, it is an important part of the history of exploration. The Norsemen were fierce and blood-thirsty warriors; they were also cruel slaveholders. But the Vikings also left behind a legacy of fearless and heroic seafarers who overcame great obstacles to find and colonize new lands. And as they traveled the seas, they spread Scandinavian influence across half the world, from the ancient city of Baghdad to the northeastern coast of the **New World**.

WORLD WIDE WEB SITES:

http://collections.ic.gc.ca/vikings
http://www.nlc-bnc.ca/history/24/h24-1210-e.html
http://odin.dep.no/odin/engelsk/norway/history

Alfred Russel Wallace

1823 - 1913
English Naturalist, Explorer, and Geographer
Explored the Amazon River, Indonesia, and Malaysia
Developed a Theory of Evolution

ALFRED RUSSEL WALLACE WAS BORN on January 8, 1823, in Monmouthshire, Wales. His parents were Thomas and Mary Anne Wallace. Alfred was the eighth of nine children. The family was poor, but the home was filled with books. Wallace's parents encouraged their children to read and study the natural world around them.

ALFRED RUSSEL WALLACE WENT TO SCHOOL for just six years at a one-room elementary school. He left school at 14 to go to work.

FIRST JOBS: Wallace moved to London, where he lived with his brother John. He learned to be a surveyor and worked for his brother William's surveying business. Over the next ten years, he surveyed sections of England and Wales. When William died in 1845, Alfred took over the business.

Wallace's surveying led him to spend most of his time outside. He loved to collect and study plants and animals. Around this time, he met a naturalist named Henry Walter Bates. He and Bates decided to travel to South America. They planned to collect specimens to sell to museums.

EXPLORING THE AMAZON: Wallace and Bates left England in 1848. For most of the next four years, Wallace explored the Amazon River region. He collected plants and insects, while mapping the area. He also filled notebooks with his findings.

Wallace and Bates split up and explored sections of the Amazon area alone. Wallace discovered many new species of butterflies. He noted how different species of plants and animals grew in different regions. Like **Charles Darwin**, Wallace was fascinated by their origins and development.

In 1852, Wallace headed back to England. Then disaster struck. The ship he was sailing on caught fire. The crew and passengers were rescued, but Wallace's specimens and journals went up in flames. Four years of work had been reduced to ash. But he was able to recall enough important aspects of his journey to write two books.

EXPEDITION TO INDONESIA AND MALAYSIA: Wallace next journeyed to the the thousands of islands that make up modern Indonesia and Malaysia. From 1854 to 1862, he explored nearly 15,000 miles of territory. He studied and collected more than 125,000 plant and animal specimens.

Wallace also wrote important essays on the origin and development of species. He thought that species developed over time — evolved — to adapt to their environment. Animals and plants competed for food and habitat. The strongest survived; the weaker died out. He sent his findings in a letter to Darwin.

DARWIN AND THE THEORY OF EVOLUTION: Wallace didn't know it, but his theories were strikingly similar to Darwin's. Twenty years earlier, Darwin had explored South America and the Galapagos Islands. Like Wallace, Darwin had been struck by the wide variety of species of animals. From these observations, he developed an important theory. He saw that animals had to compete for food, space, and habitat. The animals that had the greatest chance to succeed were those who could adapt, or change, to suit their environment.

Over time, the most successful species would survive. Those that were less successful would die out. Darwin called this theory "natural selection." Darwin was reluctant to publish his findings. But when he received Wallace's letter, he changed his mind. He knew it was time to let the world know of their joint discovery. In 1858, Darwin published a paper outlining their findings, under both their names.

Darwin's and Wallace's theories of evolution were revolutionary — and controversial. At that time, many people believed that the world was only about 6,000 years old. They believed that all animals, plants, as well as the mountains and oceans, had been created at the same time, 6,000 years ago. They believed that all living creatures had not changed since their creation. For them, the Bible story of Creation was the truth. But what Darwin and Wallace had discovered challenged these beliefs.

The two men became famous. They also faced ridicule and anger from people who refused to accept their theories. Yet as scientists read their work, they became convinced that the theories were true. Wallace and Darwin had started a revolution in science. Over the years their findings have become widely accepted. There are some groups that continue to oppose their theories, but most modern evolutionary theory is based on their work.

A FAMOUS NATURALIST: When Wallace returned to England in 1862, he was a famous man. He spent the next 40 years writing more than 20 books and hundreds of articles. He wrote about natural science and his evolutionary theories. He contributed important books on animals and habitat. He also became involved in many different political and social causes. He fought for new laws and for women's rights. He even commented on the possibility of life on Mars.

ALFRED RUSSEL WALLACE'S HOME AND FAMILY: Wallace married Annie Mitten in 1862. They had three children, Herbert, Violet, and William. Wallace died on November 7, 1913, at the age of 91.

HIS DISCOVERY: Wallace is remembered for his theory of evolution, based on his explorations of the Amazon, Indonesia, and Malaysia.

WORLD WIDE WEB SITES:

http://www.win.tue.nl/~engels/discovery/index.html
http://www.wku.edu/~smithch/wallace/top.htm

Francis Xavier
1506 - 1552
Spanish Missionary Who Traveled to India, Indonesia, Japan and China

FRANCIS XAVIER WAS BORN on April 7, 1506, in Navarre, Spain. His last name is pronounced ZAY-vee-uhr. He came from a noble family. He was educated in Navarre.

BECOMING A JESUIT: In 1525, Xavier went to Paris for college. He was planning to become a priest, and Paris was a major center of religious education. There, he met a young man named Ignatius Loyola. Loyola was then founding the Jesuit group within the Catholic Church. Xavier joined the group, called the Society of Jesus. One of their purposes was to serve as missionaries. They wanted to spread their Christian faith to people all over the world.

In 1537, Xavier became a Jesuit priest. He studied, taught, and prepared for his first mission. King John III of Portugal was looking for missionaries who wanted to serve in India, where Portugal had several colonies. King John chose Xavier, and in 1540 he left Europe for India and his life as a missionary.

IN INDIA: Xavier arrived in Goa, on the western coast of India, in 1542. There, he set a pattern of missionary work that has been followed by Jesuits for centuries. In his work with native peoples, he strived to preserve their culture and way of life. This was unlike the Spanish conquistadors and others, who more often destroyed the cultures they encountered.

Xavier saw his mission as adapting his teachings to the culture of the native people he taught. He learned the local language and customs. He established schools so that native priests could be trained in the Catholic faith and continue religious teachings.

Xavier served for three years in southeast India, teaching the Paravas people about Christianity. He had translated the Catholic catechism into their language. He used the translation to reach out to thousands of people. Xavier then traveled to the southwest Indian coast and lived with the Macuan tribe. He converted some 10,000 of them to Christianity. He also planned schools for them.

IN THE MALAY PENINSULA: In 1545, Xavier traveled to the Malay Peninsula. There, he taught Christianity to the people, including those on the Spice Islands. He returned to India in 1548 and oversaw the development of a college to train native priests.

IN JAPAN: In 1549, Xavier traveled to Japan. He had met and converted a Japanese man named Anjiro while he was in the Malay Peninsula. Now he wanted to meet the Japanese in their own country. Japan had only recently been discovered by Europeans, and they knew very little about it.

Xavier was fascinated with the Japanese. He called them "the best people yet discovered." His letters from Japan to his superiors in Europe were full of information about how the Japanese lived and what their country was like.

CHINA: From the Japanese, Xavier learned about the Chinese. He wanted to go to China and set up missions there. In 1552, he began his journey to China, but he never reached the mainland. He became ill and died on an island off the Chinese coast in December 1552. By the time of his death, he had converted about 30,000 native peoples to the Christian faith.

HIS DISCOVERY: Unlike others who explored foreign lands in his time, Xavier was inspired only by his desire to spread his faith. He firmly believed in respecting the customs and languages of the people he worked to convert. He also believed in the training of local, native priests. Those principles are still used by Jesuits in their missions around the world.

For his work as a missionary, Xavier was canonized a Catholic saint in 1622.

WORLD WIDE WEB SITE:

http://www.newadvent.org/cathen/06233b.htm

Xenophon

430 B.C. ? to 350 B.C.?
Greek Historian and Military Leader
Explored Ancient Iraq and Turkey
While Leading 10,000 Soldiers Home from War

XENOPHON WAS BORN in Athens in Greece around 430 B.C. His name is pronounced ZEN-uh-fuhn. His parents were wealthy and he grew up in a comfortable home.

XENOPHON WENT TO SCHOOL and studied with the great Greek philosopher Socrates. He was interested in the military from an early age. He also didn't get along with the government of Athens.

MILITARY CAREER: At that time, Greece was not a unified country. It was made up of many "city-states" that were often at war. One of Xenophon's first military positions was part of the calvary defending Athens.

In about 400 B.C., Xenophon left Greece. He joined a group of paid soldiers who fought for a prince from Persia (modern-day Iran). This prince, Cyrus, established an army to fight his brother for the kingdom of Persia. Xenophon took part in this battle. Cyrus was killed in combat.

Cyrus's death left nearly 10,000 Greek soldiers stranded 1,500 miles from home. The soldiers, known as the "Ten Thousand," elected Xenophon to help them get back to Greece.

XENOPHON AS AN EXPLORER: The Greeks didn't want to return across the deserts and plains they'd crossed already. They decided to head north, toward Greek settlements on the Black Sea.

Xenophon led his men home through an area that was unknown, and hostile. They started their journey from an area near the ancient city of Babylon, in southern Iraq. Following the Tigris River north, they had to fight their way through some sections of their journey. They endured hunger and intense cold in the mountainous regions. Nearly 4,000 of the soldiers died.

After traveling through modern-day Turkey, the soldiers finally reached a Greek settlement, Trapezus (now Trabzon, Turkey). From there, they traveled to a city near what is modern-day Istanbul.

Xenophon returned home, but learned the Athenian government had banished him. He moved his family to another city-state, Sparta. There, he served the local government and began writing books. His book about his amazing journey home from war was called the *Anabasis*, which means "The March Up Country."

Xenophon's book was studied and admired for hundreds of years. It shows his bravery and intelligence in leading his men to safety. It was also used by geographers to create maps for later travelers.

LATER CAREER: Xenophon went on to write many books. He wrote histories, biographies, and other works. He lived on an estate near the Greek city of Olympia. Later, he moved to a home in Corinth, where he died around 355 B.C. Near the time of his death, he completed a work called *Ways and Means*. In it, he stated that the Greek states should live together in peace.

XENOPHON'S HOME AND FAMILY: Xenophon was married to a woman named Philesia. They had two sons.

HIS DISCOVERY: Xenophon is remembered as a great historian and strong military leader. Leading his men through unknown and hostile lands, he was an early explorer of the Middle East.

WORLD WIDE WEB SITE:

http://www.liv.ac.uk/~gjoliver/xenophon.html

Zheng He
1371 - 1433?
Chinese Diplomat and Admiral Who Led Sea Voyages to Southeast Asia, the Middle East, and Africa

ZHENG HE WAS BORN in 1371 in Yunnan, China. His name is pronounced "jung huh."It is also spelled "Cheng Ho." In Chinese, a person's last name appears first, so the last name of this early explorer was Zheng.

GROWING UP: Zheng He was from a Muslim family. His Muslim name was Ma He. When he was growing up, Yunnan was ruled by the Mongols. When he was 10, the Chinese conquered Yunnan.

Zheng, 10 years old, was taken prisoner and made a slave in the Chinese army. Over the next few years, he was first a servant, then a soldier.

AT THE COURT OF THE EMPEROR: Zheng was taken to the court of a prince named Chu Ti. There, he learned the ways of the court. He became very popular with the prince. Around 1402 the prince became the Emperor. Emperor Chu Ti wanted to show the power of his court to the world. He wanted the people of the world to pay tribute to him.

LEADING EXPEDITIONS: The Emperor chose Zheng He to lead sea expeditions to spread the word of his greatness. From 1405 to 1433 Zheng led seven voyages. He was in charge of the largest fleet ever put together in China. His expedition was made up of more than 27,000 men in more than 300 boats. The boats were called "treasure ships," and they brought back wonderful riches to China.

Zheng traveled in boats called **junks**. These boats were large and could carry heavy loads. Some were 400 feet long and 150 feet wide, and were set with many sails. They were much larger than the **caravels** used by the Europeans of the Age of Exploration.

Zheng's ships carried soldiers, sailors, traders, cooks, religious men, and astrologers. Some of the ships could carry over 1,000 men. These magnificent ships were called "swimming dragons." They often had dragon eyes painted on the outside.

Over 28 years, Zheng led his fleet to over 40 countries in Southeast Asia, the Middle East, and Africa. On their first journey, they stopped in what is now Vietnam, Ceylon (now Sri Lanka), and Indonesia. Zheng dealt with a revolution in Indonesia. He captured a

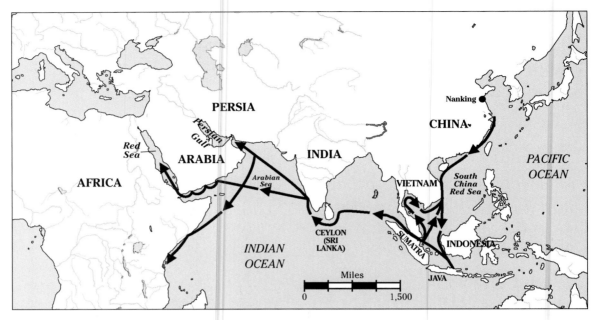

Zheng's voyages, 1405-1433.

Sri Lankan king. Everywhere he went he asked for "tribute." That meant he expected the people of the countries to offer gifts for Zheng to take back to the emperor. Most agreed.

On later trips, Zheng traveled to Indian ports on the Arabian Sea. Journeying across the Arabian Sea, they reached the Middle East. Zheng led his men to the east coast of Africa. There, they stopped in the port cities of what are now the countries of Somalia, Tanzania, and Mozambique.

The emperor wanted to impress the world with the wealth and power of his fleet. Zheng and his men met with leaders of the places they visited. The leaders sent gifts to the emperor with Zheng when he returned home. Later, they established trade with China.

Zheng brought back unusual gifts. From Africa, he brought back the first giraffe ever seen in China. He also brought back lions, leopards, zebras, and ostriches.

THE DEATH OF ZHENG HE: In around 1433, while traveling back to China, Zheng He died. He was probably buried at sea, although a tomb was built in his honor in Nanjing, China. By the end of his life, he had traveled more than 180,000 miles for the emperor.

Shortly after Zheng He's death, China changed in many ways. The country no longer wished to be a sea power. Large, ocean-going ships were destroyed. It became against the law to have a boat with more than two masts. The time of Zheng He and the grand explorations of China came to an end.

HIS DISCOVERY: The accomplishments of this brave explorer are generally unknown today. Many years after his death, when Portuguese explorers like **Bartholomew Dias** rounded the southern tip of Africa, they thought they had "discovered" the Indian Ocean. But Zheng He had been there before them.

WORLD WIDE WEB SITES:

http://www.pbs.org/wgbh/nova/sultan/explorers2.html
http://www.mariner.org/age/china.html

Photo and Illustration Credits

Columbia Crew: Courtesy NASA
Alexander the Great: Courtesy of the Library of Congress
Roald Amundsen: Courtesy of the Library of Congress
Neil Armstrong: Courtesy NASA
Vasco Núñez de Balboa: Courtesy of the Library of Congress
Robert Ballard: Courtesy JASON Foundation for Education
Joseph Banks: Courtesy of the Library of Congress
Vitus Bering: Courtesy of the Mariners' Museum
Isabella Bird Bishop: Courtesy of the Library of Congress
Daniel Boone: Courtesy of the Library of Congress
Etienne Brulé: Courtesy National Archives of Canada
Richard E. Byrd: Courtesy of the Library of Congress
John Cabot: Courtesy of the Library of Congress; Courtesy of the Mariners' Museum
Sebastian Cabot: Courtesy of the Mariners' Museum; Courtesy of the Library of Congress
Kit Carson: Courtesy of the Library of Congress
Jacques Cartier: Courtesy National Archives of Canada; Courtesy of the Library of Congress
Samuel de Champlain: Courtesy of the Library of Congress; Courtesy National Archives of Canada
William Clark: Courtesy of the Library of Congress
Christopher Columbus: Courtesy of the Library of Congress; Courtesy Jay I. Kislak Foundation
James Cook: Courtesy of the Library of Congress; Courtesy of the Mariners' Museum
Francisco Vasques de Coronado: Courtesy of the Library of Congress
Hernando Cortes: Courtesy of the Library of Congress; Courtesy of the Mariners' Museum;
    Courtesy Jay I. Kislak Foundation
Jacques Cousteau: Courtesy of the Library of Congress
Vasco da Gama: Courtesy of the Mariners' Museum
Charles Darwin: Courtesy of the Library of Congress
Alexandra David-Neel: Courtesy of the Alexandra David-Neel Foundation, Digne les Bains, France
Hernando de Soto: Courtesy of the Library of Congress; Courtesy of the Mariners' Museum
Bartholomew Dias: Courtesy Publius Historicus
Sir Francis Drake: Courtesy of the Library of Congress; Courtesy of the Mariners' Museum
Sylvia Earle: Courtesy Dr. Sylvia Earle; AP/Wide World Photos
Leif Erikson: Courtesy of the Mariners' Museum
Matthew Flinders: Courtesy of the Library of Congress
John Franklin: Courtesy National Archives of Canada
Simon Fraser: Courtesy National Archives of Canada
John Charles Frémont: Courtesy of the Library of Congress
Martin Frobisher: Courtesy Robert McGhee
Yuri Gagarin: Courtesy of the Library of Congress; Courtesy NASA
John Glenn: Courtesy NASA
Louis Hennepin: Courtesy National Archives of Canada
Prince Henry the Navigator: Courtesy of the Mariners' Museum
Matthew Henson: Courtesy of the Library of Congress

PHOTO AND ILLUSTRATION CREDITS

Herodotus: Courtesy of the Library of Congress
Henry Hudson: Courtesy of the Mariners' Museum
Alexander von Humboldt: Courtesy of the Library of Congress
Mae Jemison: Courtesy NASA
Louis Jolliet: Courtesy National Library of Canada; Courtesy National Archives of Canada
Rene-Robert Cavelier, Sieur de La Salle: Courtesy National Library of Canada
Meriwether Lewis: Courtesy of the Library of Congress
David Livingstone: Courtesy of the Library of Congress
Alexander Mackenzie: Courtesy National Library of Canada; Courtesy National Archives of Canada
Ferdinand Magellan: Courtesy of the Library of Congress; Courtesy of the Mariners' Museum
Jacques Marquette: Courtesy of the Library of Congress; Courtesy National Archives of Canada
Fridtjof Nansen: Courtesy of the Library of Congress
Mungo Park: Courtesy of the Library of Congress
William Edward Parry: Courtesy of the Library of Congress
Robert E. Peary: Courtesy of the Library of Congress
Ida Pfeiffer: Courtesy of the Library of Congress
Zebulon Pike: Courtesy of the Library of Congress
Francisco Pizarro: Courtesy of the Library of Congress
Marco Polo: Courtesy of the Mariners' Museum
Juan Ponce de León: Courtesy of the Library of Congress
John Wesley Powell: Courtesy of the Library of Congress; Courtesy of the National Parks Service
Ptolemy: Courtesy of the Mariners' Museum
Sir Walter Raleigh: Courtesy of the Mariners' Museum
Sally Ride: Courtesy NASA
James Clark Ross: Courtesy of the Library of Congress
Sacagawea: Courtesy Denver Public Library, Western History Collection;
    Courtesy Bismarck- Mandan Convention and Visitors Bureau
Robert Falcon Scott: Courtesy of the Library of Congress; Courtesy of the Royal Geographical Society, London
Ernest Shackleton: Courtesy of the Royal Geographical Society, London
May French Sheldon: Courtesy of the Library of Congress
Alan Shepard: Courtesy NASA
John Hanning Speke: Corbis
Henry M. Stanley: Courtesy of the Library of Congress
Valentina Tereshkova: Courtesy of the Library of Congress
David Thompson: Courtesy National Archives of Canada
Amerigo Vespucci: Courtesy of the Library of Congress

Glossary

This Glossary contains terms used in the entries on the explorers. It includes descriptions and definitions of navigational and technological items and concepts relating to exploration. Glossary terms are in bold-faced type in the entries.

ASTROLABE: The astrolabe was an ancient tool used to measure the height of the sun or stars above the horizon. It was used by Greek astronomers and sailors as early as 200 B.C. Simple, early versions were used by sailors to establish **latitude**. The astrolabe was replaced by the **quadrant** and later the **sextant.**

CARAVEL: The caravel was a wooden cargo ship originally built in the 1300s rigged with two masts. In the 1400s, the Portuguese expanded the design to hold more cargo and handle rough weather at sea. This model included a third mast with both square and triangular sails. Caravels were swift and sturdy and could endure storms and ocean crossings. **Bartolomeu Dias** used a fleet of caravels in his travels, as did **Christopher Columbus**.

CHRONOMETER: The chronometer was the first instrument to allow an accurate measurement of time, which is necessary in determining **longitude**. This was important to sea exploration, because ships' clocks couldn't keep time accurately and were affected by weather and the movement of the ship. One of the best chronometers was invented by John Harrison in the 1760s. It allowed mariners to determine longitude with greater accuracy than ever before. It helped in mapmaking and also made sea travel safer.

COMPASS: The compass is an instrument with a magnetic needle that points to the Earth's magnetic fields. One end of the needle points to the **North Pole**, the other to the **South Pole.** One of the earliest compasses was invented in Europe in the 1100s. Mariners discovered that a piece of lodestone (a piece of iron ore that is naturally magnetic) attached to a stick and floated in water would always point north.

CONQUISTADOR: "Conquistador" is the Spanish word for "conqueror." It is used to describe Spanish explorers of the 16th century who conquered the peoples of America, especially in Central and South America. They often brutally destroyed the native people and cultures. **Hernando Cortes** and **Francisco Pizarro** were both conquistadors.

DEAD RECKONING: Dead reckoning was a method used to determine the position of a ship at sea without using the stars or sun. It required careful measuring of distance and speed. The navigator measured the course and distance. To measure the course, the navigator used a compass. To measure distance, he kept track of time and the speed of the ship.

It is hard to imagine how the early explorers measured time and speed, because they didn't have our modern inventions. There were no speedometers to calculate speed. Instead, a ship's speed was measured by throwing overboard a log attached to a line of rope with knots at specific distances between them. The sailors would count how many knots would pass by in the time it took the sands to empty from an hourglass. They used an hourglass because there were no clocks that could measure time accurately. **Christopher Columbus** and other early explorers used dead reckoning to navigate.

DHOW: The dhow is a cargo ship that has been used in the waters around the Middle East since ancient times. Dhows have one or two masts and sails. They were first used by Arab merchants and explorers, and later throughout the Mediterranean and Asia.

JUNK: Chinese cargo ships, junks were ships with masts used by the Chinese to transport cargo. In the early 1400s, **Zheng He** led a huge fleet of more than 300 ships, mostly very large junks, to explore Southeast Asia, the Middle East, and the eastern coast of Africa.

KNORR (also spelled "knarr"): A knorr was a **Viking** cargo ship. Unlike the swift **longships** used for raids and travel, the Viking knorr was used to transport large loads of goods. It was shorter and wider than the longship, with high sides. Built for sturdiness rather than speed, these ships were used to carry people, livestock, and supplies. They needed wind for power, because they were too heavy to row. **Eric the Red** used knorrs when transporting the founding colony of people who settled Greenland.

LATITUDE AND LONGITUDE: Locations on sea and land are determined by the coordinates called latitude and longitude. If you look at a globe or map, you will see regularly spaced lines that run north and south, and lines that run east and west. These lines represent latitude and longitude.

Latitude is the name of the horizontal measurement lines that run north and south of the equator. The lines of latitude are called "parallels." Latitude is measured in degrees, from the equator north to the **North Pole** and south to the **South Pole**. The equator is 0 degrees, the North Pole is 90 degrees North, and the South Pole is 90 degrees South. Each degree of latitude is about 69 miles. These are further divided into minutes and seconds.

Greek astronomers from 200 B.C. used an ancient instrument called an **astrolabe** to measure latitude. By the Age of Exploration, explorers and mapmakers were able to determine latitude using an instrument called the **quadrant**.

Longitude lines, called "meridians," are the vertical lines on a globe or map. They measure distance from an imaginary line that runs through Greenwich, England, called the "Prime Meridian." Longitude is measured in degrees that run east or west of the Prime Meridian. The globe is divided into 360 degrees of longitude, 180 degrees run west of the Prime Meridian, and 180 degrees run east of the Prime Meridian. Like latitude, the degrees are further divided into minutes and seconds.

To measure longitude, you need an accurate measure of time. This wasn't possible until 1762, when John Harrison developed an accurate **chronometer**. That has enabled modern people to pinpoint, with great accuracy, a more exact location of places.

LONGSHIPS: Longships were long, narrow boats made of oak used by the **Vikings.** The front of the ship was carved with a fierce dragon's head, often painted red and inlaid with gold. The ship used one large, square sail. The longships also had oars, so the ship could move when there was no wind. The longships were swift, light, and easy to launch and land. They were used by the Vikings in their raids on Europe and the British Isles and later in their travels to Iceland and Greenland.

NASA: NASA stands for the National Aeronautics and Space Administration. It is the U.S. agency that coordinates the program for the exploration of space. NASA is responsible for choosing and training astronauts, developing space craft and satellites, and planning the manned and unmanned missions into space. It also oversees research into the origins of the universe and our own solar system. NASA developed and launched the first manned flights in the Mercury Program, the Apollo program that landed humans on the moon, and the current **space shuttle** program. Using the shuttle, NASA astronauts conducts missions to and from the International Space Station as well as scientific research to continue the exploration of space.

NEW FRANCE: The term "New France" referred to the lands in North America claimed by the French from the 1500s. It included much of the St. Lawrence River valley in what is now Canada, Newfoundland, Nova Scotia, parts of the Great Lakes region of the U.S., Louisiana, and parts of the Mississippi valley. The land changed hands over several hundred years as the English and French fought wars to claim the lands.

NEW SPAIN: The term New Spain referred to the region in North America claimed by the Spanish from the 1500s. It contained the lands north of isthmus of Panama, including what is now Central America, Mexico, and most of the southwest United States, from Florida to California.

NEW WORLD: The term New World referred to the lands of North and South America explored by the Europeans of the Age of Discovery.

NORTH POLE: The Earth actually has two sets of Poles. The North and South *geographic* Poles are located at the northern and southern end of the Earth's axis. The geographic North Pole lies in the Arctic Ocean, about 450 miles north of Greenland. The geographic South Pole lies in Antarctica, about 300 miles south of the Ross Ice Shelf. At both the North and the South Pole there are six months of complete sunlight and six months of complete darkness. **Robert E. Peary** claimed he reached the North Pole in 1909. **Roald Amundsen** reached the South Pole in 1911.

The *magnetic* Poles are the northern and southern points that magnetic compasses point to. **James Clark Ross** discovered the magnetic North Pole in 1831. The crew of **Ernest Shackleton's** *Nimrod* expedition located the magnetic South Pole in 1909. Because the Earth's magnetic fields change over time, the north and south magnetic poles do not remain constant, but change in reaction to changes in the Earth's magnetic fields.

NORTHEAST PASSAGE: In the 1500s, Portugal controlled the sea routes from Europe around the southern tip of Africa to the riches of the East. Other countries, especially England and the Netherlands, wanted to find a sea route to Asia by a northern route, following the Russian coast of the Arctic Ocean. Early explorers like **Sebastian Cabot** of England and **Willem Barents** of the Netherlands traveled north from Europe and explored the Arctic looking for the passage. After hundreds of years of failed attempts, the Northeast Passage was discovered by **Nils Nordenskiöld** in 1879.

NORTHWEST PASSAGE: From the early 1500s, many people believed that a water passage from Europe to Asia existed through what is now Canada. They sought a sea route that could be used for trade linking the Atlantic and Pacific Oceans through the islands of the Canadian Arctic.

In the late 1400s, Portugal established and controlled trade routes from Europe around Africa to the riches of India and the East—gold, spices, silk, and other treasures. At the same time, Spain claimed and controlled the route that led from Europe to North America, and the route leading around the tip of South America and on to Asia.

Thus, from the 1500s, Spain and Portugal controlled the major sea routes used for trade with the East. England and France wanted to find a route that they could use for trade. Early explorers from both nations headed to the coast of North America, then north into the Canadian Arctic. They explored what we now know as the Davis Strait, Baffin Bay, the Hudson Strait and Hudson Bay, pressing west through the many inlets and islands of the Canadian Arctic. The waters are blocked by ice almost year round. Many expeditions faced great hardship in trying to make the journey from the far eastern shores of Canada all the way to the Passage's end–the Bering Strait, which separates Alaska and Russia and leads into the Pacific.

For 400 years, explorers sought — and died — looking for the Northwest Passage. Among those who searched for the passage were **Jacques Cartier, Martin Frobisher, Henry Hudson, William Baffin, James Cook, George Vancouver, William Edward Parry,** and **John Franklin.** It was finally navigated by **Roald Amundsen** in 1906.

QUADRANT: A quadrant is a device used to measure the height of the sun or stars. Developed in the 1500s, the quadrant was more accurate than the **astrolabe** in measuring the altitude of objects in the sky. Through measuring the altitude of the sun or a star, a mariner could establish **latitude.**

SEXTANT: A sextant is a device used to measure the height of the sun or stars to establish **latitude.** It was developed in the 1700s and was an improvement on the **astrolabe** and **quadrant.** Mariners would measure the height of the sun or stars, then, using a chart, be able to determine from that measurement the latitude of a position.

SILK ROAD: The Silk Road, also called the Silk Route, was a network of paths and trails that connected what is now eastern China and the Mediterranean. It was actually a group of routes by which people traded goods, from silk to spices to foods, as well as ideas and religions. It was the main trade route from Asia to Europe for centuries, from around 500 B.C. to about 1400 A.D. By the 1400s, traders were using ships and sea routes instead of overland trade routes to transport goods.

The Silk Road started in the city of Sian, in eastern China, and spanned over 4,000 miles, ending in the cities of Constantinople (now Istanbul, Turkey), and Damascus, in modern-day Syria. From those cities, good were shipped as far west as Venice and Rome.

The main product shipped to the west from China was silk. Silk is made from the cocoon of the silkworm. It has been valued for centuries for its beauty.

When the Silk Road was first created, only the Chinese knew how to make silk. They carefully guarded their secret for years. The Chinese also traded spices and jade to people in the west. From Europe, merchants sent gold, silver, horses, and foods along the Silk Road to trade with the merchants of Asia.

No single trader traveled the whole distance of the Silk Road. Instead, people would travel several hundred miles, then pass their goods on to other traders. The merchants often traveled by caravan, with goods loaded on the backs of camels. The Silk Road was a dangerous route. Bandits sometimes preyed on the caravans and stole their goods. Some rulers demanded money or goods as the caravans passed through their lands.

Traders, travelers, and explorers all used the Silk Road. Perhaps the most famous explorer to travel the Silk Road was **Marco Polo**, who followed part of the route on his journey to China in the late 1200s.

SOUTH POLE: *see* **NORTH POLE**

SPACE SHUTTLE: The space shuttle is the vehicle used to transport astronauts and materials from the Earth into space. At launch, the shuttle is attached to a large, high-powered rocket that takes the shuttle into the outer atmosphere, where it begins to orbit the Earth. Aboard the shuttle, the astronauts conduct scientific experiments, launch and repair satellites, and deliver people and supplies to the International Space Station.

TREATY OF TORDESILLAS: In 1494 Portugal and Spain signed an agreement that divided the world between the two countries, allowing them the right to claim the lands they discovered in the **New World** and in Africa. The treaty created a line running north and south about 1185 miles west of the Cape Verde Islands. That allowed the Portuguese to claim the lands of Africa and most of Brazil in the New World. It allowed the Spanish the right to claim the islands of the Caribbean, all of North America and Central America, and most of South America. It also limited the rights of other nations, including England and France, to claim lands for their countries.

In 1533, King Francis I of France had the treaty changed so that it covered only lands already discovered. After that date, other nations could claim lands not yet discovered by Spain or Portugal. That opened the door for France and England to claim and colonize the New World.

Explorers by Nationality

American
Armstrong, Neil
Ballard, Robert
Boone, Daniel
Byrd, Richard E.
Carson, Kit
Clark, William
Earle, Sylvia
Frémont, John
Glenn, John
Henson, Matthew
Lewis, Meriwether
Peary, Robert E.
Pike, Zebulon
Powell, John Wesley
Ride, Sally
Sacagawea
Sheldon, May French
Shepard, Alan

Arab
Ibn Battuta
Leo Africanus

Austrian
Pfeiffer, Ida
Belgian
Hennepin, Louis

Canadian
Fraser, Simon
Jolliet, Louis

Carthaginian
Hanno

Chinese
Fasian
Hsuan Tsang
Zheng He

Danish
Bering, Vitus

Dutch
Barents, Willem
Tasman, Abel Janszoon

English
Baffin, William
Banks, Joseph
Bell, Gertrude
Bishop, Isabella Bird
Burton, Richard Francis
Cook, James
Darwin, Charles

Drake, Francis
Flinders, Matthew
Franklin, John
Frobisher, Martin
Hudson, Henry
Kingsley, Mary
  Henrietta
Parry, William Edward
Raleigh, Walter
Ross, James Clark
Scott, Robert Falcon
Shackleton, Ernest
Speke, John Hanning
Thompson, David
Vancouver, George
Wallace, Alfred Russel

Finnish
Nordenskiöld, Adolf
  Erik

French
Brulé, Etienne
Cartier, Jacques
Champlain, Samuel de
Cousteau, Jacques
David-Neel, Alexandra

La Salle, Rene-Robert
  Cavelier, Sieur de
Marquette, Jacques

German
Humboldt, Alexander
  von

Greek
Alexander the Great
Herodotus
Ptolemy
Pytheas
Xenophon

Italian
Cabot, John
Cabot, Sebastian
Columbus, Christopher
Polo, Marco
Verrazano, Giovanni da
Vespucci, Amerigo

Norwegian
Amundsen, Roald
Erik the Red
Erikson, Leif
Nansen, Fridtjof

Portuguese
Cabral, Pedro Alvares
Da Gama, Vasco
Dias, Bartholomew
Henry the Navigator
Magellan, Ferdinand

Russian
Gagarin, Yuri
Tereshkova, Valentina

Scottish
Livingstone, David
Mackenzie, Alexander
Park, Mungo

Spanish
Balboa, Vasco Núñez de
Benjamin of Tudela
Cabeza de Vaca, Alvar
  Núñez
Coronado, Francisco
  Vázquez de
Cortes, Hernando
De Soto, Hernando
Orellana, Francisco de
Pizarro, Francisco
Ponce de León, Juan
Xavier, Francis

Swedish
Hedin, Sven Anders

Explorers by Area of Exploration

This section includes a listing of major geographic areas, subdivided into categories corresponding to the areas explored by each explorer. Individuals who explored more than one geographic area (i.e., Roald Amundsen, James Cook) are listed in more than one geographic area. The list is divided by continent, then by region ("Central America") or country (Canada, United States). In the case of the United States, the country is further broken down into regions ("Great Lakes"). Place names reflect present-day usage, with the exception of "Northwest Passage" and "Northeast Passage," which are areas of historical significance to exploration that are no longer known by that name. There is a special section at the end of the list for Ocean and Space explorers.

AFRICA

Central Africa

Burton, Richard
  Francis
Kingsley, Mary
  Henrietta
Livingstone, David
Speke, John Hanning
Stanley, Henry M.

East Africa

Ibn Battuta
Sheldon, May French
Zheng He

Nile River

Burton, Richard
  Francis
Herodotus
Livingstone, David
Speke, John Hanning
Stanley, Henry M.

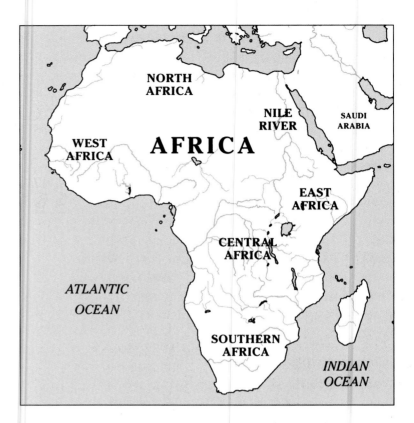

North Africa

Alexander the Great
Benjamin of Tudela
Herodotus
Ibn Battuta

Southern Africa

Dias, Bartholomew
Livingstone, David

West Africa

Hanno
Kingsley, Mary
  Henrietta
Leo Africanus
Park, Mungo

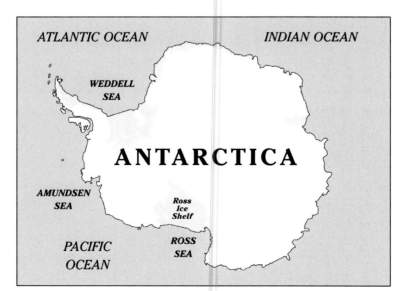

ANTARCTICA

Amundsen, Roald
Byrd, Richard E.
Ross, James Clark
Scott, Robert Falcon
Shackleton, Ernest

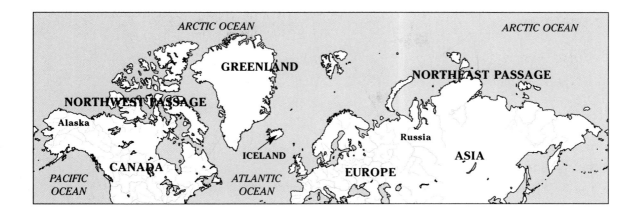

ARCTIC

Greenland

Erik the Red
Henson, Matthew
Nansen, Fridtjof
Nordenskiöld, Nils
Peary, Robert E.

North Pole

Amundsen, Roald
Byrd, Richard E.
Henson, Matthew
Parry, William E.
Peary, Robert E.

Northeast Passage

Barents, Willem
Bering, Vitus
Hudson, Henry
Nordenskiöld, Nils

Northwest Passage

Amundsen, Roald
Baffin, William
Cabot, Sebastian

Cartier, Jacques
Cook, James
Franklin, John
Fraser, Simon
Frobisher, Martin
Hudson, Henry
Mackenzie, Alexander
Parry, William E.
Ross, James Clark

Russian Arctic

Bering, Vitus
Nansen, Fridtjof

AUSTRALIA

Banks, Joseph
Cook, James
Darwin, Charles
Flinders, Matthew
Tasman, Abel Janszoon

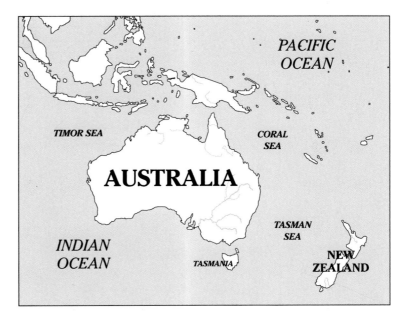

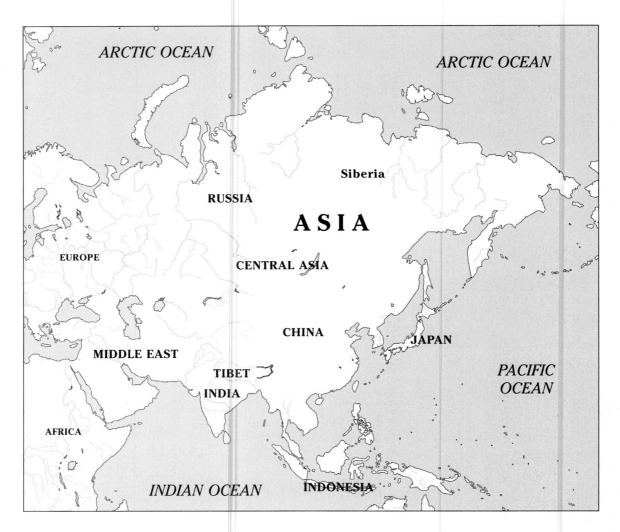

ASIA

China
David-Neel, Alexandra
Ibn Battuta
Polo, Marco

Central Asia
Alexander the Great
Faxian
Hedin, Sven Anders
Polo, Marco

India
Alexander the Great
Da Gama, Vasco
Faxian
Ibn Battuta
Xavier, Francis

Indonesia
Wallace, Alfred Russel

Japan
Xavier, Francis

Malay Archipelago
Wallace, Alfred Russel
Xavier, Francis

Middle East
Alexander the Great
Bell, Gertrude
Benjamin of Tudela
Burton, Richard Francis
Herodotus
Ibn Battuta
Xenophon
Zheng He

Russia (Siberia)
Bering, Vitus

Southern Asia
Zheng He

Tibet
David-Neel, Alexandra

NORTH AMERICA

CANADA

Brulé, Etienne
Cabot, John
Cabot, Sebastian
Cartier, Jacques
Champlain, Samuel de
Erikson, Leif
Fraser, Simon
Frobisher, Martin
Hennepin, Louis
Hudson, Henry
Jolliet, Louis
La Salle, Rene-Robert
  Cavelier Sieur de
Mackenzie, Alexander
Marquette, Jacques
Thompson, David
Vancouver, George

CARIBBEAN
Columbus, Christopher
Ponce de León, Juan

CENTRAL AMERICA

Panama
Balboa, Vasco Núñez de
Columbus, Christopher
Drake, Francis
Pizarro, Francisco

MEXICO
Cabeza de Vaca, Alvar
  Núñez
Coronado, Francisco
Cortes, Hernando
Humboldt, Alexander
  von

UNITED STATES

Atlantic Coast
Brulé, Etienne
Champlain, Samuel de
Hudson, Henry
Verrazano, Giovanni da

Great Lakes
Brulé, Etienne
Champlain, Samuel de
Hennepin, Louis
Jolliet, Louis
La Salle, Rene-Robert
  Cavelier, Sieur de
Marquette, Jacques

Mississippi River
Jolliet, Louis
La Salle, Rene-Robert
  Cavelier, Sieur de
Marquette, Jacques

Northwest
Carson, Kit
Clark, William
Frémont, John Charles
Lewis, Meriwether
Sacagawea
Thompson, David

Pacific Coast
Cook, James
Drake, Francis
Vancouver, George

Southeast
Cabeza de Vaca, Alvar
  Núñez
De Soto, Hernando
Ponce de León, Juan

Southwest
Carson, Kit
Coronado, Francisco
Frémont, John Charles
Pike, Zebulon
Powell, John Wesley

PACIFIC ISLANDS
Banks, Joseph
Cook, James
Drake, Francis
Tasman, Abel Janszoon

SOUTH AMERICA

Banks, Joseph
Cabeza de Vaca, Alvar
  Núñez
Cabot, Sebastian
Cabral, Pedro Alvares
Columbus, Christopher
Darwin, Charles
Humboldt, Alexander
  von
Magellan, Ferdinand
Orellana, Francisco
Pizarro, Francisco
Raleigh, Walter
Vespucci, Amerigo
Wallace, Alfred Russel

OTHER:

Oceans
Ballard, Robert
Cousteau, Jacques
Earle, Sylvia

Space
Armstrong, Neil
Gagarin, Yuri
Glenn, John
Jemison, Mae
Ride, Sally
Shepard, Alan
Tereshkova, Valentina

Timeline of World Exploration

c. 1100 B.C. Phoenician culture flourishes in present-day Lebanon, Syria, and Israel. They begin trading and colonizing throughout the Mediterranean.

c. 814 B.C. Carthage is founded by the Phoenicians in present-day Tunis.

c. 500 B.C. Hanno (Carthaginian) explores the western coast of Africa.
The Silk Road becomes a major trade route between China and the Mediterranean.
Buddhism becomes an influential religion throughout Asia.

c. 400 B.C. Herodotus (Greek) explores the Middle East and North Africa.

Xenophon (Greek) explores present-day Iraq and Turkey.

334 B.C. Alexander leads his army on a 10-year campaign of conquest and exploration through the present-day countries of Turkey, Lebanon, Egypt, Iraq, Iran, Afghanistan, and India.

c. 325 B.C. Pytheas explores the Atlantic coast of Europe and the British Isles.

146 B.C. Carthage is destroyed by the Roman army.

27 B.C. Caesar Augustus becomes the first Roman Emperor.

c. 6 B.C. Jesus is born in Bethlehem.

c. 30 A.D. Jesus dies in Jerusalem.

c. 100 A.D. Ptolemy publishes maps that will be used by navigators for the next 1,000 years.

399	Faxian travels from China to India.
c.750	Vikings begin raiding the British Isles and the northern coast of France.
c. 870	Vikings settle Iceland.
986	Erik the Red establishes first European settlement on Greenland.
c. 1000	Leif Erikson sails from Greenland to North America.
1066	The Normans (Vikings from northern France) conquer England.
c. 1150	Benjamin of Tudela writes about his travels throughout Europe, the Middle East, and North Africa.
1271	Marco Polo begins his journey to China, a trip that will last 24 years.
c. 1360	Ibn Battuta writes about his 24 years of travel from Spain to China.
1405	Zheng He begins his voyages of the Asian seas.
1419	Prince Henry the Navigator sponsors the first of several expeditions to explore the coast of Africa.
1488	Bartholomew Dias becomes the first European to sail around the southern tip of Africa.
1492	Christopher Columbus sails across the Atlantic Ocean and becomes the first European to discover the New World.
	King Ferdinand and Queen Isabella expel all Muslims and Jews from Spain.
1497	John and Sebastian Cabot sail across the North Atlantic Ocean to North America.
	Vasco da Gama becomes the first European to sail around Africa and on to India.
1499	Amerigo Vespucci explores the coast of South America and the Caribbean. He is the first European to suggest that these lands are not part of Asia, and are instead new continents in a New World.

1500   Pedro Alvarez Cabral is first European to discover Brazil.

1513   Juan Ponce de León is first European to discover Florida.
Vasco Núñez de Balboa becomes the first European to reach the Pacific Ocean.

1519   Hernando Cortes conquers Mexico.
Ferdinand Magellan begins the first expedition to sail around the world.

1520   Leo Africanus writes about his travels through Africa.

1525   Giovanni da Verrazano explores the Atlantic shore of North America, from North Carolina to Newfoundland.

1528   Alvaro Núñez Cabeza de Vaca begins his seven year exploration of Florida, Texas, and Mexico.

1532   Francisco Pizarro conquers Peru.

1534   Jacques Cartier explores St. Lawrence Bay in northern Canada.

1540   Francisco Coronado explores the Southwest United States.
Hernando de Soto explores the Mississippi River.

1541   Francisco de Orellana explores the Amazon River.

1549   Francis Xavier travels to Japan.

1576   Martin Frobisher explores present-day Baffin Island in northern Canada.

1577   Sir Francis Drake sails around the world.

1585   Sir Walter Raleigh establishes the first British colony in America at Roanoke, in what is now North Carolina.

1594   Willem Barents begins the first of three voyages in search of the Northeast Passage to China, exploring the Arctic region.

1595   Sir Walter Raleigh explores the Orinoco River in present-day Venezuela.

1608   Samuel de Champlain explores the St. Lawrence River in Canada, and founds the city of Quebec.

1611	Henry Hudson dies in search of a Northwest Passage to Asia. During his voyage, he explores the waters of northern Canada now called Hudson Bay.
1615	William Baffin, while searching for a Northwest Passage to Asia, explores the region between northern Canada and Greenland now called Baffin Island and Baffin Bay.
	Etienne Brulé explores the Great Lakes.
1624	Abel Tasman explores the South Pacific Ocean and is the first European to discover Tasmania and New Zealand.
1668	Jacques Marquette explores the Great Lakes.
1673	Jacques Marquette and Louis Jolliet explore the Mississippi River.
1678	Louis Hennepin explores the Great Lakes with Rene R.C. de La Salle.
1680	Rene R.C. de La Salle begins his voyage down the Mississippi River. He reaches the Gulf of Mexico in 1682 and claims the territory for France, calling it Louisiana.
1728	Vitus Bering explores the western coast of Siberia and the waters that separate Asia and Alaska. The Bering Strait and Bering Sea are named after him.
1768	James Cook begins his first voyage around the world. He explores Tahiti, Australia, and New Zealand.
	Joseph Banks travels with James Cook and studies the plants in Tahiti and Australia.
1769	Daniel Boone explores the Kentucky territory.
1772	James Cook begins his second voyage around the world. He explores the waters off of Antarctica and many islands in the Pacific.
1775	Daniel Boone blazes a trail through the Cumberland Gap in the Appalachian Mountains. This opens the Kentucky Territory to settlement.

1776   James Cook begins his third voyage. He explores present-day Hawaii and then the Pacific coast of North America. Hostile natives in Hawaii kill him in 1779.

1776-1781 American Revolutionary War.

1792   George Vancouver explores the Pacific coast of North America.

1793   Alexander Mackenzie, while searching for the Northwest Passage, explores the rivers of northwest Canada to the Arctic Ocean, as well as present-day British Columbia and Alberta. The Mackenzie River is named after him.

1795   Mungo Park begins explorations of the Niger River in Africa.

1799   Alexander von Humboldt explores the Orinoco River in South America.

1801   Matthew Flinders begins circumnavigation of Australia.

1804-1806 Meriwether Lewis and William Clark lead the Corps of Discovery on an expedition to explore the western U.S., from St. Louis to the Pacific Ocean. They hire a Shoshone guide, Sacagawea, at Fort Mandan, in modern-day Bismarck, North Dakota.

1806   Zebulon Pike explores Mississippi, Kansas, Nebraska, and Colorado. In Colorado he sights and climbs a mountain later named Pike's Peak for him.

1807   David Thompson begins a four-year expedition to map the Columbia River.

1808   Simon Fraser, searching for a water route to the Pacific Ocean, navigates a river from Fort George, British Columbia, to modern-day Vancouver. The river is later named the "Fraser" for him.

1819   Sir John Franklin begins first of two overland expeditions to find the Northwest Passage in the Canadian Arctic.

         William Edward Parry begins the first of three expeditions in the Canadian Arctic to find the Northwest Passage.

TIMELINE OF WORLD EXPLORATION

1829-1833   James Clark Ross explores the Canadian Arctic in search of the Northwest Passage. He finds the North Magnetic Pole.

1831   Charles Darwin serves as the naturalist on board the *Beagle* on its five-year journey. His discoveries in South America and the Galapagos Islands lead him to his ground-breaking theories of evolution.

1839-1843   James Clark Ross explores Antarctica.

1841-1853   David Livingstone explores Africa, while building Christian missions and fighting the slave trade. He is the first European to discover Lake Ngami, the Zambezi River, and Victoria Falls.

1842-1843   John Charles Frémont, with Kit Carson as his guide, explores and maps the Oregon Territory.

1845   Sir John Franklin's final expedition to find the Northwest Passage becomes lost in the Canadian Arctic. The quest to find them becomes one of the most famous in the history of exploration.

1848-1852   Alfred Russel Wallace explores the Amazon River. On the basis of his discoveries in the Amazon and Indonesia, he develops the theory of evolution, published in 1858 with Charles Darwin.

1856-1858   Richard Francis Burton and John Hanning Speke search for the source of the Nile. They are the first Europeans to discover Lake Tanganyika. Hanning reaches the Nile's source, Lake Victoria, on July 30, 1858.

1861-1865   American Civil War.

1866-1873   David Livingstone searches for the source of the Nile. He is not heard from for years and is presumed lost. In 1871, Henry Stanley finds him.

1854   Isabella Bird Bishop begins her travels, and in 1856, her travel writings. In 1892, she becomes the first female member of the Royal Geographical Society.

1869   John Wesley Powell navigates the Colorado River through the Grand Canyon.

1878-1879   Nils Nordenskiöld navigates the Northeast Passage.

1886   Robert E. Peary begins his first Arctic expedition.

1890   Sven Anders Hedin begins his explorations in Asia.

1891   May French Sheldon explores East Africa.

1893-1896   Fridtjof Nansen sails across the Arctic Ocean in the *Fram*.

1894-1895   Mary Henrietta Kingsley explores West Africa.

1900   Gertrude Bell begins to explore the Middle East, taking photographs and going on archeological digs. She participates in establishing the political boundaries of modern-day Iraq.

1901-1904   Robert Falcon Scott's first expedition to Antarctica.

1903-1906   Roald Amundsen is the first to successfully navigate the Northwest Passage.

1907-1909   Ernest Shackleton leads the *Nimrod* expedition to Antarctica. They are the first to reach the magnetic South Pole.

1909   Robert E. Peary and Matthew Henson reach the North Pole on April 6, 1909.

1911   Alexandra David-Neel begins a 14-year exploration of Asia.

1911-1912   Roald Amundsen and Robert Falcon Scott race each other to the South Pole. Amundsen reaches the Pole on December 14, 1911. Scott's crew arrives in January 18, 1912. The crew perishes on the return journey.

1914-1917   Ernest Shackleton leads the *Endurance* expedition to Antarctica.

1914-1918   World War I.

1926   Richard E. Byrd is first to fly over North Pole. Roald Amundsen flies over the Pole in a blimp, the *Norge*, shortly after Byrd.

1928   Roald Amundsen perishes in the Arctic while on a rescue mission to find Umberto Nobile.

1929   Richard E. Byrd is first to fly over South Pole.

1933-1955   Richard E. Byrd leads four expeditions to Antarctica. His crews explore and map the continent and collect scientific data.

TIMELINE OF WORLD EXPLORATION

1939-1945   World War II.

1946   Jacques Cousteau converts the *Calypso* into a floating exploration ship. He begins to explore the oceans and to film his discoveries.

1957   The Soviet Union launches *Sputnik*. The Space Race begins.

1961   On April 12, Yuri Gagarin of the Soviet Union becomes the first person to travel in space.
On May 5, Alan Shepard becomes first American to travel in space.

1962   On February 20, John Glenn becomes the first American to orbit the Earth.

1963   On June 16, Valentina Tereshkova of the Soviet Union becomes the first woman to travel in space.

1969   On July 20, Neil Armstrong becomes the first person to walk on the Moon.

1979   On September 9, Sylvia Earle dives 1,250 feet deep into the Pacific Ocean, the deepest dive anyone had made to date. She plants a U.S. flag on the ocean floor.

1983   On June 18, Sally Ride becomes the first American woman to travel in space.

1985   On September 1, Robert Ballard finds the *Titanic*, the first of many famous sunken ships to be found and explored by him.

1992   On September 12, Mae Jemison becomes the first African-American woman to travel in space.

Subject Index

Adventure 156

Alexander the Great **1-5**

Alvin...32

Amundsen, Roald **6-13**, 489, 490, 498, 501, 573, 574

Apollo 11 ....16, 18-20

Apollo 14 510

Argo...34

Argus..32

Armstrong, Neil **14-22**, 216, 510

Baffin, William..............**23-25**, 398, 574

Balboa, Vasco Núñez de **26-29**, 422

Ballard, Robert **30-38**, 218

Banks, Joseph **39-42**, 153, 236, 395

Barents, Willem **43-45**, 298, 387, 573

Beagle 184, 187

Bell, Gertrude...............................**46-48**

Benjamin of Tudela **49-50**

Bering, Vitus........................**51-54**, 159

Bismarck 35

Bishop, Isabella Bird **55-59**

Boone, Daniel..............................**60-65**

Brulé, Etienne **66-69**, 117, 119, 376

Burton, Richard Francis **70-74**, 359, 514, 516

Byrd, Richard E.....................13, **75-80**

Cabeza de Vaca, Alvar Núñez ...**81-85**, 162

Cabot, John **86-91**, 255

Cabot, Sebastian........43, 90-91, **92-96**, 298 , 573

Cabral, Pedro Alvares **97-99**, 181, 203, 546

Calypso 175

caravel....................138, 201, 563, 569

Carson, Kit **100-105**, 249

Cartier, Jacques......**106-112**, 115, 255, 362, 574

Challenger 22, 465, 466, 467, 468

Champlain, Samuel de...............67, 68, **113-120**, 376

Clark, William ..**121-132**, 398, 341-352, 364, 417, 477, 478-485, 533

Columbus, Christopher.......27, 87, 88, 89, 93, **133-150**, 166, 202, 203, 231, 368, 373, 423, 435, 438, 450, 452, 454, 544, 546, 547, 569, 570

Concepcion 368

conquistador............26, 161, 165, 194, 421, 570

Cook, James..........39, 40, 41, **151-160**, 289, 340, 346, 407, 537, 574

Coronado, Francisco Vázquez de ..84, **161-164**

Cortes, Hernando....148, **165-171**, 570
Cousteau, Jacques **172-176**, 218
Cumberland 238

Da Gama, Vasco....97, 98, 99, **177-182**, 203
Darwin, Charles......**183-189**, 308, 553, 554, 555
Dauphine 540
David-Neel, Alexandra............**190-193**
De Soto, Hernando....84, **194-199**, 425
Dias, Bartholomew 97, 98, 136, 178, **200-203**, 285, 367, 565, 569
Discovery (Baffin) 24, 25
Discovery (Cook)............................158
Discovery (Glenn)...........................271
Discovery (Hudson)..........24, 301, 302
Discovery (Scott)....................487, 495
Drake, Sir Francis............**204-211**, 459

Earle, Sylvia.............................**212-219**
Endeavor (Cook) 153, 154, 155
Endeavor (Jemison) 318
Endurance..................495, 497, 498-501
Erebus 241, 473, 475
Erik the Red....**220-224**, 225, 228, 230, 232, 550, 571
Erikson, Leif 86, 89, 223, **225-232**, 550

Faxian................................**233-234**
Ferdinand and Isabella..........136, 137, 142, 144, 336
Flinders, Matthew 41, **235-238**, 239, 240
Fram............10, 381, 382, 383-384, 385
Franklin, John.............7, 236, **239-243**, 473, 474, 475, 574

Fraser, Simon **244-247**
Freedom 7................................507, 509
Frémont, John Charles..102, 104, 105, **248-252**
Friendship 7 ....268, 269, 271
Frobisher, Martin **253-258**, 362, 574
Fury......................400, 401, 471, 473

Gagarin, Yuri......17, **259-263**, 267-268, 508-509, 529
Gemini VIII......................................18
Gjoa..8, 9
Glenn, John **264-271**
Golden Hind 207, 208, 210
Grande Hermine............................111
Griffin....................279, 331, 332, 333
Griper..398

Half Moon 299
Hanno **272-274**, 414
Hecla............................398, 400, 401
Hedin, Sven Anders................**275-277**
Hennepin, Louis **278-281**, 331, 332, 333
Prince Henry the Navigator....97, 136, 178, 200, **282-285**, 367
Henson, Matthew **286-290**, 404, 407
Herodotus **291-293**
Hopewell......................................298
Hsuan Tsang 234, **294-296**
Hudson, Henry 24, **297-303**, 362, 574
Humboldt, Alexander von......**304-309**

Ibn Battuta **310-314**
Investigator..................................236

Jason...34, 37
Jemison, Mae.......................**315-319**

Jolliet, Louis............**320-324**, 330, 375, 376-379

Josephine Ford.................................77

junks 563, 570

Kingsley, Mary Henrietta........**325-328**

knorr 223, 571

La Salle, Rene-Robert Cavelier, Sieur de.........278, 279-281, **329-335**

latitude........24, 89, 451, 452, 455, 569, 571, 574

Leo Africanus...........................**336-338**

Lewis, Meriwether ...121, 122-131, 308, **339-352**, 365, 417, 477, 478-484, 533

Livingstone, David .275, **353-360**, 503, 517, 518-519, 521, 523

longitude......24, 25, 451, 452, 569, 571

longship 221, 223, 227, 549, 571, 572

Mackenzie, Alexander 122, 245, 341, **361-365**

Magellan, Ferdinand 94, 149, 207, 208, **366-374**, 423, 547

Marquette, Jacques 320, 321-323, 330, **375-379**

Matthew 88

Maud 12

Nansen, Fridtjof.....7, 10, **380-385**, 389

NASA............15, 17, 21, 22, 35, 266, 270, 317, 319, 464, 466, 468, 506, 510, 512, 572

New France.....67, 68, 69, 113, 115, 119, 120, 278, 320, 321, 330, 331, 333, 376, 572

New Spain...82, 84, 161, 162, 169, 170, 171, 195, 197, 390, 572

New World 26, 27, 28, 67, 84, 85, 86, 91, 93, 94, 99, 106, 107, 114, 115, 116, 117, 133, 140, 141, 143, 147, 148, 161, 166, 170, 195, 198, 203, 205, 211, 226, 227, 229, 230, 231, 255, 258, 278, 301, 303, 320, 334, 376, 392, 422, 438, 452, 459, 460, 462, 540, 542, 546, 547, 548, 550, 551, 572, 575

Nimrod.............................496, 501, 573

Niña................................137, 138, 141

Nordenskiöld, Adolf Erik..............275, **386-389**, 573

Norge..12, 13

North Pole 9, 10, 12, 13, 77, 240, 286-290, 298, 381, 382, 387, 401, 403-409, 451, 455, 471, 472, 475, 570, 571, 572-573

Northeast Passage.........12, 43, 51, 96, 297-300, 386, 387-389, 572, 573

Northwest Passage..............7, 8, 9, 13, 23, 24, 25, 92, 93, 94, 96, 107, 114, 118, 119, 122, 128, 158, 159, 236, 239, 240, 241, 244, 245, 253, 254, 255, 258, 300, 301, 341, 348, 351, 361, 362, 398, 399, 400, 402, 470, 471, 481, 536, 538, 573-574

Orellana, Francisco de............**390-393**

Park, Mungo......................41, **394-396**

Parry, William Edward.....25, **397-402**, 470, 471, 473, 574

Peary, Robert E. 10, 286, 287-289, 290, **403-408**, 573

Pfeiffer, Ida **409-413**

The Phoenicians 272, **414-415**, 453

Pike, Zebulon **416-420**

Pinta.........................137, 138, 140, 141
Pizarro, Francisco....27, 149, 195, 373, 390-91, **421-427**, 547, 570
Polo, Marco......134, 276, **428-436**, 575
Ponce de León, Juan..............**437-441**
Powell, John Wesley **442-449**
Ptolemy 134, **450-452**
Pytheas...............................**453-456**

Quest.......................................500

Raleigh, Sir Walter................**457-462**
Resolution............................156, 158
Ride, Sally....................**463-468**, 531
Roosevelt.............................288, 406
Ross, James Clark......9, 241, 242, 398, 401, **469-476**, 487, 496, 573

Sacagawea 126, 128, 131, 345-346, 348, 351, **477-485**
St. Paul..52
St. Peter....................................52, 54
San Antonio............................368, 369
Santa Maria...................137, 138, 141
Santiago.................................368, 369
Scott, Robert Falcon...10-12, **486-492**, 495, 496, 501
Shackleton, Ernest...10, 489, **493-501**, 573
Sheldon, May French..............**502-504**
Shepard, Alan.....17, 18, 266, 267, 268, **505-512**
Silk Road 276, 430, 574-575
South Pole 6, 10, 11, 13, 77, 80, 287, 406, 451, 472, 473, 475, 489, 490, 491, 496, 497, 498, 570, 571, 573,
space shuttle....22, 271, 317, 466, 468, 572, 575

Speke, John Hanning 72-73, 359, **513-516**, 520
Sputnik................17, 261, 267, 508, 529
Stanley, Henry M.....353, 359-360, 503, **517-523**

Tasman, Abel Janszoon.................152, **524-527**
Tereshkova, Valentina 466, **528-531**
Terra Nova 489
Terror.....................................241, 473
Thompson, David............246, **532-536**
Titanic.............................30, 34-35, 37
Trinidad 368, 372

Vancouver, George...........41, 122, 341, **537-539**, 574
Vega.......................................387, 388
Verrazzano, Giovanni da.......106, 115, 300, **540-542**
Vespucci, Amerigo...........99, 149, 373, 423, **543-548**
Victoria 368, 370, 372
The Vikings.....221, 223, 226, 228, 231, 456, **549-551**, 571, 572
Vostok 1 ....17, 261, 267, 509, 529
Vostok 6 530

Wallace, Alfred Russel....188, **552-555**

Xavier, Francis **556-558**
Xenophon...............................**559-561**

Zheng He **562-565**, 570

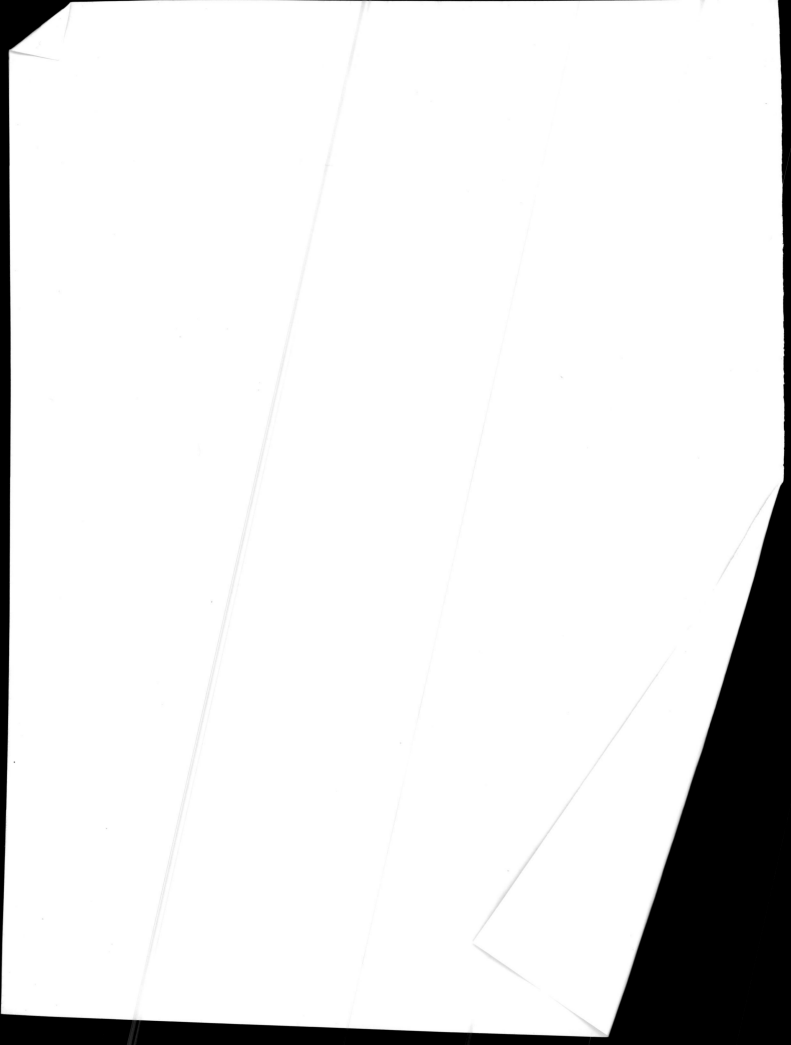